FOUNDATIONS OF
INDIAN POLITICAL THOUGHT
— AN INTERPRETATION —

(From Manu to the Present Day)

FOUNDATIONS OF
INDIAN POLITICAL THOUGHT
— AN INTERPRETATION —

(From Manu to the Present Day)

V.R. MEHTA

MANOHAR
1996

ISBN 81-7304-157-1

First Published 1992
Revised Edition 1996

Published by
Ajay Kumar Jain for
Manohar Publishers & Distributors
2/6 Ansari Road, Daryaganj
New Delhi 110 002

Typeset by
A J Software Publishing Co. Pvt. Ltd.
305, Durga Chambers, 1333, D.B. Gupta Road
Karol Bagh, New Delhi 110 005

Printed at
Print Perfect
Mayapuri
New Delhi 110 064

FOR
PRATAP AND RAJE

CONTENTS

CONTENTS

PREFACE

The book seeks to be an introduction to the evolution of Indian political thought in terms of its continuities as well as discontinuities. This is not to claim that this is a historian's history of Indian political thought. Rather it is an attempt to articulate, explain and examine the concepts of state in politics used by an ongoing tradition of enquiry. Tradition here is not to be confused with the past or with the series of immutable and monolithic precepts. It is a set of ongoing, even contradictory practices and arguments which engage each other through shared concepts. Thus the presence of plural interpretations of concepts and ideas cannot be considered a good argument against the existence of a tradition. On the contrary, it is the hallmark of a mature tradition of enquiry that many voices prevail. This book admittedly does not give an account of *all* the voices or shades of thought on the tradition, but it does aim to give some sense of its internal possibilities.

There are many scholarly works but as they are mostly either good summaries of the main texts or concentrate exclusively on describing the administrative system; they do not deal adequately either with the relationship of political concepts to general philosophical concepts or with the social background which conditions thought. To be more specific, sufficient attention has not been paid to the concept of the state in Indian political thought in relation to other wholes and practices in society. The book seeks to fill this gap in a modest way. It must, however, be confessed that the knowledge of the historicity of the texts is woefully inadequate and therefore one is forced to supplement our existing knowledge by locating both concepts and history within the text itself.

The book seeks to look at the evolution of the Indian social and political thought, particularly in the context of the state, through an exposition of the ideas of some representative thinkers. Thus in the middle ages Barni and Abul Fazal have been given priority though there were many other thinkers who influenced the age. In the modern period, greater emphasis has been given to exposition of the ideas of the thinker rather than his contribution to the ongoing process of Indian politics. Those who are interested in the later part may refer to my other book *Ideology, Modernization and Politics in India* (Manohar, 1983). Throughout it has been our aim to describe the ideas of great thinkers or texts, to relate general concept of the state to society as well as the subjective and the objective conditions of the time. The book views Indian society as a great civilization and seeks to understand continuities and discontinuities in the development of political thought with a view to discovering points of signification for the present.

In the process of writing this book there have been many points where simplification and over-simplification have become inescapable, particularly in the absence of a reliable historical data. Sometimes, there has been so much concentration on the exposition of concepts in the texts that minor points, contradictions and cleavages have been overlooked. But since this is meant primarily to be an introduction, it will have served its purpose if it stimulates interests in the students and researchers alike in the discovery of primary sources. In fact, the purpose of the book is to remind students of Indian politics that while the study of Western thought is important, the study of Indian thought can no longer be ignored if they want to understand their present, which itself is a result of historical development of the dominant tendencies in the classical and medieval thought. As the crisis of the Indian state deepens, the more is the need for a thorough understanding of the traditions of political thought in India in reference to the state, in our search for a coherent relation between the individual and the state— a relationship, which should enable the Indian state to cope with the problems of the modern world and yet sustain the Indian society in terms of its own peculiar identity.

I must gratefully acknowledge my debt of gratitude to my father and to my wife, in whose company I have lived the continuity of tradition and innovation which go to make an enlightened Indian household a literal paradise on earth. The book is for my sons Pratap and Rajesh and their tribe, too, in the hope that they will be able, to use Oakeshott's expression, to pursue 'intimations with tradition' of political thought in India—in the direction of a more just and differentiated political order.

I am grateful to Mrs M.K. Singh who typed and retyped the manuscript. My thanks are also due to Professor Daya Krishna for all his encouragement. I am also grateful to Shri B.P. Srivastava for reading an early draft and suggesting several changes. I am thankful to Prof. D.B. Mathur for preparing the index.

I am also grateful to the participants of International Colloquium on Political Philosophy held in London, particularly Prof. Noel O'Sullivan and Prof. Bhiku Parekh for their comments and suggestions which enabled me to revise and improve my last chapter.

The author is indebted to the University Grants Commission for creating this opportunity by inviting the author to write this book.

V.R. MEHTA

CHAPTER 1

INTRODUCTION

Politics is an activity between human beings by which diverse and conflicting claims of various wholes in a polity are conciliated, redirected and, at times, reorganized for the welfare of all. The need for such reconciliation arises because, as the ancients thought, the more powerful wholes are apt to transgress into the spheres of the less powerful and the right is often identified with the interest of the strong. Although there is politics in all wholes and structural arrangements of society, in family, village and industry, the one whole in which political activity is pre-eminent in relation to community is the State for in it alone politics acquires unique importance: it seeks to mediate between order, change and history. Each conciliation, reconciliation and reorganization may not be final but so long as it endures it secures some order by means of which men relate to each other in society; when this order is lacking life cannot go on smoothly. The role of political activity can indeed be compared to the activity of the stomach in the human body which is to reconcile the demands and needs of different organs of the body and to supervise productive and distributive activities in accordance with general rules of hygiene. Political activity is a managerial activity of this sort which seeks to organize and conciliate different interests, claims and demands of the various wholes in society by supervising its productive and distributive apparatus.

It is, therefore, natural that people must have thought about and debated issues pertaining to it right from the beginning of conscious existence on this planet. There was Chinese political thought, Greek political thought and Roman political thought. We speak of modern Western political thought. Likewise Indians also developed their own kind of political thought which in due course acquired its own identity. When we emphasize the separate identity of Indian society or traditions of thought in India, we do not mean that Indian society exists or has existed in isolation from other societies. Indeed, in diverse ways the growth and development of Indian society, as well as its decay, have been shaped by outside influences which have come to us from time to time. We can mention the influence of earlier prehistoric civilizations such as the Egyptian, the Persian, the Chinese with all of which there is a close resemblance. Then came the Greeks, various tribes, people from Persia, Iran and other Arabic countries which brought with them the richness of their culture, and finally the Western culture which has enriched the ever flowing stream of national consciousness in so many ways. In certain cases, the influence was decisive in giving a new direction to the already existing thought. But pervasive influence from outside does not mean the non-existence of our own personality. Each society has a personality of its own. It can develop only when it accepts those influences which suit its requirement at a particular point of time and which it is in a position to assimilate. When the external influences become overpowering, or the body is not able to assimilate them, certain tensions are generated which in due course lead to its decay. The subject of the interaction of outside influences with the total personality of the society and various traditions within it can be a fascinating subject of study. This interaction helps each society to be conscious of its distinct personality, gives a new meaning to its own civilizational experience, and suggests various ways and means, options and choices by which the society can cope with its own problems. The study of western political thought is therefore important not only because in a certain measure it is already part of our total personality but also because its very creativity suggests ways and options open to us after a century of give and take. What is, however, unfortunate is the little attention being paid in university courses to the development of social and political thought in India. Our students know more about Rome and England than about their own country with the result that they remain largely ignorant about their own traditions of thought. This is responsible for much of the alienation of the Indian intellectual from his own society.

It would be worthwhile here to ponder a little more deeply in order to identify the distinct features of the Indian civilization, particularly in terms of political thought. Such distinctness comes to light only at the deepest level and not on a superficial appraisal. The peculiar situation of India which makes it a neat geographical unit as well as the socio-religious structure in the country have provided a certain stamp of unity. This unity is to be found at the deepest level in the social and philosophical orientation of the people which provided legitimation as well as viability to its ongoing social progress from the earliest period. There are doubtless various cleavages within this process, between the various wholes which compose it, but there is a pattern of thought which is common to all and which made it possible for people to talk simultaneously of the world, the cosmic process and transcendence. Indian languages may vary, but their approach, grammar, and vocabulary have been strikingly similar throughout the country specially when it comes to enunciation or explanation of such concepts as caste, duty, worldly process, kindness, justice, rights, which are either directly based on the Vedic world view or are derived from it through translation while the roots remain the same. This is of course true for worshippers of the Mother or Siva or Krishna or Christ for each occupies a sacred place in different parts of the country. The Puranic heritage is common to an overwhelming majority. There are cleavages between Hinduism and Islam. But the Bhakti movement within Hinduism and Sufism in Islam tried to bridge them by emphasizing the similarities and creating points of contact in terms of which a common identity could emerge. There have been many leaps and setbacks in this process but on the whole Indian civilization has marched on from one crisis to another in search of a composite culture. It may sound simplisitc, but as a rough generalization one might say that most of our philosophical notions today come from Sanskrit, ideas about justice and fairplay from Urdu and Persian, and legal and political words from English. The philosophical and social unity of the Indian civilization far preceded political unity. This philosophical unity has assumed different forms in diverse customs and cultural practices, structures, and languages and modes of social living, though all have an underlying unity as if they were different branches of the same tree. It has yet to find a meaningful expression in the political field. This very cleavage between the inherited philosophic-social system and the political system based on the Westminster model is one of the most important political problems facing India. The former is rooted in the pre-historic period; though it has been sustained and consolidated by diverse people in diverse ways; they have shared meanings, symbols, myths, languages and cultural idioms. Urdu added yet another flavour to the simmering brew, and gave a new meaning to the common experience. Indian civilization has successively assimilated various people and tribes, most of them coming from the west, various ideas and cultural practices, some with unitary forms, some with a world view; the Vedic world view, the Upanishadic philosophy, the Buddhist, Jain, Sikh and Islamic religious traditions are undoubtedly the most significant later developments of this assimilation.

We are emphasizing this in order to question the commonly held view that there is no continuity in the development of Indian thought. Indeed, one can confidently assert that there is a remarkable continuity in the development of ideas about action, duty, caste, cosmic process and even justice and the state. Then there are breaks as when Islam entered India or Christian and Western cultures came in. But in these periods also, there was an attempt to combine the earlier ideas with Islam, an effort to tide over the gaps so that the old thread was recovered, resurrected or reinterpreted in a new form. In the medieval period, there was a lull in Hindu political thought but some of the ideas were absorbed by people like Abul Fazal. In another sense, there was an effort to preserve the dominant tradition through such epics as Tulsidas' *Ramcharitmanas*. We do not propose to gloss over the fact that there was very little political speculation in the medieval period. In this sense there was of course a break in continuity. While the civilization continued, politics assumed different forms; in the medieval period politics actually broke down and then resumed with a different flavour. But this did not long endure and with the advent of the Europeans, particularly the British, a new political idiom emerged and took hold of the minds of the people. However, if we do not take into account the rich contribution of Islamic law and world view, their ideas about justice and equality which entered in legal and various other institutions, reinforced by the adoption of Urdu and Persian as court languages, we shall not be able to properly understand the modern Indian psyche. It is true that Islamic political thought rested mainly on Greek and Persian antecedents. But in another sense, though this has yet to be established, the traditional Indian ideas about social order, justice, kinship, equality which might have profoundly influenced Greek thought of Hesiod, Plato and Aristotle, came back home, albeit in a new form, via Persia, through Islam, for there was a close resemblance between these ideas and Barni's ideas on these topics, notwithstanding his contempt for Hindus, on traditional notions of good and evil, and the need for moderation and justice in a well governed state. In any case, when the modern Renaissance began in the nineteenth century, there was a Herculean effort to recover the spirit of the ancients, to combine it with that of the medieval, and to integrate both to suit the needs of the moderns. The Renaissance reformers and thinkers looked back at the past, identified what was living and dead in Indian tradition.[1] There was remarkable revival of the ancient thought. Their debates are intelligible only in terms of the historical context of an ancient society awakening itself to new light and glory in a colonial situation. This was true of Aurobindo, Gandhi, Ranade and Tilak right down to the present time.

It must be confessed that the continuity of the socio-religious tradition is quite in contrast to the breaks in political traditions,[2] where there are tensions, short cuts, regressions as well as jumps. The foundational experience received as severe setback first with the advent of Islam and then with the introduction of English education in the nineteenth century. The adoption of the Westminster model with its justificatory liberal theory was yet another departure from existing thought and practice. It is from this angle that one can say that tension between society and politics is one of the unresolved problems facing us even today. It is as a result of so many ups and downs, twists and turns that we cannot share the western notion of history as progress. In our case it has been a cyclical, almost a zigzag movement in which earlier insights are given up under pressure of a new wave of thought and reintroduced and reinterpreted at a subsequent moment to accommodate yet another set of changes which have come upon society. This has made the development of the Indian personality a far more complicated process than in the West where one can legitimately speak of progress through the Reformation, the Renaissance, and the industrial revolution to the present space age. This complexity becomes all the more glaring when one is told of manuscripts lost or still untranslated, making one wonder whether these manuscripts had any importance, and if so why they were lost or condemned to oblivion. Obviously if they were important once and then lost, one may be inclined to think there were breaks in the development which made them irrelevant or unsafe.

Recently there has once again been talk of the absence of unity in this tradition, or traditions, in India, thus discrediting the view of continuity in or cohesiveness of a social centre in society such as emerged in the late nineteenth and early twentieth century. But on the whole Indian society has up to the time of Gandhi, worked and operated with a conviction of such a continuity. In other words, we have always taken India to be a case of unity in diversity.[3] Throughout our history we have constantly referred to the past writers, habitually quoting or citing Manu, Valmiki or Vyasa, as though these people shared the same idiom of thought. Even Abul Fazal undertook the translation of the *Mahabharata*. The influence of earlier ideas is writ large in his writings. Similarly, writers like Aurobindo and Gandhi constantly referred to the past view; others like M.N. Roy refuted the dominant tradition but only to draw our attention to the materialist tradition in India. Mazumdar's and V.P. Varma's books have emphasized this historical continuity in the past or the present in which the older ideas are seen in terms of timeless and permanent trends which still have some relevance.

II

Even the most timeless truth has to be integrated with the development of time, place and situation, or the idea of historical development as the moderns would put it. We cannot all the time hark back to the past. It is not possible to revive it either. As a condition of survival, we must have knowledge of the present and confidence in the future. Change is the irresistible law. The zigzag progress of society itself demonstrates that nothing remains static. What is born has to grow up, reach manhood, die and take a new birth. Ideas are both relative and autonomous. They are relative in regard to subjective, objective and ethical factors operating at a particular time. They reflect historical stages in the growth of society. They arise because there is a tension which has to be resolved. But they have an autonomy of their own in the sense that parallel to the history of society, there is also a history of ideas which has its own momentum. Doubtless this history is influenced by developments in society but it also influences them. This happens because in this way man's effort to relate the world to the spirit beyond is revealed, and in the process there are laid bare a variety of choices and options in terms of which a historical actor finds illumination and acts. It is true that while the Greeks of their time found Plato and Aristotle largely irrelevant, yet their ideas caught fire in thirteenth century Europe to shape a new civilization. But one can never be sure that the same ideas will influence all societies in the same way. For instance, Aristotle came to India during the same period through Islamic writings but the influence took an altogether different form. This is the contextualist approach which has recently found much support in historical conferences. The attempt here is to look at philosophers in the context of special situations and specific audiences to which these writers were addressing themselves. It is believed that great writings do not always have a universal message. They are not always a search for Platonic 'essence' or 'forms'. One must, argues Skinner,[4] go beyond the text and context and recover the authors' intentions; the historian must have insight into the language, ideas and symbols of the time because philosophy is expressed through words which are located in the language of a particular time. This philosophical position is right in so far as it insists on the importance of context, but it ignores the fact that the history of ideas in due course acquires its own autonomy and whatever the language or words or historical context, certain ideas or concepts are common to all mankind. They persist across time. Otherwise Plato's *Republic*, Kautilya's *Arthasastra* would be simply incommunicable to us. The dilemma which haunted Arjun on the battlefield still confronts us. We are able to appreciate and sympathize with it. And it is this which explains the enduring influence of these classics and provides a legitimacy to all attempts to seek permanence amidst change and flux. It is one thing to emphasize the importance of context and another to make the context absolute at the expense of the text. The context is important because it helps us in two ways. First, it throws a new light on some hidden meaning in the book which would not otherwise be revealed. Secondly, it is important insofar as it emphasizes the totality of social process in which the world is integrally related to consciousness as a part of this process. Political thought cannot be divorced from political experience. Therefore it is incumbent on us to understand the context of ideas and issues in their age if we wish to properly appreciate Aristotle or Kautilya. They were debating issues which were important to their contemporaries. In that sense they were addressing particular audiences of their time. To this extent the totality of historical process provided the background to their political thought. It would, for example, make no sense to argue about imperial administration before Kautilya or about liberal democracy before the modern experience. The emphasis on the context of the historical process must make us very careful in our evaluation of historical personages. Rana Pratap and Shivaji appear as reactionaries from the point of view of the present but in the context in which they were placed, their struggles had a definite significance.

Context has two aspects. First comes objective and subjective apparatus and second, the intellectual history of the society. We must reiterate that while the objective and subjective factors condition men they do not determine all that they do. Though human life may not provide much choice, man has a certain autonomy and responsibility for conscious actions. Political thinkers like individuals are moral beings insofar as they make conscious decisions and are responsible for these decisions. They cannot be condoned on the pretext that they thought in a particular way because of the compulsions of the situation in which they were placed. Rules and institutions of society may be laid down but human beings are endowed with the capacity for making conscious choices, either of conforming to these rules or changing them. The historical process has its own flow but individuals have the capacity to give it new direction. The individual may not always succeed. There may be, as the ancients believed, an element of *rita* or inexorable destiny or conspiracy of circumstances. Every writer or thinker grapples with this to find out where changes or jumps are possible. In that sense while every man is a creature of his age, he is also a creator. There are so many instances of people who were weak in their personal life yet became most powerful and positive leaders, heroes or philosophers. There is a need to explain the reasons for this incongruity in their lives. The context may help us to find out why a particular philosopher said a particular thing. The value of this personal or historical experience is limited by the fact that he tries to transcend the immediate experience in terms of search for permanence. The greater his effort to transcend the immediate in order to change, revitalize or reshape it,[5] the greater is his stature as a man or a thinker. This is what is meant by a great thinker or hero. Both often appear irrelevant to their contemporaries. A great thinker is indeed one who transcends the immediate constraints to create something which connects him to the past, the present and the future. Of course, even here there are limits beyond which a thinker cannot go if he wants to be understood or appreciated. That is why we have Don Quixotes too. But between these two points of immediate environment and historical sweep, there are many options and choices available to thinkers in terms of which they can communicate their message. The cherished ideals of truth, justice, freedom, equality may vary from society to society but there is hardly a society which would deny the importance of these ideals, specially the importance of speaking the truth. Certainly some ideas are more important in one tradition than in another and authors must be related to this distinctness in their traditions, but the greater the attempt one makes to transcend the boundaries of one's tradition and formulate a universal discourse, the more enduring is one's stature as a thinker. That is why, as we have already said, Plato or Kautilya still make sense to us.

Moreover, a purely historical approach will make us antiquarians rather than political theorists. As political theorists we are interested in the past in so far as it illumines our own situation and predicament, gives us new insights into the human situation or throws new light on its constituents. After all, the vision of a right order or dharma or of a good person such as Rama has provided meaning and substance to the developments of our national ethos. These visions grew in a particular historical setting constituted by both the material situation and the intellectual history of society. But once they arose, they acquired an autonomy of their own, transcended history to become part of the evergrowing corpus of ideas and became integral to the intellectual background of every subsequent generation. It is in this sense that the ideal of *Ramarajya* in *Ramayana* or of *karmayogin* in *Gita* make sense to us; the principles of dharma or justice in the middle ages provide a background against which we react. It would be impossible to understand the integralism of Aurobindo or the notion of *Ramarajya* of Gandhi without understanding their basis in the ancient thought. Every age has its epochal characteristics. Some of these features are given up in the course of historical development. Others are retained because they are found to be either useful or conforming to deeper human experiences. A sense of history is important because it helps us to disentangle these features. In the subsequent pages we shall not be asking questions of past thinkers about things which did not directly concern them nor shall we quote them out of context. A historical sense makes us humble and more sympathetic to their predicament. It also helps us to identify those features of human situation which have changed and consequently necessitate a new answer. In this respect, a study of history of political thought does two things: it gives us a knowledge of the past, its ideas and their relationship to concrete political activity in terms of continuities and discontinuities; second, it helps us to understand ourselves and our predicament better by sharpening points of similarities and differences between the past epoch and ours and highlighting human possibilities for the future. It embodies traditions of society, its past aspirations and achievements, present crisis and future promise.

III

A word must be said about the study of context in the classics in ancient India. Historians differ widely and almost acrimoniously about the dates of different books. Archaeologists may have one view, students of literature another. And those who would like to date these works according to the vast and staggering astronomical data mentioned in these books constitute yet another category. While the descendants of the Greeks and the Romans and the Chinese have no difficulty in deciding the possible dates of their classics, the Indians find it almost exasperating. There is no need here to go into the possible reasons, or even motivations of the scholars, for these controversies. It is partly a colonial heritage in which one group is out to demonstrate that all that is best in that West today existed in ancient India, and the other is equally vehement in its debt to the West. Then there are liberal historians, Marxist historians and the supporters of orthodoxy. In part, the fault lies with the manuscripts as they exist today. They have been subjected to almost genetic mutations from time to time to suit the interests of a particular class or age. The result is that the profound and the banal are so inextricably mixed that it becomes a difficult task disentangling them. However, it is our belief that while these classics bristle with inconsistencies and incoherencies, there is a philosophical core which can be disentangled once we take into account their linkage with the general development of philosophical and religious thought. Similarly, each classic has a certain historical sequence of events within it which may not be authentic from the view of exact dates but may nonetheless provide us with sufficient insight to reconstruct the context in which these classics were written. From the Western experience we know that there is certain correspondence between development in the field of ideas and concepts on the one hand and society on the other. Individualism gives rise to one kind of society, collectivism to another. In some cases changes in ideas precede social changes, in other situations social changes precede changes in ideas. Advances in mathematics are reflected not only in changes in physical sciences and technology but also in philosophy and vice versa. Indian society too must have gone through a process in which changes took place in conjunction or concert with each other and not in isolation. A certain level of technology must give rise to a certain philosophical system and vice versa. When we refer to the Western process we do not mean that Indian society passed through exactly the same stages. This would be too simplistic a picture of a process which has been far more complex. But study of the process in the West can certainly illuminate the linkages which might have existed between politics, society, economy and philosophy in the past. It is our belief that once these linkages become clear a certain story of the evolution of ideas in India with all its continuities and discontinuities, begins to appear. And it shall be our endeavour to pursue the course of this story as revealed by history, myths, legends and symbols.

NOTES

1. See, V.R. Mehta, *Ideology, Modernization and Politics in India* (New Delhi, Manohar, 1988).
2. Ibid.
3. Ibid.
4. See Q. Skinner, "Meaning and understanding in the History of Ideas", *History and Theory*, VIII, No. 1, 1969, pp. 3-53. Also B. Prakash and R.N. Berki, "The History of Political Ideas: A Critique of Q. Skinner's Methdology", *Journal of History of Ideas*, 34, 1973, pp. 163-84. Q. Skinner, "Some Problems in the Analysis of Thought and Action", *Political Theory*, 2, No. 3, August 1974, pp. 277-303. Richard Ashcraft, "On the Problem of Methodology and the Nature of Political Theory", *Political Theory*, 3, February 1975.
5. Michael Oakeshott, Introduction to Thomas Hobbes, *Leviathan* (Oxford, Blackwell, 1957).

CHAPTER 2

THE COSMIC VISION: MANU

The actual origins of Indian philosophical and political thought are shrouded in mystery. It certainly emerged from the political experience of various kingdoms which were diverse and free, spanning the entire land peninsula from the Himalayas in the north to the Indian Ocean in the south, the Persian empire in the west to the land of enchantment and mystery now known as Assam in the east. The first known formulation came to surface in the Vedas and the next during the legendary wars of the *Ramayana* and *Mahabharata* when presumably one era of history merged into another. This vision which was more in the nature of a foundational experience, became the bedrock of all subsequent thought, was perfected by Kautilya to suit the needs of a pan-Indian kingdom, found its echo in the writings of Kalidasa, Kamandaka, Brihaspati, Sukra, and Somedeva, in Buddhist and Jain thought, and was replaced in the end by the emergence of medieval sects. Although the formulation of political thought in the *Mahabharata* and later of Kautilya was an exciting departure, it was the product of a long process of development, both in ideas and social life, in Indian society. Who were the original inhabitants of the land is a controversial question on which there is no settled opinion. Certainly there was a long process of change and stability, migration and settlement. Quite early the inhabitants, whether they were indigenous or from outside, came to regard themselves as belonging to Bharata, looking down on others as 'barbarians' or '*mlechas*'. They were conscious of their superiority in intellectual and moral fields and gave expressions to it in their writings, such as the Vedas, in which they regarded themselves as Sons of Gods enjoined to conquer the world. They had links with Iran, Persia and Egypt. They also developed military and governmental organizations. It is not precisely known whether they were purely agricultural communities or whether they had also developed urban civilization. The Mohenjodaro and Harappan cultures as well as some references in Vedic literature point to the fact that urban civilization had come into existence quite early in the life of the society. Even if the Mohenjodaro civilization had perished, it must have left some residue in the civilization and culture to follow. Rich resources and innumerable rivers favoured the development of trade and commerce. The discovery of copper, iron and steel led to an early development of civilization. If myths and fables are to be believed, quite large kingdoms came into existence. These were more or less economically self-sufficient units which were called by various names resembling modern states. In some cases these kingdoms consisted of a single tribe, in others they were a mixture. On the whole it was a stratified society in which perhaps the labour of some was used by others to maintain the system. Society comprised men of knowledge, warriors, merchants, peasants and those devoted to menial labour. It was believed that where rulers work in concert with men of knowledge, the world turns holy and Gods dwell in it. The various storms in the life of the nation resulted in the disappearance of most of the records, but some of these were fortunately preserved culminating in the Vedas, epics and Puranas. As the earlier period receded in time, the people became less aware of the past which they thought was intimately connected to the other world. But as new social and political structures began to take shape, the contrast with the earlier periods became more pronounced. However, memory of the glories of their common past held together the various communities which inhabited the land.

There are no straightforward pictures of life in these kingdoms. It varied from state to state and depended very much on the king. In most cases these states were ruled by kings with the support or benediction of priests. There were some instances of democracies also. But the general system was that of constitutional monarchy and it must have worked well to lead Aristotle to quote in *Politics* (Book VII, Chap. 14) a remark of an old traveller that rulers in India were on the whole better and morally superior to the general population. This was certainly so in the period of the *Ramayana* which has come to be seen by posterity as the ideal state. A famous paragraph in *Srimad Bhagwat* sums up the ideal of a good king in ancient India. It proudly refers to the devotion of the king for his subjects, a state system which existed to protect the week, the old and women, and respect for popular will. There were no thieves, no crime; everything existed in abundance and nature herself was bountiful. Man was free from fear of everything that he is now afraid of. Working for the welfare of the people was seen as the hallmark of a great king, while selfishness and greed were the greatest blemish on his character. The learned were advised to be guardians of right and virtue, they were expected to be vigilant.

It is not easy in the case of ancient Indian history to establish the precise relationship between theory and practice. The historical data is so inadequate and confusing. But there is no doubt that following the principles of right in life was always considered important and it was thought that kingship is the basis on which such a life can be built up. The king was considered a bridge between this and the divine world.[1] In *Rig Veda* the doctrines of *rita* (cosmic law) and *dharma* (right) were clearly asserted and they later found expression in the *Satapatha Brahmanas*. Preference for monarchy had also been stated but the supremacy of *rita* or *dharma* was given greater importance and the Vedas went so far as to assert that *rita* preceded society, not historically but logically. The implication was that before there could be cosmos there must be regularity which provides inherent equipoise to the cosmic process.[2] It is during this period that the germinal ideas of subsequent civilizations emerged, an image of a life patterned on the rhythms of nature, the institutions of caste and kingship. Civilization found its governing principles in the organic ideas of society as distinguished from the state, and of the king on whom devolved the responsibility of maintaining the system. The process of creation in the realm of the world, the in-between and the Beyond reflected the historical development of social life as distinct from the political forms found in Egypt and Mesopotamia. The creation of the cosmos in Indian mythology was a complicated process in which man and society were ultimately made safe as a result of the conflict of order and disorder. It is for this reason that though society was always considered important, politics had its own place. While on the one hand the king was a choice of God, on the other he was made responsible to the people. He was required to fight the forces of disorder. People always feared that the forces of disorder might gain an upper hand because obedience was problematical and good and evil were inseparable in life.

II

Legend elevates Manu as the first legislator who laid down the form of social life and practices later embodied in various *Dharmasastras* and Samhitas. The *Manusmriti* laid down the rules to be observed by a righteous person including a righteous king. Like all ancient texts the exact period of the writing of the *Manusmriti* is not known. The dates vary from twelve hundred BC to the second century AD. Some commentators even speak of an earlier and a later *Manusmriti*. For instance, Saletore's view is that there is an earlier version which belongs to a much earlier period. This view seems plausible, when one looks at the description of India in *Manusmriti* and compares it to that of Kautilya's *Arthasastra*. While Kautilya included the whole of India, south of the Himalayas, Manu had in mind only the *Aryavarta* extending from the Himalayas in the north to the Vindhyas in the south and from the western sea to the eastern sea.[3] This is also substantiated by the fact that *Manusmriti* pays more deference to the Vedas than to other works. As in the Vedas, Manu also continues to see human life, or even the cosmic process, as a whole. Although the date of *Manusmriti* is disputed, mythologically Manu is supposed to have been the first teacher of mankind who revealed the knowledge of man in society to Bhrigu. Maharshi Bhrigu was one of the seven sages entrusted at the beginning of the cosmic cycle with the task of preservation of right in the world. Siva and Parvati were asked to set the process in motion. They therefore became the symbols of the world as well as of transcendence. The seven *risis* were then entrusted to safeguard dharma. It may be remembered that such beliefs were legion in the ancient world. Even in Greece of the seventh century BC there were similar myths about seven sages and Solon was considered to be one of those sages assigned the task of preservation of right in the world at the beginning of the cosmic process. In any case from the larger angle the debate about the actual date of the composition of the *Manusmriti* can be left to historians. This is not to deny the importance of context in analysis as well as evaluation of the classics but only to suggest that in the absence of an agreed date, we should postpone the issue involved in relating them to the context to some more appropriate time. The more important thing is to discern the basic principles, system and truth and establish coherence in divergent and conflicting aspects of *Manusmriti* in order to fathom its essence.

Every great system of thought starts with a certain view of the man-comsic relationship. Since no book of rules has been more influential in guiding the actual conduct and ways of life of generations of people than this one, one could say that it must have had a powerful philosophical and ideological basis to it. The *Manusmriti* is a mixture of the lofty and the mundane. On the one hand, it gives a very profound account of creation, on the other, it delves deep into the most ordinary details of daily life. The philosophical basis of *Manusmriti*, and indeed of the entire epic and Puranic tradition, is neither idealism nor materialism. Consciousness is neither separate from the world nor is it a mere epiphenomenon of matter. The cosmos is a process, Voegelin's "In Between", in which consciousness and matter, form and emptiness, are blended together in a search for Beyond. These are not bipolarities. Both are implied all the time. First, there is a Beyond, a supreme Brahman. Second, there is also the differentiated reality which is an extension or manifestation of the supreme Brahman. Third, there is all the time an effort to connect the cosmos with the Beyond, something in which man participates. The Beyond cannot be fully comprehended, it can only be experienced. Sometimes the Vedic seer became a sceptic and declared:

> That from which this creation came into being,
> Whether it had held it together or it had not,
> He who surveys it in the highest region.
> He, truly, knows it, or may be He does not know it.[4]

The *Manusmriti* begins with the concept of *Nirguna Brahma*[5] as the causeless cause of the universe and then goes on to describe the process of manifestation, which, according to it, is a product of a series of individuations and differentiations leading to the formation of many worlds and levels and varieties of existence. The cosmic process emerged back in the age of primeval chaos. The cosmos came into existence when God awakened from the primeval sleep. A part of the supreme cosmic reality *Nirguna Brahman* becomes manifest in the endless cosmic cycles, the rest of it remains unmanifest. The unmanifest is *noetic* and cannot be known, but the manifest which is *pneumatic*, and includes the differentiated creation, can presumably be known because the manifestation follows certain rules which God also himself accepted as binding on himself when he created the world, so that there could be some order in the cosmic process. The *noetic* is mysterious. It is unmanifest and can only be experienced with the aid of practices in breath regulation (*pranayama*), prayer (*japa*) and meditation on the foundational syllable 'Aum'. But differentiated reality can be known and communicated with the help of reason and experience of which positivism too forms an important part. Yoga and *tantra* provide integrative knowledge of the differentiated reality and yet are both positivist and mysterious representing a link between it and the unmanifest. The third practice *tapa* (penance) deals with the 'In Between' and is the connecting rod between the manifest and the unmanifest.

It is from this viewpoint that the seven sages are supposed to give guidance in the process of sustenance of the world. It is believed that they have knowledge of the rules and principles which govern the world and its processes. Man can also know some of these rules because human beings are gifted with *buddhi* which is the highest faculty of integral reasoning. But only that communication or form of knowledge is important which helps us to explore the structure of reality.

Man's existence has significance in so far as he participates in the process of reality. That is why *karma*-yoga is the most important yoga as it includes all other yogas. According to the *Manusmriti* it includes both *paravartt* and *nivritti*. The first means regulation of desires and the latter their total eradication. Indeed there is no antagonism between the two. The first also connects us to the reality which is Beyond. Thus practice of virtues includes various forms of *tapa* (penance), *dhyana* (meditation) and *japa* (prayer) which must never be abandoned by those engaged in action because the aim of all action is to move beyond as an experiential reality. Myths, legends, rituals and symbols are all different facets of this experiential reality. Even those who renounce the world still continue to participate as seers, not with a view to controlling the cosmic process but to participate in its flow. Others prefer a path of asceticism whereby instead of leaving the household they stay in it without any attachment to the fruits of action, ever taking delight in the cosmic process that goes on.

It would also appear from the *Manusmriti* that the world, its sustenance, expansion and development are the basic values. It is created in time and as time goes on, there is decline from pure to impure, from the age of truth and innocence to the age of anarchy and chaos. The author of the *Manusmriti* indeed had a moral view of history in which a certain notion of right order is considered a necessity for the sustenance of the world. Virtues like love and charity have a value because they enable the world to continue. So great is the concern of the author with the sustenance of the world that even a search for the ultimate should be deferred as long as the father, mother and guru are alive. Their service alone is dharma; so long as they are alive one need not bother about God or the intra-cosmic Gods at all. Contrary to the philosophy of Sankaracharya who regarded the world as an illusion, the life of the householder in the *Manusmriti* occupies an important position because it alone enables other ashramas such as, *brahmacharya* and *sanyasa* to continue; what is more, according to the *Manusmriti*, we can all know the rules and principles which govern life and its interrelationships. The presumption is that, while the highest reality is incomprehensible, beyond logic and reason, the process of its manifestation (*prgata*) and development is within the reach of human comprehension.[6] Its knowledge can be acquired and imparted.

The whole physical process as presented in the *Manusmriti* is a mixture of fact and fiction. It describes in great detail the picture of cosmic relationships; good and evil, truth and untruth are inextricably mixed in this process. Both these tendencies according to Manu found expression in the development of 'ego' as an element of human psyche. The formation of earth is a process of integration and differentiation of which human being is the highest manifestation. According to the *Manusmriti*, what distinguishes human beings from others in nature is the fact that human beings have the faculty of integral reasoning with the help of which they can acquire knowledge and wisdom, while other beings in nature merely respond to the outer world stimulus. Human beings have the capacity to transcend the realm of necessity and identify with the realm of freedom which is identical to experience of 'the Beyond', the other creatures are lower in the scale and are enslaved to the realm of necessity. It is because of this integral reasoning that human beings can discriminate between good and bad, just and unjust, desirable and undesirable. It is because of this again that they are able to devise a mode of existence which would enable them to experience freedom. This is so because man is endowed with will and activity in terms of which he can attain his desires and accomplish his ambitions.

Nature as well as society is governed by certain laws. In the Vedic period the word '*rita*' came to mean cosmic law. Later on it was replaced by the word '*dharma*'. The entire literature of the period incorporated the current language. Although Indian philosophy was speculative and metaphysical it never lost contact with the real life of the people because it always conceived of the world as a process towards the Beyond. The word '*rita*' which stood for natural order came to be identified with *dharma* which in the English language might be translated as the 'principles of right'. The precise distinction between *rita* and *dharma* remains elusive. Why did the latter term replace the former? We feel that the earlier term referred to natural causality in the sense in which Kant used this term. The latter refers specifically to 'moral concerns' of the human world. The idea presumably was that nature follows certain fixed laws. Human beings insofar as they are biological creatures, are parts of the natural process. But besides breath (*prana*) they also have a 'mind', a 'soul' and 'integral reasoning' in terms of which they can transcend or attempt to transcend the world of natural causality and be able to give a new direction to their past *karmas* for future life. It is in this sense that the concept of responsibility is applicable to the human world. Since man is not completely incorporated into the world of natural causality, and since he can have motives which may go beyond the immediate concerns of life, he may be moulded by his environment and not determined by it. He has his nature given to him at birth, but also acquires a temperament in the course of his living. Some concept other than that of *rita* was needed to ensure that the concept of human responsibility is not evacuated under the pretext of inevitability in the process of nature. Dharma was one such concept. It emphasized the importance of the distinctness of the individual temperament, motives, reasoning and action and yet connected them all into a grand architectonic designing of cosmic order. A Vedic hero, when acting according to dharma, acted with the best of motives, directed to a well-being beyond himself and assumed total responsibility for his motives and intentions but not so much for the consequences of his action which depended on a very complex set of socio-biological variables present in nature and which no man could always master. What enabled man in this way to break the bounds of natural causality (*rita*) was his soul (*atmana*), integral reason (*buddhi*) and motives (*mana*), an ability to grasp the necessary conditions for survival and an obligation to work for the good of others in terms of those conditions regardless of the fruits thereof. The form of a good act was an act performed with such motives and in such a manner as would lead to the sustenance and development of the individual living in society; a basic requirement for evaluating whether the action is according to dharma or not. According to the *Manusmriti*, one could discern this from the practices of good people who are free from attachment and hatred. The customary morality found in the scriptures is also of help. But in the final analysis each man will have to decide for himself on the basis of conscience because everything arises from *sankalpa* which is the idea of an end to be realized through action. This concept was developed in the *Mahabharata* later. The key precondition for an individual to perform such acts was the fact that though man neither fully knows the working of natural causality (which was also later on identified with 'fate' and 'time') nor could he ensure that the results of his actions would always be good, he was fully autonomous insofar as his motives and reasoning were concerned. In fact, this autonomy imposed an obligation on him to work with sincerity and integrity. The duty to work for others (with the best of intentions) regardless of the consequences, was clearly established and lay at the basis of the concept of the hero in the ancient world. It also found its eloquent expression in the Vedic lore of Vali who, despite the fact that he knew that Lord Vishnu was deceiving him, preferred to stick to the promise he had made, an act by which even the Gods were bound. In terms of philosophical development it was embodied later in Krishna's enunciation of '*nishkama karma*', doing one's duty with equanimity and without caring for the fruits thereof. There are apparent difficulties in this concept.

What happens if each individual defines his own moral values? The ancients were aware of this end, and therefore, they laid stress on customary morality. But is customary morality absolute? Such are the questions to which we shall return later. But is whatever the answer, they believed that it was possible for man and society to devise a mechanism for the transformation of human temperament towards achievement of normatively defined goals.[7]

One great merit of the *Manusmriti* is that forms of actions which are desirable and actions which are undesirable have been described in great detail. There are three concepts which are important here. As pointed out earlier, in *Manusmriti* there is a continuous effort to connect man as a part of the differentiated reality to the Beyond, the unmanifest. The supreme Brahman, who in Puranic literature is Vishnu, differentiates himself in a process called history. This process of differentiation is stated in the very beginning in the story of genesis which is repeated with slight modification in all Puranic literature. In the process of history man discovers reality to be engaged in a movement towards the Beyond. This process begins from the Divine, which differentiates itself in time, and then returns to the Beyond in the form of a series of cycles, at the end of which all are merged in the Brahman till a new cycle starts. History is, therefore, a zigzag process in which there is continuous fall from the age of truth termed *Satyayuga*, to the age of iron, called *Kalyuga*, through the intermediary stages of *Tretayuga* and *Dwaparyuga*. The first is the age in which truth reigns everywhere, while in the last it is completely destroyed and is replaced by the rule of the organised mighty (*Sanghu Shakti*). In *Satyayuga* man had long life, principles of right governed, and, as a result, justice prevailed everywhere and each caste followed the duties of its station. In *Kalyuga* man has short life, the principles of right are replaced by the principles of dominance of power and wealth and as a result there is no justice and caste disappears.[8] Then the cycle begins again. There is a certain inevitability in the decline but all is not resigned to fate. By appropriate action (*purushartha*) it is possible to have *Satyayuga* even in *Kalyuga*. Much would depend on the character and the disposition of the ruling classes. And hence the importance of politics (*rajniti*) and the system of punishment (*dandaniti*).

There is a functional division in society. According to Manu, men are equal not in their executive capacities but in terms of their enjoyment of desires. Since the executive capacities vary, each person must perform the functions for which he is naturally fitted.[9] People must be given different powers and stations in proportion to the qualities and talents they possess.

Manu divides society into four castes namely, *brahmanas, ksatriyas, vaisyas, sudras.* While the *brahmanas* are devoted to knowledge and pursuit of virtue, the *ksatriyas* are devoted to protection of others. The *vaisyas* are engaged in the production of services and goods and *sudras* are supposed to devote themselves to the service of others by performing manual labour. In this functional division is also implicit a social hierarchy in which the *brahmanas* occupy the highest position and *sudras,* the lowest. The *brahmanas* are considered superior to others because they are supposed to be completely selfless in pursuit of knowledge and wisdom and ever concerned with the welfare of others. They are like Plato's philosophers who are constantly in communion with the light and who have a complete notion of right. Second in order are the *ksatriyas,* in whom the will to protect people is combined with some selfish interest or personal ambition. In *vaisyas,* there is mostly self-interest in the form of hankering after accumulation of wealth. The fourth caste tends to the realm of necessity and therefore serves all the rest. It is in terms of this qualitative division of society that Manu argues that while the service of *brahmanas* is the best, the service of *vaisyas* is the worst. While *brahmanas* are completely selfless creatures ever concerned with the welfare of others, the *vaisyas* are just the opposite since their sole concern is with the accumulation of property unmindful of the effects such accumulation would have on others. Money-lenders were a typical example of this. Thus the man of property is contrasted to the man of knowledge, the commercial society based on the domination by property to the aristocratic society resulting from rule of knowledge. The idea that knowledge should rule follows directly from the basic position taken in the *Manusmriti* that if knowledge of the world is possible, and if *brahmanas* possess this knowledge, they deserve our reverence. A man who has experienced the light is virtually God and his advice merits the highest respect of all others.

Yet it must be pointed out that some of the passages refer to the hereditary basis of the caste system also in which the *brahmanas* are forbidden to have any social relations with *sudras.* Manu laid down a strict code of conduct for the *brahmanas* for the pursuit of penance, meditation and yoga. According to Manu, a *brahmana* must practise control of the senses by being of pure mind and pure action. Manu declares that the *brahmana* should never hurt others. A *brahmana* is even expected to learn from *sudras.* So great is Manu's emphasis on purity of principles that he declares that if a *brahmana* does not know the Vedas and still performs 'saradha' (a ceremony in honour of the dead) for others, he goes to hell and receives severe punishment. At another place Manu declares that if a *brahmana* deviates from the strict code of duty assigned to him he is not a *brahmana* and will suffer thousands of hells. He definitely does not deserve to be treated as a *brahmana*. This principle obviously contradicts the hereditary basis of the caste system. Indeed the whole idea of a *brahmana* is of a man who is capable of pursuing knowledge without any attachment, which is considered as the highest ideal, while the members of others castes have this kind of attachment. That is why priests were regarded as inferior because they used the money gifted to the temples.

It must be stated that the legitimation of *brahmanical* superiority still bristles with many contradictions. It is nowhere shown how the brahmanas are selected. Should one lack the *brahmanical* qualities, how can he be downgraded from the caste of *brahmana* to that of *sudra*. In the absence of such a mechanism it was natural that in due course, the principles of functional division of society and proportional justice were destroyed in favour of the most reprehensible system of *brahmanical* domination in accordance with principles of heredity.

Conflict between good and evil is a fact of nature. And good implies participation in the cosmic process in our effort to move Beyond. Nowhere does the value of participation appear more clearly than in the doctrine of repayment of debts to Gods, teachers, parents and society at large. To pay back this debt is called human endeavour. The first stage in this endeavour is to serve one's immediate superior, that is one's master and one's mother and father. In fact, according to Manu, service to each of these has priority over meditation and prayers, for they are considered veritable Gods. Intra-cosmic Gods (*devas*) are the ones who give, and since parents give us life, they all deserve our gratitude and respect. Then comes one's family. Indeed, the family is the foundation of the Hindu social organization. It is believed that if one cannot find happiness within the family, it will not be found elsewhere. Therefore, it is considered that both husband and wife must keep each other happy and satisfied. The wife is the very soul of her husband, but since she is physically weak and vulnerable, she should be protected by father, husband and children at different stages in her life.[10] There are, however, contradictory ideas on the place of women in society. On the one hand, the *Manusmriti* declares that the intra-cosmic Gods do not dwell where women are not respected, on the other women have been denied the practice of the *upanayana*. On the one hand, it is considered obligatory for both husband and wife to keep each other satisfied, on the other she is ever in a state of dependence on her father, husband and sons. She has been given complete charge of the internal management of the households and, yet it is not clear what is meant by this. It can, of course, be argued that these ideas are based on the functional division of labour between different components of the household, in an environment of mutual affection and love. Woman is neither an object of enjoyment nor a wage earner, but the very basis on which the glory of the household is built. The argument acquires some plausibility when we compare the position of a woman in the ancient world to the position of a woman today when she is becoming more and more either an object of lust or a competitor to man in all aspects of life, depriving the household of the necessary privacy and gentle care of the earlier system. However, it must be confessed that in the edition of the *Manusmriti* available to us there is definitely a shift from the Vedic ideal of complementarity to a new ideal of relative dependence which in years to come became more important and was one of the main factors responsible for the decline of the ancient civilization.

The family is central to social existence in the same way in which the heart is central to the body. The family is the institution which enables people belonging to other institutions to perform their functions. The good household is that in which there is mutual accord and which serves students, old people, the forefathers and Gods. But the chief aim of the family is not domination of others. There is realization that both power and wealth are necessary for the efficient management of the household. But both these should not become instruments of domination over others. They should not lead to pride and unrighteousness. Manu declares that a household commits sin by accumulating more property than is required by the end of fulfilment of needs and performance of one's duties towards one's parents, teachers and society. A craze for property merely becomes the cause of unhappiness. One should not merely follow one's own interest, or what satisfied oneself. Manu declares that one must strive to attain the happiness of others.

But what happens when there is a conflict of interest between duty to one's parents and the larger interests of society?[11] Manu's reply is simple. The basic governing principle of dharma is the welfare of others (*upkar*) and the welfare of the larger group must get precedence over the smaller group. The good of society is to be preferred to the good of one individual. The underlying belief is that while man is ostensibly related to others in various relationships, he is alone in the results of his actions; others do not participate in them and therefore he should not abandon the path of virtue for the sake of obliging his kith and kin. It is the pursuit of virtue alone which elevates the soul to the Brahmanhood. Manu advises that one must follow the obligations of one's station and household in a spirit of equanimity and slowly seek to earn spiritual merit. By doing so, one establishes firm links with the divine order and attains '*moksa*'. One may become a veritable God in this world itself. It is important to note here that there is no contradiction between '*moksa*' and '*dharma*', because the basic governing principle in both cases is sustenance of the cosmic process. Dharma is important because it enables people to sustain and develop the world towards the Beyond and therefore naturally it leads to *moksa*. The entire emphasis is one of coming to terms with life as it is. There are layers, levels and stages of existence and each one of us must try to experience it in our own way so that in due course (there is no hurry, it may take many lives), we experience the 'Beyond'.

This pragmatism of Manu nowhere comes out more clearly than in his ideas on kingship and international relations. In fact the most striking feature of the *Manusmriti* is that it conceives of politics as integral to society, as a basic factor without which society cannot function. Manu also subscribed to the then prevalent notion of the stronger fish devouring the smaller in the absence of politics. He was convinced that without a king there would be anarchy in which order would perish, the strong would devour the weak, no one would be able to perform his obligations and live a happy existence. Manu linked politics to ecology also and said that in the absence of the king even the trees would be felled. In fact this last point highlights the basic difference between the Greek and ancient Indian political thought clearly. The ancient Greeks were concerned with the individual's relationship to the cosmic order in which the community is an important link but not the end. According to the *Manusmriti*, the task before the government is the regulation of relationships of the entire manifest world in which even tress occupy a place important to the unmanifest. Governments must ensure that no one is able to dominate the others. It is in this sense that the view of the individual in Indian thought is very different from that in the West. According to Manu, if everyone fulfils his obligations, this must also ensure the good of all. A good state must be judged not only by the services rendered by it but also by the quality of people inhabiting it, for Manu says a good kingdom is that in which many saintly people live, there is no disease, fruits and vegetables are grown in plenty, people are polite and fearless, there are good crops and easy commerce. The main duty of the king is to protect good people and punish the bad ones. He must remove the thorns in the path of good life. There is no place in his state for smugglers, profiteers or blackmarketeers. The whole emphasis is on the idea that the community cannot be divorced from the cosmic relationship. The powers of the king are limited by the purpose for which the kingdom has been created. A kingdom in which there is theft or dacoity or which is full of smugglers cannot survive.[12] To protect the weak, specially orphans, widows and the old is the supreme duty and the highest religion of the king.[13]

A selfish king eventually becomes a cause of his own destruction. The king is enjoined to protect people and not violate dharma.[14] We must ensure that the strong are not able to exploit the weak.[15] A kingdom in which the weak are exploited perishes.[16] The king must ensure that evil persons are contained and that every man is motivated to the pursuit of right.[17] In exercise of whimsical authority, the king is destroyed with his relatives, for this leads to trouble not only for the people but also for saints and other cosmic beings.[18]

Manu's ideas on social organization aimed at establishment of order in terms of a certain notion of proportionate justice. He envisaged courts of justice in which judges are appointed on the basis of their character and experience by the king. The decisions of the judges should be based not only on equity (*dharmam sasvatam asritya*) but also take into account diverse customs and practices of different castes, regions and even families. This once again highlights the acceptance of the differentiated reality by the author. Kingly power is conceived as originating in the authority of God Vishnu, though for its day-to-day performance it is dependent on the approval of the elders including the *brahmanas* and seers in the state. Manu tries to reconcile the authority of the king with a social system in which the authority of the *brahmanas* is accepted as supreme and pure. He enjoins that the two castes, the *ksatriyas* and the *brahmanas*, must act in concert with each other to ensure order in society. Though the king derives his authority from Vishnu, he is also regarded as subordinate to the authority of *brahmanas* and loyalty to him is always conditional on the fact that he would maintain the *varna* system in society. Manu could not separate politics from socio-religious practices of the time, the two were clearly tied to each other. It is argued that the king's power grows only when he maintains the *varna* system and ensures that everyone follows his duties. At one place, Manu goes to the extent of postulating that the opinions of the *brahmanas* must be respected and even what one *brahmana* learned in the Vedas declares to be the dharma must not be disputed.[19]

According to Manu, a good king alone is not enough. He must be assisted and advised by good and truthful ministers and civil servants. Manu says that in the discharge of his duty the king must be guided by the advice of his ministers and wise men. He must ensure that his ministers are firm in truth and firm in action. He lays down elaborate rules for the selection of ministers. Exercise of whimsical authority destroys the king and his relatives. It is for this reason that Manu elaborates a system of education for the king. The objective of this education is not merely to provide knowledge, but also to teach the king how to control his senses.

Manu was pragmatic enough to be conscious of the fact that sometimes evil methods have to be employed in politics to gain good ends. But he wanted the king never to forget that it is in truth that the ultimate victory lies. For the fulfilment of the ends of the state, Manu recommended the following types of structural arrangements:

(i) Organization of the State (Rajyamsamgrahyam)

The organization of the state is recommended in terms of ascending cycles of villages, districts and provinces. This is an arrangement which would roughly correspond to our system of administration at district and village levels. It is interesting to point out that the basic governing principle of this organization is that the larger group must deal with a problem only when the smaller group fails. It is better to solve problems, as far as possible, in the place where they arise. Some such principle of decentralization has always exercised a fascination over the Indian mind and this presumably originated in the belief that such a large and diverse country cannot be governed except by organizing the state in terms of smaller units.

(ii) Taxation

The system of taxation should be such as would increase the national wealth. Manu is very clear in his mind that a kingdom in which people starve perishes sooner or later. The king is entitled to 1/50 of the gold, 1/6 of crop, 1/12th of the commerce. He must see to it that people are not over-taxed for these very people are the ultimate source of his wealth and property. Though Manu recommends harsh measures against anti-social elements, he seems to be convinced that unless people are given sufficient autonomy, the economy would not flourish.

(iii) Wages

Wages should be fixed in accordance with the merits of the earners. Manu is not in favour of distributing positions and honours in the state on the basis of heredity alone though he recognizes that since certain traits of character are passed on from generation to generation, the principle of heredity should not be disregarded altogether.

(iv) Public Opinion

For organization of public opinion, Manu contemplates an assembly of the learned as well as the officers of state. In the assembly, they are expected to decide issues on the basis of dharma. The members of the assembly are expect to speak their minds without fear and favour, for anyone who does not do so is, according to Manu, an evil person. When people refuse to speak their minds, Manu argues, the truth is destroyed and the whole assembly along with the king perishes. Once again it is emphasized that it is virtue alone which is a true friend, everything else perishes, and, therefore, one should not leave the path of virtue for the sake even of one's children, wife and relatives. Not making known one's mind and not making right judgement, both lead to the ruin of the kingdom. It is not clear whether sudras were forbidden to take part in deliberations of the assembly. Perhaps it was an aristocracy which Manu favoured. Whatever it was, the king and his assembly were expected not to violate dharma. Manu clearly states that the king is subject to law which is framed by the learned, not by the king himself, and anyone who defies this law deserves to be punished. In fact people are justified when the king deviates from dharma or disregards the joint advice of his ministers and councillors, even in killing the king. Obedience to the king is necessary but it is conditional on the king's performance of this functions.

One can see that the important principles of the organization of the state in the *Manusmriti* are decentralization and welfare activities. In Manu's scheme, the village and district authorities have been given sufficient autonomy to control their affairs as it is supposed that the king shall not interfere in their affairs until he discovers that they are unable to solve their problems at their own level. Further Manu's state is not a police state; the king is supposed to undertake various welfare activities in the interest of all. The king should also involve himself in the process of production and distribution in society. There is a general injunction that the king must increase the wealth of the society and distribute what has been increased. It is indeed astounding to know that very early in the development of Indian political thought, the ideas of decentralization, welfare state and public opinion are so clearly spelled out. In fact a strong philosophical defence of these ideas in terms of differentiated reality in the process of the movement towards the Beyond has been provided; this view of a multi-dimensional, multi-structured reality, at different levels and stages of growth, yet united by the *noetic* principle of 'the Beyond', inevitably leads to the doctrine of the welfare state in terms of a differentiated society. There are apparent difficulties in Manu's ideals about individual '*karma*', social relationships and political order. What happens if each individual defines his own role independently of society? Since he is responsible for his own '*karma*', will there be no conflict of wills? What is the role of customary morality in relation to abstract principles of right and justice? Is it absolute or relative? Whatever the answer, it was a great leap forward for the human mind to think that it was possible for man in society to devise with the help of politics a mechanism for transforming human life towards the achievement of normatively defined goals.

NOTES

1. A. V. VII, 105
2. Betty Hermann, *India and Western Philosophy*, p. 35.
3. *Manusmriti* II: 22.
4. RV X: 129.7 quoted and translated A.C. Bose, *Hymns from Vedas*, (New Delhi, Asia, 1966), p. 305.
5. *Manusmriti*, I: 97, 98.
6. Ibid., I: 8, 9.
7. Ibid., I: 21, 22, 26, 28-30.
8. Ibid., I: 83, 84, 86.
9. Ibid., I: 3, 160.
10. Ibid., IV: 111, 112, 116.
11. Ibid., IV: 240-42.
12. Ibid., VII: 27, 28.
13. Ibid., VII:143-44.
14. Ibid., VII: 14.
15. Ibid., VII: 75.
16. Ibid., VII: 20.
17. Ibid., VII: 22.
18. Ibid., VII: 29.
19. U.N. Ghoshal, *A History of Indian Political Thought* (Oxford, 1959), p. 160.

CHAPTER 3

THE HEROIC VISION: VALMIKI AND VYASA

The earlier writings had sought to explore the structure of reality. They started with the presumption that no absolute knowledge of God was possible. All the time we live in a state of uncertainty and imperfect knowledge of God in which at every moment the experience of the 'Beyond' is being expressed through language, thoughts and symbols and yet is never fully encompassed. But while the unmanifest, noetic supreme Brahman was beyond the reach of senses, the manifest world of intra-cosmic Gods as well as the material world constituted by the three qualities of *sattva* (truth), *rajas* (energy), and *tamas* (inertness) could be known to some extent. There was always the possibility that the mysterious would burst forth in unexpected directions and, therefore, one could not be fully certain about what was absolutely good or false, or even about the possibilities of existence. As a process of creative evolution, life was supposed to be full of immense possibilities in which the best option man had was to perform his duty with happy spontaneity (*sahaja karma*) regardless of the consequences of his action on himself. Beyond it there are layers, levels and stages of existence in which each one of us is given to experience the reality in our own way.

This outlook nowhere comes out more clearly than in the epic literature which was a combination of myths and mysticism on the one hand and the world of intra-cosmic Gods and human beings on the other. Both *Ramayana* and *Mahabharata*, therefore, seek to emphasize the coming to terms with life as it is. The qualities of a true devotee expounded in the Gita point to this fact. They emphasize complete surrender of the consequence of ones' action to God. But it seems that along with the unitarian view of the Vedas, there had also developed two antagonistic philosophies of idealism and materialism creating a chasm between man, nature and God. The idealist thought found its culminating point in the Upanishadic philosophy. There

were obviously several stages in the process, many points of development
and regression. Our knowledge of the exact process of the development of
ideas in the period is grossly inadequate. There were schools which
preached the immortality of the soul amidst three levels of existence,
namely, gross, subtle and causal in the cosmic process of the philosophies
of *karma* (action) and *sansar* (worldly process), ideas which through the
Upanishadic philosophy and the *Samhitas* and *Srutis* became the
cornerstones of Indian civilization. The materialist doctrine had its
beginnings in the Vedas but reached its apogee in the philosophy of
lokayata. Besides their spiritualism, to the Vedas are also attributed the
first questionings about the world of 'in Between' explicable in terms of
such positive sciences as mathematics, astronomy and medicine. The
overall impression was that the cosmos could be understood as a structure
within a process, consisting of various levels and hierarchies: hierarchy in
the divine, in the human, in the animal world, as also in the planetary
systems. In their search for underlying principles the ancients recognized
the One in the many and many in One, and from the Vedas came the view
that knowledge is the power through which the cosmic process could be
understood. In these early writings also we find the beginnings of a
rudimentary atomic theory of the universe, which received its culmination
in the writings of Aryabhatta and Bhaskaracharya later on. It must,
however, be added that for various reasons the materialist doctrine never
received great impetus. The *lokayata* and *kapalika* or even tantric traditions
always existed on the periphery of ancient society. Their general approach,
however, was later incorporated in the positivist traditions from Kautilya
to Somedeva, namely that knowledge acquired in terms of known objects
was useful and especially for those entrusted with the task of ruling.

It appears that during the period preceding the *Ramayana* there came
into existence some schools which doubted the basis and authority of the
Vedic view of life and tried to demolish it. This trend of course later on
found its expression in such philosophical movements as in *lokayata* and
kapalika. Tradition has been very harsh in its treatment of these movements.
It would appear that while they were utilitarian they were not subversive
of the existing systems in spite of all that their denigrators have told us from
time to time. Although they are credited with the adage that since there is
no after-life, we should 'eat, drink and be merry', they do not seem to have
questioned the commonsense notions of the society in which they lived.
However, they were disliked because they denied the three cardinal tenets
of the Vedic view, namely, God, cosmic process and *karma* and made a
distinction between nature which is purely a physical process and society

which is human creation. They had perhaps noticed the diversity in customs and laws, the exploitation of the masses in the name of transcendental doctrines and were naturally sceptical of the whole of tradition, the authority of laws, the truth of religions, and believed in the class basis of justice and virtue. During the decline of the ancient Indian civilization, they perhaps lashed out against the authority of religions and priests, of the institutions of the family and state, the alleged superiority of Aryan culture over non-Aryan.

II

The *Ramayana* is a reassertion of the unitarian view of the cosmic process of a movement towards the Beyond. There is one difference of course. While in the earlier writings principles were baldly stated, in these two epics there is sometimes a discussion to emphasize the sovereignty of dharma. Both the *Ramayana* and the *Mahabharata* refer to war and periods of relative uncertainty in which power in all its forms had come to plague men. And both make an effort to transcend this sordid condition of mankind by stressing that there are certain principles of nature to which man must conform. Rama is the first king around whom a whole new concept of life, society and politics emerges in the writings of Valmiki. It seems it was written at a time when the materialist outlook had gained the upper hand, leading to violence and corruption. One does not know whether the story of the *Ramayana* was fact or fiction. Some writers have questioned the authenticity of the story. But there is no doubt that in Rama and Ravana were created two powerful personalities centring round dominance or subordination of ethical principles to materialist reality. Ravana was a man possessed of immense knowledge and power. He ruled over Lanka which was unequalled in wealth and splendour. And yet because he had become arrogant and transgressed into the spheres of everyone else, he had to suffer the fate of all tyrants. His besetting sin was that he succumbed to the temptation of the material world, became arrogant and denied the supremacy of 'the Beyond'. Rama, on the other hand, was bound by the customary morality and worked for the welfare of his subjects by upholding it.

Whatever the twists and turns of the story, there are elaborate discussions of polity in dialogue form. The political thought in the *Ramayana* was more a synthesis of conventional wisdom. The virtue of adherence to conventional morality was stressed. Valmiki accepted the possibility of two kinds of life embodied in the respective personalities of Rama and

Ravana, but his intention was to uphold the superiority of the ideals cherished by Rama whose whole life was depicted as an effort to establish the supremacy of right.

Not much is known about the life of Valmiki. It is said that he was given the foresight to see the events before they actually happened by Brahma, the creator of the universe, when he presumably asked the latter about the ideal king. Myth and legend tell us that he was a dacoit who later on became a sanyasi after being questioned by his family members, at the behest of the sages particularly Maharshi Bhrigu, as to why when they shared his ill-gotten wealth they were not prepared to partake in his sins. There is no doubt that he was far more influential in shaping the notions of life of ordinary Indians than anyone else. With him the notion of an ideal state found its clearest expression and became the reference point for all subsequent political thought. There are various reasons for this. The text of the book was assiduously preserved and passed on from generation to generations. Another notable feature was the elegance of the writing itself which tried to express not only the life of Rama but also abstruse and profound truths of philosophy in elegant poetic form. Also noteworthy was the humanism embedded in his ideas which presented a mirror to life. It is no exaggeration to say that both the epics, the *Ramayana* and the *Mahabharata*, have been more influential in shaping the currents of life in India than all other philosophical texts put together. Their fascination for any student of politics in India increases when we consider that ordinary people in India still believe that Rama was an ideal king who laid the foundations of social morality for eternity. There is a grain of truth in this belief because the *Ramayana* laid the foundations of a world view which was to dominate all subsequent thinking on social relationships in India. Valmiki's *Ramayana* established the image of Rama as an ideal ruler. He was also an upholder of the supremacy of public opinion. It is said that he banished his wife, Sita, from the kingdom because a dhobi in his realm doubted her character. It was certainly a poor way of showing deference to public opinion and Rama has been reproached by many writers for this, but considering the fact that Rama did not marry again and suffered the pangs of separation, there is no doubt that it at once and finally established in the public mind the idea that for the rulers public opinion is more important than anything else. It is in this light that the feeling that the state envisioned in the *Ramayana* was an ideal state is not without foundation. Rama was a symbol of an enlightened king, who would subordinate his own interest and that of his nearest and dearest to the interest of the people. To quote the *Ramayana* about his qualities: "He is upright, true to his vows, modest and a preserver of law. His character is high and pure. He is famous, wise and possesses the knowledge of all. He is the protector of all, defender of religion and the caste system. He is the supporter of his kinsmen and friends. He is like Prajapati himself. He is the supporter of all and destroyer of his enemies. He always gives shelter to his devoted followers. He is deeply versed in the Vedas and Vedangas. He is highly skilled in archery, and his valour is admitted by his dying foes. He has great fortitude. He is a genius and possesses excellent manners, is profoundly learned in all the sacred lore. He is wise, compassionate and valiant. Everyone is fond of him ... he meets out equal treatment to his friends and foes."[1]

Rama was not the only king whose example was often quoted, though his was the most shining. Prithu was also idolized as one who saved people from both the tyranny of the king Vena and the resultant chaotic conditions. Vena disregarded customary law as embodied in the Vedas and claimed full sovereignty for himself. All principles of moral life were thrown to the winds and the strong began to oppress the weak. So despicable were conditions that even the sages reminded him though in vain, of his agreement to protect his subjects. When Vena replied by claiming absolute sovereignty and his right to create law, he was belaboured by the angry sages. Out of his right arm was born Prithu who was then installed as king.[2] The interesting thing about both Prithu and Rama is that both accepted the supremacy of customary morality as enunciated by *brahmanas* and seers. Kings were ideal in so far as they elevated the concept of public welfare above personal welfare.

The foundation of the state in the Valmiki *Ramayana* is dharma which is "the prime object and basis of truth".[3] Dharma is used in different senses in different contexts, sometimes with the meaning of right and justice, and sometimes right order. In Valmiki it had replaced the Vedic concept of *rita*.[4] As already pointed out in the previous chapter, *rita* referred to regularities in the whole cosmic process whilst dharma had specific reference to the human context of those regularities. Sometimes, it was thought to be a fixed principle. At other times, it was identified with customs, convention, usages and the system of religious beliefs prevailing then. But on the whole it was believed to be the knowledge "directed to the achievement of desired happiness here and hereafter".[5]

The real driving force of Valmiki's vision is not social but transcendental too. Like all ancient thinkers, he looks beyond this life to liberation hereafter and believes firmly in the immortality of the soul. The pursuit of dharma enables one to attain that state. In fact, there is a tension between the ideal of renunciation and the ideal of performance of one's obligations;

hermit might represent the former and kings like Janaka and Rama the latter. There are various sections which allude to the final bliss which is available to the virtuous. But on the whole it is the ideal of dharma, due performance of one's duties, which wins. It occupies the highest pedestal because it alone successfully conceptualizes the differentiated reality to the 'Beyond'.

There is an interesting discussion of the relative merits or demerits of righteous conduct. At one place Lakshmana revolts against dharma and repeats all the arguments which would normally be found in the bag of a *carvaka* philosopher. He says, "nature is happy without any morality: so created beings can also be happy without any religion whatsoever".[6] Another person who argues in the same way is Javali.[7] He gives epistemological, ontological and ethical arguments in support of his views. He argues that since dharma cannot be perceived, while other objects can be, it does not exist. Moreover, in the world, the unrighteous people live happily while the righteous suffer. The two standard arguments in favour of dharma were those of destiny and soul. Lakshmana repudiates both of them. He says that if one is slain at the order of destiny then "it is destiny which is touched by the sinful act and not the doer".[8] Predetermination absolved men from all responsibility. As far as the soul is concerned, there is no need to worry about the consequences of good or evil because the soul neither suffers nor enjoys. In the context of Rama's banishment, he says that since observance of truth was dharma Rama was not bound by it. According to him even Dasratha was not bound by it. In fact, referring to history and mythology, he argues that history is full of instances when people who could not follow the righteous path (*dharma*) followed the unrighteous one (*adharma*). He gives the example of Indra killing Vishvarupa muni and then performing sacrifices. On the other hand, he asserts that actions leading to loss of wealth lead to one's annihilation and adds: "A man who has wealth has friends, he who has riches has relatives, he who has wealth has individuality in the world, he who has wealth is a learned man, powerful, intelligent, mighty, armed, full of fortune and graces . . . and has dharma, desires attend to him, he is auspicious."[9]

One of the most astounding things is that there is no immediate attempt to reply to Lakshmana. But in general Valmiki took the position that all creatures are bound by both general and specific dharma. He gave the following arguments in favour of dharma:

(i)   Dharma can be known. He believed that man can discern it with the help of their intelligence.[10] He was aware that it is difficult to understand but it is there in the heart of everyone. To quote, "It is the soul of all beings which discerns good and evil."[11]

(ii) Dharma cannot be divorced from prosperity and pleasure. He felt that there is no opposition between prosperity (*artha*), pleasure (*kama*) and right (*dharma*). Each has its own importance in different times, seasons and contexts.[12] But dharma is supreme because it regulates both our quest for prosperity and for pleasures. It also defines satisfaction of immediate desires. Prosperity does not mean acquisition of all kinds of wealth. It only means acquisition of wealth with spiritual intent. This should obviously mean that it is dharma which relates prosperity and pleasure to their objectives. We can know true interest or true prosperity only through dharma.

(iii) Since time and fate play an important role, in the ultimate analysis, dharma also implies purity of mind. Man may not be responsible for what happens around him, but he is certainly responsible for his own mind which he should seek to control.[13] Indeed this argument has a streak of existentialism in it, so far as it identifies the authentic life with the heroic life, in which the hero works with the best of motives, unmindful of the consequences of his action on others.

(iv) Dharma is also necessary in order to create order in society. Order is necessary for the sustenance of society. It is the basis of the welfare of all. Valmiki wrote: "Pious men living with vicious men will meet destruction for the sins of others, though they themselves did not commit any misdeeds, like unto fish living in a lake where snakes dwell."[14] It was perhaps the strongest secular argument in favour of right. Valmiki is clear that we need dharma because in its absence there would be anarchy and the weak would perish.

(v) Valmiki was not sure of the strength of these arguments against the position of the materialists. He, therefore, added that those who follow right go to heaven, and even to *brahmaloka* which is the seventh or eighth heaven in the Hindu system. On the other hand, those who go against it go to hell.

There is always a tension between differentiated and integrated reality which later on assumes the form of a tension between dharma and *moksa*. But Valmiki tries to resolve this tension by returning to experiential reality. Both human effort and divine grace are incomplete by themselves. Since men's rationality is limited, whatever men do is limited. In this scheme, there is no place for arrogance or dogmatism. Dharma is believed to be the right order which sustains society. The Vedas are presumed to contain a compendium of the rules of dharma. All those who do not accept them are condemned to go to the nether world. Valmiki demolished the *lokayata* argument, which was destined to play an important role later on. *Lokayata* had asserted that there was nothing like dharma, it was man made, and generally served the interest of the strong. It seems this view was held by a group of people, it certainly lay at the root of what Ravana was trying to do; right was accepted as subservient to what was expedient. Another source of evidence for this appears in Javali's account of the *caravaka* position. When he implores Rama to return to Ayodhya and not to renounce his ancestral kingdom, he argues that man is born alone and dies alone. Attachment to others is a sign of insanity. Good people are never attached to others. There is no point in suffering because everyone is going to be annihilated by death. He rejects the principle of life after death and mocks at the ceremonies of the dead. These arguments about gifts and penances, he says, have been devised by clever people to rule over others, to make them submissive and disposed to charity. According to him, there is neither an afterworld nor any religious practice for attaining it. He tries to support this argument by a doctrine of knowledge which presumes that there is nothing beyond experience, and consequently one should not think or act in terms of what lies beyond it.

Rama, however, replies by saying that the Sastras have supremacy over experiences and anyone who preaches against them is not honoured. It is one's conduct which decides whether one is high born or low born. If one acts according to the doctrine propounded by Javali, mischief will ensue. There would be anarchy in social life. If acting according to one's own precepts is accepted as right even a bad person would be able to justify his conduct. Rama particularly stressed the supreme importance of *myths* as a basis for the existence and survival of all worlds. He further argued that worldly possessions as well as spiritual gifts are bestowed on those who follow truth. Devotion to truth is the highest of all spiritual faiths.[15] He realizes that it is not always easy to follow the path of truth but argues that it is one's adherence to the principles of truth which decides one's nobility. He eloquently says, "Noble men have always borne its burden."[16]

Both Lakshmana and Javali have powerful arguments. But both are rejected. The dialogue form has its advantages, and allows the writer to advance his own point of view. Sometimes Valmiki glides nimbly over some of the crucial issues and ironies of actual social and political life. At other times he accepts the actuals of life but fails to reconcile them with the high moral principles he seeks to espouse. The actual is contrasted with the ideal and the ideal with the actual as and when it suits him. The result is that at times we are made to accept without good reason the inequality among human beings or the banishment of Sita.

However, the main attempt of Valmiki was to establish that dharma is objective, real and rooted in the very order of the cosmic process of 'In Between'. He refers to the origin of the state, the ingredients of the ideal city. The presentation is clear and straightforward. The State arises out of our desire to escape from natural anarchy in which the strong eat the weak, as larger fishes eat the smaller ones. It is a kind of contract theory in which rulership is a creation of human convention. But this is also wedded to the idea that once the ruler is installed he becomes the embodiment of Lord Vishnu, the supreme ruler of the Universe, and must be obeyed. Thus while the state arises from human need it derives its legitimation from the sordid fact that life would not be possible without it.

But from another angle, society precedes the emergence of the state and has its own form of organization independent of it. Men have different natures and temperaments, skills and capabilities and society is a mutual exchange of services. There is a natural division of labour for the merchants, warriors, priests, farmers and others, which provides the material base of society. These are the arms, legs, and head of society. The state emerges in order to reconcile their respective claims. Such a society in which there are different kinds of people with their own skills and interests could not exist without the state. Since there is no end to man's cupidity, and since the goods are limited, people come into conflict with each other. They covet each other's wealth and wares leading to conflicts and wars. This leads to anarchy and necessitates a central controlling power which would reconcile the claims of all in society.

In Valmiki's state the upper level is composed of the king, council of ministers, and sages who are generally *brahmanas* and the base is constituted by those who are actually engaged in the task of production. The most important thing, Valmiki believes, is that there should be a clear distinction between all castes. The possibility of movement from one caste or *varna* to another is not ruled out. Membership of the caste depends on one's qualities, but there are two constraints. First, it must be accepted that no one is fit to perform all functions. Men are endowed with different qualities, depending upon their nature and temperament, and therefore, they should not meddle with the business of others. Very few people are really fit to govern. Secondly, since this is so, too much intermingling of the castes ruins the state. We might say that Valmiki was laying the foundation for the class privileges of an aristocratic society. However, it must be realized that the scheme of functional division envisaged by him was subordinate to a vision of moral life in which there are so many constraints on the ruling classes. A life good for merchants cannot be good for the brahmanical class. One of the safety valves in his scheme is the denial of right to wealth for *brahmanas*. Even more striking is the system of constraints to which a king is expected to conform. He is expected to be in complete control of his senses and compassionate towards all creatures. Behind this social structure lay the belief that human society can function properly if it follows the pattern of order found in nature. The task of a good ruler lies in discerning the structure of this natural order, relating it to human beings and enforcing it with severity. Just as the Sun is the central point of nature, the notion of dharma was seen as the driving force which, when properly enforced by the central powers, keeps all planets as well as individuals in society in their respective places. Real knowledge consists in knowledge of the structure of the cosmic process and the principles governing it. The highest virtue consists in following laws which conform to this pattern. Anything which goes against it is condemned. Valmiki advocated the caste system because he believed that it conforms to the natural hierarchy; the rulers are there to keep everyone in his proper place. They are themselves subject to natural laws and cannot claim absolute power because this would disturb the natural order of things where everyone has his appointed function in accordance with his nature and temperament. The whole emphasis was on creation of right order.

Indian society by the time of Valmiki had already come to accept this division; Valmiki was merely giving expression to it. He was providing legitimacy to the system which practical experience had taught him was functional. The crucial thing according to him is that everyone in society must perform his functions, the rulers are no exception; they too must operate the system to uphold the sovereignty of dharma in terms of the guidance they receive from men of knowledge and wisdom. This doctrine is important because it made the office of kingship dependent on something outside itself. Politics is autonomous in relation to the productive and distributive apparatus of society; but as far as the determination of law is concerned, it is dependent on other spheres of social life. Indeed law and society are prior to the state. In ancient India the principles of dharma had existed from time immemorial. They had the sanction of custom. The kings did not make law; they merely executed it. Their actions were judged in terms of customary law. Whether there were constitutional checks on the exercise of powers by the king apart from *sabha* and *samiti*, or moral injunctions laid down in scriptures, we do not know. But the very presence of these bodies and the emphasis on dharma meant that the kings had to be careful; beyond a certain point they knew that people would not tolerate injustice.

It is not possible here to provide a detailed critique of the social and political ideas of *Ramayana*. The entire modern thought in India is an attempt in this direction. We shall allude here to two points of historical importance. First, the point that salvation consists in due performance of one's own function has had an extraordinary appeal in the development of Indian society and has found its resurgence in recent times in the ideas of Vivekananda and Tilak. Second, the concept of the ideal ruler, who subordinates his own welfare to the happiness of the people, who yields power as a matter of duty, looks after the interests of the community, of the old, the weak and the women, has been the aspiration of all subsequent political thought in India and found its echo in the Gandhian concept of *Ramarajya*. Both these ideals had a certain philosophical finality about them. From the point of view of philosophical argument, it was not a very systematic attempt. But it was not philosophy but the reality of the experience with which the poet was concerned and he was able to express this experiential reality through myths and symbols in a manner rarely equalled in the history of human literature. The entire vision was a synthesis of the ideal of individual salvation and that of community welfare. By postulating a disinterested performance of duties by the king as well as his subjects in the welfare of all, Valmiki made it possible to transcend this dualism of consciousness and material world in our journey towards the unmanifest.

It must be added here that such a system has mostly been an aspiration and very rarely, if at all, has it been realized in practice in known history. Most people who accepted this vision turned it into a system which served the interests of the dominant castes, became rigid in due course, and led to agonizing experiences for the downtrodden. History is replete with examples of kings refusing to listen to the voices of sanity, when politics became a game of power with bigger armies and more wealth. In so far as the myth of the enlightened ruler was established, the concern for building institutions for expression of the voices of sanity was pushed into the background. The unfortunate result was that when the moral fabric of society began to disintegrate, the real power passed into hands of the king and his advisers who then took every advantage of the powers they acquired to aggrandize themselves at the expense of others. Yet it does not detract from the value of the ideal of *Ramarajya* as a standard in terms of which all states, and particularly the ruling classes, must be evaluated; if man has not fulfilled his promise so much the worse for him. Subsequent writers made an attempt to moderate the ideal of *Ramarajya* so that it would become practical. The first full effort in this direction is found in Vyasa's *Shantiparva*.

III

Vyasa's *Mahabharata* is an account of a legendary battle which took place possibly about 3102 BC. Once again the date is not certain: some have even questioned the historical authenticity of the work. But be that as it may, it remains the most powerful legend in the minds of Indians. So great is its importance that it is considered the fifth Veda. Some even believe that the *Ramayana* war took place after the *Mahabharata* war. Whatever the historical truth, there is no doubt that the *Mahabharata* story is far more complex. It is the largest single poem in the world. Whereas the *Ramayana* story gives the impression of having been a part of an agricultural, rural society of small townships, the *Mahabharata* is located in a truly urban civilization with all its complexities. How the change came about, what events intervened, we do not know. The authors of both the works shared most of their values and assumptions, such as belief in a cosmic process and the caste system and faith in the superiority of aristocratic rule. Whatever the quality of the intervening period the philosophic vision of the two is broadly similar. The main difference lies in emphasis. The *Ramayana* is more idealistic whereas the *Mahabharata* is more practical. In that sense the two together constitute the twin pillars on which stood the entire structure of ancient Indian civilization. The *Ramayana* is simple, sober, written in an elegant and musical style which spontaneously wins our heart. The hero Rama is the archetype of an Ideal King. The *Mahabharata* is musical too, but it is too complex, at times jarring to the ears; it is a turbulent sea beside the calm waters of the *Ramayana*. If stories are to be believed, some of which appear truly fanciful, the age of the *Mahabharata* must have witnessed many developments in the field of astronomy, embryology and medicine. Science had definitely made great strides. There are separate chapters devoted to a summary of the prevalent views on these subjects. From a historical viewpoint, it is considered to be a record of the second battle (the battle of *Ramayana* being the first) which was of more than local or regional significance. Some of the events were even recorded in terms of planetary movements such as the death of Bhisma. It also contain descriptions of lands and people known to the heroes of the *Mahabharata*.

The political philosophy is mainly found in *Shantiparva*, though there are interesting discussions elsewhere too. At the end of the war, one of the heroes Yudhistira, who succeeds to throne, goes to Bhisma, his grand sire, who is awaiting his death in the battlefield, for instruction in statecraft. The result is one of the most comprehensive and profound discourses on kingship, the duties of subjects, and indeed the whole historical process which alternates between order and anarchy, the mainfest and unmanifest. Vyasa's discussion of virtue, right, astronomy and other sciences was extremely comprehensive. He was a great compiler of all aspects of life. There is scarcely anything which escaped his attention; he wrote on almost all subjects. As regards the general view cf the universe, his ideas dominated Indian thought for a considerable time. Though the moral vision of the *Mahabharata* has been alternately admired or rejected in recent times, it remains a mirror to the glory that was India.

The influence of the *Mahabharata* is all the more remarkable because we do not have the original copy. There have been so many additions, alterations and interpolations that one does not really know which part is authentic. This makes the *Mahabharata* one of the most enigmatic writings in the history of ancient India. Whatever the nature of the controversies surrounding its authorship,[17] there is no doubt that the discussion of moral and political ideas in the *Shantiparva* is eminently readable, reflecting a profundity and depth of vision about the organization of political life not matched elsewhere. The overall message remains clear. The recommendations are sharp and categorical, though complex in so far as they seek to cope with the complex structure of the differentiated reality in relation to the Beyond. It is a remarkable treatise written with complete scientific detachment and existentialist anguish at the human predicament. Both the victors and the vanquished are described with all their virtues and vices, fads and foibles, perhaps conveying the notion that what counted in life was neither victory nor defeat but the capacity to lead a heroic life of authenticity. This comes out very clearly in two facts. Krishna who was considered the incarnation of God had also to witness in his own life the destruction of his capital and tribe; he even met death at the hands of an ordinary bowman. Similarly, Arjun who had won the war and was the greatest of archers, finally had to suffer an ignominious defeat at the hands of Bhils on his way back to Hastinapur from Dwarka where he had gone to escort the wives of Krishna after the latter's death.

Vyasa's general position was almost an extension of the general position of the Vedic and post-Vedic literature such as the *Ramayana*. He also subscribed to the earlier theory of the four types of activities: devotion to knowledge, ruling, production, and menial labour. Corresponding to these are four kinds of virtues such as establishing relationship with the divine, pursuit of right, prosperity and satisfaction. Right (*dharma*) is the activity which maintains balance and harmony among all other activities and thereby sustains them and leads to the supreme good of all. In society, there are four classes corresponding to the four activities described above namely, *vaisyas* who are engaged in agriculture, rearing of cattle and trade, *ksatriyas* engaged in providing protection, *brahmanas* devoted to the Vedas, knowledge and the science of morals and *sudras* engaged in the service of others. It is declared that when each class performs the functions for which its members are by nature and temperament fitted, there is right in society.[18] One can see the lines of similarity between this and the view taken in the Platonic dialogues. It was rooted in the general picture of a harmonious and integrated cosmos as a process in which everything has its appointed function. There is obviously nothing beyond the reach of man if he properly understands the pattern of an intricate, inter-related and hierarchically ordered cosmos, where there are many levels and practices and everything is justified in terms of its own level of development. The process according to the *Mahabharata* is made up of our beneficial and sinful actions, neither of which exists without the other. Human life is itself a precarious balance between good and evil, between tendencies which uplift us towards the Beyond and those which take us downwards. The first were called *daivic* (divine) and the second *asuric* (demonic) tendencies. In this process everyone has his potential in accordance with his own nature, temperament and the level of development he occupies in the cosmic process. The development for the individual as well as the family consists in making the *daivic* potential actual—a view which is almost similar to the Aristotelian view. There are sentences and passages in the *Shantiparva* where the similarity to the ideas of Plato and Aristotle is astounding. A view of change is clearly implied in the views expounded in the *Mahabharata*.

Cosmic process for Vyasa consists of various wholes—on the lines of the planetary systems. His perspective is hierarchical and in it there are superior and inferior, good as well as evil beings. Starting from inanimate objects at the bottom he moves up through human beings and on to the realms of various intra-cosmic gods, monsters (*daityas*) and devils (*asuras*). Although reality is basically integral, it is, in its manifestation, multi-dimensional and differentiated. There are structures representing different stages in human organization. There are many practices and stages of development in terms of a set of normatively defined values from the inert and impure to the active and pure. Different individuals are at different levels of development. Each one expresses different aspects of reality. In the cosmic process, each of these is autonomous and yet is related to others. This was not merely an intellectual conception. It was believed that one could come face-to-face with the Supreme in its various forms, the most general being light, through the practice of penances, sacrifices and yoga. But this path, for the author of the *Mahabharata*, is open to only a few true yogis. As far as the mass of mankind is concerned, they should lead their normal worldly life. What a yogi attains through meditations is attained by an ordinary mortal through sacrifices, penances and prayers. In fact, there is a long discussion in this point. Distressed by the manslaughter during the war, Yudhistira wanted to give up the throne and take to a life of renunciation. At this point Bhisma brings home the significance of the life of the householder which maintains both the student and the renunciator and enables the cosmic process to go on. Since all this depends on the king, according to Bhisma, he comes to acquire the pivotal position; he becomes the basis on which people can earn spiritual merit in terms of their distinct potential. The king not only helps others but also thereby helps himself. He acquires a hundred times more merit than a yogi, and goes to heaven in the same fashion in which a yogi does, by protecting his subjects. This view later became an important aspect of Indian tradition and found its clearest formulation in the writings of Kalidas.

The *Mahabharata* was perhaps a response to an age of decline or transition when society was facing a crisis of values and entering into the age of the *Kalyuga*.[19] The poet not only describes events but also makes an attempt to preach a set of values, even an ideology in terms of which the broken mosaic the society could be recreated. He avowedly accepts the view that the world is a *lila* of the Supreme *Brahmana, Narayana,* from which everything in the cosmic process has sprung. He is the source of creation, sustenance and destruction. In the *Mahabharata*, the nature of this origin is described in detail to Yudhistira by the sage Markandeya, who was supposed to have witnessed the great cataclysm. The Supreme Brahmana is the supreme being of the *Manusmriti*, he is man and universe locked in the process of time and space which are all his creation.[20] He is also near and far, manifest and unmanifest, here and beyond. The *Mahabharata* also accepts the earlier view of the ages of mankind, the total period being of twelve thousand years—*Kreta* of four thousand years, *Treta* of three, *Dwapara* of two and *Kalyuga* one, and also transitional phases in between comprising in all ten months.[21]

Two points must be noted about the general perspective of the

Mahabharata. First, we should note that the picture of the universe was deeply rooted in socio-religious traditions. The release of creative energy is evident in this work. It is through the various characters, specially Krishna, that the epic became a vehicle for the expression of a new symbolic form of a dawning faith in an age when the old certainty was no longer valid. Second, man's autonomy is asserted in a profoundly new form. It is true that intervention by cosmic forces still an important role, and life is still controlled by external factors; yet the idea of man as a hero emerges in very forceful way: the idea that despite the constraints of time and past *karma*, man is responsible for his own actions. Vyasa says, "This world rests on the arms of heroes like a son on those of his sire. He, therefore, that is a hero deserves respect under every circumstance. There is nothing higher in the three worlds than heroism. The hero protects and cherishes all, and all things depend upon the hero."[22] Mortals are bound by fate which fixes the limits of human action but within these limits man has definite choice. Though time and fate are important elements man can through a combination of his effort and divine grace change his destiny. The final merit leading to heaven or to transcendence of causality depends on the feelings with which one seeks to go beyond oneself. As one identifies himself with larger and larger entities by working for their welfare, the cosmic process being the final end, one ascends in the hierarchy leading to identification with the unmanifest. In the famous section known as the *Bhagwadgita*, a full justificatory theory for a life of detached action is provided. Man's glory consists in exercising choice in the larger interest. Through meditation, man could participate in the divine drama, consistent with dispensation granted to him. It is for this reason that Yudhistira refused to enter heaven unless his own dog was also admitted. It is for this reason again that Karna brushed aside the advice of the Lord Sun that one was not bound by higher moral principles if it endangered one's own life, to uphold the sanctity of the principle of charity. In lives of all these heroes, specially Arjuna and Krishna, the autonomy and responsibility of the individual is emphasized and the limitation of fate universalized and dramatized as the parameters of human salvation.

Krishna appears like a god because he does not accept any limitation, he castes aside all the constraints of customary morality and emphasizes the potentialities of human endeavour. He becomes a symbol of a new moral life in an age of uncertainty, that moral life which is rooted in the sustenance of the world order. The war was not fought for political order as such, it was the result of the internal crisis of certain individuals, such as Duryodhana, which had led to the breakdown of norms required to maintain the social order. According to Vyasa, although men are restrained by pity and concern for stability, natural arrogance, pride and greed make them blind to right. Such a deviation should invite punishment. Human beings may try to acquiesce in the situation with fortitude as Yudhistira did. But once tyranny reaches a certain limit, and the king deviates from the path of right, severe punishment must be meted out to such a man regardless of filial or other considerations. Arjun becomes the vehicle of this. It is either arrogance of power or obsession with personal interest which offends against the right order, as when the Yadavas became slaves of pleasure, and Dwarka went up in flames. All men have to die, the fate of Arjun in the battlefield was not unique. The dilemma of Arjun is the dilemma of all who face concrete life; like a mortal he is driven by pity and filial affiliation and like a hero he must wage a war for the everlasting fame of his deeds. It is this obsession with duty regardless of the consequences which leads Krishna to give up his kingdom after the death of Kansa, to act as a mediator between Kauravas and Pandavas to avert a war, not to try to save his kith and kin in Dwarka who had run amok with power. He wanted to sanctify the life of heroic action, without the arrogance of power that normally goes with it. His message was that man has a choice between two kinds of life, but it is a life in pursuit of right which alone secures immortality. It is violation of dharma which leads to disorder and this violation is sooner or later bound to disrupt social harmony. Disorder is the result of unrighteousness and arrogance of power in the ruling class. Indeed, the whole purpose of this epic is not so much to describe the transcendental life, which of course forms an important part of it, but to import moral teaching. For while *Satyayuga* has already passed it can yet be a future order, albeit for a short time when justice will reign and order appear. Such a possibility is metaphorically presented in the identification of the quality of the king's reign with the quality of the epoch. The *Mahabharata* was a response evoked by a society in crisis and it succeeds in imparting to the unique otherwise perishable action of men a measure of permanence. It is this concern to develop heroic life by a combination of human effort and divine grace which connects the ideals and practices in the epic.[23]

As in the *Manusmriti*, here also there is clear recognition of the importance of this world. Mysticism is not rejected but is not given the same importance which it received in the Upanishads. In *Srimad Bhagwat*, which is almost a footnote to this great epic, it is clearly stated that anyone who offers prayers (*puja*) without noticing that God is manifest in all creation doesn't deserves spiritual merit. It is enjoined that one must look upon all creatures with love and humility since they all have divine spark in them. Anyone who hates others or looks down upon them cannot attain spiritual merit. Indeed, no one can realize God unless he experiences his presence in all beings. To quote, "In human beings, *brahmanas* are the best. In *brahmanas* those who know the Vedas are superior and within these those who know the meaning and essence of the Vedas are the best. Those who are able to remove doubts are better than those who merely know the essence, and to them those who follow the duties of their station or *varna* are superior and to them again those who perform their obligations without any attachment to the fruits thereof are superior. And there is no equal to those beings who completely surrender all the bodies, actions and the consequences to me and act with non-discrimination towards all creatures." In the *Shantiparva*,[24] also, "when one seeth creatures of infinite diversity to be all one and the same, to be but diversified emanations from the essence, one is said to have attained Brahma."[25]

Knowledge pertaining to politics is called 'political right'. This is the refuge of all creatures as it is a means of regulating interrelationships in the world. Without politics, declares Vyasa, there would be anarchy and the caste order would perish. And in this respect it is a gift of Gods to mortals. One might call it the basis of all other activities. It is vital to the sustenance of society. It deals with the means by which the unacquired is acquired, the acquired is guarded well, and the guarded is distributed well.[26] Vyasa goes to the extent of saying that the king is the maker of his epoch: the various epochs such as *Kreta, Treta, Dwapara* and *Kali* progress according to the way in which the science of politics is properly or improperly applied to human affairs.[27] However, one point must be noted here. Though the science of polity has been given great importance as the condition of all other sciences, of individual security and social order, it does not exhaust the entire social life, nor does it enjoys the kind of supremacy which politics enjoy in modern political thought in the West. In Indian thought while politics can legitimately regulate life, the principles and the objectives of regulations are decided outside politics. The supremacy belongs to the social whole on the one hand and the needs of the individual soul on the other. By regarding it as the condition of other sciences Vyasa is merely referring to the functional importance of political power in the maintenance of social fabric. The main concern of Vyasa is for the establishment of righteousness but this depends on individual happiness and security on the one hand, and stability of the social order on the other. Politics is important because without it righteousness is not possible. In its absence, society would be a conflict of wills and anarchy would ensue, a condition which all political writers of the period so much dreaded.

The main concern of Vyasa is not, therefore, with what men ought to do, but how best to create an order which would facilitate the individual pursuit of happiness and finally supreme bliss. The pursuit of pleasure or happiness is taken to be natural human instinct, though there is always a feeling that some kinds of pleasure are higher and the other lower. Sacrifice, giving gifts, asceticism, knowledge of the Vedas and adherence to truth are the five virtues ever present in good people. Indeed, truthfulness and abstention from doing injury to others are justified not only because they are good for the subject but also because they are beneficial to all. The highest pleasure, therefore, would be consonant with righteousness and lead to the supreme good of all. There are higher kinds of pleasures to be found in the lives of great men such as Rama, and lower kinds of pleasures found in the lives of *asuras* and *daityas*. The disposition to pursue higher pleasures is present in all, but can be acquired only by deliberate and conscious efforts to control propensities to evil. Man is endowed with a free will and has the capacity to choose between various options and the more moral options he exercises, the greater he becomes.

Pursuit of pleasure must involve human endeavour leading to activity. No one can perpetually remain inert. Even Gods are ever active. True there is time and fate to provide limits to our efforts to transcend the force of circumstances. But a man can, as pointed out above, attain merit by performance of his own functions and duties, determined according to his own nature, temperament and potential (*swadharma*), in a spirit of philosophical detachment and equanimity. This is sometimes identified with the avoidance of excess. The virtues which Vyasa stresses are, of course, the virtues of an ascetic or heroic life; but there is no contempt for the lower types because one must perform one's particular functions.

There is a general rule at first enunciated in the *Manusmriti*, that one must, while pursuing one's own happiness, try to identify himself with larger and larger social wholes such as the family, the village, the caste and so on. The larger the identification, the more authentic is one's life. The highest life is that of the sage who is a seer and is able to rise above narrow applications and sympathize with human misery in general in a spirit of equanimity. The best life for man is to adopt the attitude of a sage, to perform duties with equanimity in pleasure and pain, victory and defeat. Human life cannot be completely free from unpleasant events. The best of heroes, including incarnations of God like Rama or Krishna, had to face severe adversities. It is a mixture of both happiness and unhappiness. But a man can make the most of it by inculcating the spirit of a yogi, by learning to control his senses and feelings. It is this kind of happiness alone which is enduring and lifts man above the twists and turns of ephemeral reality. It is this attitude again which can be combined with other kinds of activities and can enable man to identify himself with others without incurring any sin in the process.

There is, according to Vyasa, no conflict between the life of a yogi and the life of a householder. It all depends on one's own nature and temperament. While some are good in meditation, others are capable of reaching the same end by penance (*tapasya*) and prayers (*japa*). The regular injunction is that one should aspire for only those things for which one has the potential and should not imitate the duties of others because in spiritual terms all functions have equal importance. Spiritual merit depends not so much on the kind of function one performs but on the spirit with which it is performed. Some attain salvation through meditation, others through performance of their own function in a spirit of equanimity. In fact, as already pointed out, while a yogi nullifies or transcends his past *karma*, by coming face to face with the Light, the householder does so through suffering (*tapasya*) and prayer (*japa*). In fact the life of the householder has the additional merit in that it enables a man to pay the debts due to intra-cosmic Gods, parents, and society. Indian thought has often been accused of adopting an attitude of life-negation. But if the *Ramayana* and the *Mahabharata* are taken as the finest examples of the Indian mind, one would have to conclude that the seers were deeply in love with the life in this world which was considered sometimes an extension, or a play or a product of the very nature of God, reaching out to him through the process of history. In the *Shantiparva* the life lived in accordance with right receives the highest place.

IV

Turning to politics, in order that righteousness can be practised, that different wholes may not trespass beyond their limits, and people have a chance of experiencing the divine in their own way, it is necessary to control their evil propensities with the help of political power and institutions of justice so that interests are conciliated and the guilty punished. Tension is endemic in both the cosmic and the human world. Just as various intra-cosmic Gods govern the cosmic process, rulers, who are also to that extent divine, govern and regulate human life. It is clear that both do so in the interest of commonality, God protects the manifest world (*khil jagat paripalanaya*) and the rulers protect the human world. "Protection of his subjects", says the author, "is the highest duty of the king, since compassion to all creatures and protecting them from injury has been said to be the highest merit."[28] The purpose of power is protection of the good and punishment of the wicked. It is punishment alone which in the ultimate analysis prevents mischief in society. In this sense the science of punishment is a means to the achievement of higher ends: individual security and social order. Here the state plays a positive role, it secures justice, preserves what society has, takes steps to increase it, keeps the four castes within their bounds, and ensures security and welfare to the people. In this sense, the author says, people can sleep in their houses with the doors open, women bedecked with their ornaments can walk along the street without fear, and the people can practice virtue.

There are three aspects of the *Shantiparva* which make it different from the preceding literature on politics. First, the emphasis on the ideas similar to contract theory is more pronounced. The word 'contract' has not been used, but the description of the origin of the state more or less resembles the description found in Hobbes. There are two stages or contracts envisaged. In the first stage there is mutuality, reciprocity, love and peace. It is a state of cooperation. But it does not last long because under the delusion of greed and passion men are prone to self-aggrandizement at the expense of others. People kill one another as stronger fish devours the weaker. Tired of this, people decide to enter into a compact that none should injure others. Brahma codifies the law and writes the first book on polity. But, in the absence of a known power, it was impossible to implement the law or the rules given by Brahma. People then decided to approach God who sent Manu for the purpose. It seems Manu was reluctant to accept the task in view of the general deceit in human nature. But when the people made an agreement with him assuring him of their support, he accepted. After this Manu was able to subdue the forces of anarchy and establish order. This story is repeated at various places in the *Shantiparva* in various forms. It is not that the earlier emphasis on the divine origin is given up. Even in this section, Manu derives king's authority from God. But the divine authority is used as an additional support to the idea of contract presumably because the author realized that without the sanction of the divine authority, the contract would be too weak an instrument to secure human obligations. When at one place it is asked, why the king is respected as a divine personage, the answer is given with reference to the role which the king performs in the maintenance of peace and order. This explanation obviously relates the importance of the king to the function he performs in the polity.[29] It is the idea of what would be termed as contract which gets precedence and apportions the rights and duties of the king as well as of the subjects. For instance, when the king acquires the right to command obedience from his subjects, a claim to one-fifth of their live stock and cash, and one-tenth of their crop, he assures them in return protection of caste order, individual security and social stability. The story of king Vena's failure to establish a reign of peace is also alluded to. This story highlights the need to keep his obligations to his subjects on the part of the king. King Vena was unrighteous and self-indulgent and ignored the injunctions of the Vedas. When the sages learn of this, they killed Vena as retribution for his tyranny and installed in his place Prithu who took a solemn oath to protect the latter. This oath is a testament of the idea of contract and highlights the duties of the king more than his rights.[30] The idea of mutuality in the confiscation of the property of the people by the king during emergencies also emphasizes the contractural nature of the enterprise.[31] The king is also warned against oppression of agriculturists as well as traders. As if this was not enough, the author of the *Shantiparva* went a step further to say that a good king earned all the good merit gained by his subjects, and if he fails in his duties, the state is afflicted by robbers for want of protection, the sin of all this stains the king himself. So scared was the author of the state of anarchy that he went to the extent of saying that it was better to maintain the king first and then wife or property or should there be no king, there would be no wife or property.[32] The contract enjoined that the king should fearlessly implement dharma regardless of personal likes and dislikes, should be impartial to all and protect his subjects and should promote everything which leads to righteous conduct including the obligations of the caste system. *Ramarajya* is once again held as an ideal.[33] The author says that in his rule "the clouds, yielding showers seasonably, caused the crops to grow abundantly. During the period of his rule, good was always abundant in his kingdom. No death occurred by drowning or fire. As long as Rama governed it, there was no fear in his kingdom of any disease. Every man lived for a thousand years, and every man was blessed with a thousand children. During the period of Rama's sway, all men were whole and all men attained the fruits of their wishes. The women did not quarrel with one another, what need then be said of the men? During his rule his subjects were always devoted to virtue. Contented, crowned with fruition in respect of all the objects of desire, fearless, free, and wedded to the vow of truth, were all the people when Rama governed the kingdom. The trees always had flowers and fruits and were subject to no accidents. Every cow yielded milk filling a dorna to the brim."[34] The protection of the weak is the special responsibility of the king. "The eyes of the weak, of the Muni, and of the snake of virulent poison should be regarded as unbearable", says the author. He further advises, "Do not, therefore, come into (hostile) contact with the weak. Thou should not regard the weak as always subject to humiliation. Take care that the eyes of the weak do not burn the race to its very roots. Weakness is more powerful than even the greatest power. Take care that the eyes of the weak do not burn like a blazing fire." Again, "when a weak person fails to find a rescuer, the great rod of divine chastisement falls (upon the king)."[35]

It must be remembered that the outcome is once again a combination of noetic and pneumatic, human and divine. The state emerges to protect the weak but as the authority of divine grace. Human action alone is not enough without the grace of God. But there is a difference here between this theory and the theory of the divine origin. According to the theory of the divine origin of kings, all kings are representatives of God; according to the Indian view only good kings are true representatives of God and they remain good by discharging their obligations to their people. Indeed, in the origin of the state is defined both the nature and purpose of the state also. Since the state comes into existence to protect the weak, it is good only so long as it does that. Hobbes' account of the state of nature was quite similar to that of the state of nature in the *Mahabharata*. But the concept of the protection of the weak was missing, with the result that the state became a mighty Leviathan. On the other hand, in the *Mahabharata*, the concept of sovereign power is missing since the state is the outcome of both human effort and divine intervention, and furthermore, since it is specially charged with the responsibility of the protection of the weak, it can regulate but can never dominate others who owe their origin to different sources. It cannot trespass on other spheres. Even the law which it executes is made elsewhere by people who have experienced reality at its deepest. It can regulate different spheres so that they do not trespass on each other and the welfare of all (*loksamgraha*) is secured. What specific project the state should undertake cannot be answered in the abstract. A concrete question can be decided with reference to a fine balancing of dharma keeping in view the specific needs of time, place and circumstances.

What happens if the king violates his agreement? The earlier writers were silent on the point. But the *Mahabharata* is clear and unequivocal. In case the king fails to give protection and anarchy comes upon society, people are justified in devising ways and means to get rid of the king. Such a king who is dishonest and unrighteous and plunders their wealth, or whose officers act from lust or avarice, or when he does not maintain the caste system, may be slain because if it is not done, argues Vyasa, there would be complete anarchy in which women will be forcibly abducted and property plundered. The people are authorized in such eventuality to rise in armed rebellion and kill the king as if he were a mad dog afflicted with rabies. In such emergencies even *brahmanas* are enjoined to give up their functions and work for the common cause by providing the necessary leadership to overthrowing the king. The *Mahabharata* is full of passages which emphasize that the rod of chastisement is not "intended for self-aggrandizement". It says that those who seek to enlarge their fortunes by afflicting their kingdoms in unscrupulous ways very soon come to be regarded as vermin in a dead body.[36] Indeed it is justified to kill them. Vyasa says that the king who acts according to the counsels of a vicious and sinful minister becomes a destroyer of dharma and deserves to be slain by his subjects with all his family. That king who is incompetent to discharge the duties of statecraft, who is governed by caprice in all his acts, and who indulges in beastfulness, soon meets with destruction even if he happens to be the ruler of the entire earth.[37] At another place, "That crooked and covetous king who suspects everybody and who taxes his subjects heavily, is soon deprived of life by his own servants or relatives."[38] Krishna even advised the assembly of the Kuru elders that they should kill Duryodhana. Krishna had declared "Even this is a great transgression of which all the elders of the Kuru race are becoming guilty, that they do not forcibly seize and bind this wicked king in the enjoyment of sovereignty. If this is done, it may still be productive of much good."[39] In pursuit of virtue the subjects were justified in rebellion. It is for this reason that the practice of anointing kings developed whereby the seers and priests solemnly confirmed the elevated character of the king; it meant bestowing of community powers on the king. The custom was evolved further whereby certain families became the repository of the king's power as a result of his ascendency to the throne confirmed by the priests and elders. The ruling in general became hereditary. Theoretically, however, this was not always to be the case. There are examples of election of kings. Indeed the principles of contract and divine ordination were combined to legitimize his authority. In fact the whole idea of divine ordination was supposed to apply to the office and not to a particular king. It might not be out of place here to refer to the commentaries of *Mimansa* authors like Sabara and Kumarila. These refer to various usages of the word *rajan* (king) and tend to identify kingship with a ruler who pleases people.[40] The word *rajan* is derived from two roots, *runja* which means to please and *rajr* which means to shine. There is reference to a counter opinion which tended to apply the notion of kingship to the *ksatriyas* only but even these people, applying the principles of substitution, admitted non-*ksatriyas* who were kings within the fold of *rajas*. These ideas later found their echo in the *Sukraniti* which made a distinction between a righteous and an unrighteous king in terms of threefold qualitative division of *sattva*, *rajas* and *tamas*. Only the righteous king could claim ordination by God. In this sense, legitimacy, according to Vyasa, was made dependent on the actual performance of a particular king; it was certainly the principle, though seldom the practice, to rule in a manner which would ensure individual security, social stability and general well-being. A king could become absolute if circumstances warranted but not tyrannical as Vena or Nahusha tried to become; in such cases deposition was justified. The office of kingship in India bordered on tyranny perhaps only in the middle ages with the introduction of Persian ideas and emergence of the period of feudal uncertainty.

The passages relating to the episode of Vena in both the *Mahabharata* and the *Srimad Bhagwat* are remarkable for three reasons. First, they carry further the distinction between society and the state. The state is merely a means to an end. It almost appears as an artefact created by human beings to serve a definite purpose and that purpose is to please and win the hearts of the people. The king can conciliate but cannot dominate unless the latter is necessary to effectively achieve the former.[41] And if the state fails in due performance of the functions for which it is created, and if anarchy actually comes upon society, people are justified in disobeying it. Obedience is contingent upon the king keeping to his part of the contract.

Secondly, the state becomes delinked from the king. It becomes a locus of political power of which the king is perhaps the most important element but not the sole element. In the state the king is distinguished from six other elements, i.e. the people, the ministers, the army, the treasury, the system of justice and his friends and these elements are regarded as parts or limbs of the body which are mutually interdependent; it is argued that even a minor defect in any of them may be inimical to the whole body.[42] This was a great leap forward towards the conceptualization of the state which becomes an institution distinct from both rulers and subjects. That is why the king cannot use the state treasury for personal pleasure. If he does so he is regarded as a thief. The king is compared to a pregnant woman who is ever concerned for the welfare of her child. The king should show utmost compassion to his people who constitute, according to the *Mahabharata*, "the most impregnable fort".[43] Whether these constitutional checks on the exercise of the powers of kings worked in practice or not, we do not know. The bodies such as *sabha* and *samiti* or panchayats, *srenis* or laws such as *jatidharma* were perhaps too weak to prevent abuse of authority. Otherwise

Duryodhana would not have been able to ride roughshod over all else. Nevertheless the very fact that such a theoretical possibility existed meant that rulers had to keep a finger on the public pulse; at a certain point they knew that obligation to obey would cease, the contract would be abrogated, and people would be justified in disobedience and even overthrow of government.

Third, Vyasa and other writers accepted that true law is higher than the king. The concept of true law of dharma was not very satisfactory, either in pure logic or in the political field. It is over-general, vague, almost axiomatic which may lead to awkward subjectivity in its interpretation. For example a liberal might think that the right to property is necessary for the sustenance of the world. A communist might argue that this right is a great threat to human civilization. Despite this, it was a valuable concept in so far as it implied something wider and more moral than the human law created by the king. Without this, the doctrine of checks on the authority of the king could not have been justified. It implied that all states rest implicitly or morally, that is according to dharma, upon contract. If it were asked why there where restrictions on the authority of the state, it could be answered that dharma "implied the advancement and growth of creatures" and the king should act according to the dictates of dharma for benefiting his subjects.[44] A king who disregards dharma and acts with force alone loses both righteousness and profit. The oath taken by *Prithu* contains very explicit reference to the king's duty to observe law and administer justice according to the principles of dharma. The entire process of governance is seen as an activity to ensure a government of law. The word 'law' of course is used here in the medieval sense as something discovered by sages to be in accordance with the natural order of things. It had therefore as much majesty, if not more, as the majesty of the king himself. When later on Sukra referred to barbarians (*mlechas*), among other things he identified lack of law as one of the characteristics of their organization. This belief in the existence of a higher law has been the saving of mankind in all times. The feeling that there is something higher than the authority of the state, and to which it must conform has been the basis of all civilized existence.

It is in this context that the discussion of the merits of various forms of government in the *Mahabharata* becomes important. There is particularly a contrast between monarchy and democracy which highlights the conceptual shift from the time when the state was almost synonymous with the king to that in which it becomes a distinct constitutional structure in which the rulers are enjoined not to look to their own welfare but the welfare of all, "to eschew evil passions, practice charity and do good to their subjects".[45] Bhisma recognizes the strength of democracy since it inspires all to work for the state. But he feels that such a state is very difficult to administer. The republics can be sustained only in terms of moderation, fellow feeling and equality, forbearance and self-control on the part of its leaders. Otherwise they are prone to internal dissensions and sometimes even the voice of the wise ruler is not heard. Since the number of executives is large, it is difficult to keep secrecy in deliberations. People seized by greed and anger tend to inflict injury upon each other by espionage, intrigue and corruption, by force, fraud and intimidation until the republic, which can survive only on the basis of unity and consensus, disintegrates and succumbs to outside pressures. It is only through concerted action that republics can be maintained. When the divisions become sharp, the principle of equality which regards everyone equal regardless of their intelligence and material possession becomes a liability and anarchy overtakes society. In such a situation the wise are enjoined to come to the rescue of the people and republics are replaced by aristocracies in which a few leaders are entrusted with political power on the basis of their wisdom and capacity to carry on the important business of the state in secrecy. The citizenship is also restricted to people of learning, known for their adherence to righteous customs and moral training.

Another important departure from current thinking is the political realism in the *Shantiparva*. The *Ramayana* on the whole emphasized righteous means to achieve righteous ends. When Javali tried to persuade Rama to return to Ayodhya on purely materialistic grounds, Rama emphasized the importance of truth as the sustenance of the cosmic process, the eternal virtues of the duties of the king based on truth and compassion, and argued for the duty of the king to work for the establishment of truth.[46] On the other hand, while praising truthful action, the *Mahabharata* permits the use of all such means as would secure the end with minimum cost and hardship to all concerned. The author makes a sharp distinction between normal and exceptional times. In the latter the use of evil means is permitted if it secures the result. The king is enjoined to be neither too strong nor too mild, a combination of lion and fox, of the creator (*Brahma*), the protector (*Vishnu*) and the Destroyer (*Siva*). He should appear to be fearless even though afraid, while distrusting others appear to be trustful, for "one who is heedful never trips and tripping is never ruined". "In interstate relations particularly, use of fair or foul means would depend on the actual conditions obtaining at the time of the action. The emphasis is on victory. For instance, the king should destroy the enemy not only by fire and sword, poison and drugs but also by sowing seeds of dissension among his councillors and courtiers. And in case of impending defeat, the king must be quick to bend as if he was bending before the current."[47]

There is no hard and fast rule. It all depends on who does it, for what purposes it is done, and in what spirit it is done. Sometimes it is moderation which is better and sometimes ruthlessness. Bhisma declares that anyone who practices non-violence gives life breath to *mother earth*. There is a whole chapter in *Srimad Bhagwat* in which those who practice violence and particularly those who indulge in animal sacrifices are despised. Such people are according to the author, tormented by their victims in the same way in which they have tormented them. But in actual practice it is admitted that it is always a choice between more or less as no one can be absolutely non-violent. Agriculture is good but it involves harm to animal life. In the process, numberless creatures on the ground are destroyed. Similarly, there are innumerable creatures living in trees, in fruits and in water. Even in the process of walking, we tend to kill countless organisms. There is indeed not a single person who is free from doing injury to others. The sage Markandeya declared, "the ways of the righteous are subtle, diverse and infinite. When life is at stake and in the matter of marriage, it is proper to tell an untruth. Untruth sometimes leads to the triumph of truth, and the latter dwindles into untruth."[48] The only guiding principle is that with gratefulness and with malice towards none, one must try to do what is good for all because the wise man delights in virtues and lives by righteousness.

The author is thus very clear that where there is danger to life, there is no harm in departing from truth. What one has to keep in mind is that one must do so only to better perform the duties of his station. Moral precepts are subtle and one can be righteous by integrating scriptural knowledge, customary practice and force of circumstances. One is also entitled to follow expediency if demanded by conditions of the times so long as it is for the achievement of public goals, the condition is that one must not appropriate any profit to oneself. The supreme goal, as is clear from the parable of sage Visvamitra, is the preservation of life. When Yudhistira compares this morality to the one practiced by robbers,[49] Bhisma replies by saying that morality is not only derived from canons but is also a product of wisdom and its precise form can be discerned only by great effort. The king who has integral reason (*buddhi* and *pragya*) alone succeeds in the end, for he alone has the capacity to choose between alternative options. Wisdom is compared to a river with devious flowing currents. Canon does not speak for itself. It has to be interpreted. In the hands of an angry and selfish man, it may mean one thing, in the hands of a wise man another. The greater the integral reasoning one has, the more beneficial will be the results.

There is a certain amount of awe at the complex character of the world where it is not possible to know all the variables; sometimes action made with the best of intentions leads to harmful results and vice versa. This comes across particularly in the discussion of the relationship between ends and means. There are ample instances where there is a clear warning not to expect a simple answer to the actual problems of living. Moral principles have their own place but ultimately their precise application will depend on the nature of circumstances. The guiding principle in such cases is to follow the path trodden by great men who have preceded us. This discussion is significant because it makes the *Shantiparva* a link between the *smriti* tradition and the *Arthasastra* tradition which was later to receive its full narration in Kautilya.

This must lead us to a consideration of what exactly constituted the good state which Vyasa had in mind. There is no one place where we find a systematic discussion of it. In fact, at times the discussion is quite confusing. But there is no doubt that an attempt is constantly made to relate the principles of right to political life. Secular conditions which would facilitate their implementation are laid down in great detail. Vyasa, like other authors in the *smriti* tradition, thought that the ideal state is one in which all castes perform their functions and do not meddle in the affairs of the state. The state on its part must maintain the system, protect family and the property of all, provide individual security and conditions of social stability. The ruling class is recruited on the basis of heredity as well as merit. The state must protect the weak, the aged, women and children, and dumb, lame and poor, and sanyasins. The state is required to help the cultivators by providing means of irrigation. Sometimes even financial assistance is made available to them as well as to artisans and traders. In emergencies such as famines, floods or epidemics, the king is enjoined to undertake relief work. The epic considers it disgraceful for the king if his subjects suffer for want of foodgrains.[50] It envisages "alms" and "feeding" houses for the destitute. The same concern is shown for the health of the subjects. Almost all the tasks of the modern state such as construction of roads, parks, gardens, digging of wells, tree plantation, construction of water reservoirs and rest houses are mentioned. The state is also required to encourage education by maintaining brahmanas as well as by patronizing arts and culture. It even maintains play houses (*natyashalas*). In this sense, the theory of the state in the *Mahabharata* is the theory of the welfare state. It is true that the lower classes do not get their due and this is reflected in the story of Eklavya. It appears that the caste hierarchy was enforced with rigour. Such discriminatory view cannot be acceptable to us, but the ideal of the welfare state is relevant. One can hardly disagree with the saying that the best state is one in which men live fearlessly like sons living in the house of their father,[51] in which the state provides for the maintenance of the poor, the helpless and the aged. There are beautiful passages where the poor are extolled as deserving of the first attention of the king; the king's supreme duty consists in wiping the tears of those who are poor, helpless and aged and in bringing happiness to men. Anything which serves this purpose is justified. In the *Mahabharata* there is a special connection between the origin of the state and the protection of the weak. Indeed, the state comes into existence because in the state of anarchy the strong exploit the weak and the helpless. It is, therefore, the first duty of the king to ensure that such a thing does not happen and the weak are able to lead a secure life. The idea of contract may be a weak basis of men's obligation to obey but the idea that the state originates to protect the weak is a powerful idea which must inevitably lead to a welfare polity.

This brings us to the last point: How is the system of property envisaged? The author is clean that property is one of the basic conditions for the expression of one's personality. One of the reasons for man's flight from the state of nature is that property is not safe there. But there is no absolute right to property. Property in itself is neutral. It depends on who uses it and for what purpose. While the protection of property is one of the fundamental duties of the state, the *Mahabharata* is very clear that by this is meant the property of the good, the righteous and the deserving. It is only property founded on virtue which is the necessary element of life and not that based on sin. The author warns against two evils which often go with prosperity, namely pride and unrighteousness, which inevitably lead to loss of spiritual merit.[52] While the king is enjoined not to seize the property of the good,[53] he may confiscate that of the wicked. In fact, confiscation of the property of the wicked has a dual merit. First, its distribution to the good and deserving saves them from their misfortunes. Secondly, it strengthens the king's treasury. However, there are a few contradictory passages here which may be later interpolations and do not conform to the general tenor of the argument. They breathe contempt for the lower classes and tend to protect the *brahmanas* at any cost. While the ruler is enjoined to exact agricultural tax from those who do not study the Vedas and made offerings to the sacred fire, he cannot touch the property of *brahmanas* in any case, even in periods of dire distress. Though the impact of this is softened by stressing that the king can take away the property of those who do not follow their duties as *brahmanas*, the sting nevertheless remains. One may then wonder whether any man of property is entitled to be called a *brahmana* because the *Mahabharata* says, "If a *brahmana* acts otherwise, he should be punished like a *sudra*." Such a *brahmana* deserves no respect.[54] However, the moral is clear that the state must not permit acquisition of property by unrighteous means, that by treating the unrighteous as one treats gnats and mosquitoes, righteousness is achieved.

To pass judgement on the *Shantiparva* would be presumptuous. It must be said that some of these ideas have become a part of our modern thinking on the subject. On other points, the insights and aphorisms are highly malleable, they have a rare quality of suggestiveness as well as being full of ambiguity. Two points, however, should be mentioned. First, the idea of inequality is thoroughly outdated. Even if it is natural, the justification provided is too weak to be acceptable. It became a part of tradition and we are too well aware of its consequences which led to the abominable degeneration of the caste system in the middle ages. There is a more profound notion of equality implicit in the *Mahabharata* but it is never fully worked out. Be that as it may, our generation has opted for equality. Doubtless, different people have different capacities in realization of their potential. But such a view need not necessarily lead to a doctrine of inequality. In fact, it should lead to a realistic doctrine of equality in terms of equality of opportunity to realize one's potential. It would mean not the recognition of equality in terms of capacities which are truly unequal, or to be more accurate, dissimilar, but equality in the right of each to preserve and pursue his own autonomy. Men are equal not in their capacities or inclinations but in terms of their right to perfect their specific capacities. This, however, is hinged upon the recognition of equality of opportunity to everyone to be able to identify his potential, and equality of social conditions so that the potential is finally actualized. But what is important is that the Indian view respects diversity both at the level of individual and social existence. It acknowledges that the distribution of benefits and rewards, goods, and things, will depend on specified circumstances. The ideal arrangements should be such, as would enable each differentiated whole to perfect its own autonomy in order to be able to pursue the law of its own being. The differences and inequalities should be justified not in terms of hereditary or ascriptive rights but in terms of specificities of different individuals, occupations and practices, all existing as "wholes within wholes" organized in terms of the doctrine of spiritual equality.

In the philosophical position of Vyasa, one consideration ought to be kept in mind. The emphasis on the qualitative basis of caste rather than the

hereditary basis must have appeared quite progressive to his contemporaries
and a significant challenge to orthodox opinion. The hereditary basis had
come to be accepted as a part of life long before the *Mahabharata* was
written. The plea for political and economic equality was certainly absent
then. In fact it enters Indian thought only in the late nineteenth century.
This caveat is necessary to put the *Mahabharata* in its historical perspective.
The author of the *Mahabharata* was primarily writing for his contemporary
audience. This scheme of qualitative and functional division has not lost
its force completely; its revival decisively influenced the attitude towards
the caste system of our leaders towards the late nineteenth and early
twentieth centuries, and was accepted even by Gandhi. In fact, a point can
be made that Vyasa's emphasis on righteous rulers and their obligation to
protect the people on the one hand, and the right of the people to resist
illegitimate authority on the other, making political relationship a matter
of contract, should make all ruling classes who are interested in their own
welfare quite uncomfortable. It remains a matter of speculation as to why
these ideas on political obligation were not taken up and further developed
by subsequent writers on polity?

NOTES

1. M.L. Sen, *The Ramayana of Valmiki* (Delhi, Munshi Ram), 1978, p. 2.
2. U.N. Ghoshal, *A History of Indian Political Thought* (Oxford, 1959),
    p. 331.
3. Valmiki, *Ayodhya Kanda*, Tran. M.N. Dutta, 21-41.
4. A. Keith, *The Religion and Philosophy of Veda and Upanishads* (London,
    Oxford University Press, 1925), Vol. II, p. 454.
5. Vaisesikasutra, I. ii.
6. *Ayodhya Kanda*, 506.
7. M.L. Sen, op. cit., pp. 149-51.
8. *Ayodhya Kanda*, op.cit., pp. 149-51.
9. Ibid., 83: 31-49.
10. *Aranya Kanda*, 66-15.
11. *Kishkindha Kanda*, trans. M.N. Dutta, 13-15, 6.
12. *Ayodhya Kanda*, 100-62, 63, also, *Ayodhya Kanda*, 63-6.
13. *Ayodhya Kanda*, 116-8, 9.
14. *Aranya Kanda*, 38-20.
15. M.L. Sen, op. cit., p. 150.
16. Loe at.
17. See I.W. Mabbet, *Truth, Myth and Politics in Ancient India* (New Delhi,
    Thompson, 1972).

18. *The Mahabharata,* trans. P.C. Roy (Calcutta, Original Publishing House), Vol. II, Sabhaparva and Vanaparva, p. 453.
19. G.C. Aggarwal, *The Age of Bharat War* (Delhi, Motilal, 1979), p. 30.
20. *The Mahabharata,* op.cit., Vol. III, (Vanaparva) Sec, CL, XXX, VIIL.
21. Ibid., III, CLXXX.
22. Ibid., VII, XCIX.
23. See the chapter on Hesiod in John H. Gunnel, *Political Philosophy of Time* (Conneticut, Wesleyan University Press, 1968). The similarities between the ancient Greek and the Indian Tradition are striking.
24. *The Bhagwatpurana,* Hindi trans. (Gorakhpur, Geeta Press, 1981), pp. 161-62.
25. *The Mahabharata,* op.cit., VII, XVII.
26. Ibid., VII, Slokas 122-25.
27. Ibid., VII, X.
28. Ibid., VII, LXXI.
28. Ibid., VII, LXVIII (68).
30. Ibid., VII, LIX (59).
31. Ibid., VII, LXXXIX.
32. Ibid., VII, LXVII (67).
33. Ibid., VII, XXXXIV, V, LLXXXVII (137).
34. Ibid., VII, XXIX.
35. Ibid., VII, XCI.
36. Ibid., VIII, LLLXXV (135).
37. Ibid., VIII, LXXXXIII. Also see, Spellman, *Political Theory of Ancient India* (Oxford, 1964), pp. 233-45.
38. Ibid., VIII, LLLVI (156).
39. *Mimamsasutra,* II, 3.2.
40. *The Mahabharata,* op.cit., VII, LXXXVIII.
41. Ibid., VII, LVIII (57).
42. Ibid., VIII, LVI.
43. Ibid., VIII, XC.
44. *The Mahabharata,* op.cit., *Yoga Parva,* 126.44.49.
45. Ibid., VIII, 93.
46. Ibid., VIII, LVI.
47. Ibid., VIII, CXIV (114).
48. Ibid., VIII, Vol. II, p. 460.
49. Ibid., VIII, 140.
50. Ibid., *Udyogparva,* 39.
51. Ibid., VIII, 57.
52. Ibid., VIII, XC.
53. Ibid., VIII, 57.
54. Ibid., VIII, LXV.

CHAPTER 4

THE MORAL VISION:
SUKRA AND BRIHASPATI

According to mythology, Sukra was disciple of the great sage Bhrigu. It is believed that he was a teacher of *Asuras* and in his treatise he distilled knowledge about polity and morals for *asuras* from the ancient treatise uttered by Brahma for the benefit of mankind. Although the *Sukraniti* in its present form is considered to be of a later period, the ideas contained in the first chapter are so humane that they could not be easily reconciled with the kind of political philosophy prevalent in later times when the concept of the accountability of the king receded into the background. The distinction between a good and a bad king, the need for a clean administration, are all stated with remarkable clarity and force.

Like many ancient authors Sukra too considered politics an aspect of ethics. He, too, called it moral science (policy science would, however, be more appropriate) (*nitisastra*) which he considered as the basis of virtue, wealth, enjoyment and salvation. According to him, it is with the help of this science that a ruler can conquer a foe and win a friend. While all other sciences deal with their respective spheres of action, it is the supreme science because it deals with all of them. While grammar deals with words, logic with material substances, *mimamsa* with religious ritual and *vedanta* with the fraility and destructibility of the material body, the policy science deals with moral philosophy without which no stability can be maintained in human affairs.[1] It plays the same role in human affairs as that played by food in the maintenance and preservation of the human body. In this sense it is superior to other sciences because it aims at the fulfilment and achievement of the desires and interests of all that man seeks, the happiness which is their chief end. *Nitisastra* tells us the method to achieve this end. Complete control of oneself and independence from others is the supreme form of happiness both for the individual and the king. He declares in a sentence reminiscent of Plato that "Great misery comes of dependence on others. There is no greater happiness than that from self rule."[2] For the achievement of this Sukra concludes, *nitisastra* is indispensable to the prince who is the Lord of all. The two primary functions of the king are protection of subjects and punishment of the guilty and both these functions, according to him, cannot be adequately performed without *nitisastra*. When the ruler does not follow *niti*, writes Sukra, "the kingdom is weakend, the army is inefficient and the civil service is disorganized; other elements of the state get topsy turvy; in short evil prevails everywhere".[3]

Unlike the earlier writers, Sukra does not insist on a properly appointed ruler. All that he seems to say is that the ruler should rule his subjects in accordance with moral principles. According to him, there can be three kinds of kings, namely *sattvika, rajasika* and *tamsika*. *Sattvika* king is one who is constant in his duties, protects his subjects, performs all sacrifices, conquers his enemies, and "who is charitable, forbearing and valorous, has no attachment to the things of enjoyment and is dispassionate".[4] *Tamsika* king has the exactly opposite characteristics and such a king according to Sukra goes to hell. A king in whom passion rules, who is attached to the world and its gifts, and who is not respectful of morals, who is of an intriguing disposition is a *tamsika* king. Nowhere is the distinction between a good and bad king stated so clearly in the ancient literature as in this treatise. Sukra goes to the extent of saying that the *sattvika* king enjoys the blessings of the Gods, the *rajsika* those of men, and the *tamsika* those of mere demons. He is very clear that a ruler cannot take shelter behind necessity by advancing the plea that extraordinary situations require extraordinary solutions. As soon as the king is installed as king, he is obliged to act according to moral principles.

The threefold classification of the kings corresponds to the threefold classification of the individuals in terms of the *sattva, rajas* and *tamas*. The law of action (*karma*) is tied to this classification and everyone reaps the fruits of his actions either in this life or the next. It is by virtue of one's actions that one is born in the caste of *brahmana, ksatriya, vaisya, sudra*, or *mlecha*. It is interesting to note here that Sukra is very clear in his mind that membership of different castes should rest more on qualities that we possess than on colour or descent. A *brahmana* is a *brahmana* because he is devoted to Gods and knowledge and has a predominance of *sattva* in him. A man who can protect others, is restrained and full of valour is *ksatriya*. The *vaisya* is one who is expert in purchase or sale of commodities, who makes his living by commerce or agriculture. The people who serve these three classes are *sudras*. This caste would, according to Sukra, also include the drivers of the plough and the hewers of wood. Sukra also adds one more caste to the traditional four *varnas*, namely, that of the *mlechas*. These are the persons who do not perform their duties, who are greedy, unkind and troublesome.[5]

Sukra subscribed to the doctrine of *karma* which unfolds itself in diverse ways through many life-cycles until man is either liberated or condemned. According to him, most people reap the fruits of their actions according to their behaviour in their previous births (*prarabhda*). Yet Sukra does not want them to resign themselves to fate. He declares that while people with character respect energetic action, others who are weak worship fate. Following the heroic tradition, he says that everything that we do in the world is founded on a combination of fate and enterprise, on divine grace and human endeavour. The strong seek to make their own destiny in this world itself. We may not be able to see the consequences of our actions in this life, but whatever we do shall definitely determine the curve of life in the next incarnation. When fate is favourable even small exertions result in great achievements but when it is unfavourable, great efforts end in naught. The examples of Vali and Harischandra are cited in support of the argument. But despite this Sukra insists that one should face life with enterprise and apply remedies whenever one can.

Sukracharya accepted the traditional nation of the kingdom as an organism with seven limbs, namely the sovereign, the minister, the friend, the treasury, the state, the fort and the army. The sovereign is the head, the minister is the eye, the friend is the ear, the treasury is the mouth, the army is the mid-region, the fort is the arms and the state is the legs. The bond between the king and his subjects is indissoluble. One of the great merits of Sukra is that he again and again emphasizes the distinction between a good and a bad king and argues that a good and just king not only saves himself but also his subjects, while a bad king goes to hell like the great Nahusha. In this sense he assumes that the state is a natural organism and it cannot function properly unless there is a harmony of interests between all the organs of the state or the nation (*rastra*). Sukra repudiates the belief that every king is endowed with the power of Gods and declares that "the prince who is virtuous is a part of the gods. He who is otherwise is a part of the demons, an enemy of religion and oppressor of subjects."[6] A good king combines in himself the attributes of seven persons: father, mother, preceptor, brother, friend, Kuvera and Yama. The book is full of details of administration which do not concern us here. We shall devote ourselves only to general principles.

The king is enjoined to protect the weak and be merciful even to his enemies. A long list of do's and don'ts is prescribed. The king should also shun passion, specially for women, gambling, and drinking. It is not that every pleasure is forbidden completely. The injunction is to avoid excess in enjoyment of pleasures and to act with moderation. A distinction is, for instance, made between wife and women. While the company of a wife is for his happiness, that of other women can be cause of his ruin. Emotions as pleasure and anger should be duly used, the former in the maintenance of the family and the latter against enemies. There is nothing inherently good or bad in such values. They are instrumental and their relevance would depend upon the object in view. Pleasures are good or bad according to circumstances as well as in proportion to the object to be achieved. Sukracharya's moral code is thus calculated to create a system which would lead to a harmonious development of our personality. Pleasure with one's own wife is good, with another's wife it is not, heroism is good but oppression of one's own subjects is not. The main functions of the king are six in number, namely punishment of the wicked, practice of charity, protection of the subjects, performance of sacrifices, equitable realization of revenues, and extraction of wealth from the land. If the princes fail to perform these functions, they are no better than fools.

His state is ever respectful of public opinion. Gods ruin and cast down a king who is not a protector. The king is enjoined to know the minds of the people through a network of spies. But the difference between Kautilya and Sukra here is that while Kautilya would plead for wanton destruction of all opposition, Sukra would first advise the king to be mild and compassionate. According to him, the king should rectify his own faults and should never punish the people for holding opinions opposed to his.[7] A king who hides his own faults is wicked. Nowhere in Indian thought, after the *Ramayana* and the *Mahabharata*, is so much stress laid on a king's own discipline and his responsiveness to public opinion than in *Sukraniti*. Sukra argues that although it is difficult not to be angry on hearing disparagement of oneself, the king should try to be merciful and affectionate. This is so because if a king is uncharitable or insulting or deceitful or cowardly or passionate he is liable to be deserted by his own subjects.[8] Only a king who avoids sensuousness, anger, ignorance, cupidity, vanity and passion, can hope to rule better and for a long time as kings like Jamadagny and Ambarisha did. In order to discipline the king Sukra, like all law givers, recommends that the king should train himself in material science including logic, the Vedas, economics and law.

The king is particularly expected to look after the weak and the poor. He should treat poor people with kindness. He should abstain from oppression of the poor people. "For they", says Sukra, "dying through repression, ultimately ruin the king." There is no better art for winning over people than the practice of mercy, friendship, charity and sweet words. For this the king is also enjoined not only to protect the existing wealth but also to take steps to increase it. Without income not even the God of wealth can survive for long. It is interesting to note that the classification of the status of the king is directly related to the revenue realized in his kingdom. While the income of the *virat* is about 50 crores, that of a *samrata* is three lakhs. In between are the *mandalika* with 10 lakhs, the *raja* with 20 lakhs, the *maharaja* with one crore, the *sivarat* with 10 crores. Over and above all these is the *sarvabhauma* who is the lord of the earth and the seven seas. In exceptional circumstances the king can levy extra taxes. But, Sukra is convinced the ruler who extracts his share through cupidity is ruined with his subjects.[9]

Sukra describes a whole hierarchy of offices, those of the priest, the viceroy, the prime minister, the secretary, the minister (*mantri*), the judge, the scholar, the controller of finance (*sumantra*) and the controller of land records (*amatya*). These are the executive officers (*prakritis*) to advise the king. It is remarkable that Sukra assigns them a very crucial place. He says, "If the king fears their control, they are good ministers."[10] He further asks, "Can there be prosperity of the kingdom, if there be ministers whom the ruler does not fear? Such ministers are to be gratified like women with decoration, liveries of honour, etc." The king is also to ensure that wages are paid according to the rules in force at the time. There is a very elaborate discussion of the wage policy in the *Sukraniti*.[11] The king is enjoined neither to stop or postpone payment of salary. It is a measure of his concern for the popular welfare that according to him even a moderate wage would include supplies of indispensable food and clothing. He believes that low wages are a cause of social and moral turmoil. His definition of 'indispensable' would include all the basic necessities for all the dependents. He also provides for different kinds of leave, pension, gratuity and even compulsory deposit, for he says, "He (the king) should keep with him (as deposit) one-sixth or one-fourth of the servants' wages, he should pay half of that amount or the whole in two or three years."[12]

Sukra goes into great detail about the construction of the city, the palace and the council chambers and enjoins the king to maintain roads, rest houses, forests and also to provide protection against the misuse of metals, ghee, honey and milk, and to control gambling, drinking, hunting, use of arms, sale and purchase of animals, jewels, and ornaments. He must inform the people of laws in advance. He should hear the petitions of the people and should punish his officers, including his spies if they have committed wrong and should be wary of flatteres. In case of conflict between his officers and the subjects the king is enjoined to side with his subjects.[13] He even suggests that an officer, who is accused by one hundred men should be dismissed. Indeed, a wise ruler should ever abide by the well considered decisions of his councillors, office bearers, subjects and other members, attending a meeting and never by his own opinions.[14] These are known to be the eyes and ears of the king. Sukra is convinced that a monarch who follows his own will brings misery upon himself and his subjects are soon alienated from him. Such actions on the part of the king lead to disasters, poverty, crime, division within the kingdom and ultimately rebellion of the subjects.[15] The state administration is to be run on the basis of efficiency. In such matters no notice should be taken of caste or family. Sukra says, "work, character and merit, these three are to be respected neither caste nor family. Neither by caste nor by family can superiority be asserted."[16] According to him, these considerations are reserved for dinner parties and not for matters of the state. The offices of the state are not to be given to each and everyone. The king should select such officers who can advise well, and bear pain, who have virtuous habits and who by the strength of their wisdom can deliver a king who has gone astray; men who are pure, and who have no envy, passions, anger, cupidity and sloth.[17]

The ideas on the relationships between ends and means are the same as in the *Mahabharata*. While in national matters the welfare of the subject is the goal, in international matters scant regard is paid to it. It appears as if the sole aim is the aggrandizement of the king. In such matters, in order to conquer enemies the king can make use of peace, force, punishment and division. If necessary he is enjoined to make peace with his feudatories. Sukra says, "Property never deserts a man who bows down to the powerful at the proper time, just as rivers never leave the downward course."[18] In warfare due consideration is paid to time, region and army. War is to be picked with a weak and never with strong one who has powerful army.

Sukra belonged to the tradition which recognized the importance of the ideal of *moksa* but not at the expense of three other activities, namely, *dharma, artha* and *kama*. He declared, "Let not one try to get *moksa* without trying to acquire the other three (*dharma, artha* and *kama*) and let him constantly follow (the path of) *moksa* without discarding the other three. This is the (golden) mean in all religions."[19] The wise man should never disregard the wife, the child, the diseased, the slave, the cattle, wealth, studies and attendance to good.[20] He says in his characteristic manner, "What is the good of crying at a place where the mother does not nourish in infancy, the father does not educate well and the king is the robber of wealth?" Sukra was conscious of the importance of wealth. He was of the view that while in general wealth of learning is superior to all other kinds of wealth, the material wealth is respected by all. A man without wealth is deserted even by his wife and son and lack of wealth forces one to become a slave. Therefore one should practice whatever is necessary to make one wealthy. But like all law givers Sukra also makes a distinction between wealth earned by right means and that earned by wrong means. He emphasizes that one should try to earn wealth only by good means, e.g. by good service, valour, agriculture, storekeeping, arts or begging. It is ironic that even usury, which Aristotle found repugnant, was considered a part of good means. However, he says, "One should lend money to friends without interest."[21] He also says that a man of wealth must maintain his family. Indeed, such a man should not pass even a single day without giving away something.[22] On the whole Sukra would follow the doctrine of the mean. According to him "Excess is ruinous. So one should avoid it."[23] He further says, "People get exasperated through harshness, cast abuse on miserliness, do not reckon anybody for his mildness, and insult a man for his overstatements." Further, "Poverty comes through excessive charity, insult through excessive cupidity, and foolishness is begotten of excessive zeal."[24] That activity, according to Sukra, is good which does not lead to failure in one's duty. There are many things in *Sukraniti* which cannot be reconciled with the high minded concern about virtue evinced in the first chapter. As one moves on the rest of the book, there appears to be so much variance in the overall tenor and attitude that one begins to wonder whether the author is the same. Whatever the case, *Sukraniti's* distinctive contribution is its explanation of the central importance of the state and the relation of the concept of the organic state to the welfare of the citizens. Moreover, he specifically makes politics transcend the special concerns of all other sciences in the interest of all.

II

Brihaspati was one of the great sages and according to legend and the Vedic texts this was the name of the teacher of intra-cosmic Gods. There are two books associated with his name. One is the *Brihaspati Sutra* and the other is the *Brihaspati Smriti*. The consensus of opinion is that while the first belongs to the eleventh or twelfth century, the latter is of much earlier origin, probably of the second century BC.[25] It is unfortunate that there is so much difference between the two books. It is certain that

Brihaspati was a great teacher of politics because he was referred as a great authority on statecraft by almost every writer on Indian polity in the ancient world, including Vyasa and Kautilya. It is also possible that the *Brihaspati Sutra* in its present form is of much later date and might have been compiled by someone who wrote in the name of Brihaspati, a common practice in the medieval period. But when we read the context within the text, it is certain that Brihaspati's writings belonged to a turbulent period when strife and forceful seizure of power were frequent. For instance, in his writings the earlier fear of anarchy is repeated with much concern. He accepts the view that in the beginning there was a golden age which was based on justice and right. Thei was no king and every man followed his or her own good sense. There was of course a social hierarchy in which there were masters and servants. But the whole mechanism worked spontaneously.[26] Everything was well in society in which there was an atmosphere of cooperation and harmony. But two things led to its degeneration: human ego and cupidity; the ancient falsehood and vice versa. Knowledge, sense of right and wrong and social cooperation disappeared. They were replaced by the law of jungle in which the more powerful survived at the expense of the weak. Following tradition, he also repeats the ancient concept of "the law of fishes" in which the larger fish devours the smaller ones. There was then no agriculture, commerce or trade. The caste system disappeared. In certain cases there were kings but they were unable to enforce law.

It is at this point that the need for kingship was felt. According to Brihaspati, without fear of authority, there can be no order; in its absence people fight and destroy each other. The strong devour and exploit the weak. People begin to appropriate everything to themselves. The world disappears. The family ties no longer operate. And the notion of rights and duties disappears too. This gives rise to anarchy and natural calamities. Brihaspati argues that in order to escape from such a terrible state people meet and elect a person who is already endowed with divine qualities. It must be pointed out here that the emphasis clearly shifts from contract to divine ordination presumably because he thought that no government can be sufficiently strong on the basis of contract alone. Thus, Brihaspati also subscribes to the ancient view that the state results from man's selfishness and cupidity and the escape from this lies in checking man's selfishness and seeing that right prevails in society. This is the aim for which the state comes into existence. All this is a repetition of the doctrine of the *Mahabharata* that the state is united by the ends it serves, the chief end being to see that people follow the duties of their station.[27]

What distinguishes Brihaspati from Vyasa, however, is that he had no theory of political obligation and he completely ignored the contract part of the origin of the state and relied exclusively on divine intervention. According to Brihaspati, God created the king in his own image for the creation of order in society. In his scheme, the king is given power to punish those who create a threat to social peace. Fear alone can provide a legitimate basis of obedience in which people do not deviate from their duties.[28] The greater emphasis on divine origin by Brihaspati makes the king far more powerful than he is in the *Shantiparva*. Brihaspati has no theories of disobedience and rebellion as enunciated by Vyasa. The mere fact that the king combines in himself all the powers of the intra-cosmic Gods guarantees him super human character and any act of disobedience against him could be an act against God, apart from making man liable to punishment in this world. He of course makes a distinction between good and bad kings but does not take this to its logical end. It is not clear what are the rights or obligations of the people when kings deviate from the path of dharma. Indeed, so strong is the emphasis on the need of fear of force that it can safely be presumed that according to Brihaspati, any act of disobedience makes man suffer in this world as well as in the next.

It is another matter that the king is enjoined to practice the doctrine of the *mean*. There is an elaborate chapter on the duties of the king. It is specifically laid down that a good king goes to heaven and a bad one to hell. People pay revenue and in return the king is enjoined to serve them. It is only in service of the people that the king flourishes. Any king who ignores their welfare does so, according to Brihaspati, against the will of God. Indeed, he goes on to say that divinity lies not in the king himself but in his acts. Specially those acts which lead to protection of the good people and punishment of the unrighteous. A good king must give charity, protect the wealth of the people, help in the development of their wealth, and create a reign of righteousness, love and charity. It is in this sense that he combines in himself the special features of *Brahma* the creator, *Vishnu* the preserver, and *Siva* the destroyer. Brihaspati's doctrine of the welfare state is more or less the same as that of Vyasa. But while in the *Shantiparva* there is a clear connection between the factors leading to the origin of the state and the theory of rebellion in the case of the state deviating from its primary task, in the works of Brihaspati the two stages run in opposite directions. If the cause of the establishment of the state is the need for protection which was lacking previously, then obviously the state ought to be limited by the conditions of its origination. If, on the other hand, there is a divine hand alone in the foundation of the state, then it is irrelevant whether there is anarchy or not. Brihaspati is not able to decide which is of primary importance. He wants a good ruler but does not want to legitimize any dissent or rebellion should that ruler turn bad. There is another important departure at this point. The weak are fulcrum of the state in the *Mahabharata* whereas in Brihaspati they are more or less absent. This fact obviously points to changes which might have taken place in Indian society in the intervening period.

One thing must be made clear before we can make a further assessment, namely who selects the ruler. There is a concept of popular election embedded in the earlier writings but Brihaspati does not give it much importance. There is no explicit statement on this theme. At the time of the primeval anarchy, when people are at each other's throats, election is mentioned but then who could believe that these people would be able to consult among themselves and elect a common superior. Once they acquire the capacity, they paradoxically lose this right. There is no subsequent mention of it. Indeed, the whole weight of the argument appears to be in favour of the powers that be. The doctrine of hereditary descent is given full support. Brihaspati was definitely in favour of monarchy and once again did not ask the question which would have logically followed from his ideas on the origin of the state, namely, how does it matter who governs, so long as the government is able to maintain law and order, whether the government is monarchical or democratic so long as it is acceptable to the people. The citizens are given respect but they have no opportunity to express their wishes.

Within this limited framework, the king is supposed to have education, wealth and property, friends and good officials. There are detailed references to the education of the prince, his coronation and the duties of the king. The whole purpose seems to be to make the king leader of the people so that all follow the duties of their stations. Brihaspati also thought of the king as one who pleases people rather than one who administers through force alone. According to him, the king must protect his subjects from three things, namely, external danger, thieves and dacoits, and the more powerful. The king can best do this by preserving the caste system so that everyone follows the duties of his station. It is for this that the king is entitled to one-sixth of the produce. Brihaspati is also in favour of a positive rule. The king must give encouragement to increase in agriculture, commerce and trade. He must give protection to the learned and participate in the social life of the community. Since the king alone cannot look after all the aspects, he must have good ministers and subordinate officials who must accept him as their mother and father and leave no stone unturned to implement his ideas. Brihaspati introduces the idea of conducting tests to select the right officials and ministers on merit by taking into account their virtue and excellence. So influential is the position of the ministers that they are considered as one of the important elements of the state along with the king himself. In fact, the king exercises his powers formally, in reality they are exercised by the ministers. In a certain sense these ministers are expected to act as the mother and father of the king because in their absence there cannot by any proper organization of the state. It must be stressed here that the emphasis on merit does not mean equality of opportunity despite references to merit. The *Sukraniti* does not conform to the pattern of hereditary office-holding, not in terms of the employment of the sons of the officials, certainly not in terms of the offices being distributed according to caste. Indeed, contrary to the *Sukraniti*, the political organization of *Brihaspati Sutra* is that of the dominance of the caste system in which *Brahmanas* occupy the highest and most elevated status. Most officers are to be selected on the basis of their caste and Brihaspati is very clear that members of the lowest caste are not to be made ministers. Distinctions of status are clearly indicated, and the king is enjoined not to ignore them. The system is elitist to the core. There are doubtless references to merit but the principle applies only to the upper castes and not to all castes. Within the upper castes, however, the selection is based on merit and the application of rational standards for determining talent is emphasized. What Brihaspati would detest is politics favouring relatives and personal friends on these grounds alone. But as far as caste boundaries are concerned, they are important and cannot be ignored.

What is significant in Brihaspati's political ideas is his enunciation of an elaborate system of justice. According to him, justice is so important that on its proper administration depends the king's future. He argues that justice must be administered in accordance with the codes and scriptures and no transgresser, even if be a brother or sister of the king himself, should go unpunished. The ultimate aim of justice is to create such an atmosphere in which the king is able to satisfy all. There are also elaborate details of the rules for detection of crime, collection of evidence and examination of witnesses, etc. Judgement should be based on a thorough examination of the contentions of both sides backed up by evidence. He recommends an elaborate hierarchy of courts and suggests that the judgements ought to be based on equity arrived at through consensus. The judges must be of good character. They must invariably be *brahmanas* or they must belong to good families but never from the lower castes. They must also be paid sufficient emoluments. The machinery of justice is decentralized and enough respect is shown to assemblies administering justice at the village and district levels. The whole system of course culminates in the court of the king himself. The lower courts are competent to hear new cases and review old ones. The high court is competent to review the judgements of the district and lower courts. In the system of justice Brihaspati contemplates such things as examination of evidence, time for asking question, production of fresh evidence, cross examination of witnesses and oaths. It is also enjoined that the courts can take into account local customs, local traditions. The aim of justice is the search for truth, punishment of the guilty and elimination of the cause of misery of the people on the side of truth.[29] There are four sources of law, right (dharma), conduct, character and the orders of the king. Right is based on scriptures, conduct on prudence. Scriptures without prudence only lead to destruction of right. There is no straight road to the determination of right. Character is based on conventions as also the customs of society and family. The last source is the order of the king. Here again one can see the change. In Vyasa, the king was merely a recipient of the laws created outside the realm of politics, in Brihaspati, he himself becomes an important source. This was indeed of momentous importance because once the right of king to create law was recognized, there was no going back. The king, from the sheer fact that he had a monopoly of coercive power, could interfere in all aspects of life, including how the *brahmanas* ought to interpret the scriptures. This idea found its clearest expression in Narada and later in Kautilya.

Another important aspect of the state is the treasury. Without wealth no kingdom can survive. It helps to stabilize kingdoms, build dams, encourage commerce and makes people loyal to the state. As in the *Mahabharata*, to protect wealth, increase it and to spend it for the right purpose is one of the ideals of kingship. This would of course very much depend on the character of the people incharge of the treasury. If the treasury is not protected enemies overwhelm the kingdom. Brihaspati gave elaborate details for the organization of the finance department. He also enunciated a system of graded taxation so that the sources of income are not dried up and the wealth of the state is increased.

Brihaspati also recommends a system of proportionate punishment. The idea is that people should not deviate from their duties as prescribed by their caste status. What is significant is that no person is above the law, however, powerful he may be. But punishment is to be given in accordance with caste and status. In this scheme *brahmanas* come out better than members of all other castes (It is true that he said *Sudras* could not be fined but this could be due to the fact that they did not own any property).[30] For instance, a *brahmana* cannot be given death penalty. The worst punishment for him would be to cut off his hands and banish him from the kingdom. Brihaspati contemplates four types of punishment: warning, dishonour to remind people of their duties, fines, and the death penalty. While the first two were in the jurisdiction of the *brahmana* courts, the latter two were in that of the king. It must be remembered that the fourth category not only meant death penalty but also physical hardship and torture. This would particularly be applicable to the lowest castes. Some of the varieties of punishment in this category would now be classified as barbaric. These recommendations were also symbolic of the departure from the heroic tradition of compassion and forgiveness to subjects. However, it must be said in favour of Brihaspati that he lays equal emphasis on the prevention of crime and reform of the criminal, and suggests measures to that effect.

The idea that the *brahmana* shares the power of punishment given to the king was a regressive step. It amounted to the mixing of the *brahmanical* and *ksatriya* realms. It is further not clear whether *brahmanas* can interfere in temporal matters. There was no development of the doctrine of the two swords in India as there was in Christianity in medieval Europe and the authority of the *brahmana* encompassed, at least in theory, the authority of the *ksatriya*, but it is doubtful if the former could administer punishment independently of the state. Once we accept the doctrine of simultaneous jurisdiction, so many insuperable difficulties crop up. In any case, Brihaspati was scarcely aware of these problems.

III

Sukra and Brihaspati were the two most important of the thinkers who represented the last stages of the development of the *smriti* literature. Both Brihaspati and Sukra thought of the king as raja, i.e. one who pleases, rather than as an autocrat. Despotic rule was detested, it was associated with *tamas* concept which implied personal and arbitrary rule which was quite opposite of *sattvic* rule. With some difference in emphasis, both kept priest and king quite separate, though both were expected to be in consultation with the other. Both praised those who disparaged tyrants or persons who were too arrogant with power. In this context, it is significant that for all their praise of the king, they did not turn to the state control of religion or education. These were left in private hands.

The king was also enjoined not to interfere with the family. He was to take special care to see that the quarrels between husband and wife, father and son, or brother and brother are not exploited. Indeed no Indian thinker could have thought as Plato did of a good state which rested on the destruction of the family; nor could they have argued like Aristotle that only the state is a whole and family only a part. Both were considered wholes within wholes. In Indian society family life, combined with caste obligations, remained far more important than in early Western thought. The principles of ethics and systems of law were built around the two institutions of the family and the caste.

Unlike the Romans, who retained the 'amateur' tradition in which there was no specialization, the Indians, particularly Sukra, recognized difference in nature and levels of excellence in different individuals and, as a result, pleaded for an almost professional civil service and professional army in which each incumbent was trained in his respective sphere. While in Brihaspati we have professionalization of judicial procedures, in the case of Sukra, there is great emphasis on the professionalization of the state services. All this was perhaps responsible for the development of a mixed sort of polity in ancient India in which the principle of kingship was made dependent on the priest and the *brahmana* on the one hand and the councillors and ministers on the other. Following the earlier traditions, the poor and the weak were considered important aspects of polity who required the attention of the prince and yet they never assumed supreme power. It is nowhere clear how are they to get themselves heard, yet through spies, the council of ministers and occasional rebellions people seemed to have conveyed their resentment against tyranny which partly explains the special concern of Sukra that the king should take every step to make himself acceptable to the people. The constant references to the exile of Sita in deference to the wishes of the citizens, however barbaric in the light of present day notions, symbolized the extent to which a good king was expected to bow to public opinion. The will of the ruler is not the only law, the best law. The ruler has authority because either the people or Gods or both have given him to rule and Sukra's distinction between the *sattvik* and *tamsik* exercise of power makes it abundantly clear that the authority is given only because it serves a higher principle, namely the welfare of all as in the case of Manu, and not merely because it is exercised as in Kautilya. Sukra actually insisted that Ravana and Nahusha both lost their authority because they deviated from the ideal of the public good.

It must, however, be said that distinctions of this kind are not accompanied by any discussion of institutional controls over the exercise of power by the king, a charge which can be laid at the door of all thinkers in the ancient world. In the absence of such institutional safeguards theoretically rule according to the principles of truth and the will of the people were almost taken for granted but rarely existed in practice. Deference to the people was theoretically accepted but in paractice the ministers and the councillors turned to be bards. The stories of Rama and Prithu were found to be a make believe. Yet the very fact that these myths were widely shared was of some importance, and the concepts they contained inspired many people in medieval times to create barricades against feudal tyranny.

NOTES

1. *The Sukraniti*, trans. B.K. Sarkar (Allahabad, The Panim Office, 1923), I: 20-22.
2. Ibid., III, 646, 652-53.
3. Ibid., 37-38.
4. Ibid., I: 59-62.
5. Ibid., I: 87-88.
6. Ibid., I: 139-40.
7. Ibid., I: 260-66.
8. Ibid., I: 277-80.
9. Ibid., I: 421-22.
10. Ibid., II: 168.
11. Ibid., II: 788-83.
12. Ibid., II: 834-35.
13. Ibid., I: 75.
14. Ibid., II: 5-6.
15. Ibid., II: 5-6.
16. Ibid., II: 111-12.
17. Ibid., II: 11-18.
18. Ibid., IV: 292.
19. Ibid., III: 4, 5.
20. Ibid., III: 85, 86.
21. Ibid., II: 382-83.
22. Ibid., III: 413-14.
23. Ibid., III: 438.
24. Ibid., III: 439-42.
25. *Brihaspati Smriti*, Intro. 1-80.
26. Ibid., I: 1-2.
27. Ibid., I: 9.
28. Ibid., I: 6-8, 38.
29. Ibid., I: 77-78.
30. See R. Vajpayee, *Brihaspati Rajya Vyavastha* (Varanasi, Chokhamba, 1968).

CHAPTER 5

THE PRAGMATIC VISION:
KAUTILYA AND HIS SUCCESSORS

In the period between 321 and 185 BC we can detect the culminating points of the tendencies towards orderly speculation on politics. The *Mahabharata* had identified the state as something different from both the prince and the populace. Now its complete autonomy became the chief focus of political thought. The idea of *dharmasastra* for the time being receded into the background. Its place was taken up by the *arthasastra* tradition which was more pragmatic in outlook. It is true that colours and shades of this tradition are also found in the earlier thought. It would be sheer intellectual contortion to prove that the *Ramayana* or the *Mahabharata* belonged purely to the *dharmasastra* tradition; both were equally concerned with the preservation and development of the kingdom by whatever means the king thought expedient. The same could conversely be said of the *arthasastra* tradition. Presumably it drew heavily on the *lokayata*, but its concern with the establishment of 'right' was no less. In truth, both the traditions were found inter-woven with each other. If there were other books upholding either of these traditions in pure form, they have been lost to us. However, what is germane here is that the *arthasastra* tradition takes precedence in the ideas of Kautilya.

A picture of India during this period is found in the travel records of Megasthenes. The account (from a little before 302 BC) is of course a mixture of observation and fables but certain facts emerge with stark clarity. First, there appears to have been no institution of slavery. Though inequality in property was permitted, there was some sort of equality before law. People had equal right to all possessions.[1] This concern for equality obstensibly was an out-growth of the moral principle of equanimity in life because, according to Megasthenes, people believed that the ideal situation was neither one of domination nor servitude but of self-regulation. Second, the law did not play much part in the lives of ordinary Indians.

People seldom went to the courts; there were few suits or depositions.[2] It appears that men of wisdom were highly respected and still played an important role. Thirdly, the state had come to assume a variety of functions. There were different departments looking after not only law and order but also things like trade, commerce, weights and measures, systems of production and regulation of price,[3] care of markets and regulation of labour relations. This complex character of the state apparatus is amply reflected in Kautilya's *Arthasastra*. But it is equally evident that this was also a period of intrigues because one thing which Megasthenes prominently mentions about the daily life of the king is that he was shifed from palace to palace at night to portect him against possible plots to kill him. Fourthly, the tension between the spiritual and the material had come to the surface. On the one hand, Megasthenes refers to the doctrine of unity which held that the world had a beginning and is liable to destruction, and is in shape spherical, and that the Deity who made it, and who governs it, is diffused through all its part. On the other hand this Vedantic view had to contend with the principle that the world consisted of five basic elements which included water and ether. There are also ideas about immortality and future judgement after death. God was viewed as Light and Word whose hidden mysteries were known only to *Brahmanas* because they alone, wrote Megasthenes, "have discarded vanity which is the outer most covering of the soul".[4] Since people believed in the immortality of the soul, death was regarded with contemptuous indifference. A belief in the reality of existence could be discerned in the idea that God is corporeal "that is (God) wears the body as its external covering and when it divests itself of the body, it becomes visible to eyes".[5] To this was connected a pessimistic view of life in which, similar to Platonic ideas, it was believed that there is a constant war going on between good and evil in the body, between such things as anger, grief, sexual appetite, on the one hand, and the principle of good, on the other. The body is a prison house and we must escape from its fetters to be able to come face to face with God as pure sunlight. Megasthenes found the resemblance between these ideas with those of the Pythagoreans as well as Plato startling. Indeed, the ancient seers had tremendous zest for life. They enjoyed the beauty of the sunrise and delighted in the enjoyment of the pleasures of the world though in due proportions. Now it seems that this worldview was slowly giving way to the view that the world is a prison house, the enjoyments of body are an obstacle to the realization of God and must therefore be curbed. This partly explains the respect which people came to bestow on Buddhists. However, this tendency did not perhaps become predominant until much later. In the meanwhile, there was perhaps a reassertion of the reality of the world as reflected in the *Samhkya* system. Kautilya's emphasis on *Arthasastra* is perhaps representative of this trend. Lastly, a definite all-India view seems to have come into existence because Megasthenes speaks of India as consisting of indigenous people who were neither conquered by others nor sought to conquer others. Lastly, kings during this period were still under discipline. Athenaeus quotes Daimachus' *History of India* to argue that in India while people drink, it was not permitted for the king to get drunk.[6]

Alexander's invasion had given a severe jolt to the complacency of the Indian mind which had begun to prize mystic communion more than the achievements of the earthly life. Buddhism and Jainism had also their share in strengthening the belief that the concerns of the after-life supersede the concerns of this world. In contrast there was renewed interest in the secular and humanistic traditions, towards positivism and science, which reached their apogee in the development of *vaisesika* doctrines in the first century AD as also in the great achievements in the field of medicine in the hands of Caraka. In the field of politics, Kautilya wrote his famous *Arthasastra* as well as the *Chanakyaniti*. It is often argued that they were not the work of the same person, but even a casual glance at the two would leave very little doubt about their authorship. *Chanakyaniti* provides the background and *Arthasastra* the specific application to the state of the principles developed in *Chanakyaniti*. However, we shall not enter into this debate. Tradition has viewed them as the writings of the same person.

At the time when Kautilya was living, India consisted of a number of small states which were constantly at war with each other. There was very little peace within the states either. Intrigues and murders were quite common. The peace which Vyasa had so much yearned for in the *Shantiparva* was nowhere in sight. It was the time of Alexander's invasion in north-west India and in contrast to the authoritarian rule he established, there was much disunity. Undoubtedly, in the field of literature, art, philosophy, there was much sophistication but since the political centre in India was weak, there was very little political organization. Alexander's invasion might have provoked some rethinking. It at least produced one great political thinker Kautilya, who has not been superseded in depth of thought and breadth of vision by any subsequent political thinker in India. Kautilya is credited with being the founder of the *arthasastra* tradition as distinguished from the *nitisastra* tradition. He was the first to make Political Economy an independent discipline; while paying lip service to the ideal of right, he propounded a theory of politics which dealt with the immediate practical concerns of polity. He was known for his exceptional, frank and candid ideas. He wrote with complete detachment, and sometimes cynicism, about issues of politics. It is remarkable that while Machiavelli who had views similar to those of Kautilya, was denounced throughout the seventeenth and eighteenth centuries, Kautilya was generally admired and revered in ancient India as the greatest of authors on politics except by Visakhadatta in his play *Mudraraksas*. For the first time he emphasized the need for a strong political centre in India. He even outlined a structure of government which would enable society to create this centre.

II

One of the basic presuppositions of Kautilya's thought is his acute awareness of the dangers of anarchy as well as the absolute necessity to transcend it by establishing order in society. The first book points to the dangers of anarchy. Kautilya too used the simile of larger fish eating the smaller when anarchy prevails. In order to escape from it, Kautilya emphasizes the need for a strong ruler capable of creating order. He discusses in detail the consequences of such a society, the dangers it entails not only for the social system of the castes but also for the individual's sense of security and his yearning for pleasure. Living at a time when the discipline and might of Alexander's army was in contrast to the decadent character of the state authority under the Nanda dynasty, he had sensed the impact of national humiliation when India had narrowly escaped being overrun. He may have also learnt a lesson from Bhisma in the *Mahabharata* who had emphasized the tendency of all kingdoms to slip into anarchy in the absence of a strong political order. This fear finds its echo throughout Kautilya's writings. Whatever the reason, he was convinced that society can never hope to be in peace without a strong state. With this as the backdrop to his ideas, he repudiated any idea of attacking the state authority or slaying the ruler. He had come to regard excessive concern for the individual as the greatest threat to the peace of the kingdom. This attitude comes out most clearly in the advice given by him to the rulers to maintain themselves. He is conscious that a weak king encourages impoverishment, greed, disaffection in his subjects. When people are impoverished they become greedy and overturn the state. But instead of expounding the idea that the people had an obligation or a right to resist the authority of the state, or get rid of bad rulers as in the *Mahabharata*, Kautilya puts more emphasis on the need for the rulers to curb the unrighteous and to protect the righteous, by respecting the leaders of the people and not deposing the worthy.[7] He perhaps felt that the main purpose of the king is to see that such an eventuality when people rise in revolt against the king should never arise because anarchy is worse than the highest tyranny. Kautilya even goes to the extent of saying that a diseased king is better than a new king. This position was almost a reversal of the position taken by Manu and Vyasa. Kautilya gives two reasons in support of this contention. First, while the diseased king is well versed in tradition and is bound by it, the new king, since there are no traditions to follow, acts without restraints. Secondly, Kautilya generally preferred kings of high birth because, according to him, people obey high birth more readily and tend to waver in their loyalty to a king who is low born. These arguments obviously involved a strong defence of the dynastic principle. Once the idea of the supremacy of the king is granted, Kautilya becomes quite liberal and warns against tyrannical tendencies which eventually incur popular wrath and destroy the kingdom: "It is unrighteous to do an act which causes popular fury: nor is it an accepted rule."[8] It is to be noted that he is respectful of popular fury not because of any moral consideration as in the *Mahabharata*, but because as an exponent of *real politik* he accepts the substantial importance of keeping people happy. He adds, "when people are impoverished, they become greedy, when they are greedy, they become disaffected, when disaffected, they voluntarily go to the side of the enemy and destroy their own master". He further adds, "hence, no king should give room to such causes as would bring about impoverishment, greed or disaffection among his people."[9]

Although Kautilya was in favour of a strong king, it may be doubted whether he was in favour of an absolute monarchy.[10] In his state the king had to work under so many restrictions. But from another angle, there is no doubt that the emphasis shifts from a contract as in the *Mahabharata* to the assertion of the authority of the king and from the popular assemblies to the council of the king.[11] All questions of political importance used to be discussed in the two houses of *pura-janapada* which were a powerful instrument to curb the king's authority. He further held that the king was never the proprietor of the soil and hence could not be called absolute. But in Kautilya the state had become highly bureaucratic. Indeed the bureaucratic apparatus described in Kautilya's *Arthasastra* very closely resembles the bureaucratic structure we have today.[12] The type of government suggested is so complex that it would be wrong to categorize it in terms of either absolute monarchy or oriental despotism or constitutional monarchy. Kautilya says that while a strong enemy of the wicked character should be opposed, when a virtuous king is attacked, he should be helped. In certain circumstances, he is even prepared to permit the ruler of another state to invade. He also accepts the *Mahabharata* vision of the contract theory. At another place he calls the king " a wage earner equal to other wage earners in the state" and declares that the kingdom is to be enjoyed by all.[13] He says, "In the happiness of his subjects lies his happiness, in their welfare his welfare, whatever pleases himself he shall not consider as good, but whatever pleases his subjects he shall consider good."[14] The imprint of the *dharmasastra* tradition is unmistakable.

But he is convinced that the state is sovereign and with it the king must be supreme. The king is above all other elements. After giving eight elements of the state such as the king, the minister, the country, the treasury, the fort, the army, the friends and the enemy,[15] he declares a good king can improve even the most defective constituents. He makes or mars other elements. Kautilya repudiated Bhardwaja's view that the calamity of the officials is of greater importance than that of the king. The king alone selects his officials, rewards and punishes them, endows prosperity on any one he likes, Kautilya even makes a categorical assertion about the transcendental character of the king's authority. Though he repeats the contract version of the *Mahabharata*, he tends to emphasize that the king derives his authority not so much from the popular contract as from divine benediction. This makes any idea of revolt against the king doubly difficult. The kingship is a result of the escape from the state of nature in which laws of the jungle prevailed. As a result, any state is better than no state which throws people back into anarchy. It is almost the Hobbesian dilemma which haunts Kautilya. The authority of the king and his right to collect taxes, etc., are in the interest of the people themselves. To reinforce this, the concept of divine ordination is also added. He writes: "Kings are visible dispensers of favours and disfavours, and as such they are in the position of the Gods Indra and Yama respectively: he who despises them is visited with divine punishment." Perhaps Kautilya added the second argument only to use religious superstitions in the service of the state because he says, "Thus the lowly folk should be silenced." In any case, so ardent is his partiality towards a strong king that he even pleads for modification of social customs and practices by royal inervention, though always keeping in mind that it should not be at variance with the rest of society. He refers to the authority of canon law, customary law, usages and logical principles. He argues that in case of conflict of interpretation, the king should himself decide the dispute and his interpretation is to be upheld as final. Even his executives' edicts have the force of law. The king can bestow rewards and punishments upon his servants, he can honour anyone or grant remissions, he is empowered to attest the act of a subordinate and offer safe conduct to travellers. He guides the works of various administrative heads of departments and panels of magistrates incharge of adminstrative courts.

This constituted a further development on the doctrines in the *Shantiparva* and *Brihaspati sutra*. While the earlier literature had subordinated the king to brahmanical authority, and the *Shantiparva* gave the king some discretion, when we come to Kautilya, we find that the king is given the last say in all matters. This emphasis on the principle of the kingship became the basis of consolidating perhaps the first centralized government in India. It is true that at several places where Kautilya pays deference to tradition, he recognizes the authority of sacred canon, customary law and usage and argues that the king should settle disputes in accordance with these. He even asks the king to respect the laws of *sanghas*. When a king acquires a new kingdom, he is enjoined to respect the customs and usages of the conquered territory. But sometimes, and specially in the case of acquired territories, the king is authorized to abrogate all those customs which are against his interest or contrary to righteousness. This shows that the governing assumption is that the state is supreme. Nowhere does this come out more strongly than in his insistence that since rogues and charlatans roam in the garb of *sanyasins*, all the *sanyasins* must be registered.

In Kautilya's book the idea of a welfare state is repeated with great force. According to him, the king must ensure that people of the four castes and four orders of life keep to their respective path, respective duties and occupations. He clearly states that it is the responsibility of the kings to maintain the safety and security of their subjects, "and of being answerable for the sins of their subjects when the principles of levying just punishment and taxes have been violated".[16] The king has to be dynamic in order to ensure that his subjects are likewise dynamic. If the king is reckless, they will also be reckless and will eat into his works. He warned that a reckless prince will easily fall a prey to enemies. There is nothing more important for a king than enterprise, wakefulness and concern for the welfare of his subjects. These are the three virtues he admired most. He enjoins that the king must provide for the orphans, the aged, the helpless and the afflicted. Helpless women must be provided subsistence by the state when they are pregnant. The king is also required to construct dams, rivers, and roads, to maintain forests, and provide help and superintendence to places of pilgrimage. He is also to supervise the reservoirs constructed by cooperative enterprises of the people and to ensure that those who do not work, do not gain from them.[17] The king must protect agriculturists from molestation and other kinds of oppression, forced labour and oppressive taxes.[18]

During famines, the king is asked to help the people by providing seed and provision. He declares, "A wise king can make the poor and miserable elements of his society happy and prosperous, but a wicked king will surely destroy the most prosperous of loyal elements of his kingdom."[19] He was convinced that a vicious and unrighteous king who ignores the welfare of his subjects would fall a victim to popular fury or become vulnerable to enemies. Such a state in which people are not happy is a weak state. On the other hand, "a wise king, trained in politics, will, though he possesses a small territory, conquer the whole earth with the help of the best elements of his sovereignty and will never be defeated".[20] It is a measure of tribute to Kautilya's administrative genius that there is an elaborate discussion of the state structure, the organization of various departments, the centre and the state governments.

In fact, the *Arthasastra* is more of treatise on administration than on politics and statecraft. The administrative principles are discussed with such insight as to make us wonder whether there has been any real progress in the science of administration since then. The idea of a positive state is taken up and the king is authorized to create conditions for a good life not only by digging wells, canals, and constructing dams, planting trees, preservation of forest but also by providing the infrastructure for trade, commerce and industry through construction of roads and providing an impetus to navigation. There is an elaborate discussion of the methods by which harmful tendencies in these activities can be regulated in the interest of all, and suggestions of ways and means to achieve this. He even argues that evil and adulterous persons should be arrested in the name of security and public interest. We shall not go into the details here.

The most interesting point is his reference to republics which he felt were difficult to conquer. He gave various reasons for this. First, the subjects are very rarely oppressed. According to him, such governments are free from the vices of single rulers.[21] Second, the collective actions impart strength to them. But like the author of the *Mahabharata*, Kautilya too felt that such governments are difficult to administer and very soon disintegrate because of internal dissensions in the ruling class. He seems to think that such governments can be easily subverted by the use of spies. In fact, it would appear that Kautilya had a very poor opinion of the masses. He thought that the masses are more often swayed by popular slogans than by reason. Therefore he enjoined statesmen to take advantage of this to win them over by following a policy of conciliation where needed and force when necessary.

He was the first thinker who consciously thought of an all-India state or even empire.[22] In a good state it is not only necessary to have right laws and institutions, honest and clean administration devoted to public welfare but the right kind of relations with other states. It may be remembered that both a freind and an enemy are constituent elements of Kautilya's concept of sovereignty. The exposition of state relations with other states occupies much space in the book.

The relations with other states are important because no state exists in isolation; in fact every state is competing with every other for land. This is the natural order where none is content with what he already has. This implies that no state can be stable unless it takes care of its foreign relations. If such relations are ignored, argues Kautilya, the state will soon fall a prey to conspiracy hatched by other princes. The only solution is to be wakeful and to treat offence as the best defence, to ensure that the state is not only capable of defending itself but also inflicting damage on others when need arises. It is only victories which can ensure stability. The field of relations between states is like a jungle, only the strength of a lion can prevail there.

In this enterprise, Kautilya advises, the king must first use right means, but if they fail he must use intrigue and treachery. The whole idea is to increase the sphere of the influence of the king. He identifies a *chakravartin* with one who rules the entire land south of the Himalayas, which would cover the whole of the present day India. The objectives of foreign policy has to be from equilibrium to progress. The success of a foreign policy would very much depend on a combination of sound counsel and material resources which would include revenue, army and enterprise. He discusses in detail the policies to be adopted by the king in dealing with a strong, an equal and a weak kingdom. The general feeling is that it is easier or preferable to deal with an unjust king however strong he may be than with a weak just king because while in the case of an attack on the unjust king, the population would desert the victim, in the case of a just king it would be the reverse. However, the details of the policy, when to attack, opt for a compromise or surrender should depend on the relative strength or weakness of the enemy. For instance, should the enemy be strong compromise is recommended. Again, the king is enjoined to expand his kingdom whenever he finds that there is sufficient economic prosperity and a strong army or when he finds that the enemy's state is divided. Kautilya is categorical that if progress of a kingdom is equally attainable through peace, or war, then peace is to be preferred thereby saving the state from unnecessary expenditure on men and material. In any case, before an action is taken, there should be an assessment of the relative strength of one's own position in relation to the enemy in terms of such factors as power, time, place, the time for mobilization of troops and the prospective loss of men and material. In these ideas, Kautilya is very refreshing in suggesting that a wise policy is to be preferred to one based on purely military or financial considerations, and that the latter must get precedence over the king's own volition. A policy based on wisdom can achieve the same, and perhaps even better results than a policy based purely on military or financial considerations. He is very clear that if a king is to become a *chakravartin*, he must have all these three assets, namely, military power, financial prudence, and wisdom. But ultimately the quality of good advice based on wise assessment of the situation matters more than anything else. It is this consideration which leads him to conclude that it is better to enter into a compromise with superior forces. This also explains why he suggests a policy of treachery and intrigue against a stronger adversary. The king in such cases may enter into a compromise and then wait for the opportune moment to arise in order to detach himself.

Kautilya is convinced that although a good and wakeful king is necessary, this alone is not sufficient to ensure a well ordered state because people are generally selfish and tend to give more importance to their own selfish interests than the interest of the state. There is a general tendency among administrators and ministers to alter the state of things in their favour by practice of bribery and corruption, which if allowed unchecked, can wreck a state. To meet this situation, he suggests two things. First, the king must be aware of the motives and activities of his council of ministers. He must not consult more than two ministers at a time. Ministers must be selected on the basis of their talent, character and loyalty. From time to time the king must test their integrity and loyalty by offering them temptations through his spies. They must be kept under constant watch so that they are not able to wield undue influence inimical to the king. In cases of corruption, the king must impose the severest penalties and in certain cases he is even enjoined to get rid of such ministers. He admits that such a step might be cruel, but adds that this is the only way in which thorns in the state can be weeded out. Such severity is indispensable for public welfare. If these people are not handled in this manner, they will conspire to rob the public of its wealth and the king of his state.

On the other hand, the king must reward all those who show integrity and are deserving. Loyalty is very high on the list of merits which enables the king to decide who is deserving. Such people are necessary to save the state from falling apart in times of emergency. Public life is governed by envy and jealousy. Therefore if loyal people are slandered in public, the

. accusers must be forced to bring charges against them, investigation must be held, and if such charges are proved untrue, those who bring the charges must also be given severe punishment.

Kautilya discusses in detail how corruption arises, what are its various forms, and what is needed to keep the state free of it. He also discusses the special procedure to be applied in such cases: he suggests that a panel of three magistrates with the rank of ministers should be entrusted with this task. He had perhaps a system of administrative courts in mind because for this task judges are not recommended.

Kautilya was not only concerned with corruption of officials but also of everyone in public life.[23] For instance, there should be a superintendent of merchandise to exercise control over trade practices so that traders are not able to oppress the people. The king is enjoined to punish thirteen types of criminals after ascertaining their activities with the help of the spies. This list includes manufacturers, traders, corrupt officials and judges. Corruption includes not only material gratification but also abuse of authority. All these criminals are to be tried by special tribunals according to a fixed procedure, a common practice it seems, in the Mauryan empire.[24]

Kautilya's vision was undoubtedly rooted in the classical ideas of virtue and he admired courage, truth, fortitude and valour in all. He did not have much interest in pure philosophical speculation but was more concerned with practical moral virtues. He thought that a minister possessing only theoretical knowledge was likely to blunder.[25] He understood politics essentially in administrative terms, of good and bad administration, recognizing the former as necessary to the foundation and maintenance of a good state. A good administration is necessary in order to ensure individual security and social stability. Even military adventures against enemies are justified because there cannot be order in states which are threatened by others. He also believed in the force of fate and time and enjoined that astrologers must be consulted before embarking on any military adventure. But on the whole he had greater faith in man's capacity to rise above circumstances and shape them. To be able to do so is the mark of a statesman.

It is significant that in his writings the state becomes the supreme association and religion a private affair. Indeed, the secularisation of political life was achieved nowhere better than in Kautilya. His plea to have the *sanyasins* registered was a clear demonstration of this. He was aware of the religious corruption of the times. He goes to the extent of saying that if someone becomes an ascetic without making provision for the maintenance of his wife or children, he shall be punished along with the person who converts him.[26] Among his spies are included the false hermits, the false ascetics and the false mendicants. They are also enjoined to exploit popular superstitions in the interest of the king. If it is necessary for the preservation of the state, he authorizes the use of temple money on flimsy pretexts. Religion is useful to the king because it can be a powerful instrument in the service of the state. This may sound trivial to us, but at the time when the authority of religion was respected, it was truly an attempt towards secularisation of the state power.

So great is his concern for the stability of the state that he thought that even the powers of the king are justified because they lead to the good of the state. To ensure rightful exercise of powers by the king, Kautilya gives elaborate instructions on the education and training of princes, which almost remind one of the education of the Guardian class in Plato. He also imposed severe curbs on the king's expenditure in the civil list.

His concern for the stability of the state comes out most clearly in his ideas on the sanctity of a treaty. He declares[27] that a treaty based on truth and solemn affirmation is immutable both in this world and the next. Even a treaty supported by a security and a pledge must also be respected. It is the duty of the king to make the state safe from all kinds of evil men. For the preservation of the state, Kautilya was convinced that the ruler had to ignore the ordinary conceptions of morality; he had to have recourse to the most evil methods. His remedy was to utilize evil for the good of all. He suggests every evil method to extirpate thorns from the state—the use of spies, deceit, treachery, sex, violence and murder. In a number of suggestions which are ingenious, Kautilya lays the foundation of the science of statecraft, despicable by our standards, which was to dominate actual political life in India later when princes employed every trick suggested by him for self aggrandizement. Since Kautilya often confused the preservation to the state with the preservation of the king, he virtually gave a blank cheque to the princes to commit all sorts of cruelties.

III

Kautilya made politics autonomous. He divided human knowledge into four sciences. Philosophy deals with reasoned argument and makes one steady in weal and woe. The sacred canon gives us knowledge of the four castes and their respective duties the performance of which leads to heaven. The science of political economy leads to better agriculture and production of metals and forest products. The science of politics deals with reward of the good and punishment of the wicked. In this sense it is the most important of all the four kinds of knowledge because it leads to acquisition and preservation of them all. On this depends the sustenance of life. Indeed this flows logically from the priority to prosperity accorded in his thought. He is of the view that any one of three elements, namely right, prosperity and sensual pleasure, if enjoyed in excess destroys "not only the other two but also ifself". He goes on to say that prosperity is the most important because on this depends pursuit of right as well as satisfaction of desires.[28] Therefore, he further says that politics deals with "the acquisition of what has not been gained, the preservation of what has been acquired, the increase of what has been preserved, and the bestowal of the surplus upon the deservers." This makes the scope of political science truly comprehensive and humane because it is not merely concerned with law and order but also with preservative and development functions as well as with distributive justic so that the surplus is bestowed upon the deserving. It is in the pursuit of this humanistic aim that Kautilya has discussed almost all political variables which might lead to the rise or decline of the state including influence of the stars, mystical numbers, religious superstitions and social practices. It was his singular achievement to weave the influence of geopolitical factors into his science of administration which is truly inductive in character. He was perhaps convinced that the existence of a central authority in India was a necessary condition for the continuance of the civilization. Incidentally, it is in his book that for the first time we find a description of India which survives until modern times. We find a vision which characterizes our thinking. His chief concerns—preservation and development of the state in terms of a certain concept of distributive justice, security of subjects and stability of society—have beeen clearly stated, concerns which much remain with all those who are interested in theorizing about India. In many ways his vision is unique. While his excessive emphasis on the use of evil methods survives in later periods in the bedevilment of relations between princes and their subjects, his emphasis on the establishment of a powerful administrative structure gets a new lease of life with the modern awakening of India. In a way he cut through pious wishes and moral principles, and reached the pivot of *real politik* directly. What is significant is that while he recognized the corruption and degradation of his contemporary society, he also wanted to ensure that out of this emerged a powerful administration which would found the state on a strong basis and forever banish the scourge of insecurity and instability. He paid a great deal of attention to the creation of various structures of administrative authority in this direction.

He even retained a significant number of constraints on the exercise of power by the ruler. He continued to regard the ruler as a servant of the people.[29] He also recognized the distinct character of the popular will and warned rulers against the dangers of disregarding it. Though the decision of the ruler was final, the ruler is enjoined to administer justice according to sacred law, customary law and usage. The king was bound to regard sacred law as upholding the system of justice. This crucial limitation is enunciated at a number of places with great emphasis. The ruler is above others but not above right (dharma) and is, therefore, bound to obey the customary and sacred law except in extreme cases. Kautilya also laid down an elaborate system of constraints on king's behaviour, for he must uphold sacred law, protect the property, family and life of the people and, maintain the caste system. The general position is that there is nothing more sacred than the people's welfare.

Though Kautilya through his advocacy of evil methods for good ends has come to be compared to Machiavelli, we must pay greater attention to his administrative system particularly in the context of the emergence of a vision of an all-Indian state. We must also not forget the context in which the *Arthasastra* was written. Kautilya was trying to create, almost single-handedly, order out of chaos, peace out of war, a public state out of a corrupt one. That is why his ideas were extremely complex. On the one hand he had suggested the use of all evil means, on the other hand he was obsessed by the idea of creation of a neat administrative system, town planning, problems of mines, rural and urban colonization and settlement, with the creation of dams and canals no less than with a monetary system and control of wieghts and measures. Obviously, such a man could not be preaching political gangsterism; he is not preaching that the end justifies the means, the only end which justifies the means is the preservation and development of the state, punishment of the wicked and protection of the good. His great insight lies in the discovery that any agency entrusted with the task of maintenance of order, acquisition of what has not been achieved so far, and distribution of surplus to the deserving in society, requires creation of an agency or authority which cannot be a common standard to evaluate all human action, namely, the imperative of life in society (samsar), to continue without hurting anyone in the process. Consequently, it means that non-violence is good because as Bhisma said in the *Mahabharata*, anyone who is non-violent gives life breath to the universe. In other words, it enables life to go on. But he also recognized that absolute non-violence is impossible. Even the very fact of being in itself would involve some sort of violence. There he concluded that it is not a choice between pure violence and pure non-violence, between white and black as it were. In fact there are many strands in between. The value of an action is to be judged with reference first to its objective which ought to be the preservation and development of human life, and secondly, to the adoption of those means which would do the minimum of harm to the parties concerned and help in the achievement of the objective.

According to all these writings, the customary morality is not binding in all cases. It is to be respected because it is a product of ages of human experience. But there may be situations when it may be required to depart from it in the larger good of society. The lives of great men always break the bounds of custom in order to provide new direction to human life or a new insight into a human situation. Rama and Krishna were considered such personages. We are living in a hostile world and we do not know all its intricacies. The best we can do is to lead an authentic life which is the life of a hero, by following our conscience on these points. There is no good or evil as such. It all depends on the objective and the circumstances in which we are trying to achieve it. Another element which was important was the motive. Since we do not have any control over outer conditions, we are permitted to act according to time, place and circumstances so long as our motive, over which we have absolute control, is clear, transparent; so long as we are inspired by the idea of the welfare of all (*loksamgraha*) and not personal gratification, we are permitted everything. In formulating the entire statecraft on this principle, his system has not been superseded by any subsequent thinker. This was no doubt a departure from popular notions but in the time in which the idea of *Loksamgraha* was expressed, it had surely radical implications, decisively influencing the organization of the central state in India during the Mauryan and Gupta periods. By renouncing all forms of accommodation with the wicked and corrupt, and by outlining a strong state structure, he was laying down the foundation for a possible national state. Perhaps it was some such effort which made the glory of the Mauryan and the Gupta period possbile. No wonder all later writers on statecraft either condemned him or adulated him out of all proportions. Writers like Bana and Magha denounced the doctrine, in *Kadambri* and *Sisupalvadha* respectively,[30] as a grossly materialistic doctrine of deceit rooted in the worship of wealth and worldly success, to the nefarious influence of which was attributed the increasing hypocrisy of political life in which kings yielded rule to their confidants and indulged in orgies of dissipation. On the other hand, he was eulogised by Kalidas and Visakhadatta and Somedeva as the greatest authority on statecraft.

IV

Kautilya's *Arthasastra* was a product of a period of turbulence. It came to terms with the problems presented by a mercantile society torn asunder by the ravages of wars between princes and external attack. There was no other independent work on politics of comparable significance until much later. Bana and Magha do provide a critique of Kautilya but nothing more. The summing up of the best in ancient thought is found in the works of Kalidasa. He achieved a synthesis of all traditions of political thinking that preceded him with rare literary finesse in the *Raghuvansham* which deals with the rise and fall of the Raghu dynasty of Ayodhya and also with the statecraft practised by their kings. Kalidasa cannot be called a political thinker in any sense of the term. We would not have included him but for two reasons. First, he has evoked and inspired the imagination of the modern Indian mind about the glory that was India more than any other figure of the period. Second, he in a way sums up the ideal of the good state which was never again matched either in grandeur or in depth by any subsequent thinker.

Kalidasa belongs to the more settled reign of Chandra Gupta Vikramaditya, under whose patronage he flourished. This was a period of great intellectual achievements in the realm of philosophy, art, science and medicine. In astronomy great strides were made by the authors of *Jyotisha Vedanga* and the *Suryaprajapati*. Aryabhatta made a major breakthrough in the field of astronomy in AD 499. He calculated the value of Pi to 3.416 and the length of the solar year as 365.3586805 days. His calculations are remarkably close to those of our own time. Varahamira systematized all the five schools of astronomy. There was a close exchange of ideas with the Greeks. The great stories of *Shudraka* and *Panchatantra* also belonged to the same period. Fahien, a Chinese Buddhist pilgrim, left detailed accounts of the life of the people during the period. He testifies to the fact that the life of the average man was quite happy and contented. The same is also reflected in the writings of Kalidasa himself. In *Abhigyan Shakuntalam* and *Meghaduta* and *Kumarsambhava* we find rare glimpses into the pattern of contemporary life with all its delicacy and gentleness. The *Shakuntalam* came to be known in Europe and exercised a great impact on Goethe who opined that if there was heaven in literature, it was in this play.

Kalidasa emerged as a conscious advocate of traditional Indian values and institutions and a supporter of the theory of enlightened constitutional kingship expressed in the *Ramayana* and the *Mahabharata*. He described the kings of Raghuvansha because he thought that they consciously tried to emulate the teachings of *Smriti* and followed Kautilyan standards of just wars and righteous victory. He was strongly influenced by the ideal of moderation and praised these kings because they practised virtue without avarice, and enjoyed pleasure without being addicted to it. According to him, kings must try to become perfect embodiments of harmony and balance, avoiding the extremes of both severity and mildness.

He accepted the ancient Indian ideal that each individual has his own end and the supreme end is liberation (*mukti*), possible through the pursuit of righteousness (dharma). The aim of life is the fullest awareness of this. He goes on to demonstrate that only in a good kingdom can this be realized. The role of a good king is to make this kind of life possible; as Lord Vishnu is the protector of all universe, so the king is the protector of all people living in his kingdom. According to him, under a bad government, nature revolts and men suffer untold misery, but under a good government, nature becomes bountiful and men righteous. Of course, he identified good government with monarchy. But the mere existence of monarchy was not important. He was more concerned with the purpose for which the monarchy existed. It is the supreme concern for the welfare of people which made Rama unique or the supreme capacity to stand for certain ideals which made Raghu and Harischandra great. The kings of Raghu dynasty were the noblest, of all kings, because in conquering the world, they subjected themselves to moral principles and a certain notion of the public good.

Indeed the ideal of the king as father finds eloquent expression in him. The sole object of statecraft, we are told, is the good of the subjects. The internal government must be marked by mercy and compassion. The king should neither be severe nor mild but should combine in himself all the virtues and administer laws with impartiality so that people gain prosperity, and the obstacles in the path of their spiritual growth are moved. The king is not above law but is bound by customary law. A good kingdom is one in which subjects live without fear and get protection in return for the taxes they pay. It was indeed a plea for a complete merger of the king's own interest with the interests of the subjects. It was in effect the acceptance of the principle of the supremacy of virtue. The king should punish criminals for the preservation of order. He should distribute property. Even marriage has a public function because the king is expected to marry for the sake of welfare of his kingdom, so that both the pursuit of pleasure and property become a means for the practice of political virtue. The king is permitted to conquer other territories but only for righteous purposes. In all these we discern audible echoes of ancient literature.

There is no novelty in all these writings except that they express the earlier ideals of the *Smritis* in a more effective and elegant style. Kalidasa is one with Valmiki and Vyasa that man should lead his life with zest and complete faith in the order of being. There is a realization that the fullness of life consists in a harmonious development of the multi-dimensionality of our being. Despite the Buddhist context, the argument remains valid; it is a clear expression of the political aim in the ancient world. The social harmony is the condition of such a fulfilment and can only be attained by the authority of a king who subordinates pursuit of power to ideals of truth, righteousness and sacrifice. To this extent he reflected a fine synthesis of classical thought.

At times it appears that Kalidasa had the potential to give us a justificatory theory for some of these ideals, but, being a poet, the task does not interest him much. This leads to a more general point. What was the contribution of the literature of the classical period to the development of political thought? We are here including various *Puranas* which from time to time contain references to the state, though here is very rarely a systematic discussion of it. While no one would doubt that the writers like Kalidasa and Bana were eminent and profound and from time to time provided rare insights into political matters, it seems from available evidence that this period did not produce any outstanding political philosopher, certainly not one to match the authors of the *Shantiparva* or the *Arthasastra*. There are stray manuscripts such as that of Kannanda, but it is doubtful whether they contained anything original. Mostly these works repeat earlier ideas without incorporating any new element. This is reflected in their attitude to customary law. In the earlier period, law was supposed to be derived from natural principles which governed the cosmic process and, since they were objective, could be discerned by yogis and seers. The principles of dharma were thought to derive their authority from the principles embodied in nature itself. That is why Bhisma could say that it is these principles which hold the worlds together. Some of these were turned into non-rational principles which derived their authority not so much from natural or cosmic order as from scriptures, customs and usages. Upanishadic seers, later on quoted by Gautama, could preach that nothing could be taken as certain unless it was verified on the authority of scriptures alone. This shift expressed the ways of life followed by people in later times. If those who compiled them had their own interests to serve, the literature and usages were changed. Thus the legitimation of beliefs was simply based on their existence. These writings embodied traditional beliefs of thinking and action within society. In the process there might have developed the curious phenomenon of addition, alteration and interpolation, for after all the rewards of life depended on what was written in these works. From Kalidasa onwards, from the point of view of political thought, we find blank pages in much of Indian history up to the advent of the Muslim period, of course with the exception of a few excellent arguments in *Agni Purana* and Somedeva Suri's *Nitivakyanmritam* which we shall discuss later.

We would hazard a conjecture on the reasons for this phenomenon. All the dominant philosophers of the period, those of Vedanta, Buddhism and Jainism shared one common feeling, that the life of quietude could not be combined with the worldly life, much less with the life of the state which was full of deceit and treachery. This contempt for politics was reflected in the writings of the famous Buddhist thinker Asvaghosa in the fifth century AD. Sankaracharya who was unmistakably the greatest and the most visionary of our mystical thinkers lived during this period. Since men of talent and thought would not think about man's relationship to the state, the field was left to compilers, systematizers, and commentators who, as best as they could, tried to preserve the sayings of the ancients. It is one of the great mysteries as to how a civilization which produced such a prodigious literature in music, art, aesthetics, astronomy, all of a sudden turned its back on this magnificent heritage, stopped asking new questions and giving new interpretations to the old truths. It is true that this systematization became the basis of the legal and judicial system in later times. Generations of commentators provided the basis for the state to build on. But a sharp distinction had been drawn between the life in this world and the other, between the life of renunciation and the life lived according to the compulsions of the social system. In the earlier period, even a *risi* or seer had a social role to play. Once he had seen the Light, he was expected to return to the Platonic cave, as it were, in order to guide others in their quest for the spiritual truth. Since he had seen (that is why he was called *drista*) the basic structure underlying all forms, he was, it was believed, in the best position to guide others so that they could attain happiness without hurting themselves. The *risi* had his own timetable to follow. The idea of a Tirthanker or a Buddha was the same. Having attained knowledge of the past, the present and the future (*trikaladarshi* or *kaivalya*) the Tirthanker had the ability to help others. But henceforth the true philosophic minds left the world to itself, or to priests and kings who interpreted the ancient ideals to suit their narrow interests.

But when all is said against the systematizers, there are three points which must be said in their favour. First, important distinction between executive, legislative and judicial powers came to be made. The council of ministers and the officers of the state, all later came to wield unlimited powers as the actual politics became more Kautilyan and divorced from moral life. But none of these systematizers and poets such as Bhartrihary and Bhairavi considered rulers above law or dharma which, they also believed, provided legitimacy to secular authority. Even in these dark ages, the notion of right and law served at least as a fiction. To this were anchored in the later medieval period the rules of *noblesse oblige* and *ma-bap sarkar*. It served to provide some sort of constraints, albeit moral on the exercise of political power in the medieval period. The vision of the systematizers provided the framework in terms of which political authority could be exercised. Second, they also retained the appreciation of power which the ancients had. Power was considered necessary for the maintenance of life. It was never condemned as evil. There were varieties of power, namely, economic power, physical power, political power, spiritual power and all these were found to be necessary for the preservation and development of life. Nowhere does this appreciation come out more clearly than in the *Markandeya* and *Devi Puranas* both of which are a form of prayer to the Mother who is considered the veritable embodiment of the highest powers. The sytematizers were also aware of the possibility of misuse of power. They often remind themselves of the legendary examples of the great but perverted yogis such as Hirnyakashyapu and Ravana. But they also emphasised that power should be used for the welfare of mankind. In fact, without it there was no possibility of happiness in this world. This notion was relegated to the background as the gap between the wheel of cosmic order (*samsar chakra*) and the wheel of right order (*dharma chakra*) widened and the first was condemned as illusory and ephemeral. The third thing which finds its clearest expression in the Puranas is the zigzag view of history in which one epoch is succeeded by another in the order of *Kreta, Treta, Dwapara* and *Kalyuga* and then another cycle begins. Within each epoch, they did not rule out the possibility of a short-lived *Treta* or *Dwapara*. Such a transformation was thought possible if somehow the kings and rulers became good and sincere in their devotion to public welfare. In fact the connection between the quality of political order and the nature of the *yuga* was considered extremely important. Most authors dread the advent of *Kalyuga* which, following the author of *Vishnu purana*, was identified generally with the rule of wealth and then of the labouring class or with anarchy. The description of *Kalyuga* given in *Bhavisya purana*, for instance, is reminiscent of the Platonic description of anarchy. In the earlier epochs the ruling

classes were identified with knowledge and valour. In this whole pro°ss
of existence apprearance of divine forces in human form from time to ti. .e
was considered a unique event in human history, specially the incarnations
of Vishnu or the advent of a *Tirthanker*, which they thought gave a new
direction to the course of human history. The belief underlying this view
of history was the permanences of change and the essential tendency of
social formation to corruption. To stop the tendency towards corruption
and decay, divine intervention from time to time was required. A certain
moral relativism also followed from this point of view because with each
successive epoch there is an inevitable decline of right (dharma).
Recognizing this inevitable tendency to decline, the Puranas yet declared
that each earlier epoch was better, meaning thereby a society in which
knowledge and valour rule is better than one in which wealth rules, though
such a form is capable of realization only when people adhere to right. All
of them sing the praises of earlier period, specially of Ramarajya, where
the happiness of people was considered sovereign, and where citizens
armed with virtues and guided by sound leadership, found glory and
satisfaction in pursuit of right and just conquest of other territories.

They preserved the great visions of the authors of the *Ramayana* and
the *Mahabharata*—the vision which, despite all the tumultuous changes
which had come upon the Indian scene never lost its appeal and received
a fresh impetus during the renaissance in the nineteenth century. It
surfaced in the writings of Dayananda, Vivekananda and Aurobindo. In a
world in which philosophy in general breathed an air of pessimism and
resignation, it provided an incentive to action in term of which social life
could proceed. The medieval interpreters certainly failed to provide a
rational system. They at times got swept off their feet by their faith in fate
and the supernatural. They perhaps reconciled themselves to decay: the
inevitability of a fall after one had reached the climax is noticeable in the
thought of Sri Harsha. The general feeling became one of awe against
powers they felt they could not control. The actual corruption and decay
of social life was only matched by a very profound sense of futility which
characterized the writings of some of these thinkers; the search of intellect
to achieve material prosperity gave way to efforts to escape from the world.
For instance, the famous poet Bhairavi, though still adhering to Kautilya's
doctrine, took the position that not kings but sages attain success through
self restraint. He pleaded for the adoption of a policy of indifference by
wise men in his *Kiratarjaniyam*.[31] *Smritis* and the *Arthasastra* came to be
divorced from the larger purposes of individual and social welfare and
were identified solely with the preservation and expansion of the powers
of the king. This trend paved the way for heroism without purpose with

which the middle ages abound when politics became, as the Buddhist canonists thought, a dismal science concerned with one's own aggrandizement at the expense of social welfare.

NOTES

1. *Ancient India as Described by Megasthenes and Arrain,* trans, J.W. Macrindle (London, Trubner & Co. 1977), pp. 35-40.
2. Ibid., p. 70.
3. Ibid., pp. 86-87.
4. Ibid., p. 120.
5. Ibid., p. 121.
6. Athenaeus, *Dei Dnosophists,* trans. Charles Burton Gulick (London, Heinne), vol. IV, MCM, XXVII.
7. Kautilya, *Arthasastra,* chaps. 5, 276.
8. Ibid., I. V, 6.
9. Ibid., I. VII, 5.
10. V.A. Smith, *Indian Constitutional Reforms Viewed in the Light of History* (Oxford, 1919), p. 55.
11. Kautilya, op. cit., p. 97.
12. See, B.G. Gokhale, *The Making of Indian Nation* (Bombay, Asia Publishing House, 1960), p. 201. K.M. Pannikar, *A Survey of Indian History* (Bombay, 1957), p. 29.
13. Kautilya, op. cit., X. 3.
14. Ibid., I. IV. 9; XVIII. 12.
15. Ibid., I: VI, 1.
16. Ibid., p. 24.
17. Ibid., p. 51.
18. Ibid., p. 52.
19. Ibid., pp. 309-11.
20. Ibid., p. 311.
21. Ibid., XI, 1.
22. See D.D. Kosambi, *An Introduction to the Study of Indian History* (Bombay, 1956), p. 205.
23. Kautilya, op. cit., IV, 2.
24. V.A. Smith, *The Oxford History of India,* 1919, p. 89.
25. Kautilya, op. cit., p. 14.
26. Ibid., p. 51.
27. Ibid., VII: 17.
28. Ibid., P. 12.
29. Ibid., I: 3.
30. U.N. Ghosal, op. cit., pp. 353-54. Also 1778.
31. Bhairavi, *Kiratarjaniyam,* II-8-10, 12.

CHAPTER 6

THE SRAMANIC VISION
MAHAVIRA, BUDDHA AND SOMEDEVA

Not much is known about the precise contours of what happened between the war of the *Mahabharata* and the rise of Buddhism and Jainism. Literary sources survived but not the knowledge about the succession of events. There is no doubt that it must have been a period of turbulence with kingdoms at war with each other. In politics, while the general pattern was that of monarchies, there were certain regions in the Eastern sector, specially near the hills, where the republican form of government flourished. There are references to these even in the *Mahabharata*, but such references become more pronounced in the Buddhist literature. These republics included those of the Shakyas, Koliyas, Mallas and Vrijis. It is debatable how far they would resemble republics in our times or whether they were tribal organizations or had any well defined constitutional system at all. We also do not have full details about their origins. It appears that sometimes they were founded by persons of loyal lineage who abdicated their throne for a variety of reasons. At other times, they were a product of a concrete application of the older Vedic ideal of acting in concert with assemblies of elders and people. There is not much evidence available about the actual procedure which might have been followed by them in the determination of public issues. It appears that assemblies consisting of the heads of families were organized under the leadership of some person who was called the *raja* or *pradhan*. These assemblies took decisions after due deliberation of all the points at issue. The emphasis was on unanimity, failing which issues were put to vote. It would appear that in these states there was greater individualism and respect for heterodox opinions. It is ironic that the leaders of both the Jaina and Buddhist traditions came from these republics.

To be sure, the individualist mode of thinking had already appeared in Jaina thought which dated back to the Vedic period in the form of *Sramana parampara.* In the genesis story repeated in the *Puranas*, there is a reference to Sanat Kumars. They were the first offsprings of Brahma. But when Brahma asked them to become householders and help him in the process and the expansion of the world, they refused because they thought that they would thereby incur sin and fall from their state of perfect bliss by so participating in this process. In a sense, they were the paragons of *nivritti*. Brahma was distressed at their reply and then came Rudra who agreed to oblige him. In a sense, the *Sramana parampara* symbolised the revulsion of Sanat Kumars at the ways of the world and their yearning for nothing less than perfection.

The first tirthanker Rishabdeva was the sixth *avatar* of the *Smriti* tradition. Both Jainism and Buddhism were extremely critical of the brahmanical system, the hereditary basis of caste and animal sacrifices and other rituals attendant on them; both did not care much about the intervention of intra-cosmic Gods and both preached the value of a moral life in terms of the theory of *karma*. So great was their contempt for the system of brahmanical dominance that while Buddha accorded the first place to *ksatriyas* in the state, the Jains declared that tirthankers would never be born in a *brahmana* family. There is a story that the foetus of Lord Mahavira had to be transferred from the womb of a *brahmana* lady in accordance with this injunction. Some of their followers went further in rejecting political and social life altogether, their advocacy of a life devoted to moral principles was considered inconsistent with such a life. The influence of these people grew more in the trading communities which had by the time come to acquire a powerful position.

Both Mahavira and Buddha lived in the sixth century BC. In their teaching the existence of intra-cosmic Gods as higher beings was considered more or less irrelevant, as a causal factor for individual salvation, because man could transcend *karma* by his own efforts alone. Although they recognized functional Gods, it was stressed that the universal process (*samsar*) was a result of certain immutable laws of action (*karma*) resulting in progress and decline. Jainism argued that the world was composed of infinite souls which were trying to purify themselves of action particles (*karma*). These action particles bind the soul, which is consequently embodied in different incarnations in a cycle of birth and rebirth. The soul acts and suffers the pangs of the body in which it is clothed. The present life is determined by our past *karma* which survives the decay of the body and clings to the soul in its new incarnation. The doctrine of *karma* is extremely complex and well developed in Jainism. Be that as it may, both subscribed to the ideal of liberation by one's own individual effort as transcending the evergoing cycle of birth and death and rebirth. Both stressed that every soul, or link in the causal chain as the Buddhists viewed it, by its own effort, regardless of the grace of God, could achieve this by acquisition of right knowledge which had many sides. The highest knowledge was *kaivalya jnana* in Jainism and *nirvana* in Buddhism.

Both were largely a product of revolt against the system of animal sacrifice which had crept into brahmanical rituals. Jainism developed a marvellous epistemological theory called *anekantvada* and wedded it to the doctrine of non-violence. Following the story of the elephant and the six blind men, it was argued that it is very rarely that one side is completely right and the other side completely wrong in a dispute. The world is not divided between absolute right and absolute wrong. There are many shades and levels in between. It was argued that one should, therefore, try to understand the truth in its totality which is a result of total understanding of different viewpoints. If this is so, one has no option but to be non-violent. Purification of the soul is the result of balanced life possible for a monk only. The emphasis on non-violence was carried to such an extreme that even unconscious killing of germs while walking or speaking was considered wrong as it became a sin and, as a result, the possibility of Jains adopting an agricultural profession was ruled out, since cultivation and digging of wells would obviously entail violence. No wonder Jains took to trade and commerce and flourished. They reaped the benefits of an urban civilization. They took to maritime commerce and money-lending. There is a certain amount of individualism even in the *Manusmriti* in which definition of dharma as *upkar* is followed by the statement that man alone is responsible for his actions. Even the Puranic tale of Valmiki's conversion to the life of purity brings out this moral eloquently. But the salvation of the individual as a whole is tied to a combination of salvation of other wholes as well as divine grace. That is why there is the long story of Brahma and Siva leading the Saptarishis for the continuance of the cosmic process in terms of due performance of one's social obligations. But in Jainism these obligations pale into insignificance before the ideal of liberation by one's own effort. In fact, so rugged is the individualism in Jainism that one's involvement with these obligations is considered dangerous to the pursuit of supreme happiness. Individual souls are regarded as essentially separated and unconnected. It is only in their physical embodiment as a result of past actions that they get related. The most complete statement of individualism is to be found in the following extract:

Individually a man is born, individually he dies, individually he falls (from his state of existence), and individually he rises (to another). His passions, consciousness, intellect, perception and impressions belong to the individual exclusively. Here indeed the bonds of relationship are not able to help or save one.[1]

Two points should be emphasized here. First, the Jain principle of many-sided knowledge was similar in substance to the Vedic principle of *'neti'*, *'neti'* (this is not, this is not) or the Upanishadic principles of relativity. That is one reason why Jainism in practice could not always distinguish itself from other practices. In fact, with the passage of time even forms of worship, *mantra* and *tantra* found their way into Jainism. Second, in the beginning Jainism was a non-political, but not an anti-political doctrine. It did not contain any political statement of individualism or human equality. Even democratic ideology was wholly absent from it. Since it regarded the world as a bondage, the whole emphasis was on man's efforts to find release from the world to gain salvation by practising sacrifices and penance. The idea of renunciation received its full expression in Jainism; the world was a cave from which men had to escape in order to find release.

According to Jainism, as a slave to pleasures of the senses man accumulates infinite misery for these pleasures are transient and there is no end to their accumulation. This leads to attachment of *karmic* particles which, in turn, lead to infinite cycles of life and death.[2] The search for self-knowledge and self-realization is the only way to transcend this world and attain liberation. This is the true welfare of all which can be attained by leading a life of self-abnegation, severe penances, absolute non-violence and by cultivating an attitude of compassion and equality towards all creatures.[3] The Vedic vision of unity in diversity was relegated to the background and a sharp cleavage was created between man and nature. "The spiritual quest of the Sramanas", writes G.C. Pande, "was thus purely negative, viz., to transcend the realm of suffering and transcience. In a sense, it could also be called subjective since it required man to withdraw from all contact with society and nature."[4]

For the most part there was an acceptance of the traditional forms of the *nivritti* path towards happiness and unhappiness. From the attitude of 'life affirmation' there was a shift towards an attitude of 'life negation'. There is an interesting conversation recorded in *Uttaradhyana* between a saint king and Lord Indra in which the saint king emphasizes the futility of the life of a king in contrast with the life of renunciation which alone can lead to one's liberation from the cycles of birth and rebirth. When Indra enjoins the king to establish peace by the use of his powers, the king replies that the rod of punishment is a mere delusion because sometimes the guilty are left free while the innocent are punished. To the advice that the latter must conquer other kings, the reply is that the one who conquers himself is far superior to the one who conquers millions of warriors. To quote Mahavira, "Fight the self alone, what is the benefit in fighting external forces. Man attains happiness only by conquering his self by soul."[5] Anyone who aims at less than liberation remains tied to the process of life and birth with all its attendant happiness and unhappiness. Such a man would never be satisfied even if he gains dominion over the whole world. The more the profit the more will be his greed and cupidity. Therefore, a person who desired *moksa* should renounce it in the spirit of a monk. Such a man alone is able to destroy his *karmic* particles.

Buddha too preached non-violence. There is a striking resemblance between the life of Buddha and that of Mahavira. In fact, the Jain school of thought after Mahavira was led by a saint called Gautama who is credited with having recorded his conversations with the master. While the doctrine of many-sided truth enables Jainism to come to terms with brahmanism later, the Buddhist doctrine had a different epistemology which could not adapt itself to the brahmanical position. While the Vedas believed that the intra-cosmic Gods were also real, they represented the primal fire from which the whole universe originated, Jainism so emphasised the importance of *karma* that these Gods became more or less irrelevant; these Gods were themselves in the process of ascent towards complete liberation and hence could not be of much help in spiritual ascent. Thus, while brahmanism emphasized mutual dependence of intra-cosmic Gods and men, Jainism brought into bold relief the majesty of the human souls which had the potential for perfection. Buddhism emphasized the importance of the psychic transformation for the attainment of *nirvana*.

Buddha was deeply struck by the fact of change in human life. He thought permanence was merely a mental construct. It was not a quality of the cosmic process, which was a result of the constant working of the human mind without any permanent spiritual substance. Buddhists even denied the existence of a soul passing from life to life in fulfilment of its past actions. There was no such spiritual substance. Personal identity was merely a result of the process of psychic life which continued from birth to birth binding actions in terms of their moral consequences. While it accepted the force of actions, it developed altogether a new view of the agent who is, according to Buddhism, indistinguishable from his actions and experiences. Mind then becomes a purely causal process unadumbrated by the idea of the soul acting upon natural elements. Dharma stood for principles which brought about order in these elements. Buddha, on the whole, declared metaphysical questions irrelevant and emphasized the importance of a simple moral life in accordance with the four noble truths, that is, the world is full of suffering, suffering is caused by human desires, the renunciation of desires is the path to salvation (*nirvana*), and salvation is possible according to eight principles, namely right views, right resolves, true speech, right conduct, livelihood, effort, recollection, and meditation and the middle way which would avoid the extremes of sensual indulgence and asceticism. Buddhism adopted a rational position, namely, that human life is governed by causal principles and not left to divine intervention. This law prescribes that man should follow the eight-fold path. Attachment to the world is irrational and should be suppressed. The only virtuous way is one which allows withdrawal from the world. Buddhism also rejected the hereditary basis of the caste system and since it considered the world irrelevant, caste also became irrelevant. This appealed to the lower castes. Its universalism made it acceptable to peoples across civilisational boundaries and so it soon became a universal religion.

Early Buddhist thought despised politics as a necessary evil. There is no full-fledged treatment of political ideas in Buddhist literature of the period. Some hints and suggestions are contained in *Digha Nikaya* and the *Jataka* stories. Two features stand out very clearly. First, Buddhism subscribed to the contract theory of the origin of the state. It is not difficult to see the connection between this and the association of Buddhism with the republics of the period. According to it, everything was well in the beginning. But with the origin of property and family began the fall of man as it led to the feelings of mine and thine, to conflict, rule and subordination. There is an eternal law to govern the behaviour of individuals. But in the absence of a ruler to enforce it, it is not followed. At this point people decide to enter into contract with each other and entrust power to a king who governs the others in accordance with dharma. Then followed the caste system, Buddhism also accepted the functional basis of the caste system. A person who has, as a monk, destroyed all moral taint and has reached a stage of equilibrium in good and bad actions is to become the ruler, for he knows what is dharma. In so far as the divine basis of royal power is given up, it was a step towards emphasizing the contractual character of political obligation.

The second important principle is the emphasis on ethics as the basis of politics. While the *Mahabharata* admitted the importance of connecting morals with experience in the establishment of order in the state, Buddhist literature tended to emphasize the absolute value of no-violence as well as the importance of moral principles in the governance of society. It did not recognize the autonomy of public or political morality and declared: "A king is unrighteous if he does not follow dharma." The consequences of such a rule would be that all his subjects and ministers would become unrighteous; nature would not follow its course; there would be no rain and so no crops.[6] Sometimes Buddhism also conceded that it is necessary to practice evil but the general impression one gets is that there is a contempt for politics which is considered a game of deceit and treachery. The *Sadharma Pundrika* went to the extent of saying that the Buddhist monks must not join the presence of kings or princes, and royal officials.[7] Politics, thus, far from being the condition of all other activities, became an abode of delusion, an obstruction to righteousness, contrary to the practice of dharma which demands quietude. This is well brought out in Asvaghosa's *Life* of *Buddha*.[8]

What strikes one in Buddhism and Jainism is the utter contempt for the normal activities of life. They rejected property, sex, power, all of which according to them, lead to the plight of the soul. They may be natural to human beings but we ought to forgo them in order to gain a higher satisfaction. They are ephemeral and transient. Sex more than anything else is the supreme manifestation of our unbridled nature. They rejected the *Lokayata* view of pleasure and its attendant materialistic doctrine. They also rejected the rationalistic basis of the Vedas and thundered against idolatry and superstition. They exposed the systems of animal and human sacrifices. For them, living for the body became a sign of corruption, and living for the mind a brahmanical vanity. What was important was the cultivation of the soul or the 'psyche' through the practice of moral principles.

Some aspects of this doctrine were harsh and one sided, meriting the critical assaults of Shankaracharya later on. As a result, Jainism revised its view. Buddhism did not, and the consequence was that it disappeared from the land of its birth. People have exaggerated the difference between brahmanical and sramanic traditions. To us it appears that there was only a difference of emphasis. While the brahmanical tradition accepted the value of divine grace, it did not disregard the force of *karma* whose consequences one had to face by one's own effort. Similarly, while the Jains praised individual effort they in the later phase did not completely disregard the role of intra-cosmic Gods, indeed during the eighth to twelfth centuries, which was in many ways the golden period of Jainism, it too developed *mantra, tantra* and cosmological views almost similar to those of the brahmanical tradition. The writings of Amitgati and Kundacharya would fall into this category. Their greatness lay in their emphasis on the value of the individual's own effort to attain his salvation, in the special emphasis on non-violence and specially in the case of Jainism, in providing philosophical basis for logical thinking. Their writings on politics on the whole never measured up to the sweep and breadth of the *Smritis* and the *Ramayana* and the *Mahabharata*. But in a sense they mediated between the ancient and the medieval period and laid the foundation for the vision of the conflict between the life of a householder, that of a king and one consecrated to liberation. The dilemma comes out clearly in the sentence attributed to Buddha: "If a king delights in quietude, his kingdom collapses, if his mind turns towards his kingdom, quietude is ruined, for quietude and security are incompatible like the union of water which is cold with fire which is hot."[9]

No wonder that Jain canonists like Jinsena who took over the traditional concepts about the patriarchal origin of the state, on the whole took the view that the state is the cause of grief; it is a harmful drug which has to be taken as a necessity. According to him, even the king should try to get rid of it as soon as possible. Politics may provide happiness in this world, but cannot ensure happiness hereafter. It is only the life of renunciation which can do so; it alone can lead to perfect happiness. But Jainism quite soon reconciled itself to the necessity of politics. This gave rise to two of the finest pieces on statecraft, Hemchandra's *Yogasastra* and Somedeva's *Nitivakyanmritam*.

We now turn to a discussion of Somedeva's *Nitivakyanmritam* if for no other reason than because it was perhaps the most important attempt to combine the Jain and the brahmanical, the *Smriti* and the *Arthasastra* traditions during the ninth to eleventh centuries.

II

The identity of approach in political matters between the Vedic and *Sramanic* traditions is clearly demonstrated in the writing of Somedeva. Somedeva was an important political thinker at the beginning of the middle ages in India. Not much is known about his life except that he was a Jain saint and the author of a major literary work *Yasastilaka*. His famous book on political science was called *Nitivakyanmritam* and was composed eighteen years before *Yasastilaka Champu* in AD 992. His political ideas are characterized by the fact that they are directly related to life. The book was written to advise princes, specially Arikesri, on how best to govern their kingdoms. His ideas are also related to the tradition of political thinking in India going back to Kautilya, if not earlier. I mention Kautilya because he was in a way a point of departure from the earlier tradition of the *Dharmasastras*. There politics was discussed as a part of the ethics of life. Kautilya made it an autonomous discipline, thought still paying lip service to ethical principles. He was concerned not so much with the idea of good as with the formulation of concrete policies to be implemented in society. Somedeva's ideas are so similar to those of Kautilya on political matters that they are almost indistinguishable.[10] Indeed, where Somedeva does differ from him it is not so much in the substance but in the form of his style and presentation. He adopts a literary style and presents ideas, concepts and their definitions with such poetic elegance that at times he appears original. Most beneficially for us he has tried to explain Kautilya and some other authors of antiquity through passages from sources which have not come down to us. Surprisingly, these passages, attributed mostly to Kautilya, relate not to the details of statecraft as in Kautilya's *Arthasastra* but to enunciation of general rules of political conduct or some epistemological questions relating to them. In the light of his presentation, even our assessment of Kautilya should undergo considerable change.

Somedeva started with the conviction that political ideas must have direct bearing on the concrete problems of life and that life must be faced in terms of theoretical formulations of economics and political science. For Somedeva, theory and practice cannot be separated, no general theory is possible without practice and no practice can be successful without a general theory. While, on the one hand, he argues that knowledge of the science of politics is of no use to the person "who cannot understand what is political action", on the other hand he was convinced that "a wise man bereft of the knowledge of the scriptural and political science is vanquished by his enemies".[11] At another place he says, "the knowledge of sciences is the third eye of man for objects beyond the reach of senses".[12] Further, "a person who has not studied the sciences is indeed blind even though he possesses eyes".[13] Political science was always meant as a guide to political practice, and the facts of political life were important insofar as they enriched political understanding.

Nowhere does this approach come out more clearly than in his definition of knowledge. He says, "that is called knowledge, with the acquisition of which man resorts to what is beneficial and discards what is harmful to him".[14] Knowledge gives a man reason, logic and a sense of discrimination between worthy and unworthy acts, saves him from arrogance of power, and enables him to attain success, prosperity and perfection, and skill in thought and deeds.[15] He becomes conversant with the duties and practices of castes and acquires knowledge of right and wrong.[16] There is no work too small or great for him who knows "ways and means to achieve them". Success is possible if we, first, discard doubt and, second, practice positive reasoning which implies knowledge in terms of "the knowledge of the known objects as the base".[17] But the most striking difference between his positivism and modern positivism is that he never ignores the question of right and wrong;[18] the questions of the right and the best political order are central to his thinking. That is why he never thinks of politics in isolation from other forms of knowledge. He believes that the science of logic deals with metaphysical and spiritual knowledge, economics with management of agriculture and trade and other similar acts, and the science of politics with protection of the good and control of the wicked. In his book there is a conscious attempt to relate ideas about the best political order with what actually existed, for he is convinced that "there is no greater enemy of human beings than lack of discrimination and propriety."[19] It is because of this concern to relate practice to some notion of right that he condemns the *caravak* and *lokayata* philosophies which advocate the finality of worldly pleasures, as limited doctrines. He is convinced that if we adhere to these doctrines, we cannot logically banish crime from the state.[20]

Thus, the important issues to which Somedeva addresses himself are not so much questions of political philosophy at an abstract level, but those which everyone faces while living in the state. These questions have interconnections, there are primary and secondary issues too. There are some issues regarding the nature of consciousness and its relationship to the Supreme Brahman, or about the definition of right order which are fundamental questions in so far as they provide background in terms of which political action takes place. He accepts the fundamental postulate of dominant religious thinking in India that the human self is a reflection of the Supreme self.[21] It is under the veil of *maya* and its redemption lies in linking it once again to the Supreme self. This question, however, is not of great interest to him. The whole discussion is dismissed in a few stanzas. The more interesting question is that of right action and the rest of the book is devoted to a discussion of it.[22]

The need for right (*dharma*) arises from the fact that political life in particular and human life in general is characterized by a tension between good and evil, happiness and unhappiness. On one hand, each individual is an autonomous agent seeking his own pleasure, on the other, he is part of a society composed of similar individuals who, at times, frustrate his desire for more pleasure. By pleasure is meant gratification of the senses[23] and also satisfaction of mind.[24] Each man tries to seek pleasure in terms of gratification of his senses. Gratification of the senses gives happiness and its absence unhappiness.[25] It is dependent on practice which leads one to honour and fame. Practice is the hard labour which results in the accomplishment of results.[26] It sometimes leads to pride. Pride is a feeling of one's prosperity and increase in status, resulting in honour and modest behaviour of other.[27] Success lies in deliberation about the desires and the best means to achieve them.[28] Misfortune is generated by actions done in haste and without proper deliberation. Inference is the result of deliberation. It is a decision about an unaccomplished action "from among the total actions".[29] The accomplishment of one's welfare is called virtue and what flings man away from it is called vice.[30]

Thus, virtues and vices are often identified with the fulfilment of one's interest. The picture of human beings seeking pleasure painted here is very similar to that of Hobbes. But unlike Hobbes, Somedeva's individual though autonomous is related to other individuals and groups of individual such as the household and the state. He firmly believes that no action of the individual maliciously disposed to other persons can lead to his welfare.[31] The concept of household with its traditions occupies a very important place. According to him, "he who performs the obligatory duties as laid down in scriptures and righteously executes on special occasions is a 'householder'". These duties include sacrifice to Gods, service of parents, hospitality to guests and protection of the weak.[32] In order that all are able to do so, life ought to be based on the principle of give and take.[33] Here Somedeva sanctifies the principle of non-violence by asserting that its practice leads to heaven. One can see a strong streak of utilitarianism in his ideas. Non-violence is prized not because it is some transcendental principle but because its practice leads to mutual respect and enables society to go on smoothly.[34]

The other three important wholes are *janpad* (district), kingdom and the country. A country is a piece of territory where "the wealth of animals, food-grains and metals shine".[35] The tract that yields to growing authority, is ruled and has a treasure to sustain, is called a kingdom.[36] The word *Janpad* has also been used in another sense also. It is the area in which people are bound by caste obligations and seek to govern their life according to the principle of the four stages of human life in their pursuit of wealth and production of things.[37] The nearest equivalent in English would perhaps be 'civil society'. It is surprising that while his definition of the state and civil society are quite clear, there is no such clarity in his definition of the country. His definition cannot enable us to distinguish one country from another, and yet Somedeva was conscious that there were different countries separated from each other by diverse factors. It must be added that in his system all these four units are conceived almost as autonomous wholes, each with its specific characteristics and identity, and yet a part of a larger whole. Each household or country has its distinct identity and traditions and they must adhere to them.

Somedeva is quite clear that fame has no use if it does not support kinsmen and dependents or if it does not help in preventing unrighteousness in society. The emphasis is clearly on harmonious sustenance of life so that every whole is able to fulfil its needs in terms of its distinct identity. Dharma here is the principle of right conduct which leads to accomplishment of worldly success and transcendental bliss.[38] Anything contrary to this aim is unrighteousness. Following traditional thought on this point, which recognizes that activities such as pursuit of worldly prosperity and all worldly desires,[39] are necessary for pleasure, he is equally emphatic that "wealth which includes no share for refugees and dependents deserves to belong to no one at all".[40] At another place he says, "there is no prosperity for the absolutely greedy in relation to his own wealth".[41] "He is worthy of prosperity who enjoys it with rightness of means and continuity of tradition."[42] He extols those persons who assist in performance of religious and secular acts as "veritable places of pilgrimages". He is convinced that pleasures born of injustice or unrighteousness often lead not only to denial of fruits in the other world but also to a chain of unending misery in this world itself.[43] The righteous path is a means for the "accomplishment of the unattained and preservation of the attained".[44]

Jain thought has often been accused of preaching an attitude of life negation. It is argued that the mystic tradition emphasizes the essential unreality of this world which, according to it, is a prison house from which we must escape in order to be free. But it should be clear that like his mentor Kautilya, Somedeva, too, has an attitude of 'life affirmation' an attitude in which no activity or attitude is preached to the exclusion of any other. If anything, the emphasis is on the continuity of the life process in this world itself, and we are consequently enjoined not to neglect our obligations. Indian thought divides human activities into four groups, namely, pursuit of pleasure leading to satisfaction of senses, acquisition of wealth leading to fulfilment of worldly needs and prosperity, pursuit of righteousness, and search for emancipation.[45] Somedeva insists that one must endeavour to enjoy all these simultaneously.[46] Somedeva, however, does not give much importance to *moksha* in relation to the state. He confines his discussion to the other three activities only. In fact, so great is the importance attached to the task of fulfilment of needs and pursuit of prosperity that he declares "that anyone who neglects this object and resorts to righteousness alone tills a barren field abandoning a ripe crop".[47] He adopts the same attitude even with regard to pleasure. He is realistic enough to concede that a person devoid of wealth is abandoned even by his wife and children. Though spiritual emancipation still remains the final aim, it is rarely mentioned in the book. It appears that he was perhaps paying deference to the tradition rather than to the idea itself. The emphasis throughout is on the enjoyment of this world "with prosperity and sense of discrimination leading to the welfare of all".

But he knew that there are limits beyond which all these objects cannot be enjoyed simultaneously. Therefore, like Plato, he also came to regard 'right' as the architectonic principle which must define the limits of all other objects in life and create a balance. Since he is convinced that excessive pursuit of any of the three objects of life at the expense of the other two is damaging to one's ascent to salvation, he says that "a person who enjoys the fulfilment of desires consistent with righteousness and attainment of prosperity is never devoid of happiness".[48] At another place, he writes: "As a lion earns demerits by killing an elephant, so does a person transgressing the tenets of righteousness become a sharer in sins."[49] He grudgingly accepts austerity because he feels that it is the restraint of senses and mind,[50] which leads to a proper enjoyment of traditions of society.[51]

Indeed, he accepts the doctrine of equality and says that "to achieve a sense of equality among all beings is the loftiest conduct among all types of conduct.[52] But his notion of equality is different from the modern notion. He views equality not in the sense that men are physically equal or equal in opportunities, but they are equal in terms of, first, man's capacity to find his salvation, second, in their obligations to society which consists in due performance of their duties. His is indeed a spiritual concept of proportionate equality in which each individual is equal in so far as all men are creatures of God and have a divine spark in them: while they differ in their needs, they all have the same capacity to seek liberation. Whether they actually use it or not or whether they have the necessary opportunities is another matter. It is on account of this common characteristic that all men are deserving of sympathy and good will from others; they are all enjoined to look after each other's welfare. Anyone who wilfully and in narrow self-interest sacrifices others or commits violence against them cannot be right.

The need for preservation of all from the encroachment by a powerful few calls for arbitration, judgement and rightful authority. This gives rise to the state which has authority over a piece of territory and has other characteristics such as a populace, king, council of ministers, fort, army, friendly neighbours and treasury.[53] The supreme quality of the state is that it must have the capacity to protect its inhabitants. The king must be able to brighten the prospects for peaceful human life by a proper application of political and economic sciences. It is his duty to ensure law and order: "to restore order by persuasion, threat, coercion and even use of force".[54] In order to be able to do so, it is necessary for the king to administer impartial justice.[55] He must maintain the caste system and regulate the productive apparatus, agriculture, industry, trade and commerce, which, he thinks, is the basis of all other activities.[56] The king is the protector of the deserving and the castigator of all who violate their duties.[57]

Management of the state is an art. It requires certain skills in which the king and his subordinates, ministers, and civil servants must be trained with prudence and wisdom; they must cultivate the necessary sense of discrimination and propriety to deal with concrete situations. Somedeva gives a place of pride to education and argues that proper education of princes is vital for the family and worldly propriety. In the absence of education, the royal family soon disintegrates.[58] A man trained in economics and politics is one such who can give guidance to the rulers to manage the state.[59] Such people provide a correct perspective on life and its problems in different situations by relating general principles to them. Kautilya is admired by him because he gave advice which was sound for the political situation of his time and enabled Chandra Gupta to establish his empire for the welfare of all.[60]

While accepting the concept of right and social order as propounded by others, the political theorist concentrates his attention on the organization of political life. He is convinced that translation of ideas into practice is a technical problem. The king is, therefore, enjoined to gather knowledge about schemes before embarking on any new project. In relation to enemies, he must assess their strength and should he find himself powerless, he must even tolerate undesirable words uttered by the enemy.[61] He is enjoined to have an elaborate system of spies who are permitted to use the vilest of methods, including administration of poison and use of erotic charms, to get the desired results.[62] While it is better for a king to die for self-respect than to sell himself into bondage to the enemy,[63] if it is beneficial from a long term point of view, he is allowed even to take shelter with the enemy.[64] At another place, he preaches the principle of an eye for an eye and says, "A man who does not repay the treatment meted out (to him) receives neither worldly nor other worldly fruits."[65]

Somedeva views politics essentially as a skill to manage conflict in society.[66] There are permanent expedients like administration of impartial justice and proportionate punishment,[67] increasing prosperity of the state,[68] providing protection to the weak and the poor,[69] and temporary expedients such as use of spies. The king is permitted to use any tactic if he is convinced, after due deliberation with his ministers, that it will lead to the long term welfare of the state. Machiavelli also took a similar position on the issue of means. But there is a fundamental difference in the approach of Machiavelli and that of Somedeva. While Machiavelli concentrates his attention exclusively on the conditions of survival, Somedeva incorporates the condition of the good and exemplary life also. He seeks to combine both ethical and practical necessities. He accepts 'right' as the basis of politics and brings it in line with defective human nature everywhere, just as Machiavelli does in the context of 'virtue'. Both accept the need to attain perfection but are aware that it is not always possible; Somedeva admits that even the deeds of hermits are not entirely free from blemish.[70] But if the concern of Machiavelli is how to master human nature to the advantage of the prince, the concern of Somedeva is to master it so as to bring it in line with right order. Beyond mere survival, his ideas are concerned with the institutionalization of life for the welfare of all so that each individual can progress towards higher and higher levels of existence culminating in spiritual emancipation. That is why a king's powers are never regarded as absolute by him, for he says: "he alone is the Lord who inspires acceptance in many".[71] The king is free to choose the most favourable method or to wait for an opportune moment in order to create peace and order. But in whatever he does, he must try to bridge the gulf between what is desirable and what is possible in the circumstances; by relating ideas to actual conditions of life in terms of specific laws and measures appropriate in specific situations. The question which the king must ask is: How can political and economic life be best organized to create conditions based on right? Normative political science cannot be practised without positivist understanding, the latter cannot be made a vehicle for the achievement of public interest without the former; ethics, physiology, pathology, therapeutics, are all used to create a good polity.

The state conceived by Somedeva is a welfare state. While the maintenance of order makes preservation of life possible, organization of other aspects increases prosperity and founds the state on a secure basis. Thus while in Machiavelli virtue sometimes borders on barbarity, in the case of Somedeva it acquires a pleasant form in so far as it emphasizes that one's conduct should be acceptable to others. Besides, political action ought to be rooted in the traditions and moral bonds of society as expressed through caste obligations, duties of various stages of life and precepts of scriptures. These three provide a framework within which right handling of changing situations by the king becomes possible. While the king is entitled to his self-interest, the value of his achievements and their legitimation in the eyes of the people would depend very much and ultimately, upon the welfare of the people he governs. Somedeva is quite emphatic when he says, "What is the use of that prosperity of the Arjun-tree which can not be used by others."[72] It must be added here that definition of 'welfare' is not something which the king can decide for himself. It is to be supplied by the custodians of the moral sense of the community in the light of exegetic interpretation based on reason and logic. Political skill is a regulative skill, it regulates life within the state and outside with other states. As has already been pointed out earlier, Somedeva never considers rulership as absolute. There are severe constraints on the exercise of its powers. The king must have a thorough grasp of the principles of right conduct, must have courage and valour to protect his subjects and must give impetus to means of acquisition of prosperity in the state.

Somedeva's ruler is more akin to a constitutional monarch than to a typical despot. The king must have a council of ministers to advise him and, in most cases, the advice so tendered must be binding on him.[73] The constitution is of a mixed type and the ministers and judges are enjoined to perform their respective duties in the light of socially acceptable principles of right, regardless of what the king says.[74] The basic idea behind Chapter X of the book is that the best organization of the state is one which recruits the best available talent. The king is also enjoined to keep in touch with the people and their modes. Somedeva goes to the extent of laying down that "the king himself should settle the affairs of his subjects". A good ruler is one who prefers public good to his own private good and sincerely makes an effort not to allow his passions to interfere with the reason of the state. He is one who acquires a grasp of 'right' in specific human situations and has the capacity to enforce decisions with reasonable severity.[75] It is clear that such interests cannot be served by rulers of doubtful character, for a man with "good character and conduct is not naked even if he is without clothes".[76]

In fact, Somedeva goes beyond Kautilya, agreeing with Bhisma in the *Shantiparva*, in denouncing a king who has failed to protect his subjects.

Kautilya, too, despised such a king but held that a bad king is better than no king as in the absence of a king society would surely be overtaken by anarchy. Somedeva defines anarchy as that state of society in which "the stronger devours the weaker",[77] and declares that it is "better to have a world without a king than to have a world with a foolish king".[78] He thinks that there is no calamity worse than "the ruination of subjects by an evil natured king".[79] He enjoins the learned to speak the truth if the king is devoid of good qualities or is too proud and vain.[80] The ancients abhorred anarchy and feared that unrighteous behaviour by the king might prompt other people to behave in like manner.[81] It is in this sense that the king defines the state as its first and foremost element.[82] And yet, he is subordinate to traditions and the men of knowledge who interpret them for right advice and performance of sacrifices, to the rules of 'right' discerned by elders and brahmanas and for the maintenance of which political power exists. It is the combination of both men of knowledge and men of courage and valour, which can ensure order and justice, and, therefore, both must act in concert.[83]

In this discussion of statecraft, the most important place naturally goes to principles of right, for they lead to the integrated development of life and its various activities. To secure this, there should be a proper relationship between ends and means. The king must have the necessary discrimination to enforce right. But Somedeva failed to provide effective remedies against abuse of power. It seems he was scarcely aware of the pitfalls which his position entailed. For him the intention of the king is important, if the king is trying to create a better order, he is considered to be leading his society ahead. But it perhaps did not occur to him that sometimes projects started with the best of intentions might lead to the most disastrous results. That is why people have always felt a need for safeguards to reduce the operation of change of elements. Somedeva provides for the institution of a council of ministers but does not adequately succeed in demonstrating how such a council can force an arrogant king into right action, specially if he is determined to pursue his own narrow interest. Such a system might work when there are enlightened rulers and the force of public opinion is strong, but once there are corrupt and vain rulers, the safeguards he suggests are too weak. It is for this reason that thinkers like him became irrelevant in the medieval period which saw the rise of small, petty kingodms for the fulfilment of the narrow interests of their rulers. Where Somedeva's thinking is more sound, however, is that his integration of politics and morals is more realistic and reassuring in so far as he recognizes a bond between the rulers and the ruled in terms of the superiority of principles of right which are created independently of the state apparatus. Some such bond is considered as basic to good government in all contemporary thinking. Indeed, Gandhi's ideal of *Ramarajya* was a revival of this ancient belief.

When his recognition of the need for a moral bond between the rulers and the ruled is so clearly stated, one is surprised at the lack of any systematic discussion about the definition of right and its relation to the individual on the one hand and society on the other. No attempt appears to have been made to connect the ideal of the welfare state with the notion of the legitimacy of each individual to pursue his own happiness. Both do not always go together. The result is that in one part of his philosophy, an individual's happiness appears as absolute and in another the various wholes of which the individual is a part play their role. In one place, it appears that the individual pursues his happiness because it is something which is given in his biological and psychological make up. In another, Somedeva speaks of the natural character of the household and the state, their traditions and organic linkages. He fails to reconcile these two positions.

He could have adopted one of the two forms of reasoning. First, he could have accepted the idea of a complex relationship between the composite and its part as postulated by Gautama, a relationship in which while the composite appears as a single entity, parts too may have their own separate forms and importance as the constituents of the base on which the composite stands. Gautama had conceived of the composite as the superstratum (*adheya*) and the parts as the base (*adhara*). Adoption of this position would have enabled Somedeva to reconcile his concern both for the individual and the community. He could have then argued that while human associations have their own character and identity, they are integrally related to other associations in particular and society in general.[84]

Alternatively, he could have linked his ideas to a theory of evolution postulating how man's hedonism comes to be modified in stages in the course of social evolution. There are indeed connecting links implicit in this argument but they appear too tenuous in the absence of a more detailed discussion of the precise nature of their relationship. Such a discussion was necessary because in its absence, with the decay of the ancient civilization, the private and public realms became separate to such an extent that while an average Indian would be most pious in private life, he could also be most corrupt in public life. The absence of such a discussion becomes all the more intriguing because nowhere, apart from Kautilya's *Arthasastra*, are the vices of men better discussed than in his book and nowhere are remedies against such vices, such as bribery and other forms of pubic corruption, discussed at length with such elegance and moral fervour as here. It is all the more regrettable because in no other system of thought had the deeper questions of political life been secularized to this extent. If he had done it, certain incoherencies which crept into his exposition of policy could be avoided and we would have been better able to perceive the underpinnings of his repeated emphasis on a 'sense of discrimination and propriety'.

In the absence of a justificatory theory for this rather complex position on the nature of community relationships, the moral principles which he cherished were to become the first casualty; with passage of time politics lost its moral fervour and, in due course, became purely a technical activity in which princes would try to maintain themselves in power in a most ruthless manner and would then justify this enterprise in the name of dharma. The larger principles of politics were thrown overboard. Treatises such as those of Kautilya and Somedeva were seen as treatises on statecraft, providing advice to princes on how best to assert themselves in a typical situation of hostility in men and material around them. The art of governing was reduced merely to technical skill and its sole aim became how to manoeuvre human impulses towards self-aggrandizement. Instead of being a science of regulation of the wicked and protection of the good, politics became a body of tricks to control men in society. In a sense Somedeva is a trifle disappointing because most of the principles to which he devotes so much attention had already been laid down in *Shantiparva* and Kautilya's *Arthasastra*. What was required was a fuller discussion of the connecting concepts and ideas in the manner of a thinker like Plato in ancient Greece. Living in a period which saw the beginning of turbulence in Indian history, he was still living in the past. He was perhaps unaware of the enormous changes that had come upon Indian society since the days of Kautilya. Somedeva undoubtedly wrote in an elegant literary style. But he lacked the knowledge, wisdom and insight into the political process of his times which Kautilya had in such great abundance. The lack of originality is revealed in the manner in which he accepted the duties of the caste system and various other degenerated practices of his time quite unmindful of the fact that these could not be reconciled with the idea of equality which he espoused with such vehemence. Moreover, he was a Jain saint and yet he accepted all these, forgetting that some of these issues lay at the basis of the tensions and conflicts of his time.

III

The medieval Hindu sentiment received its classical exposition in the Bhakti movement. There is a sense of futility in creation and the whole creation exists in the earnest expectation of grace that will come on to devotees. It is this grace alone which will enable us to attain *moksha*. To be a good devotee means cultivation of certain virtues. In the earlier period attainment of salvation was predominantly as a result of the attainment of knowledge, though grace had its own role to play. Now it seems to rest on the cultivation of the virtues of equanimity amidst success or defeat, profit or loss as also on what Ramanujacharya called complete self-surrender (*purna samarpana*) to the supreme or one of the intra-cosmic Gods whom one takes as one's *ishta*. In one's quest from *neumatic* to *pneumatic*, most of the authors emphasise joyful acceptance of misery in this world, endurance of all that is evil, the quality of patience which in turn is the foundation of complete self surrender. The qualities of a devotee elaborated in *Bhagwat Gita* are further elaborated in different contexts in various *Puranas* and other writings of the Bhakti movement such as Tulsi Das' *Ramcharitmanas*. The idea of man as lover and God as beloved also appears and is a running theme in the entire medieval literature. *Srimad Bhagwat*, *Agni Purana* and other writings of the poets such as Surdas and Raskhan and Namdeva evoke this imagery. Chaitanya's ecstasies too were representative of this.

There is a close resemblance between the existentialist order in the Bhakti movement and that of the ancient world. It is not at all surprising because both the set of authors are responding, albeit in their way, to the larger question of the order of being. In the medieval world, the emphasis, however, shifted from a divine order manifest in the cosmos in which man attains salvation through acquisition of true knowledge, to a divine order which man cannot fully comprehend and hence can only wait in patience for salvation through divine grace. The critical difference is the treatment of *purushartha*, action. In the first case, there is a harmony between man's psyche and the divine order, in the second, man is separated from it. He is a creature of flesh and blood living in a world which is an illusion (*mithya*) and so long as he is attached to his action he cannot hope to attain identity with the supreme. The doors of *mukti* are no longer open to him in *kalyuga* (it is true of Jain thought also); all that he can hope for is the everlasting grace in cycles of birth and rebirth.

The authors of the Bhakti movement also subscribe to the directional movement in history. It is an area in which there is a constant decline in righteousness and truth. But like Vyasa they also believe that history is constantly given direction and meaning by the divine forces. There is a constant give and take between man, intra-cosmic Gods and the Supreme. But in the Bhakti movement God becomes more of man (*avtar*) who enters the historical process from time to time to set an example before others and raise others to the glory of God. The saints of the Bhakti movement were convinced that men can rise to immortality if they opened themselves to God as Prahlad or Dhruva or Radha did. In their writings, men became sons or beloved of God whom the latter raised through his divine grace. Faith in God meant participation in the same divine process (*lila*) in which Prahlad or Dhruva or Radha had participated. A vision of God or intra-cosmic Gods was the culmination of the response in a man's soul to divine presence. The form (*sakar*) and the face-to-face (*pratyaksha*) character of the vision of an intra-cosmic God is a symbol of divine grace. And any attempt to analyse it is meaningless, because the same divine presence reveals itself in differentiating consciousness differently. The intensity of the feelings of a lover or a son are subjective experiences whose importance cannot be grasped through rational or empirical knowledge. Such a devotee may even achieve a consciousness of reality which enables him to understand the world in its basic permanent as well as perishing, elements (*tattava*). He may even articulate the revealed truth. But its importance pales into insignificance before man's yearning for God through complete self-surrender. And, therefore, there is no attempt to philosophise about the structure of reality, but an attempt to win the grace of God. The *pneumena* takes precedence over the *nous*. The search of man into the structure of reality is transformed into the beauty of an encounter between man and God who reveals himself in a particular form.

With the breakdown of the earlier political order symbolised by Maurya and Gupta dynasties, the masses felt insecure and tried to recover the meaning of their existence in mystic union with God. The world became an illusion and consequently the kingdom of earth lost its earlier significance. India was divided into groups of many small warring states with shifting borders. The result was that the unity of cosmos dissolved itself into the wheel of power (*rajyachakra*) and wheel of truth (*dharmachakra*), as attested by the appearance of saints on the one hand and kings and politicians on the other with very few points of contact between them. It is true that none of the kings was in a position to challenge the importance of the religious order but nevertheless it cannot be denied that the cosmological order was sharply divided into two. The organisers of political power paid only lip service to the representatives of the spiritual order. This disjunction exercised an enormous influence on what was to follow because in the context of the conquest of India by foreigners it meant a complete dissociation of political and spiritual orders. The new political order no longer required spiritual guidance or legitimation. The principle of force and fraud swallowed up the constraints of truth and righteousness, knowledge and wisdom.

NOTES

1. Quoted in "Jain Thought and Philosophy", *Illustrated Weekly of India*, 15 February 1991, p. 19.
2. *Uttradhyan*, trans. Muni Nathmal, Ladnu, Jain Viswa Bharti, 18-14. 15. 16.
3. Ibid., 14-10.
4. G.C. Pande, *Foundations of Indian Culture: Spiritual Vision and Symbolic Forms in Ancient India* (New Delhi, Books and Books, 1984), p. 69.
5. *Uttradhyan*, op. cit., 9-34. 35.
6. *Anguttaran Kaya*, II, pp. 74-76.
7. U.N. Ghoshal, op. cit., pp. 74-76.
8. Ibid., p. 261.
9. *Loc cit.*
10. For an overview of the debate, see G.C. Chowdhary, *Political History of India from Jain Sources* (Amritsar, 1954).
11. Somedeva, *Niti Vakyanmritam,* trans. S.K. Gupta, Jaipur, Prakrit Bharti, 1987, 5. 27.
12. Ibid., p. 5. 28.
13. Ibid., p. 5. 29.
14. Ibid., p. 5. 48.
15. Ibid., p. 5. 50.
16. Ibid., p. 5. 51.
17. Ibid., p. 10. 150: 5.44.
18. Ibid., p. 5. 54.
19. Ibid., p. 10. 45: 136.
20. Ibid., p. 6.33.34.
21. Ibid., p. 11.44, 5.12.
22. Ibid., p. 5.12.
23. Ibid., p. 6.10.
24. Ibid., p. 6.11.
25. Ibid., p. 6.13.
26. Ibid., p. 6.14.
27. Ibid., p. 6.17.
28. Ibid., p. 15.1.
29. Ibid., p. 15.7.
30. Ibid., p. 16.1.
31. Ibid., p. 1.6.

32.   Ibid., p. 15.12, 13.
33.   Ibid., p. 1.7.
34.   Ibid., p. 1.41.
35.   Ibid., p. 19.1.
36.   Ibid., p. 19.2.
37.   Ibid., p. 19.5.
38.   Ibid., p. 1.2.
39.   Ibid., p. 15.2.
40.   Ibid., p. 1.6.
41.   Ibid., p. 2.4, 1.45, 46.
42.   Ibid., p. 2.2.
43.   Ibid., p. 2.5.
44.   Ibid., p. 29. 14.
45.   Ibid., p. 3.4.
46.   Ibid., p. 33.
47.   Ibid., p. 1.48; 21.9.10.
48.   Ibid., p. 3.2.
49.   Ibid., p. 1.46.
50.   Ibid., p. 1.24.
51.   Ibid., p. 1.26.
52.   Ibid., p. 1.5.
53.   Ibid., p. 5.52.53.
54.   Ibid., p. 639, 43; Also *Shantiparva*, 67.17-28, 59.13.
55.   Ibid., p. 9.2, 3.
56.   Ibid., p. 8.2.3.4.
56.   Ibid., p. 7.22.
58.   Ibid., p. 5.56, 59.
59.   Ibid., p. 5.54, 55; 10.61.
60.   Ibid., p. 10.4
61.   Ibid., p. 13.9.10.
62.   Ibid., p. 14.4, 5, 8, 9, 10.
63.   Ibid., p. 29.53.
64.   Ibid., p. 29. 54.
65.   Ibid., p. 26.13.
66.   Ibid., p. 28.4, 5.
67.   Ibid., p. 9.2.
68.   Ibid., p. 8.2.
69.   Ibid., p. 7.8.
70.   Ibid., p. 6.35.
71.   Ibid., p. 32.32; 5.33.
72.   Ibid., p. 32.33.
73.   Ibid., p. 10.58, 59.
74.   Ibid., p. 10.5. 69.

75. Ibid., p. 17.33, 34.
76. Ibid., p. 26.52.
77. Ibid., p. 9.8.
78. Ibid., p. 5.32; Also Kautilya, *Arthasastra*, 1.3.
79. Ibid., p. 5.33.
80. Ibid., p. 5.68.
81. Ibid., p. 17.31.
82. Ibid., p. 17.33.
83. For an insightful discussion of secularization of Indian thought, see D. Dumont, *Religion, Politics and History in India* (Hague, Mouton Press, 1970). Also, Radhakamal Mukerjee, *Hindu Civilization* (London, 1936), Ibid., p. 17.38, 42.
84. See N.S. Junankar, *The Nyaya Philosophy* (Delhi, Motilal Banarsidas, 1978), pp. 84-86, 89, 97.

CHAPTER 7

THE IMPERIAL VISION:
BARNI AND FAZAL

An important element was injected in political thinking in India with the advent of Islam. Political ideas in Islam had various sources. In part they came from the Hebrew prophets and from the teaching of Muhammad. From the former came the concept of one God as ruler and law giver of the world. The Muslims believed that they were directly related to this one God through their prophet Muhammad. In part it came from the influence of Plato and Aristotle who had already been embodied in the Arabic sources (an eleventh century Persian translation of Aristotle's *Politics* is available in Jaipur City Museum). There are repeated references to him in the writings of Barni. In any case, Islam in its early stages was an exclusive political doctrine. In contrast to the writings of Plato and Aristotle or the pantheistic trends in the religions of the Hindus, they had one book as the supreme directing, motivating and compelling force in their life. In this sense the early followers of Islam saw themselves as the chosen people entrusted with the task of the spread of Islam so that the earth could be saved from both infidels and rationalists such as *brahmanas*. Surprisingly Barni dubbed brahmanical system as rationalist and thought that so long as even one *brahmana* survived, it would not be possible to root out brahmanism from India. Islam, however, was not tied to any natural creed and its influences soon spread far and wide. In most countries it became the most subversive force as to the idea of the 'purified people' was added a strong universal appeal and missionary zeal. In this process of its expansion, it appears that slowly the Islamic political thought incorporated some of the teachings of Plato and Aristotle, specially their moral concerns.

The followers of Islam who came to India insisted on God as a perfect being. They insisted that Islam was fundamentally different from various sects and creeds in India. They contemptuously dismissed various practices such as idolatry and the rituals and rites of the earlier systems as superstitions.

Their belief in the universality of the law of the Koran led them to preach the doctrine of equality. Indeed they brought with them the concept of Islamic brotherhood. They believed that since all are sons of God, all are equal. Their emphasis on the ideal of equality should not, however, lead us to think that they were in any sense communists or socialists. Their idea of equality came nowhere near our modern notion of it. In fact in the political sphere, they had accepted the Greek belief in the superior and the inferior, and believed that some are born to rule and others to obey. They had also developed the theory that a king or an emperor is a representative of God on earth. In due course of time, they also incorporated some of the practices of the local sects. What, however, distinguished early Islam from the local sects was the belief in the omniscience of one book or the inspiration it claimed to receive from one man; a man who according to it, came as a prophet of God and preached his message to suffering humanity in order to purify it, a man who taught such things as that God is one. This was in stark contrast to the position of Vedanta which did not accept the final authority of either a single book or a person. Indeed compared to incoming Islam, Hinduism by this time had become a bundle of paradoxes: on the one hand, it emphasized the life of the community throughout the entire paraphernalia of what had come to be called *karmakanda*, adherence to rituals and sacrifices, on the other, it had become peculiarly individualistic in so far as any attempt to attain salvation through social or political organization was abandoned as futile. Indeed, the dominant tendency of the time was in the direction of individual salvation. It was widely held that salvation could be attained by the individual alone and never by a community as a whole. The search for inner light and personal development of the soul became more important than salvation through performance of one's functions and worldly obligations. We are not saying that all sects adopted this attitude. From time to time, such as in the *Bhagwat Puran, Vishnu Puran*, or Tulsidas's *Ram Charit Manas,* later there is ample emphasis on due performance of one's obligations to society. But on the whole the dominant tendency was towards the ideal of the individual rather than communal salvation. This notion of individual effort was viewed in terms of conscience, *karma* particles as the Jains thought or pure self-surrender which was the high point in the development of the bhakti movement.

The doctrine of *maya* led to the development of the idea of ether which can only be felt by the mind. The saints argued that He alone is real. The uncertainty of existing in the anarchic conditions of the medieval world caught hold of the people. Sensuous pleasures were considered useless because it was believed that they diminish the duration of life. All else was considered transitory. The treasury, prosperity and other things, according to the *Bhagwat*, "do little service to mortals, whose duration of life is uncertain".

The whole period was marked by an acute awareness of the new situation, the scarcity all around, the absence of law and order, breakdown of norms in which "the husbands and parents behave very cruelly". The *Bhagwatam* declares: "The Goddess of learning has now been living in the houses of *brahmanas* devoid of dutifulness, and even the best of *brahmanas* are serving the *ksatriyas* who treat the *brahmanas* with contempt."[1]

Two political principles stand out clearly in all these writings:

(i) The doctrine of the welfare state. The king loses his fame, longevity and fortune if in his state the subjects are oppressed by the wicked. According to the *Bhagwatam*, "the highest merit of a king consists in removing distress of the distressed".[2] Again, "the noblest virtue of a king consists in protecting those who follow the path of virtue and in punishing the evil workers who oppress the innocent ones without any cause".[3]

(ii) There is a contempt for things of this world and particularly property. *Srimad Bhagwat*, for instance, enjoins that no one should have more property than what is absolutely necessary for the fulfilment of his basic needs.[4] Anyone who hoards more property than that is a thief. In certain cases, specially for those who aspire to the highest spiritual merit attendant upon a person devoted to truth, it is considered as an obstacle in his spiritual progress. Thus when the great king Vali was deprived of the three worlds he commanded, Lord Hari said, "Unto whom I extend favour I take away his wealth, which creates infatuation in a person and by which he being divorced from humility, shows disregard towards me and all others."[5] The *Bhagwatam* again declared: "Corporeal beings can lay claim only to as much wealth as is enough to fill their belly for the sake of keeping their body and soul together. Those who want more than that are surely pilferers and they rightly deserve chastisement."[6]

The idea of Islamic brotherhood encouraged the ideal of freedom through communal existence. This helped Islam to be the most radical doctrine in the world at the time and gave a rare solidarity to its membership. It made Islam more dynamic.

Islamic political thought, it must be remembered, was not merely expressed by the founder but also found its embodiment in the political system he created. All subsequent political theory has been justified in terms of its relation to the events of first forty years after the *hezira*, AD 622-61, which were the years of 'Right rule' before degeneration into the supposedly wicked Umayyad dynasty. The fact that Muhammad's divine mission was integrally related to state building left Muslims obsessed by the notion of communal solidarity as well as political legitimacy in terms of it. The three basic principles which governed all subsequent political thinking were: (a) the divine law, the *Shariat* based on the Koran, (b) the historical traditions of the early years, and (c) the consensus and solidarity of the Islamic community. This meant that the framework of political thinking was for all times more or less fixed in a mould by the ninth century. No rule departing from the *Shariat* was ever justified. It was accepted as a matter of rule that the purpose of the state was always, in principle, to serve the *Shariat*.

Here the contrast with earlier systems of Indian thought is clear. While the earlier systems also accepted the authority of scriptures, they did not accept the authority of one particular scripture. This led to greater respect for diversity of political opinion and institution building in society. Since the Islamic thought accepted the finality of the *Shariat*, the role of reason was limited to interpretation of one book. This resulted in greater dogmatism of belief. There is another significant difference between the two approaches. Both of them accepted the need for authority to check the evil propensities in man. But while earlier Indian thought kept political and cultural realms separate in so far as politics could not give an authoritative interpretation of 'right' (this was assigned to the *brahmanas* who had developed an alternative centre of power quite parallel to the whole of the state) the Muslim did not develop any independent organization to further the divine ends. The result was that in Islamic theory the state was considered not only a necessary organ to check man's natural aggression, a point common to earlier thought, but a supreme organization to regulate life. It is true that the earlier thought also concentrated on the nature of authority and the boundaries in which it was legitimized. But the introduction of the idea of contract and the existence of critical factor saved it from the over-emphasis which Islamic thought came to put on the obligation to, and qualities of the just ruler. It did not, therefore, ask such a question as to whether autocracy was always necessary. It tended to take the position in common with Kautilya that a good king is better than a bad king but a bad king is definitely better than anarchy.

We can appreciate the significance of all this Islamic thought as it came to India by looking at the ideas of Barni. The first work on statecraft after the advent of the Delhi Sultanate was that of Fakhr-ud-Din called *Adab-*

Muluk kifayat ul Mumlna (Rules of the king and the welfare of the subjects).[7] The work was intended as a guide to rulers and dealt with details of administration. Unfortunately only the introduction is available in translation. It is said that the administration of Iltutmish was close to the model suggested by this author.

However, there is no work on politics which can be compared to Barni's during this period. His influence on the development of subsequent political ideas is debatable. The contemporary scholarship on Islam had tended to take the view the Barni's book *Fatwa-I-Jahandari*[8] represented his own individual view and did not make any impression on the course of development of Indo-Muslim history or political thought.[9] But this appears to be an exaggerated sectoral view. It is difficult to believe that so perceptive an author, who was also a member of the court of Ghazni, remained without any influence. It is true that he was banished from the royal court under Ghazni. But this fact itself is significant from the point of view of the influence which Barni might have exercised during his time. His bitterness against Sultan is amply reflected in his writings. In any case, there is no other work on political thought in the whole period which can rival it in both depth and subtlety of political ideas, notwithstanding his fads and foibles and strong antipathies to Hindus. It seems he was well versed in the political philosophy of Plato and Aristotle, particularly Plato, and also had deep knowledge of the basic sources of Islam.

We must note three important facts as regards the development of Barni's ideas. First, he lived in a period when Islam was finding roots in the country; it was the religion of the new rulers but the population was still hostile to it. It was a period when struggle for domination and reaction against various forms of local religions, specially Brahmanism was intense, occupying the energies of both rulers and thinkers. It seems Barni was also deeply involved in these debates, which is amply reflected is his writings. Secondly, in Islam there was a clear antipathy to local religions. In order to counteract them they needed philosophical support. Some of the contemporary thinkers were well versed in the ideas of Aristotle who had been rediscovered in the Arab world. It is astonishing how the same writer influences different people in different ways. In the writings of Barni he was seen to have supplied a rational basis for a just government. In his writings there are also references to various Arabic and Persian writers and statesmen besides Aristotle. Thirdly, Barni was a witness to the founding of so many sultanates in which religious enthusiasm was combined with messianic zeal. Barni in his work adds fuel to the smouldering fires of religious fanaticism, pleading for imposition of Islam by force.

Be that as it may, from the angle of political philosophy, he develops a theory of government albeit for Muslims only, some of the principles of which are of great permanent nature. Two ideas are particularly important, namely, the ideas of justice and moderation which are directly related to Aristotelian ideas. However, while he undoubtedly derives his political ideas from Aristotle, his perspective on immediate problems of life is based on the teachings of Islam, elements of the *Shariat*, and the distinctions which the Shias and Sunnis created within Muslim theology. According to him, God is the starting point and he created the world. He created everything in pairs of opposites such as truth and falsehood, peace and disorder, good and evil, day and night, light and darkness.[10] Prophets of God are the best and the greatest of all created beings and the success and failure of the political and administrative affairs of a Muslim king depends upon his religious faith and adherence to the commandments of the prophets. In the world of opposites, he thought, "truth must be established at the centre"[11] by the king. This would not mean that falsehood can be totally extenuated. He was convinced that even if we tried, we would not succeed. Complete destruction of evil is not possible. Evil is inescapable. And yet by following the truth shown to us by the prophets we can improve the world. "The real meaning of truth being established at the centre", writes Barni, "is that truth shall overpower untruth."[12] He identified truth with the greatness of Islam and was convinced that it would be vindicated through the humiliation and disgrace of polytheism and infidelity. One may disagree with his antipathy to Hinduism but it is more difficult to disagree with his analysis of life in terms of opposites.

In the world, he argued, there are forces of both truth and falsehood which corrupt and afflict society. Things like sex and drinking are manifestation of falsehood. Falsehood can be transcended by adherence to religious faith. It is here that he sets himself against intellectualism. Barni opines that the success or failure of a Muslim king depends upon good and bad religious faith. So strong is his faith in the Koran that he goes to the extent of saying that even enjoyment and worldly pleasures are forgiven to the king out of consideration for his firm faith.[13] In such cases a distinction is made between the personal and the public life of the king and his attempt to enforce religious principles. Barni would condone the personal sins of the king so long as he obeys the injunctions of Islam and keeps the inhabitants on the path of *Shariat*. For its enforcement, the king has the right to harass bad people. He rejected the common concept of happiness which subordinates it to sensual pleasure by saying that the king must punish tavern keepers, harlots, prostitutes and gamblers as these are against the dignity of faith. All Muslims are enjoined to perform the five basic duties of Islam which include recitation of the oath of affirmation, saying of given obligatory prayers, fasting during the month of *Ramzan* and pilgrimage to Mecca. He is against everything which leads to the sins of the flesh. In a striking passage he exposes the *Mazdak* wisdom in the acceptance of the Platonic principle of community of wives and property. He declared: "The Muslims should be brought to the highway of the Islamic faith and the non-Muslims within the domain of those who believe in God."[14]

So great was his antipathy to rationalism independent of Koranic faith that he opined that science should not be the subject matter of education at all. The only thing worth teaching, according to him, were the Koranic commentaries, the traditions of the prophets and religious law. He particularly comes out hard against *brahmanas* whom he called 'the *Kafirs*'. There is no point in repeating his arguments on this subject here; they are full of venom. But one thing which comes to the surface quite surprisingly is that he thinks that there was close resemblance between Brahmanism and the science of the Greeks which was opposed to the early commandments. Both are dubbed as forms of rational knowledge which are opposed to the traditional knowledge of Islam.[15] He repudiated such ideas as that the world is eternal or that God has no cognition of details of the day of judgement or the rising up of men from graves or even in heaven and hell. He concluded that "if these people are allowed to show their preference for the rationalistic over the traditional, how can the correct Faith be made to prevail over the false creeds".[16] A Muslim king, he declared, should establish the honour of theism and the supremacy of Islam by overthrowing infidelity and "slaughter of its leaders who in India are the *brahmanas*". Barni's identification of Hinduism with the rationalism of the Greeks may come as surprise to most people. He had perhaps in mind more the rationalism of Sankara's monistic philosophy rather than the polytheisms of various other sects within Hinduism.

The Koran showed a contempt for the use of evil methods. But Barni argues that in this wicked world a king is authorized to make use of all the means at his disposal so long as his aim is the service of religion. The governance of men is not possible without the principles of domination. He says, "No one has been able to govern the people in any other way".[17] Again, the supreme command and the *masnad* of the caliphate cannot be established or become firm without "the terror, prestige and power of kingship".[18] In fact, according to him, on the principle of domination hinges the distinction between good and bad kings. Good kings are those who have self-will and instinct to dominate, who rule on the basis of their consultations with the religious leaders, ponder deeply over the state policies and suppress disturbance in their kingdom. For this the kings are enjoined to allow frank expression of opinion on the part of men of wisdom. Besides, they should also guarantee tenure to the councillors. Barni nostalgically looks back to Solomon and Alexander. They were the chosen men of God and for both "rulership was a means for the elevation of their own spiritual status and securing the welfare of their subjects".[19]

Following Aristotle, Barni rejected despotism and tyranny because the aim of such a rule is mischief and evil and leads to public hatred, distress and misfortune. To him, the object of a good state is the welfare of the religion and the state. But it was not a plea for popular democracy, he provides justification for monarchy.

He believed that without justice, the Koranic laws are arbitrary decrees, and consequently anything against the Koran is tyranny. He went on, "You should know that from the time of Adam to our own days, the select as well as the common people of all communities, ancient and modern, are united in the opinion that justice is a necessary condition of religion and that religion is a necessary condition of justice."[20] It is the balance in which the actions of people are judged, the distinction between right and wrong is clarified. It is a necessary condition for the realization of truth and exposures of cruelty, oppression, misappropriation and plunder. It is justice which breaks the strong arms of tyranny and oppression. Justice for him is not so much a supernatural principle as a necessary condition of life because it provides sanction and legitimacy to distinctions. "If there is no justice and equity on the earth, there would be anarchy; one man's property and another's family would vanish; no time or place would be free from disorder." It includes such injunctions as helping the poor and helpless, protection of faith and raising Islam to its true glory. He respects Plato when he says that if the powers of the king are used only for the satisfaction of their desires, they eventually lose the ability to distinguish between right and wrong.

Barni's emphasis on the importance of justice was definitely a departure from the general tendency in medieval Islamic thought which tended to accept autocracy.[21] Islamic political thought had come to sanction the increasingly un-Islamic political systems people lived under, so as to preserve the fundamental moral structures of political life. But Barni's position was clear that any such attempt would take Islamic thought far from the real political problems which surrounded the establishment of an Islamic state in India, i.e. it must appear to be concerned with moral issues.

He argues that only the companions of prophets were able to combine the injunctions of prophets on property with kingship. If these injunctions are followed new kingship would be impossible. Here Barni was influenced by the Iranian ideas of empire and believed that the policy of the Iranian emperors in breaking the head-strong and subduing rebels was necessary to maintain "the traditions of the prophets."[22] He seems to view power as a necessary component of life and says that the power of kingship is necessary for protection and promotion of faith. Barni combined the Islamic idea of religion with the Iranian idea of kingship as the only way to create order in society. People are prone to evil and therefore they have to be reared in the habit of fear. Kingship means "the control which a man obtains over a territory by power and force". If there is anyone else in the kingdom who is able to have more influence than the king, the king loses his sovereignty, "the situation is reversed; the ruler becomes the ruled, the superior becomes the subordinate and the attributes of the ruler change into the qualities of the subject".[23] It is to be noted that the secular concept of sovereignty developed in Kautilya now once again gives place to the theocratic concept in which sovereignty is identified solely with the king and his power. This was in a way the legitimation of the centralization which Balban (1266-1286) had already effected. It was also the introduction of the Iranian idea of kingship which had accepted the king as the supernatural and divine force and given importance to the office of Imam as essential for the protection of the state.[24]

Three functions were considered necessary by Barni for the sovereign; (i) enforcement of the Shariat, (ii) check on immoral and sinful acts, and (iii) dispensing of justice which included appointments to various offices. He says, "all that I can do is to crush the cruelties of the cruel and to see that all persons are equal before law. The glory of the state rests upon a rule which makes its subjects happy and prosperous."[25] Barni accepted this and added his own bias to support a doctrine of personal sovereignty. He wrote, "when the kings have determined upon anything, there is not and cannot be any turning aside from it, just, as there can be no turning aside of the verdict of Destiny."[26]

However, he did not think that it was possible to attain absolute justice. With his theory of pairs, he could not have believed in such notion. As a result, he followed Aristotle and argues that in all respects moderation is the best policy consonant with both *Shariat* and Greek science. But, according to him, a king can transcend this in three cases: (i) to enforce Islam on infidels, (ii) for protection of his state, and (ii) in order to give rewards to his loyal supporters. Thus he considered it absolutely essential that in order to be just the state should have Islam as the basis. At times, he does give an impression that the state is there to secure certain essential conditions of life to all. This is a perfectly secular trend in his thought. But on the whole his conception of justice is that of a theocratic state which must be used for protection and promotion of the faith, "for fighting holy wars (*jihad*)".

He introduced the concept of individual in Indian political thought by stating for the first time the concept of rights. He regards such as recognition of rights as the basis of the state and says that if a king does not recognize the rights of the people, no trace of his kingdom will remain. He particularly mentions the rights of wife, children, old friends and well wishers, of the helpless, old servants and slaves, and the select persons of the kingdom.[27] But his concept of right is not linked to any concept of equality as in modern thought. In fact he emphatically believes that though all are equal in appearance, they differ in character. This inequality is ordained by God at the beginning of time. Each man is allotted a certain amount of virtue and vice, an aptitude for fine arts and aesthetics or for coarse things. Excellence leads to nobility. He specifically enjoins the king to create ranks and grades and to confer a portion of his own dignity and honour in accordance with their excellence. Barni had a clear contempt for the low born and went on to say, "The promotion of the low and the low born brings no advantage in this world, for it is imprudent to act against the wisdom of creation." In fact in promoting the interests of the low born, the king is a witness to his own base origin. He was convinced that human beings are unequal in nature. He particularly considers differences in character as politically relevant and recognizes that any social hierarchy based on these kinds of distinctions is legitimate. He shares with Aristotle his conviction of natural inequality. In fact it is on this basis that he also seems to justify domination of others by the king which was clearly a move away from the position taken in the Koran. The Koran, for example, had looked down upon the regalia of state with disdain, though commanding the people to obey the Caliphate. For Barni, the state is natural in so far as it is a product of the necessity to control viciousness in men, and consequently he distinguishes between good and bad governments. Besides his moralism, it was this factor which was also responsible for Barni's diatribe against *Mazdak*. He argues that if there is no private property how can the higher classes of society be maintained; if there is community of women, how can descent of sons be traced.

But he does believe that kings must ensure that no one suffers undue hardship. For this he suggests a system of price control; good management of the kingdom for him consists in ensuring means of livelihood and administration of justice to the people. When commodity sellers earn money without labour and others who have given their sweat remain poor, in distress and poverty, disorder overtakes society. This might appear a revolutionary principle, but in the context of his time, it was merely a plea to ensure the welfare of Muslims against Hindus who were controlling trade and commerce and presumably earning more profits than warranted by their exertions.

II

Thus for Barni, as for Aristotle, living within a state is natural and good, but for Barni it must be an Islamic Sate. In fact he Islamizes Aristotelian thought. The admirable concern for justice and moderation was combined with the intensity of his fanaticism. However, some of these ideas must have left their imprint on succeeding generations and must have nourished the concern for justice which later on became the glory of the Mughal state. It did not take long for Muslim rule to settle in India. The establishment of an empire by Babar was the culmination of the process. Babar was a descendent of Timur, the great central Asian ruler (1370-1405). He had been greatly influenced by both the Persian and the Mongol rulers, specially Genghis Khan (AD 1206-1227). The Mongols had conceived of the kingdom as a great fancy and it was believed that the "empire belonged not to the ruler but to the ruling family". The whole system was patrimonial. This is evidenced from the fact that the Mongols gave internal officers household names. For instance, the main incharge of Genghis' army was called a 'cook'. This idea was combined with the already existing Persian strain. It must be remembered that the Persian system of government, though paying homage to the idea of the divine character of the king, had also developed a strong bureaucratic strain. The Sasanid empire (AD 224-651) was high watermark of it. It had developed a routinised system of taxation, as tradition of centralised rule and bureaucratic administration.[28] In a way this went very well with prevalent Hindu notions. It is true that earlier Hindu thought had oscillated between the divine origin of the king and the contract theory. The powers of the king were not absolute or arbitrary. However, this evidence is not conclusive, for the actual practice in much of the later period contradicted it. By the time Muslim power came to India, kings were firmly established in their office, and kingship was held sacred, as is reflected in the Puranas. Ruling had become a matter of hereditary succession.

In matters of religion, there was a significant departure from the times of Barni. Religious fanaticism was given up. Even in earlier times, it is doubtful as to what extent it was actually practised by the emperors. As early as the twelfth century Iltutmish had declared that it was not possible for him to be "the Defender of the Faith" except in a limited sphere. For him this limited sphere did not extend beyond immediate concerns. With Balban Persian ideas of monarchy had become dominant. These were retained in the Mughal concept of royalty. But during this period a striking change took place in the relationship between religion and the state. The process of assimilation gathered momentum. The Hindus accepted some of the elements of the new faith. There were two kinds of responses. The first response was to incorporate some of the elements of Islam in order to enable Hinduism to withstand the pressure of Islam. The other was a genuine attempt to create a synthesis. People like Kabir, Nanak, Dadu and Chaitanya created a 'ferment' of ideas. Kabir, greatest of them all, wrote:

I am neither in temple nor in mosque,
I am neither in Kaaba nor in Kailash,
If thou are a true seeker, thou shall see me at once
Thou shalt meet me in a moment of time.

About Hindu-Muslim beliefs, Nanak wrote:

I will not worship with Hindu
Nor, like the Muslim, go to Mecca.
I shall serve Him and no other
I shall put my heart at the feet of one Supreme as Being.

They pleaded for assimilation of all religions and created a fertile ground for the later bhakti and sufi movements to flourish. Dadu, for instance, regarded the whole body as the rosary in which the name of One is repeated: "there is one best and there is no second, and the word (*kalma*) is He himself".

Mulk Das wrote:

Why art thou in error,
Rama and Rahim are the name of one.

Kabir was of course the profoundest and the most influential of them all. The basic postulates of this new cultural perspective were that:

(1) It is possible for everyone to approach God directly, with or without mediation of any mosque, church or temple.

(2) All human beings are knit by the bonds of brotherhood.

(3) There is a fundamental unity of beliefs in all religions.

These ideas were also shared by the Sufi movement which ultimately found its apogee in the beautiful writings of Dara Shikoh. In addition, Islam also retained some of the characteristics of Hindu society. The caste system was incorporated and Ikram tells us that Muslim castes developed as Indian Muslims classified themselves as Sayyed, Shaikh, Mughal and Pathan, though the structure was never as rigid as in Hindu society. The sufi movement particularly introduced Hindu elements in Islamic thought.

It is not certain whether there was any conscious attempt at assimilation.[29] The antipathies were not easy to overcome. What Alberuni wrote in AD 1030, that Hindus differed from Muslim in every respect, was perhaps not taken seriously but the pride and arrogance of the rulers was matched on the Hindu side by the memories of the raids of Mohammed Ghazni on the ruled.[30] Nearly three centuries after Alberuni, Ibn Battuta also noticed that Hindus and Muslims lived as entirely different communities. But there is no doubt that liberalism in thought on both sides found a reflection in Akbar's attempt to start a new religion *Din-i-Ilahi* which was, to quote Tara Chand, "not an isolated freak of an autocrat who had more power than he knew how to employ, but an inevitable result of the forces which were deeply surging in India's breast and finding expression in the teachings of men like Kabir".[31] It laid the premise on which Dara Shikoh could argue in his *Majma-ul-Bahrain* completed in AD 1655 that "there were not many differences, except verbal, in the way in which Hindu Monotheists and Muslim Sufi saints sought and comprehended truth".[32] This had led Akbar to enunciate a policy of equal treatment of all subjects which reached its eloquent expression in Shahjahan's time. No wonder Shah Muhibulla of Allahabad wrote to Dara Shikoh that the Holy prophet had been referred to as Rahmat-ul-Alim, a blessing to all the world and not merely Muslims.

Unfortunately, no book in political theory of the period has come down to us. Or perhaps society in which Iranian and Islamic ideas were fused, was not congenial to the development of such a theory. But the rudiments of this new and more liberal and humane approach are found in Abul Fazal's *Ain-i-Akbari*.[33] He was born in AD 1551 and grew up under the benign and human stewardship of Shaikh Mubarak. Later on he became a minister in the court of Akbar. He had learnt from Mubarak that all men are equal in their brotherhood, that there is a basic cultural unity in all religions, and finally, that religious differences should not be allowed to destroy the harmony of society. He attributed the quarrels between Hindus and Muslims to their different interests and perceptions.[34] to diversity of language and misapprehension of each others motives, and the distance between those who knew and the common men. He was convinced it was also a result of indolence which had resulted in the "chill blast of inflexible custom and lower flicker of wisdom". There was arrogance and self interest on both sides in which each regarded its own vision as the correct one, whilst, according to him, wisdom required that instead of wasting their time and energies on these issues, people ought to devote themselves to concerns of general welfare.

In political ideas, Abul Fazal accepted the divine inspiration theory of kingship. "Royalty", he believed, "is a light from God". He went on, "without a mediator it appears as a holy form to the holders of power and at the sight of it everyone bends the forehead of praise to the grounds of submission".[35] According to Abul Fazal a ruler acquires his qualities to rule by prayer and devotion, through a large heart and paternal love for people. An ideal ruler is compared to a father. He should fulfil his task and work for the common welfare. The king is not bound by any human law but only the law of God. He is also regarded as a spiritual guide to the people. This meant, though not explicitly stated, that subjects do not have any authority or power to check the king. Of course, in Abdul Fazal's writings there runs a contempt for tyranny which even Barni regarded as sinful; working for the common welfare was always regarded as better than working for one's own. But while there is a contempt for tyranny, there is also a strong note that a centralized monarchical form of government, above customary law, is the best. Fazal argued that for proper administration we need to divide the authority of the state and appoint various officials to look after different aspects of the state because the strength of one person is not sufficient.[36] There are, however, no clear limits on monarchical power, no special institutions of laws are mentioned as in earlier Indian thought, thereby confirming the view that people of the orient are generally slavish. There were indeed moral restraints, but ideologically, the monarch was not subject to any legal or political principles.

The pattern of administration given in *Ain-i-Akbari* is that of an empire and compares well with those given in earlier treatises on administration such as Kautilya's *Arthasastra*. The whole state was divided into many levels, each manned by officers of various kinds. What stands out most clearly is the personal interest which the king should take in the affairs of the state. All *mansabdars* reported directly to the ruler. There was of course a system of hierarchy, *nazims* and *subedars, parganas* and sub-divisional officers, *jagirdars* and *quazis*. But each was permitted to approach the ruler directly. Indeed, the ruler took such a great personal interest that he would organize bazars and feasts to feel the pulse of the people and also take an active interest in the private life of his officers.

Following Hindu thought, Abul Fazal divided society into four parts. But while Hindu thought gave first place to the men of knowledge, Fazal assigned the first place to the warriors and rulers and only the second place was given to the learned such as scholars, astronomers, philosophers and all those from whose pen there flows wisdom. He was quite poetic when he referred to the role of the learned. He wrote: "From their pen and their wisdom, a river rises in the draught of the world; and the garden of the creation receives from their irrigating power a peculiar freshness."[37] The third place was accorded to the artisans and merchants. These are the people who make God's gifts universal. The last place was given to the husbandmen and labourers. He compared them to the earth and thought that it is by their exertions that to each is brought happiness and strength. One can at once notice lines of resemblance with the caste system as well as with Plato's ideal state from which Abul Fazal derived inspiration. In the scheme, there are indeed not four classes but four different parts of a hierarchy in which the principle of rule and a subordination prevails. Nobles occupy the most important place because they belong to the first group. The notion of justice above the king creating limitations on his authority was considered bad to the maintenance of this hierarchy. Fazal wrote, "when God bestows sovereignty upon a choicest one, he exalts him with far seeing reasons, wide forbearance and the priceless jewels of justice, so that he might place familiar friends and strangers in the same balance".[38] The principles of justice were of course based on customary law; they embodied the inherited habit of the living in Indian society. But the final determination of the precise meaning of these principles was left to the emperor. The main task was to maintain peace and order. But it is nowhere discussed as to what happens when the ruler becomes a tyrant. Abul Fazal's ideas were not a synthesis but a philosophy of the co-existence of Hindus and Muslims. Hindus had already wrapped themselves in their own cocoon. This is reflected in the fact that very few cases were taken to the courts. They were mostly settled by panchayats and in caste courts which wielded enormous powers. That is why we find that what Abul Fazal was pleading for, that is co-existence, was destined, in time, to fall asunder.

III

Along with the rise of a centralized patrimonial government there came into existence during this period a system of community relationship resembling feudalism in Europe. It will not be out of place to give a brief statement of the theoretical principles governing this system. It is necessary to do so because its consequences still live with us, though there is often a tendency to misunderstand its real importance in the context of how it came into existence. The feudal system was not simple. It is a name for a variety of structures of relationship between the king and his subordinates which came into existence during this period. In the first place, it retained the important element of '*chakravartin*' from ancient India. The system of *chakravartin* consisted of a series of more or less autonomous chieftains who owed allegiance to the suzerain power mostly for the purpose of military assistance. This system continued throughout the ancient world. It did not matter who were the chieftains, whether they belonged to the nobility or were upstarts so long as they governed. In most cases, these chieftains were themselves kings in their own right. They had their history going back into the pre-historic past. Some of them claimed to be descendants of the Sun and the Moon. They had enjoyed customary privileges, had their own coat of arms, armies and customary obligations. So long as they fulfilled their obligation to come to the aid of the suzerain power in periods of emergency, they enjoyed almost absolute power within their own kingdoms. Under them there was a full hierarchy of minor landlords or landowners or chieftains, who were known as Zamindar or *jagirdars*, and the king had often to employ force to curb these chieftains. Most of these *zamindars* were connected to the king by blood ties, as in the case of the Rajputana states. It is here that along with jagirdars there also developed the *bhumiari* system in which there was direct ownership of the land by the *bhumia*. The *bhumia* did not have to pay duty for the investiture, his grants did not have to be renewed, and the ownership of most of their lands went by right of prescription. However, the ownership of such land was always inferior to that of jagirdari land.[39] There was a third category of land known as *khalsa* which was under the direct control of the king and would be mostly in the vicinity of the capital. However, the power in this system flowed from the ownership of land retained by the development of the military virtues. This system continued in various part of the country and the Muslim power did not disturb it so long as the Chieftains owed allegiance to the powers in Delhi.

Besides this, another kind of feudalism developed particularly during the Mughal period. The Mughal state was a vast centralized patrimonial system in which various kinds of ranks and hierarchies were created on the lines of the *mansabdari* system borrowed from Persia.[40] Each *mansabdar* was given certain rights and horses to command. The grant was conferred on an individual on the basis of the favour the ruler wanted to do. There were, if *Ain-i-Akbari* is to be believed, sixty-six ranks. It was a part of the system of giving gifts to the deserving. All these *mansabdars* reported directly to the ruler. In certain cases they were also given the right to collect revenue on behalf of the king. They were also known as *zamindars*, and were assigned land in lieu of cash salaries.[41] Whereas the earlier chieftains had won their right to land on the basis of their military prowess or kin relationship with the chief, perhaps in the periods of anarchy which chracterized all breakdowns of imperial authority, the new *zamindars* were a product of the central power and were solely dependent on its favours. Indeed, while the former system was organized mostly around blood ties, the latter was organized around the concept of relationship in which there was sometimes give and take for the maintenance of empire. In the first, most of the important *jagirdars*, for example Chondawat and Shaktawat in Udaipur or Asopa and Pokarana in Jodhpur, belonged to the ruling tribe. They were all of one stock and the king, therefore, was more or less *primus inter pares*; in the latter system the relationship was more in the nature of vassalage. In the former at a later stage, land grants were also given on the basis of military service, but the dominant element still continued to be that of "tenure by blood and birth right of the clan", on the other hand, in the vassalage system, the land was distributed in return either for military service or for revenue collection. The first were known as *iqtadars* and the latter as *zamindars*. In the Mughal period both came to be called *zamindars* when both became responsible for the collection of taxes on behalf of the central power. In the absence of the concept of *primus inter pares* as in princely India, these *zamindars* who had received their zamindari in lieu of pay tended to be far more oppressive than the *zamindars* who were connected by blood ties. The former often forced small holders to abandon their land, which was then absorbed in the personal property of the *zamindars*. As they became more powerful, they, in turn, leased out land to third parties, which in due course, themselves claimed hereditary right to collect taxes.[42]

Because of the survival of the traditional theory around kinship ties no system of European serfdom or slavery developed in what is now characterized as princely India. There are instances of persons living almost in bondage for generations. But in most cases they helped in the running of the households and in reality were "instruments of production" of commodities. In fact, the pangs of their servitude were further reduced on account of the fact that most of them were treated as members of family in closely knit joint family system and enjoyed certain rights and privileges. Doubtless a system resembling that of serfdom later on developed as the customary conventions became weaker and the *jagirdars* thought that they could violate the customary rules with impunity. But even such cases were protected by the system, which entitled a whole village to migrate to another village and thereby desert the *jagirdar*. This system survived even in the twentieth century. The most interesting part of this was that the *jagirdar* would then go to those people and apologise for his misdeeds and beseech them to return to his village. Needless to say that cases of violation were more common. But the very fact of the existence of a theoretical possibility of such a revolt, restrained the *jagirdar* in his dealings with villagers. The experience of such *ijaras* left its mark on the various developments in the nineteenth and twentieth centuries, in our march towards democracy and social welfare. The *jagirdars* and *zamindars* survived up to 1947. And the two together provide the penultimate points of aristocratic and democratic elements in the political life of the country today. The *jagirdari* and *zamindari* systems gave rise to the development of close knit communities consisting of the chieftain and the smaller nobility with various intermediate grades between the ruler and people. A complicated hierarchical system based on the analogy of mutual obligations of the family came into existence. The medieval Indian society therefore was turned into a complicated system of rank and status more often determined on the basis of military power than anything else. The governing principle of life was honour and status and from these two flowed a whole network of rights and obligations. Muslim rulers also created a parallel system of hierarchy by rewarding the deserving to maintain their power and preserve peace in the kingdom.

But there was another factor which made Indian feudalism *sui generis*. Whereas in Europe the individual was completely dependent on the feudal lord (the individual had to depend for his resources and livelihood on the feudal lord in the interest of land cultivation) in India the individual was for all practical purposes the owner of the land. Moreover, the natural conditions were different from those of Europe. People did not have to depend so much for their livelihood on the *jagirdar* as they did in Europe. Good weather, fertility of the land and the high level of development in agricultural technology were combined with relatively few demands of the people. The ideal of self abnegation preached by various saints helped to keep these demands low. For instance, while in Europe, a house, good food and warm clothing were necessary even for survival, in India nature made it possible for people to survive even without much of them so long as they were able to manage a few morsels of food. It is this which partly explains the fact that the Indians became indifferent to the comings and goings of empires and yet survived. In Europe, politics was important because on its better management depended the basic survival of the people. But in India it was considered marginal to the system so long as it ensured peace and order and did not interfere in their daily lives. There were doubtless elaborate retrievals of rights and obligations, but in the middle ages, partly because of the fear of Muslim intervention, and partly because of the stronger hold of social institutions such as caste and *ashram*, these rights and obligations were managed within the social framework. Occasions when the help of politics was sought were very rare. The state also did not interfere much with the distribution of justice or the management of the economy within the *jagirdari* system. In individual cases, the authority rested mainly with the panchayats. In criminal cases, the *jagirdars* were expected to consult the king but, in practice, they had enormous latitude. Even though the *zamindars*, as pointed out earlier, were far more oppressive, they, too, did not interfere in the system of justice, which, more or less, remained tenuous. As pointed out earlier, most cases were settled outside the framework of the state, in *panchayats* and caste organizations. These organizations provided mechanisms which practically sealed off Hindu society from any interference. The landowner or the *zamindar* was important but he too was assimilated into the system in so far as he accepted the customs and conventions of the people. Theoretically the *zamindar* was like a loving mother or father, in terms of his personal relationship with various groups and individuals in society. This ideal was nourished by a concern for security and maintenance of customs and usages. But in practice the ideal was rarely adhered to.

This meant that in theory the land belonged to the king, but in practice, as a result of customs, the land truly belonged to first, the village as a whole and then in due course of time to the individual cultivator. The land was mostly family property. The system of individual tenure developed much later when the chiefs claimed the right of granting an occupied land as private property to an individual. The communal ownership found its reflection in the development of such things as common grazing grounds and cooperative enterprises for the development of canals. In cases of crime and robbery, the entire village would have to pay the penalty whenever it failed to find the culprit. The idea behind all this was that the village is a community of personal relationships and if there was a theft it was everyone's responsibility. Whenever land disputes arose they were first decided in terms of customary rights and, very rarely, in terms of absolute right or wrong. This system provided a kind of security to the individual and yet at the same time a mechanism in terms of which the individual was absorbed and assimilated into the system of community relationships prevailing then. One system provided a protection against the encroachments of the other; the balance and harmony became the watch words in terms of which honour and status were maintained. The persistence of communal ownership in theory and family ownership in practice as well as popular justice were the most important factors which distinguished Indian feudalism from its counterpart in Europe.

At the same time, since the system was not confined to merely a village, it also led to the development of trade and commerce. Certain classes specialized in that. India is very rich in natural resources, and the local artisans exploited these to the full. Even as late as during the Mughal period, India was a great importer and exporter of commodities from and to the Middle East, South-East Asia and even Europe and China. It is remarkable that news of the movement of various commodities on the Kerala coast would reach Agra in a month's time. The independent village was perhaps a product of much later times. It perhaps came into existence during the period of anarchy and chaos which preceded and followed the Mughal empire. Otherwise, in peaceful times, trade and commerce flourished and gave rise to urban centres very early in the history of the life of the nation. It is clear from Kautilya's *Arthasastra* that an elaborate system of rules was framed to regulate their activities. These urban centres became the props for the royal and imperial powers. In later times, some of these traders wielded enormous powers because they used to lend money to the rulers and princes. But it must be emphasized that all this was not a uniform process. Its precise shape and character differed from region to region. In the absence of any evidence, it is not certain whether these developments had any significant impact on the nature of government. Presumably the way in which the socio-religious system developed its own centre independently of the state ensured that its effects would be absorbed in the society itself. There was no development of a united temple. Though Sankaracharya did try to establish four centres in different corners of the country, and the *Bhagwat* tried to assimilate all religious sects and traditions, including Jainism and Buddhism, into one mainstream by recognizing different religious leaders as incarnations of Lord Vishnu and accepting equal validity of different paths in the quest for truth. Hinduism, on the whole remained very fragmented and amorphous in its religious beliefs. The net result was that it did not develop a very cohesive political system which would provide an alternative to the social one. Political ambitions were diverted to concern for the salvation of the soul. The ideal of salvation relegated the importance of right here and now into the background. The preparation for the world hereafter got precedence over the world herein; the social life got absolute importance over the political one.

In fact, with regard to these matters three things deserve mention. Firstly, the social life became an independent autonomous whole which regulated the day-to-day relationships of the householders with very little interference from the state. Secondly, the politics was expected to provide law and order in society. It was also expected to be a mechanism whereby individual fulfilled political ambitions. Thirdly, it was generally emphasized that caring for the soul is more important. All principles perhaps enabled the Hindu society to protect itself against possible encroachment by the central ruler. The importance of the soul was accepted by almost all religious leaders of the period. There were certainly literary works like Tulsidas' *Manas* which reminded people of the ancient ideals by bringing them in close relationship to the imperatives of medieval society. Their influence on the life was considerable. But on the whole, finding life difficult, people tended to escape into a world of spiritualism by ignoring the importance of good life here itself. This gave rise to a feeling that there was a sphere of life, the political sphere, which was not directly concerned with the salvation of the soul, and could be left to rulers, Hindu or Muslim. People readily accepted the compartmentalization of life, and specially the idea that since rulership did not matter from the point of view of salvation, it was a necessary evil and could be left to smaller souls. The traditional writings on politics and statecraft were almost lost. Kautilya mentions about 32 such ancient texts on politics. But none of those have come down to us. The influence arising from these trends was towards the development of an attitude of life-negation. This did not of course influence the common man. He was still concerned with the problem of his livelihood. But since the mentors who had all the knowledge of the world left him to fend by himself, the poor creature was left on his own and became a passive spectator of the intrigues of the courts, of rulers and emperors. While paying lip service to high cultural principles, the ruler then utilized his status and power to further his own interest. India resembles in the eighteen century to a court intrigue in which everyone is there to outwin the other, unmindful of either the cost to themselves or the consequences to the country as a whole. It is at this point that the British power steps in, takes advantage of the political vacuum and creates yet another great empire.

NOTES

1. *The Srimad Bhagavatam of Krishna-Dyaipayana Vyasa,* Trans J.M. Snagal (Calcutta, Oriental) 1972, vol. III, p. 74.
2. Ibid., p. 76.
3. Ibid., p. 77.
4. Loc. cit.
5. Ibid., p. 83.
6. Ibid., p. 75.
7. Cf. E. Dennison Ross, "The Genealogies of Fakhr-ud-Din" in T.W. Arnold and R.A. Nicholson, ed., *A Volume of Oriental Studies* (Cambridge, 1922); Also, S.M. Ikram, *Muslim Civilisation in India* (New York, Columbia, 1964), p. 86.
8. Barni, *The Fatawa-I-Jahandari,* trans. in *Medieval Indian History Journal,* Aligarh, 1957-68. Also see M. Habid "Life and Thought of Ziauddin Barni", *Medieval India,* Quarterly, Jan-Apr 1958.
9. Ikram, op. cit., p. 86.
10. Barni, op. cit., p. 59.
11. Loc cit.
12. Ibid., p. 60.
13. Ibid., p. 19.
14. Ibid., p. 21
15. Ibid., p. 63.
16. Ibid., p. 65.
17. Ibid., p. 42.
18. Ibid., p. 50.
19. Ibid., p. 27.
20. Ibid., p. 32.
21. See A.S. Lamton, op. cit.
22. Barni, op. cit., p. 59.
23. Ibid., p. 176.
24. See D. Pandey, "Balban's Theory of Kingship", *Journal of Indian History,* April-August 1977, pp. 81-87.
25. Quoted by H.C. Roy Choudhary, R.C. Majumdar and L.R. Dutta, *Advanced History of India,* vol. III, p. 292.
26. Barni, op. cit., p. 30.
27. Ibid., p. 73.
28. See S.P. Blake, "The Patrimonial Bureaucratic Empire of the Mughals", *Journal of Asian Studies,* Vol. XXXIX, No.I, Nov. 1979, p. 88.
29. Ikram, op. cit., p. 130.

30. E.C. Sachan, *Alberuni's India* (London, 1914), I, p. 22.
31. Tara Chand, *Influence of Islam in India*, p. 165.
32. Ikram, op. cit., p. 188.
33. Abul Fazal, *Ain-i-Akbari,* Asiatic Society of Bengal, 1872, ed. Blophman, Sarkar, 2nd ed., 3 vol. 1927-1949, reprinted, New Delhi, tans. Jarsel & Sarkar, International Book Depot, 1965.
34. Ibid., III, pp. 3-9.
35. Ibid., I, Trans, Blockman, pp. 2-5.
36. Ibid., p. 289.
37. Ibid., I, p. 4.
38. Ibid., III, p. 173.
39. Daniel Thorner, "Feudalism in India", in Coulborn, *Feudalism in History* (New Jersey, Princeton University Press, 1956), p. 135.
40. Ikram, op. cit., p. 220.
41. Abul Fazal, op. cit., I, 283, II, pp. 41-42.
42. Daniel Thorner, op. cit., pp. 139-41.

CHAPTER 8

RENAISSANCE AND THE BEGINNINGS
OF MODERN THOUGHT

The three sources of the Indian thought in the nineteenth century may be mentioned here. The first was of course the impact of English thought. Unlike the previous rulers the English did not settle in India. They kept their links with home. Some of the rulers had respect for India's traditions. But most of them followed Macaulay's famous minutes of 1832, and worked for the transformation of Indian society in the image of Western Society. Bentinck, for instance thought that the primary objective of the British rule was the interest of Indians, viz., "improvement in their conditions". He declared, "I write and feel as a legislator for the Hindus, and as I believe many enlightened Hindus think and feel so."[1] Through the introduction of English system of education, the British not only transmitted the culture and temper of the European Renaissance and the Reformation and the English traditions but, more immediately, the ideas of Bentham, Mill, Carlyle and Coleridge, the amalgam of a defence of private enterprise and collective endeavour, of democracy and rule of law. Benthamism dominated the thought of the new Indian intelligentsia which had come into existence.[2]

But despite all these, the system of education introduced by the British surreptitiously but surely led to a new awareness of the value of liberty, democracy and rule of law in India. It brought into bold relief the fact that the gulf separating the rulers and the ruled was enormous. People began to compare their plight with the affluence in the West. They began to realise that while the British policy alternated between repression and liberalization, it had become a prop for the continuation of despotic rule and feudal life-styles. It made India, in due course, feel that the British colonisation in India ought to end. Indeed the emergence of the educated middle class had enormously changed the situation. Different sections reacted differently. People like Harishchandra Mukerjee, on the one hand, in an article in *The*

Hindu Patriot asserted that the time has come when the problems of India must be solved by Indians themselves. They were confident that the indigenous thought had the necessary vitality to meet the new situations. On the other hand, such people as Jogendranath Vidyabhusan quoted chapter and verse from *Caravaka* philosophy to prove the corrupt nature of the ancient Indian Brahmanism and argued that liberalism and positivism which we had learnt from our contact with the British were the coming religions of the future.[3] Another writer Surendra Mohan Tagore was also greatly influenced by Comte and Mill but instead of rejecting the tradition he tried to combine it with modernity and argued that some of these ideas were already there in the ancient texts. This line of thought based on an appreciation of the role of the British exercised a direct influence on the ideas of Ranade, Gokhale and the entire liberal schools in the country. All these people were steeped in the philosophy of freedom and justice and had great admiration for the British sense of fair-play. They also doubtlessly challenged the British imperialism in due course. But in the process they neither referred to the glory of the ancient Indian civilization and culture or to the continental traditions of thought to which more aggressive members of the middle class were turning. They quoted Paine against Burke and, to quote Iyer, "natural rights against the duties of trustees, Mill against Bentham and representative democracy against utilitarian despotism, Mazzini against Plato and natural destiny against imperial guardianship, equality under natural law against the special claims of the evangelicals".[4]

Of all such writers in the nineteenth century, Raja Ram Mohan Roy was unique. He was greatly influenced by the French revolution no less than by the ideas of Bentham. He was also responsible for founding the Brahmo Samaj. In his letters, notes and petitions he enunciated, though not in a systematic form, his own ideas about liberty. He desired independence of all colonies. Even as a boy he was not happy with the presence of the British in India. But the British seemed to him to possess qualities of head and heart which Indians lacked. He, therefore, hoped that the British rule would lead to the amelioration of the lot of Indians and would eventually pave the way for the establishment of democratic government in India. Roy's attitude was a queer mixture of concern for the establishment of democratic institutions in India and admiration for the British raj which he thought was a blessing in so far as it would bring India at par with the nations of Europe.

Roy hated despotism of all kinds and was particularly in favour of the freedom of the press. In 1832, along with Dwarakanath Tagore and others, he submitted a petition to the Privy Council for the freedom of press which he thought would not only lead to ventilation of grievances by the people but also make the government rest on secure foundations by removing discontent which leads to revolution. However, the attitude of Raja Ram Mohan Roy was feeble and timid. He had no understanding of the evil side of the Raj, did not connect his ideas to the needs of the poor or any notion of the specific identity of the Indian society. Indeed, he had invited the British planters to come and settle in India ignoring the havoc which the permanent settlement had played with the organicity of Indian life by segmenting and atomising it in the interest of the Raj. And in any case freedom of India or Indians was not to be gained by such methods. The disease was more fundamental, for mere adoption of democratic forms, unaccompanied by the disappearance of the British rule or the transformation of the Indian society, would not have been enough. The situation demanded a new and bold initiative which came later from people like Vivekananda.

The second source of influence were German ideas of Schelling, Fichte, Kant and Herder. It was natural that when a reaction stated against the British raj, people also reacted against some of the ideas of the rulers, particularly against individualism, materialism, and *laissez-faire.* In order to find a philosophical justification for some of their own ideas, they turned to German philosophy. The idea of *volk*, community, duty, nation appealed to them. It might be remembered that by this time there had been almost half-a-century of interaction between German and Indian thought. People like Goethe and Schelling had been deeply influenced by Idealism in the Upanishadic thought. Some of the thinkers and social reformers of this period in India also thought that the only way to expose the weaknesses of utilitarianism which lay at the roots of the thinking of English administrators in India was to exalt the notions of community, *volk* and obligations. They, too, desired democratic norms and various freedoms but, according to them, these must always remain secondary to the need for preservation of the Indian identity, upholding of traditional values, protection of people against economic and political domination by others. Any society which failed to do so opened the door to the possibility of continuous insult by others. They rejected outright all the social or economic advantages which came in the trail of the British Raj. They furiously rejected all efforts of the Englishmen and Westernized social reformers to reform Indian society because they thought that it would lead to an unwarranted English interference in the social life. These ideas were taken over by people like Bankim and Vivekananda and through them exercised a powerful influence on the entire philosophy of nationalism developed later by Bipin Chandra

Pal and Aurobindo Ghosh. They all pleaded that India had a unique mission, it alone could be the spiritual leader of mankind.

There was obviously too much of romanticism in this school. Their idealism also was responsible for the terrorist activities of the time. These youngmen were guided by a metaphysical religious and spiritual vision and in its name they did not shirk violence because they thought that this alone was the solution of the Indian problem. In a multi-religious society where the predominant sector was composed of the Hindus, the use of Hindu idioms and symbols also tended to encourage people tying to foment communal tensions. But in the context of the time it inspired the leaders with a new self-confidence and led to a better appreciation of the unique identity of the Indian society. The leaders of movement successfully undermined the myth of the British superiority and brought into focus the enduring elements of Indian civilization. Their exposition of the organic elements of Indian life, its metaphysics, spiritualism and aesthetics was more convincing than that given by others; they exercised an enormous influence on the people in general. Despite the religious obscurantism of some of these thinkers, they set in motion ideas which became powerful weapons in the hands of the extremists and later even in Gandhi. They made Indians aware of their national unity, and generated in them a sense of a civilized race as great as European races. They pilloried the myth of development through imitation. The growth of patriotism and nationalism brought with it, as its inevitable concomitant, a great concern to rid India of its poverty, squalor, age-old misery and degradation. The doctrine that India had a unique identity and inner purpose, as revealed in her history, and that becoming conscious of it was the best way of participating and making one's contribution, impressed a whole generation of young minds.

The third source was, of course, the traditional Indian thought. There were two kinds of reactions to this: conservative as well as radical. But the real contribution came from those who interpreted traditions in a positive way. Researches by Jones and Max Muller had already created a profound sense of admiration for the cultural traditions of the country. Thinkers of this line of thought started making distinction between an abstract concept of India and India as concrete reality. While they had every respect for the abstract concept of India, they had an equally great contempt for the actuality which they denounced in no uncertain terms. Vivekananda declared:

Sitting down these hundreds of years with an ever increasing load of crystallised superstition on your heads, for hundreds of years spreading all your energy upon discussing the touchableness and untouchablness of this food or that, with all humanity crushed out of you by the continuous social tyranny of ages—what are you?....Come, be man. Kick out the priests who are always against progress, because they would never mend.[5]

In any case, this reaction, to quote Aurobindo, "marked the beginning of a more subtle assimilation and fusing; for vindicating ancient things it has been obliged to do in a way that will at once meet and satisfy the old mentality and new, the traditional and the critical mind".

He further summed up the impact of this line of thought in the following words:

This in itself involves no more return, but consciously or unconsciously hastens a restatement. And the riper form of the return has taken as its principle a synthetical restatement; it has sought to arrive at the spirit of the ancient culture and, while respecting its forms and often preserving them to revivify, has yet not hesitated also to remould, to reject the outworn and to admit whatever new motive seemed assimilable to the old spirituality or apt to widen the channel of its long evolution.[6]

The renaissance thinkers generally turned to the thinkers of the Vedic and classical periods for inspiration. These writers had been greatly impressed by *Gita's* philosophy of action performed with equanimity in the service of others. The *Gita* had provided a particularly strong statement in support of such a position in the course of the dialogue between Arjun and Krishna on the eve of the battle of the *Mahabharata*, when Arjun was feeling weak at the sight of his relatives and friends in the other camp. In a remarkable passage Krishna highlights one's obligation to perform one's immediate duties and dwells upon the merits of such an enterprise undertaken in a spirit of "non-attachment". The Gita had indeed brought into bold relief the entire *problems* of fate in human affairs, a topic that was taken up in great detail in the *Shantiparva*. The *Shantiparva* took up an apparently contradictory position on the relative role of destiny and human will. On the one hand the importance of time and fate is emphasised and on the other man is spurred on to do his immediate duties against all odds that may be in process. But it is clear from the *Mahabharata* that the ancients never thought that everything was preordained or inevitable. In fact they saw fate as a potential friend which could be own on one's side both by prayers and sacrifices and by one's enterprise. It was felt that there were higher deities who disposed of goods on the basis of what one aspired or deserved. There was also an additional feeling that an enterprising man could even force Gods to reward him. The highest inspiration was neither pure knowledge as in the case of Aristotle nor great wealth which is something of a later addition but a heroic life combining honour, glory and position.

There was indeed the doctrine of *Karma* tied to it. Various distinctions were made between past and present *Karmas*, the enduring and ephemeral ones. It was more or less accepted that although the overall position is determined by the past *karma*, within this there is enough room for an enterprising man to mould his own future position in this life and cycle of life hereafter. People believed in astrology but astrological predictions were only indicative of tendencies inherent at the time of birth, and consequently one could modify one's fate by exertion. One quality which deserves to be rewarded is manly valour (*purusartha*) for fortune favours the brave one. It is for this reason that a hero's life was exalted in the scriptures. The underlying belief is clearly set out in the various qualities of a hero or a good prince in the ancient literature, in which the criterion for manliness is valour, and a spirit of fortitude and equanimity amidst all adverse circumstances. The implication of this was extensively explored in the development of various characters in the *Mahabharata* and the *Ramayana*, in which success or failure are not so important as the way in which one leads an authentic life by performing one's actions with the purest of motives. As pointed out earlier in the context of dharma, presumably the ancients believed that neither the ordinances of the past *karma* nor the inner movements of the natural causality were fully within man's grasp. But man had the capacity to be able to rise above them in terms of his understanding of his immediate duties and their performance with the best of motives regardless of consequences on his immediate interests. It is in this context that Kautilya distinguished between 'potency' and 'impotency'. He argued that what produces favourable results is potency and the opposite, impotency. He distinguished the two from fortune and misfortune and argued that while the consequences of fate are providential and cannot be anticipated, the consequences of human actions can be coped with in terms of 'potency', with one's strength and power.[7]

In the medieval world this classical concept was completely distorted. Fate became supreme, its laws and dictates inevitable. Men could do very little about them. Fate was depicted as benign or cruel, and hence without any logic in the bestowal of its gifts. We do not mean to under-rate here the importance of some of the saints who clung to the ideal of valour 'and thought that man was capable of moulding his destiny. But such instances were rare. This view was indeed the result of the general view on the importance of life which had, as we have seen in the previous chapters, developed in this period. People began to consider life as a wail of woe in which everything was ephemeral and transient. They believed that its operations were beyond their control; it all depended on fate and time. Man should abandon this and devote himself to the cultivation of soul. We have seen that one of the consequences of this was that politics was left to rogues. But the other more important consequence was that immediate concerns of life were relegated into background. At the highest levels there was an attempt to escape from it. Upanishadic philosophy, Jainism and Buddhism, all combined to emphasise the idea that happiness cannot be attained by the pursuit of material things. It could be acquired only by rejecting them; the search of the spiritual alone would ensure joys of heaven and transcendental life. This attitude had also found expression in the Bhakti movement as well as, though in a much subdued form, in the *Ramcharitmanas*. There were such poets as Chandbardai and Bhusan, for instance, who still preached the importance of confronting life in the face but they do not find any corresponding philosophical or religious justification in the religious philosophical movements of life.

The renaissance thinkers changed this attitude towards fate and the importance of this world. They did not deny the importance of the development of soul, but shifted the emphasis in such a way as to highlight the importance of enterprise in the service of the community. They all felt that medieval religious outlook had made India weak by inculcating fatalism. These thinkers repudiated the ideal that fate determined man's life and called on men to rise to action. A striking example is provided by Vivekananda's attack on Buddhism and other forms of what he thought fatalistic religions which declared that man could not do much about his present predicament in this world. In the writings of Ram Mohan Roy, Bankim, Dayananda and Vivekananda, there is much greater optimism about the possibility of transforming life in this world itself. In fact, all of them were convinced that India was detained to be a great nation and it was up to the people to hasten the process.

On the basis of this optimistic attitude, they were able to recapture the import of the message of the *Gita* in these matters. In fact for generations the *Gita* became the Bible of all reformers and even revolutionaries. We find this tendency in both Vivekananda's lecture on *Karma* and Dayananda's *Satyartha Prakash*. Both give call to rise, awake and devote oneself to the service of the humanity in one's own distinctive way.

II

Dayananda on whom the impact of the West was the least had already formulated a positive creed of Hinduism in his book, *Satyartha Prakash* (light of truth) published in 1875. Brahmos, notably Ram Mohan and Keshab Chandra Sen,[8] had already taken up this cause in Bengal. Vedantists had argued that the world was an illusion because it was composed of both good and evil, whereas God could only be good. Against this escapist tendency, Dayananda pointed out that the world of sense-perception is real. Even if we see God, we see Him through these very eyes. In a dialogue form he tried to refute the medieval Vedantist view that the world and its objects are independent of our perception. To deny its reality according to Dayananda, is to deny reason. It is only by recognising the world as real and relating ourselves to it, Dayananda thought, that we could talk of God giving each soul its desert. Good and evil are the fruits of past actions. The attributes of God such as mercy, charity and power could have a meaning only when we think of creation as having an independent existence of its own.[9] He argued that far from being a passive creature, God is a creative agency. How can one explain the presence of evil? Dayananda replied by saying that premordial matter existed before God intervened to set in motion the cosmic process with a view to introducing good in it. Both good and evil, therefore, constitute the reality. Similarly, souls had also existed at the time of creation. They have their own separate existence and reap the fruits of their good or bad actions in different ways. He said, "God can never become the soul, nor can the soul become God. They can never be one. They are always distinct from each other."[10] The soul earns merit or demerit according to its action. The supreme spirit is the witness who rewards and punishes according to one's deeds. And, therefore man cannot escape from action by saying that both good and evil do not exist. One can attain salvation, argued Dayananda, not by running away from the world but by performing one's actions in obedience to God's will, by "dissociation from sin, ignorance, bad company, and the promotion of public good, even-handed justice and righteous action".[11] Dayananda had a missionary zeal. He vehemently argued that Vedantism had made Hindus lazy and indolent. Public spirit must take precedence over yelling for emancipation. He was conscious of appalling degradation of Hindu Society and wanted reform of marriage, food and caste customs, saying that these had no religious significance. Religion only demanded adherence to truth, concern for justice, avoidance of evil habits and practice of "love and kindness towards all, in the cultivation of gentle disposition and in the promotion of public good etc.".[12]

Dayananda has been accused of obscurantism and revivalism. His aggressive attitude in religious matters, particularly in relation to Sikhs and Christians, was unfortunately responsible for this. He certainly lacked the catholicity of Ramakrishna or Ramanamaharishi and did not properly appreciate the importance to tolerance in the life of the nation. But, outside religion, he was the prophet of change and did more than many other social reformers to bring home to people the importance of reason and science. He was quite emphatic that reason ought to govern our life. Customs which were contrary to reason or social good had no importance. The main problem for India, according to him, was to improve the health of the nation by fostering a concern for unity and indicating great awareness of better health, clean habits and a rational approach to life. It is not that he rejected caste system. But like most other reformers of the period he did two things. First, he rejected the hereditary basis of the caste system. He also identified caste with quality of the individual mind. Secondly, he assiduously worked for the upliftment of harijans and women and went to the extent of saying that widows should be allowed to remarry. All these ideas may appear ordinary to us but at the time at which he propounded them these had revolutionary implications.

He was truly a thinker of great vigour and self-assertion who cherished a hope for India. He attributed India's fall to three reasons. First, the rise of priestcraft which led to the destruction of spontaneous action, yearning for knowledge, of power and made people fatalist waiting for an *avtar* to come to help them in their distress.[13] Second, there was a loss of character. People had lost concern for public good and had become selfish, indolent and lazy. He attributed the progress of West to their high sense of public duty and energetic temperament and, of course, adherence to their own religious principles.[14] Third, people had become insular and inward looking with the result that while they did not mind having sexual intercourse with a low caste, they refused to go abroad or have contacts with foreigners. He was convinced that no country can make progress unless its people trade with foreigners. He asked, "what can you expect but misery and poverty, when the people of a country trade only among themselves, whilst the foreigners control their trade and rule over them".[15] Lastly, according to him, India's fall was also due to the fact that Indians gave up rationalism and science and indulged in escapist mysticism. He even thought Krishna and Arjun had paid a visit in an electric boat to the present day America which he identified as underworld (*Patal*). The truth of the example is not important. What is, however important is that according to him, both boat and electricity are preconditions of advancement.

Dayanand's call to go back to Vedas has often been interpreted as an example of the revivalistic character of his thought. But we tend to forget that his call was symbolic in an age in which Indians had lost confidence in themselves. He was convinced that there is a profound knowledge of the concerns of this world lying buried in the Vedas and the resurrection of that knowledge meant the resurrection of a rational, positivist spirit in which an attitude of abandonment gives place to an aggressive and restless frame of mind, the yelling for God gives place to attempts towards a new organisation of social life. It was with this end in view that he founded *Arya Samaj* which did more than any other organisation of the time to spread modern education in Northern India, through its enterprise to launch colleges, schools and other institutions of learning. Like all social reformers, Dayananda went to extremes. He exaggerated so many of his arguments both for and against different aspects of traditions, but there is no doubt that, first, he laid the foundations of a positive approach to life sanctifying itself on the basis of reason and science; second, preached the gospel of public welfare, love and charity in the service of others; third, his concept of service encompassed the whole of India. His was perhaps the first message for a united *Aryavarta* (India in modern times). This trend of course reached its apogee in Tilak. In handling the importance of *Karma* and this world, he became a typical successor to the renaissance attitude to human life.

III

Another important feature of Modern Indian thought in the early stages is that the main focus of enquiry is not the individual but society and nation or humanity as a whole. The exponents of this line of thought do no longer conceive of society as an aggregation of competing individuals in pursuit of their selfish interests. Society is seen as more or less an organic being and individuals are supposed to be integrally related to it. There is difference of opinion, of course, whether the relationship is that of parts to the whole or what as I have called elsewhere as "of wholes within wholes". There were obviously two reasons for this kind of thinking despite the fact that there was a contractual streak in the earlier thought. First, there is a strong sense of the identity of Indian society as distinguished from other societies, particularly that of the rulers. Secondly, the idea of society as composed of selfish individuals which had resulted into the development of the philosophy of *laissez-faire* was already under attack in the current European philosophical thinking. The attention had shifted from the individual to the group or the social self. The German thought had already added the additional category of the nation.

This emphasis on the community was combined with a strong historical sense. The change in society was conceived as a change in the body politic in terms of growth, development, decay and decline. Society was conceived as an organic being determined or influenced by divine forces. It was felt that change is required if India was to contribute her best to the onward march of humanity. But the thinkers were clear that only that change will be good which will lead to the development of the distinct identity of the Indian society. Institutions cannot be implanted easily. To flourish they require a particular kind of soil and climate. And, therefore, growth meant development of institutions which would lead to the growth of the social being. In fact the writers of the period were not so much concerned with society as with the process of awakening in society. In the middle ages, as we have seen, the thought about the state had been relegated into the background. Society had come to assume more prominence. It had acquired its autonomous centre which enabled it to survive despite all the changes in politics. And, therefore, thinkers of the period where conscious of the fact that politics could no longer be divorced from social development. Vivekananda epitomised the attitude of his generation when he contrasted the East and the West in terms of the preponderance of the socio-religious factors in India. Society, according to Vivekananda, was conceived to be the centre, whilst in Europe it was politics which shaped and determined the lives of the people.

The concern now shifted to a discussion of the form of government suited to India so that the government could become an instrument of the welfare of people. While in most of the medieval political thought, politics had become irrelevant for Hindus specially, now once again there was a growing awareness that not all is well with the body politic. To Raja Ram Mohan Roy's concern for liberty was added a new concern for social justice and equality. Bankim Chandra and Vivekananda became the trumpeters of what would now be called socialist ideas. While Bankim wrote essays in favour of equality (*samya*) in terms of synthesis of Hinduism with socialism[16] Vivekananda repudiated those aspects of Hinduism which justified the inegalitarian aspects of the caste system. In his famous lecture, delivered in Madras, he gave a call to the upper classes of India to serve the poor, the scheduled caste and predicted that if this was not done, these classes would rise and destroy them all.[17] In fact he interpreted caste system to imply a theory of social change in which each caste dominates particular epoch and declared that the next epoch belongs to "the lowliest and the losts", the scheduled castes particularly, as they had been the victims of injustice of other classes in society for far too long. He declared, "All knowledge is in every soul regardless of caste order, the same power is in every man." He loved Hinduism because he thought it stood for a wonderful state of equality.[18] He repeatedly emphasised on the social reformers, "you must have hold on the masses, we must reach the masses".[19] It was realised that the individual, society and politics all are interrelated facts. Justice in the state not merely signifies the maintenance of law and order but change in the law to ensure equality of opportunity to all so that each individual has opportunities to develop his capacities. A good society is one, argued Vivekananda, which, besides maintaining order, distributes rewards equitably, specially in terms of the protection of the weak. In a way it was a recrudescence of the ancient ideal of the state that it exists to protect the weak. In this sense these elements of the new thought epitomised the resurgence and furtherance of the classical tradition in terms of the imperative of the challenge of the West. It must, however, be added that while these tendencies shaped the dominant currents in thought, it does not mean that all the thoughts accepted these elements. Indeed, there were many shades and critics within each of them. Quite often it appeared that critics did not want to have anything to do with the traditions. They were fully steeped in the western traditions and wanted them to be adopted wholesale. They had the advantage of modernity behind them. Each side in the battle provided insights into the weaknesses of the other.

Modern Indian political thought can be broadly divided into two, one of these is a tradition which continues the heritage taking into account the compulsions of modern times. The chief concern of thinkers belonging to this tradition is to think of the problems of society, state and the individual in terms of the insights contained in the Indian thought as also in the light of modern conditions as well as ideas received from the West. To this is opposed a tradition of thinking which wants to evaluate traditional thinking in the light of the paradigm of the modern West; it would apply ideas received from the liberal and the Marxist traditions to Indian conditions. It must be remembered that both these traditions are not exclusive. While the first seeks to take over the best elements of liberal and Marxist traditions and integrate them with the traditions of thought in the country itself, the latter, while taking over the western notions, seek to integrate traditional notions with them. The main difference in the two traditions, however, is in their ideas on the relationship between society and political power. While the liberals accept politics as the hinge of social process, the others regard it as one of the practices entrusted with the task of regulation of social life so that it is enabled, on its own, to achieve spiritual ends.

To understand properly these two trends we must go to the ideas of Vivekananda who for a generation epitomised the best in all traditions, who was in his lifetime, to quote Aurobindo, "the leading exemplar and the most powerful exponent of the philosophy of preservation by reconstruction".[20] We have already referred to the positive content Vivekananda gave to moral life of India. Vivekananda's political ideas were the focal point of the entire Indian political thought up to World War I. His language, social perspective and political vocabulary became the point of departure in modern political thought, and a source of immense and profound inspiration to a successor like Aurobindo. He gave a new direction to the interpretation of the earlier thought, virtually never before declared with such insight, depth and vehemence since antiquity. There is a very close resemblance between his vision and that of the antiquity: for him modernization of Indian Society meant transforming it in terms of enduring principles of antiquity. While the entire middle ages were more or less hinged on the Upanishadic or the Buddhist philosophy, Vivekananda's thought researched the foundations. His positive outlook on life and society was the first complete creative interpretation of the classical philosophy which once again sought to combine the *noetic* to the *pneumatic* through a theological argument. Vivekananda's was a very bold and sensitive mind which combined modern convictions with the ancient world view which was essentially holistic in its interpretation of the relationship between man and cosmos. From his apprenticeship at the feet Ramkrishna Paramhansa, he learnt catholicity of religious outlook and a concern for the immediate issues of life. His experience of living amidst the poverty and decadence of the nineteenth century India and his contacts with the trends of thought both religious and socialist with the outside world, reinforced his search for a moral and social vision relevant to India. As well as being a sensitive mind, he was a deeply committed religious teacher and had[21] won fame in the Congress of Religions in Chicago and later through his various lectures which were deep expressions of a man's yearning for India's resurgence. There is, however, not much of political thought in his writings except on two points, first, caste; second, political power, particularly in his essay on *Modern India*. In his lectures he argues that medieval Hinduism was responsible for the decay of India in so far at it distorted ancient values and led to a negative moral vision. He was deeply moved by "the pitiful gaze of lustreless eyes of the hunger-stricken" people of India, devastated by various diseases, famines, plagues and conditions of virtual starvation. To quote him, "three hundred millions of souls such as these are swarming on the body of India, like so many worms on a rotten, stinking carcass". According to him, "the medieval religious sects had created an unfortunate tendency to find salvation through escape from worldly experience". He snubbed Indians by saying "you cannot feed your own family, or dole out food to two of your fellowmen, you cannot do even an ordinary piece of work for the common good, in harmony with others, and you are running after *Mukti* (liberation)".[22] At another place he opined that the philosophy of the world which tells us day in and day out that the life of men's is frail and transient has weighed men down, has stifled men's concern to find peace in this world, caused them to acquiesce in their poverty and degradations, and make them lick the dust and the feet of the strong.

Vivekananda's strictures against the sordid state of affairs in society were a point of far-reaching importance because he noted the connection between bad moral life, decadent society and corrupt government. He went far more ahead in his denunciation of the contemporary Hindu Society than even the liberals of his day. His scorn was directed not against people of India but against the custodians of religion and courtiers of emperors, both of whom for very different reasons, while always talking of moral values, ignored them in practice. According to him, they practised a wrong kind of religion, the religion of what he called, "the kitchen". He said, "we are neither Vedantists, most of us now; nor Puranics, nor Tantrics". We are just "don't touchists". Our religion is in kitchen. Our God is in the cooking pot, and our religion is "Don't touch me, I am holy". He declared, "If this goes on for another century, everyone of us will be in lunatic asylum."[23] Expressing contempt for this kind of religion and society, Vivekananda contends that it is in the huts of the poor and the homes of scheduled castes and the downtrodden, and not in the religious establishments or upper class homes that we must look for the potential energy in the country which is waiting to be tapped.

Vivekananda's *Modern India* developed this line of argument in terms of development of religious thought in India as a historical analysis. He thought that religion is the basis of Indian society and changes in religion have always been the source of change in all other spheres of life. He presented a total challenge to deeply held beliefs of the then establishment. It is not that he did not care for the older ideas. But he completely reinterpreted them to preach the ethics of manliness and social concern. But he still clung to the view of freedom as freedom of the self because for him God, nature, society and body are interchangable. This freedom cannot be found in projecting it outside oneself. Freedom is always within one's own self and must be discovered there.[24] But he argued that such a freedom cannot be attained by everyone. His was not an exclusivist creed believing that some are superior and others inferior and therefore only superiors can attain salvation. It is not a question of superiority or inferiority but one's nature and temperament. While for one salvation may be attained by renunciation, for others it may be found in his daily work: both lead directly to God.

The real trouble, Vivekananda thought, arises when one kind of work is praised and other is contemptuously looked down upon. The work of a butcher is no less important and, form the spiritual angle, as much a vehicle of liberation as the work of a *sanyasin*. Therefore, he was clear, there is no need to abandon the world, one can find salvation by due performance of one's own duty done here and now in the spirit of the *Gita*. He thought that the medieval religions created false hierarchies and distinctions, gave new powers to the priests and the rich, which inevitably destroyed social harmony and man's sense of concern for fellow beings. For petty advantages these sections subjected the lowest sections, specially the scheduled castes to the worst kind of slavery and degradation. Equality, which in the earlier literature meant differing capacities to realise God, finally culminated in the legitimation of the worst kind of inequality.

What, then, is the remedy? Vivekananda never fully formulated his social vision. He preached a positive morality and a programme of national regeneration in terms of, first, a conscious policy of the upliftment of scheduled castes and, second, a social reform movement to clear the Augean stables of social life. He did not say much on political reorganisation of society except two things: first, India must develop indigenous institutions and second, these institutions must be created in terms of a diffused polity and decentralised economy which, while creating strong government would also take into account the multidimensional character of modern society. He formulated the idea of social organism and thought that change in one part of social life is linked to change in other parts. He was an uncompromising advocate of a humane society in which men had a reasonably opportunity to transcend the world in search of the Beyond.

Vivekananda accepted the principle of equality. According to him, "all evil comes from relying upon differences. All good comes from faith in equality, in the underlying sameness and oneness of things." He, consequently, rejected caste system which he thought was opposed to the

Vedanta. He noticed a strong contradiction between the true Hindu religion of Vedanta and the actual Hindu social behaviour. He lashed out against "crystallised superstition" and "the priests" who had perpetuated superstition, and tyranny in society. He declared, "No religion on earth preaches the dignity of humanity in such a lofty strain as Hinduism, and no religion on earth treads upon the necks of the poor and the low in such a fashion as Hinduism." In response to this he preached socialism. He did not make distinctions between scientific socialism and utopian socialism. His socialism was derived basically from the highest kind of Vedantism which emphasises "oneness" and "sameness" in all. Some of the important points in his agenda were as follows:

(i) Socialism is inevitable because people will want satisfaction of their material needs, less work, no oppression, no war and more food.

(ii) A time will come when Shudras will "gain absolute supremacy" in every country. In this process, socialism and nihilism are the vanguard of the social revolution. This, in essence, will mean the workers' rule.

(iii) This is so because masses have been oppressed for centuries. Now is the time for their retribution.

(iv) He considered socialism better because, according to him, "half-a-loaf is better than no bread". The other systems have been tried and found wanting. He pleaded, "let this one be tried—if for nothing else, for the novelty of the thing. A redistribution of pain and pleasure is better than the same persons having pain and pleasures. Let every dog have his day in this miserable world." He argued that the new world will spring from the grocer's shop, from beside the oven of the fretter-seller, from the factories and marts and markets.

(v) He pleaded for redistribution of wealth, elimination of exploitation based on status and privilege and equality of opportunity, assurance of the dignity of human personality, rule of the masses and socialism with a human face.

Vivekananda, however, did not give much importance to politics because he always thought that the backbone of India's national life was 'spiritual genius'. He despised both the power and the acquisitive instincts which had clearly led to the development of imperialism and commercialism in the West. He said, "Look at the Western and other nations, which are now almost borne down, half-killed, and degraded by political ambitions."[25]

According to him religion was "the one consideration in India," while "politics, power, and even intellect form a secondary consideration here".[26] Indeed he characterised parliaments as "jokes"[27] and party politics as general fanaticism and sectarianism.[28] He recognized the importance of social institutions, but in the ultimate analysis, he argued, that all good systems rest upon the goodness of men. He declared, "No nation is great or good because parliament enacts this or that, but because its men are great and good." Again, "men cannot be made virtuous by an Act of Parliament (...) and that is why religion is of deeper importance than politics, since, it goes to the root, deals with the essentials of conduct".[29] When the state tries to control actions of men through "rigid laws and threats of punishment to follow that path with unconditional obedience the destiny of mankind becomes no better than that of a machine".[30]

Vivekananda thought that the Indian history was a clear vindication of this. Through history the spiritual tradition had claimed freedom from legal oppression. "The very word sanyasin," he declared, "means the divine outlaw"[31] and since "it is freedom alone that is desirable...it is not law that we want but ability to break law. We want to be outlaws." He said, "If you are bound by laws, you will be a lump of clay."[32] He concluded, "our aim should be to allow the individual to move towards this freedom. More of goodness, less of artifical law."[33] This stand on the relationship between spiritual realm and political realm foreshadowed Aurobindo and Gandhi on the same theme. "Vivekananda's indispensable role", writes Dennis Dalton, "in the conceptualisation of politics and power in modern India, was to establish with extraordinary precision the central assumption and lines of argument."[34]

This brief evaluation of Vivekananda's thought does not do full justice to the multi-sided character of his thought. What is significant is that he resurrected the ancient connection between philosophy and theology, between this world and the other, in order to bring home to us a more holistic view of life than was the case in medieval thought. In practical terms he launched a frontal assault on corruption in society and in this sense became the true harbinger of modern India. However, there is not much of political philosophy, more of emotions and rhetorical flourish, perhaps demanded by the practical concerns of his own time. He truly highlighted the importance of social change but did not properly appreciate the importance which the ancients put on the role of politics in society. Like the medieval thinkers, Vivekananda still continued the myth that politics was not of much importance to society. He did not realise what the ancients had said that it is the supreme activity. Indeed in so far as it distributes the material goods in society and maintains law and order, it is the condition of all other activities. While he was quite emphatic in his defence of the rights of the scheduled castes, he did not realise that no other organisation in society, except the state, is powerful enough to challenge the balance of social forces in their favour. That is why his importance decreased as India moved towards political issues of constitution making and distributive justice. On a more general level, however, Vivekananda's penetrating insight into society and religion, appreciation of its structures and the importance of classical vision of moral life, proved such a valuable point of departure in the development if Indian thought that all thinkers, whether conservative or radical, could learn a great deal from him. His impatience with the decadence of society gave way later to more radical thought which combined his moral concerns with economic insights derived from Marx.

IV

A brief note should be taken here of Bankim's essay on equality. Bankim was a great nationalist. But what is remarkable is that at that early stage in the life of the freedom movement, he tried to connect the regeneration of the nation with the principle of equality. Bankim had profound admiration of Hinduism and its capacity to adapt itself to changing conditions. In his essay on "*Samya*"[35] he regarded it as the best religion. But he was also aware of the rot which had set in the society. He, therefore, made a fervent plead to reorganize civil society in India by reorganizing Hindu religion. He firmly believed that both religion and society are inseparable, the one cannot exist without the other for both are inseparable part of the process which enables us to transcend this world in search of liberation. He preferred Hinduism because he thought that it had the potential in terms of which all-round progress of people could be secured. He, however, preferred any religion to agnosticism.

He accepted the basic structure of the Hindu society but pointed out that some of its features had become redundant in the face of the movement of the contemporary society towards rule of law and equality. He pointed out both the strong and the weak points of Hinduism. The strongest point of Hinduism is that it is based on the recognition of diversity in human life and, as a result, views different individuals in terms of their own peculiar temperament. He made a subtle distinction between *Varna* and caste. *Varna* recognises diversity whereas caste stultifies society. The latter is against the principle of equality and must be given up.

Varna is a different matter. It is a mechanism to cope with natural differences in men. Since difference cannot be wished away, a system must be devised to integrate society. The caste had given importance to unnatural difference by incorporating heredity and tradition. The difference between a *Brahman* and a *Sudra*, between the rich and the poor is of this kind.

According to Bankim, equality does not mean equality of circumstances but equality in terms of equal rights—or, to be precise, equality of opportunity. The essence of this is acknowledgement of diversity which in human life leads to differentiation in society. But not all kinds of diversity occupy the same importance. The only diversity to be recognised is the diversity of circumstances. He rejects the importance of both, family and caste. The diversity of circumstances is justified not only because it is natural but because it also is the basis of human progress. He, therefore, quotes Aristotle to define equality as "the same treatment to similar persons".

By a subtle principle of substitution he wedded this principle of equality of circumstances to *Varna* system. He argued that while some are required for production in society, others for pursuit of knowledge. The conditions required for the pursuit of knowledge would naturally be different from the circumstances required for production. Following Aristotle he regarded "leisure" as essential for those who are devoted to the pursuit of knowledge. However, he did not accept hereditary basis. He was conscious of the monopolistic tendency in all walks of life, in education, bureaucracy, politics and economy. He was also conscious of the division between the rich and the poor and opposed the exploitation by both *Brahmanas* and capitalists. Both of them pursue their selfish interest at the expense of society. As a result of lack of education and privilege the rich become richer and the poor poorer, the strong stronger and the weak weaker. The caste division makes for exploitation.

Bankim's essay on "*Samya*" is interesting for both what it includes and what it excludes. In the late nineteenth century, it was a remarkable achievement for an Indian thinker to plead for a synthesis of Hinduism and Marxism. He revolted against the degeneration which had set in the caste system and was certainly far ahead of his times when he emphasised the distinction between *Varna* and caste. In that sense, he becomes a precursor of many other social reformers. Even Gandhi did not move beyond the position taken by Bankim. Indeed while Gandhi wavered between accepting the hereditary basis of caste and functional basis of *Varna*, Bankim definitely rejected the first. But Bankim did not sufficiently realise that the

Indian society required a surgical operation, almost a total revolution in relation to caste. While he criticised the inequalities of caste, he did sufficiently appreciate the inequalities as a result of land and capital—the class dimension of the problem. He was also not sure of the role which the state could play in such a system. He pinned his hopes in a Messiah—Buddha or a Jesus, who would come and purge the society of this evil. Even so, he was far ahead of his time. The very fact that he gave the title "*Samya*" to the essay was no mean achievement. Very soon, under pressure perhaps, he was led to deny the importance of the essay—may be because he didn't want the controversy over equality to divide the nationalist movement.

Bankim's essay was remarkable in three other respects also. First, it was a distillation of many cultures because he tried to combine ideas from Christianity to communism. His remarks about Christianity, Vedas, Rousseau and Marx were full of insights. But what is more important is that he tried to connect all this with Indian ideas. For instance, he wrote of Christ as follows:

The world has heard twice in its history two utterances which contain the essence of ethics and beyond which no ethics can reach. Once an Aryan *Brahmana* uttered on the banks of the Ganges: "He is learned who treats whatever or whoever exists as his own self." Once again, standing on the peak in Jerusalem, Jesus of Judea explained: "Do as you wish others to do unto you."

Similarly, he connected Rousseau to Marx and wrote:

The seed of the big tree that Rousseau had sown by saying that land belongs to the people began to bear new fruits. Communism is the fruit of this tree, so is the International.

Indeed, he tried to explain the poverty of the Bengal peasant in terms of 'profits' and 'wages', and even used the doctrine of 'surplus value'. He also used terms like *Smajik Dhana Sanchaya* (social accumulation of wealth) and *Adim Dhana Sanchaya* (primitive accumulation of wealth). Although he used the concept of class conflict, he did not think of permanent conflict between the landlord and the tenant. In this, to quote Ganguly, "... his spirit of synthesis ultimately asserts itself. He distinguishes between good and bad landlords, between good and bad tenants. His anxiety is that appropriate social conditions can be created under which conflict can be resolved in a spirit of fairness and accommodation."[36]

Second, he modified the European doctrine of "equality of opportunity" by adding "right to achieve excellence" to it. This flowed directly from his recognition of diversity in human life. Each has a special *svabhava* (temperament) and consequently, each is entitled to a different *anusheelana* or cultivation of excellence in consonance with his *svabhava*. That is why he made a distinction between caste and *varna* and tended to justify the latter at least at theoretical levels.

Third, as Ganguly has pointed out, "Bankim . . . fully understood that without the basis of real fraternity, liberty and equality would be a mirage."[37] He wedded the doctrine of equality to development of integrated personality in which different parts of one's nature—physical, moral and spiritual—converge in the achievement of a common purpose. He admired French revolution which aimed at the achievement of permanent welfare of humanity. But he also was aware of the limitations of this revolution although it tried to achieve liberty and equality, both ultimately eluded it, because the importance of fraternity was not sufficiently realized. He contrasted this with the teachings of Buddha and Christ in which, according to him, "equality" and "fraternity" were "elements harmoniously blended in a spiritual crucible".[38]

V

The persons who typified some of these ideas in practical politics were Ranade, Gokhale and Tilak. The first two belonged to the moderate group and Tilak to the extremist. Tilak rejected the moderate approach of Ranade and Gokhale. The moderates had accepted English liberalism as the basis of their creed and did not try to develop a political theory of their own. They did not differ sharply from the exponents of the British liberalism, except that people like Ranade were prepared to welcome greater state intervention to set things right in society. They had indeed argued that in order to remove poverty and squalor and lift society out of the morass of age-old customs, the state must interfere actively and creatively in social and economic life. They wanted the state to assist in the process of industrial development also. It is, however, not clear whether their plea owed inspiration to the activities of Peter the Great or Bismarck or to the writings of liberals in England. While the first showed a mixture of paternalistic concern for the lower classes coupled with centralised, aristocratic state structure, the latter were more concerned with the rights of man coupled with democratic structures. Be that as it may, Ranade favoured the idea that the state must redistribute wealth in society to ensure equality of opportunity and full employment to all. There were other more mundane reasons too for his support of the state intervention in economic matters. For instance, he realised that since the Indian industry could not flourish in competition with foreign industry in a free market, there was need for protectionist policies. He, however, did not fully accept the principle of 'self-interest' as the basis of politics[39] and, to that extent, remained tied to the Indian heritage. He wrote, "self-interest in the shape of the desire for wealth is not absent (in India), but it is not the principal motive. The pursuit of wealth is not the ideal aimed at. There is neither the desire nor the aptitude for free and unlimited competition except in certain pre-determined groups."[40]

We shall not go into the merits or demerits of this approach in relation to the political developments in India in the late nineteenth and early twentieth centuries. Some of these people spoke of the British rule as a divine dispensation ignoring the destitution and fragmentation of social life which it had let to.[41] Nor are we concerned here with the assault of extremists on their way of thinking, who, while accepting the importance of the liberal values of freedom and equality, had rejected a society based on principles of market rationality and unbridled economic competition. Tilak was one such man. His ideas were more in the nature of assertions rather than philosophical discourse, appealing more to emotions than to reason. He was not inclined to analyse political principles but to proclaim a plan of action. For him thought or intellect devoid of action (*karma*) was meaningless. He had proclaimed the supreme importance of action in his most original interpretation of the *Bhagwat Gita* entitled *Gita Rahasya*. Throughout his life he worked, organised and suffered. His life was cast in the mould of a "hero" and conveys his convictions in a way more powerful than his own words. He organized extremists, invented new forms of solidarity and protest in Shivaji and Ganesha Festivals and opposed imperialism both in form and spirit.

The central point of his political philosophy was the doctrine of self-rule (*Swaraj*). He rejected the moderate plane of a gradual introduction of democratic institutions in India and instead argued that "*Swaraj* is my birth right and I shall have it." His belief in *Swaraj* was derived from *advaita* which had taught him that moral autonomy is the very life of the individual soul which, to quote him, "Vedanta declares to be not separate from God but identical with Him."[42] According to him, this ideal of *Swaraj* applies both to the nation as well as to the individual. For the individual, the *Swaraj* meant the attainment of self-control which is essential for performing "one's duty" (*Swadharma*). It formed the very basis of the ancient Indian scheme of the triple concepts, autonomy, relations and functions in terms of which social life ought to be organised. For a nation "it (*swaraj*) means a government which rules according to the wishes of the people or their representatives."[43] Tilak wrote: "The British people select the executive through the elected representatives of the people, decide on policies and impose and remove taxes and determine the allocation of public expenditure.

Similarly Indians should have the right to run their own government, to make laws, to appoint the administrators as well as to spend the tax revenue."[44]

Tilak was clear that if the government does not feel any concern for public welfare in enacting and enforcing all sorts of laws, people should resist such a government. He juxtaposed the right of the people to resist wrongful authority (*Prajadroha*) with the government's tendency to prevent exercise of such a right by enacting seditious-acts and argued that there ought to be mutuality in the rights and obligations of citizens and the rulers. If the rulers failed to fulfil their obligations towards the people and became tyrannical, they forfeit their right to rule. It is interesting that Tilak made use of the concept of revolt against the people by the king as against the medieval concept of the revolt against the king (*Prajadroha*) by the people. He clearly emphasised the fact that sovereignty resides in the people and not in the king. He rejected the constitutional and legal methods of the moderates for fighting the British and emphasised the need for "peaceful and legitimate methods"—a phrase which was later on taken over by Gandhi. Tilak was convinced that without freedom we can not be creative. However, he always made a distinction between the King Emperor and the British bureaucracy because he feared that at the early stages, when the idea of freedom had not sufficiently captured the imagination of masses, and the Congress organization was not sufficiently strong, the freedom movement would not be able to withstand the onslaught of the British imperialism if the supporters of the movement talked of complete independence. He declared, "As an ideal, independence is alright but you cannot work for it without bringing yourself within the clutches of law."

Freedom movement had to be a movement of the whole society. Tilak argued that *Swaraj* could not be brought about without *Swadeshi*, boycott and national education. Indians must dedicate themselves to the spirit of Indianism, boycott foreign goods, encourage local products and educate themselves to foster national consciousness by which alone India could realize its own characteristic identity. While Ranade had welcomed reforms initiated though the legislature, Tilak held that reforms to be lasting should be a growth from within, that hasty measures as a result of the intervention by the British bureaucracy would only retard the cause of reform as it would encourage a mere imitation of the Western life. According to him, alien bureaucrats had no right to shape India's moral and mental equipment. He particularly lashed out against English education. It encouraged production of a class of well trained obedient and loyal clerks, but discouraged development of manliness and patriotism. Tilak was a leader whose feet were firmly planted in the soil. Thus he favoured foreign travel but was for vegetarianism. He approved marriage of child widows but equally stressed the importance of Vedic rites. He wanted female education but only if it was useful. For all practical purposes, his ideal of a social reformer was that of a Kabir or a Tukaram. He insisted that no one had any right to bring about social reforms[46] unless he lived the Indian civilization and culture in thought and practice. Reform is necessary but it must be brought about with due respect for the traditions of the society itself. The reformer must be a "stalwart Puritan man, battling for the right, trustful but not elated, serious but not dejected". He, therefore, challenged the right of an alien bureaucracy to sit in legislative judgement on the Indian society. On 1 November 1890, he declared, "We must not only see what reforms are required, but also whether and how far they are practicable and how can they be made popular for reforming society, care ought to be taken to avoid the creation of any gulf between the people on the one hand and the reformers on the other. We must always carry public opinion with us."

Thus, while Ranade was prepared to separate the need for political freedom from social reform for Tilak there was no such separation; while Ranade was prepared to use for propagation of social reform the disintegrating forces that had come in the wake of the British rule, Tilak, although wanting social reforms, believed in checking further disintegration by fostering due sense of pride for the inherited social institutions. Ranade depended much on Western education and influence, whilst Tilak wanted to synthesise the old and the new. The former accepted the state as an agent of social change, the latter rejected it on the ground that the reform to be enduring must grow from within: unless people are sufficiently prepared for due assimilation it is useless to march ahead. It was largely under Tilak's influence that "self-reliance, not mendicancy" became the watchword of the extremists. People refused to be cowed down. In social sphere, they refused to allow alien bureaucracy to sit in judgement on them. In economic sphere, the spirit of *Swadeshi* dealt a severe blow to free trade theories. People began to realize how England had strangled Indian industries. Since there was no protective tariff in the interest of Indian manufacturers, they began to boycott foreign goods.

Tilak was not merely a leader but also a movement. In political ideas he was a thorough nationalist. He appears to be a liberal in his belief in the power of education, *Swaraj* and in so many of his other ideas. He had acknowledged that democracy was important and freedom of opinion valuable. He also wanted social reform. Yet he had a vision of political independence which he thought was above everything else. He thought that such independence could only be founded on a system of *Swadeshi* and national education. For him freedom was not merely independence from the British rule but a capacity to develop India in terms of its own peculiar heritage. However, his ideas on the organic nature of society or about the role of symbols in politics were not strictly liberal. There was an uneasy tension between his ancient heritage and his indebtedness to the West. The result was that at times he made exaggerated claims for India and the Indian nationalism.

He was for the India nation because he believed that India had a unique personality of her own which could be distinguished from others. He believed that the people inhabiting this part of the globe had certain common characteristics which other members of the human group did not share. These people could realise their identity only by becoming independent of the control of others. Nationalists often turn chauvinists. But for Tilak nationalism and peace went together. He was clear in his mind that India was self-contained, harboured no design against the integrity of other states and had no ambition outside its geographical boundaries. For him the two—namely nationalism and the Vedantic ideal of human unity were two sides of the same coin. The second included the first. He declared:

The two ideals are mutually consistent and both of them demand a kind of self-control..., a kind of higher altruistic feeling by which man is impelled to ignore self-consideration and to work for persons and for objects which do not in the least favour any egotistic aim. The feeling is one of love for humanity, for the equality of man before God, and it is the spirit of that feeling that governs the two ideals, Vedantic and national.[47]

He thought that once India became free she would play a powerful role in the maintenance of peace in the Far East. Tilak, however, did not connect his ideas on nationalism and freedom to any ontological view of the order of being on the one hand and any scheme of political institutions to actualize those ideals, on the other. It is because of these limitations that his importance as a political thinker is not much.

NOTES

1. S.N. Mukherjee, ed., *Elite in South Asia* (London, Cambridge University Press, 1970), p. 30.
2. Quoted by R. Iyer, "The Political Theory of British Imperialism in India",

South Asia Affairs, No. 1 (London, Chattos and Windus, 1960), p. 14.

3. S.N. Mukherjee, op. cit., pp. 60-61.

4. Raghvan Iyer, op. cit., pp. 61-62.

5. Vivekananda, *Caste, Culture and Socialism* (Almora, Advaita Ashram), pp. 49-50.

6. Sri Aurobindo, *The Renaissance of India* (Pondicherry, Aurobindo Ashram, 4th ed. 1951), pp. 39-40.

7. Kautilya, *The Arthasastra,* trans. Shyamsastri (Mysore, Mysore Publishing House, 7th ed. 1961), pp. 312-14.

8. Raja Ram Mohan Roy is often considered a political thinker. In our view, he is entitled to a place as a great social reformer, it is doubtful whether he could be called a thinker. All his ideas are initiation of their counterpart in the insest. Besides, there is no attempt to relate conclusion to theoretical premises with the result that they almost form an incoherent whole.

9. Dayananda, *Light of Truth (Styartha Prakash),* trans. Chiranjiva Bhardwaj (2nd ed. 1915, Allahabad), p. 250.

10. Ibid., pp. 249-50.

11. Ibid., p. 270.

12. Ibid., p. 317.

13. Ibid., p. 318.

14. de Bary, ed., *Sources of Indian Tradition* (London, Oxford University Press, 1958), pp. 634-35.

15. Dayananda, op. cit., p. 317.

16. See B.N. Ganguly, *Concept of Equality* (Simla, IIAS, 1975).

17. Vivekananda, *Complete Works* (Calcutta, Advaita Ashram, 1991), V, p. 105.

18. Ibid., III, pp. 108-9.

19. Ibid., V, pp. 36, 114.

20. Sri Aurobindo, *The Renaissance on India,* op. cit., pp. 39-40.

21. Vivekananda, *The East and the West* (Almora, Advaita Ashram, 4th ed. 1949), pp. 1-2.

22. Ibid., p. 9.

23. Vivekananda, *India and Her Problems* (Calcutta, Advaita Ashram, 1967), p. 23.

24. Vivekananda, *Complete Works,* op. cit., II, p. 128.

25. Ibid., III (1960), p. 148.

26. Ibid., p. 204.

27. Ibid., p. 158.

28. Ibid., VI, p. 8.

29. Ibid., V, p. 200.

30. Ibid., IV, p. 435.

31. Ibid., V, p. 193.

32. Ibid., p. 289.

33. Ibid., VI, p. 100.
34. For a brilliant exposition of this theme, see Dennis Dalton, "The Concept of Politics and Power in India's Ideological Tradition", p. 197.
35. See B.N. Ganguly, op. cit.
36. (Simla, IIAS, 1975) op. cit., p. 89.
37. Ibid., p. 106.
38. Loc. cit.
39. See V.R. Mehta, *Beyond Marxism: Towards an Alternative Perspective* (New Delhi: Manohar, 1978), pp. 5-8, *Ideology, Modernization and Politics in India* (New Delhi, Manohar, 1983), pp. 19-49.
40. M.G. Ranade, "The Indian Political Economy", *Essays in Indian Economics* (Bombay, Popular, 1982), pp. 1-12.
41. V.R. Mehta, *Ideology*, etc., op. cit., pp. 24-26.
42. Tilak, *Speeches and Writings* (Madras, G.A. Nateson and Company), p. 254.
43. Nalini Pandit, "Tilak and Indian Nationalism", in N.R. Inamdar (ed.), *Political Thought and Leadership of Lokmanya Tilak* (New Delhi, Concept, 1983), p. 21.
44. Loc. cit.
45. Shanta A. Sathe, "Tilak's Connotation of the Concept of *Swaraj*" in Inamdar, op. cit., pp. 41-42. Also see Shay Theodre, L., *Legacy of Lokamanya Political Philosophy of Bal Gangadhar Tilak* (London, Oxford University Press, 1966).
46. See P.J. Jagirdar, "Tilak and Ranade" in Inamdar, op. cit., p. 239.
47. Quoted by V.P. Varma, "Tilak's Spiritual Nationalism", Inamdar, op. cit., p. 14.

CHAPTER 9

THE INTEGRAL VISION:
SRI AUROBINDO AND SAHU

The ideas which sought to define a separate identity of India began with
the war of independence, received a fresh impetus in the thought and
writings of people like Dayananda and Vivekananda. The ideas received
a further fillip by the nationalist upsurge in Italy, Germany and Japan. The
realization that the British power was far removed from the aspirations of
the people also set in a reaction against it and gave rise to 'romanticism'
and 'organicism' of the ideas of Bankim Chandra, Vivekananda and Bipin
Chandra Pal. The researches of Tilak and literary writings of Bankim
Chandra inspired people to the nationalist ideology. The political thought
of Aurobindo was the culmination of the process. His philosophy was a
synthesis of different strands in modern thought. In those times, politics
occupied an important place but it was still secondary to the metaphysical
questions on the one hand and those of national liberation on the other. In
general terms the chief problem before Aurobindo was, how to solve the
apparent antithesis between the order of nature as revealed by scientific
researches and the aesthetical, ethical and spiritual conception of man and
the society implicit in the ascent of man. In a half-century before Aurobindo
embarked upon his philosophical voyage, three important attempts to
resolve this were made. Hegel had shown the synthetic character of reality
in which reason and experience constitute two sides of the same coin.
Schopenhauer and Nietzsche and the entire vitalistic tradition of Bergson
has advanced the perspectival view based on the recognition of insight and
intuition against the pure rationalism of the enlightenment, which regarded
moral development as expression of an active, vitalistic impulse of man.
And at home, Vivekananda had lent credence to the ancient philosophical
and religious system by emphasising the attitude of life-affirmation
finding its expression in concrete social activity. These were the three
different strands of thought which provided a clue to Aurobindo's search

for an alternative to the liberal rationalistic creed of English utilitarians which he disliked. Aurobindo achieved a remarkable synthesis of all these trends. Reason was important but only in terms of a powerful synthetic enterprise whose ultimate aim would be the spiritual emancipation of mankind. What he planned to offer was reason as an extension or as a vehicle of intuition and integral vision. He tried to transcend the antithesis between the traditions of Hegel and Bergson, by developing an integral view of life. The chief merit of this new view, according to him, consisted in its ability to explain the many sidedness of one single central reality in terms of logical connection between intuition, reason and experience. The integral view of life hinges on the concept of 'integral reason' which transcends the one-sidedness of rationalism of Hegel, and provides direction to the vitalistic tradition of Bergson, in terms of aims and aspirations of the ancients. In the light of this, he sought to provide a new perspective in the understanding of the problems of life and politics.

Besides this, it must be emphasised that the framework of Aurobindo's thinking was not exclusively determined by mere abstract ideas. Vivekananda was already a watershed between the old and the new in India. His synthetic approach, as well as patriotism in the colonial situation in which India was placed, and overriding concern for the upliftment of India, had already induced a new ferment of ideas. He had brought into focus the value of national culture, traditions and heritage. The British rule and the arrival of modern scientific rationalism had in their own ways posed a serious challenge to the *Waltanchuung* of the nineteenth century Hindus. The reconciliation of two cultures—oriental and occidental posed a serious challenge, one which could Vivekananda had argued, be solved neither in terms of complete acceptance of western rationalism nor medieval Hindu transcendentalism. In fact, western ideas were felt to be either irrelevant or destructive of the social sense of solidarity in India. They were felt to be inapplicable to the situation of the Indian society. The same was equally true of the medieval yelling for God. To a great extent this was the estimate in which Aurobindo came to regard the two legacies. He thought that national reconstruction could start only from within the historical process taking place in India, that it would imply re affirming the finer and enduring elements of national heritage in their contemporary setting. It must be borne in mind that at the time Aurobindo was systematizing his ideas, this impulse was certainly not reactionary or conservative: it was, in a certain way, subversive, in so far as it endeavoured to demolish the whole medieval heritage in terms of rational and integral reasoning. It aimed at complete reconstruction of the Indian society. His integral philosophy in terms of ideals such as creative revolution or human unity purported to become a symbol of revolution and change. It acknowledged the basic impulse of change, the need for destruction of outdated institutions and emphasised the need to identify and harness the creative and life giving aspects of the national tradition. It is true that he subordinated philosophy to religion but in his vision both science and religion occupied an important place as two sectors of the ongoing human experience, and both were necessary requirements of the development of human society to higher and higher levels of existence, in which old institutions and ways of life continually gave place to better ones. He displayed a Faustian endeavour to synthesise human knowledge, specially the antithesis between science and religion. While his political ideas attached supreme importance to the ideal of the nation-state, these also tried to bring it in line with the grand ideal of human unity by arguing that nation-states are necessary stages in our development towards human unity. His political philosophy, thus, was neither conservative in the sense of blind adherence to the past nor revolutionary in the sense of total rupture with it; it was, in a sense, their philosophical synthesis. It may be added here that in a way there was a sharp distinction between the concerns of his early life to which most of his political writings belonged and the latter life when he had turned into a mystic and retired to Pondicherry.

Aurobindo was a radical in his youth and his political writings, starting with the famous article "New Lamps for Old" written in 1893, remain an ample testimony to that. Deeply imbued with the ancient Indian heritage, he bitterly attacked the moderate policies of the Indian liberals, not only their policy of mendicancy but also their emphasis on individualism, materialism and liberal demcracy. In close association with Bipin Chandra Pal and Tilak he provided remarkable leadership to the agitation against the partition of Bengal in 1905, and wished for the ideal of complete swaraj as a necessary condition of India's development. He thought that without swaraj India would not be able to contribute its own to the onward march of mankind. In his articles he veered to extremism which led to the Government laying a charge of sedition at his doors. It was the irony of the situation that the judge who tried the case, Mr Beachcroft, was his class fellow and had stood second to him at Cambridge. C.R. Das came forward in his defence and paid a glowing tribute to him. He said, "My appeal to you is this, that long after this turmoil and agitation will have ceased, long after he is dead and gone, he will be looked upon as the poet of patriotism, as the prophet of nationalism and the saviour of humanity. Long after he is dead and gone, his words will be echoed and re-echoed, not only in India, but across distant seas and countries. Therefore, I say that the man in his position is not standing before the bar of this court, but before the bar of the High Court of History."[1]

His main aim as a political philosopher appears to have been to lay bare the fundamental principles of the individual community life as revealed in Indian nationalism, which he thought was a necessary stage to a realisation of human unity. He sought to formulate stages of development and expansion of human soul through higher and higher groupings through which alone, he thought, its aspirations could be realised. Of his grand religio-philosophical system, which closely resembles Vedantic philosophy, two points must be noted. First, in spite of his adulation of nationalism, he still regarded the freedom of the spirit, as revealed in man's aesthetic, ethical and spiritual quests, as higher; the nation, however, is essential because different people are entitled to achieve freedoms in their own diverse fashions. In this sense Sri Aurobindo's thought is closer to the ancients than to the modern political thought which has given up the religious dimension of the soul. Secondly, Aurobindo sees history as a movement which is unfolding potentialities of different cultures. He was an avid reader of Kant, Schelling and Herder, and was particularly impressed by the exponents of the theory of evolution as that of Lamarch. This history of civilisation for him is the history of a series of national cultures, sometimes succeeding one another, at other times existing side by side, each bringing to light one particular aspect of the cosmic reality. His whole purpose was to demonstrate that in years to come it was in political freedom that the soul of the Indian nation which had hitherto remained at cultural level only, was to find its medium of expression so that it could make its timely contribution to achievements of mankind. Both these points were embodied in his political thought.

In the following discussion of his political philosophy, we shall mainly confine ourselves to his two important books—*The Human Cycle* and *The Ideal of Human Unity*—in order to highlight some of the salient features of his thought. It is not to say that these works can be separated from either his early nationalistic essays or the later metaphysical writings such as the *Life Divine*. But while the former works belong to the history of rise and development of nationalism in India, the latter to the philosophy in general. Although *Life Divine* is extremely important, a discussion of it would take us far away from our central concern, i.e. political philosophy. Both the political works mentioned here are written in a grand style and form by themselves, one complete philosophical statement, fully discussing the individual community relationship, the concept of the state and the historical process.

Aurobindo's starting point is the notion of a divine play of vacant forms in the impersonal universality of the "Absolute Brahman".[2] The historical process is a manifestation of the spirit in diverse ways. In this process, the individual has a limited role. Man may help or resist the divine plan, but "the *Zeitgeist* works, shapes, overbears, and insists".[3] He approvingly quotes *Gita*, "I am Time who wastes and destroys the people. Lo, I have arisen in my might, I am here to swallow up the nations. Even without thee all they shall not be, the men of war who stand arrayed in opposite squadrons. Therefore, do thou arise and get thee glory." He regards the entire process as a *lila* of God in which there are terrible and soft movements, oscillations between discord and harmony ultimately leading to great harmonising movements, of the world seeking to transform suffering and sin, by making men identify themselves with the permanent behind the ever changing. There is felicity or happiness only when we know and internalise the truth and know ourselves as *Sat chit ananda.* According to him, God, history, society and man are integrally related to one another. While God sets things in motion and remains as a permanent principle behind all changes and differentiations, the individual becomes the vehicle to carry further the tendencies which have been set in and which manifest differently in different societies in the light of the principle 'one in many and many in one'. This individual has a dual character. On the one hand, he is integrally related to the community of which he is a member and, on the other, he has the capacity in him to transcend the differentiated reality as revealed in community relationship and to seek identification with the Divine. The real problem of society, according to Aurobindo, therefore, is to so organise it that while social process goes on, and the individual is able to realise his purpose and aspirations which befit a divine creature. The subject matter of the *Human Cycle*, as is evident from the title itself is the cosmic process, in the rich differentiated totality of its civilisational forms, institution and ways of life. It is this process which is explained and its message for the individual community relationship is brought into bold relief.

II

The emphasis on intuition has often resulted into cult of folk or the people or the nation. In the case of Sri Aurobindo it resulted largely as a product of his studies of various cultures—the Hellenic, the Roman, the Chinese and the Indian in the idealisation of the nation. He is perhaps with Herder to whom each civilization is a progressive revelation of different aspects of the cosmic reality. Herder had believed that the supreme spirit manifests itself in diverse ways in history, in order to realise itself as freedom and bliss, an idea which he derived from his study of Vedanta. From Herder also he learnt that this reality embodies itself in different forms in different situations. All these forms are born in time and consequently are always in a state of evolution which proceeds according to the divine plan. Aurobindo's imagination had been inspired by the Indian renaissance which took place towards the end of the nineteenth century. He was convinced that the Greek civilisation was a result of craving for beauty, the Roman of craving for ethical and the Indian civilisation unfolded before the world the majesty of the spiritual. In his scheme of things the achievement of the modern scientific Western civilisation was very little as compared with those of the Greek or the Indian, and yet he thought that it has brought to man a mastery of the material world in terms of reason quite unknown to previous ages. In terms of Indian history he came to see that the buoyant affirmation of the life was as much a part of the Vedic culture as of other cultures in the ancient world, and that the attitude of life negation personified in Christianity or Buddhism was correlative with inert, narrow, inelastic forms and was a precursor of the medieval view that life is an illusion.

This reflection on early civilisation brought into bold relief the idea that in an integral view, the life with the developments in different fields must be viewed as a whole and simultaneously; the aesthetic view is necessary for the perception of beauty, the ethical for providing discipline and the spiritual for transcending the limited. It stresses that different aspects or aggregates are interrelated, as if they were parts of a whole, or more appropriately, wholes within wholes. He was convinced that each aggregate has a special mission and its history is the record of the way in which the potentiality of this mission unfolds itself and brings its unique contribution to bear on the human race.

Aurobindo held that the aim of each nation is to seek its own fulfilment, to become aware of potentiality within and to realise it as perfectly as possible. He believed that a nation like an individual has a body, an organic life, "an aesthetic temperament, a developing mind and a soul behind all these signs and powers for the sake of which they exist". He is, of course, aware of the difference between the individual soul and the group soul. The latter, according to him, is far more complex because it is composed of partly self conscious mental individuals. But according to him, when the national soul first expresses itself in the land, we begin to realise that it is people who constitute the nation. At times this soul lies dormant. But when it surfaces it begins to find expression in different individuals. The movement of Bengal in 1905 was some such event when the Bengali nationalism found its spiritual and psychological unity. When Germany became conscious it found its expression in philosophers like Kant and Hegel, in great composers like Beethoven and Wagner. He was aware of the fact that it is not always that a nation comes to identify itself with right causes. He believed that Nazism was based on the cultivation of the lower side of the soul, path full of perils, but was convinced that the misuse of great powers is no argument against not working for their right use.

Aurobindo looked forward to the emergence of India as a great nation because he believed that this was the only way in which India could bring its timely contribution towards the spiritual development of mankind and therefore he was acutely aware of the need of awakening the soul of India. He lashed out against the imitative character of the Indian nation and argued that though such imitation might have temporary success, it would ultimately lead to self-sterilization and even death of the nation.[5] The nations of ancient Europe, according to him, perished when they gave up their own individuality as the price of peace. It is only when a nation becomes conscious of its individuality and tries to make it perfect that it wakes up, captures its *clan vital*, lives and has its being. Writing in 1909, under youthful enthusiasm he said:

The nineteenth century in India was imitative, self-forgetful, artificial. It aimed at a successful reproduction of Europe in India, forgetting the deep saying of *Gita*, "Better the law of one's own being though it be badly done than an alien *dharma* well followed; death in one's own *dharma* is better, it is a dangerous thing to follow the law of another's nature." For death in one's own *dharma* brings new birth, success in an alien path means only successful suicide.[6]

He was convinced that India was struggling for self preservation against the onslaught of foreign ideas, and it was not until the balance between the two elements turned in favour of national Dharma, that the salvation of India was assured—a process which had been started by Vivekananda. It was an appeal, not to take India on the road to European path but on a path which would ensure a greater and more perfect realisation of the Indian spirit. But he was not pleading for the blind acceptance of the past either and argued that India must be on its guard against any tendency to cling to every detail that has been India. According to him, in life there are three elements: the fixed and permanent spirit, the developing soul and the brittle changeable body. While the first cannot be changed, the soul tends to develop and the body, the outward form can be meddled with:

The body must be used as a means, not over-cherished as a thing valuable for its own sake. We will sacrifice no ancient form to an unreasoning love of change, we will keep none which the national spirit deserves to replace by one that is a still better and truer expression of the undying soul of the nation.[7]

At another place he considered *yoga* as the mode of change and declared:

We believe that it is to make the *yoga* the ideal of human life that India rises today; by the *yoga*, she will get the strength to realise her freedom, unity and greatness, by *yoga* she will keep the strength to preserve it. It is a spiritual revolution we foresee and the material is only shadow or reflex.[8]

In this enterprise, the parliamentary path was only one of the methods. He accepted it in principle but rejected its form because he was convinced that India's salvation could not be achieved by enlargement of the councils alone. These things could be legitimate weapons in the political struggle. But in the ultimate analysis, according to Aurobindo, India is destined to work out her own independent life. He was convinced that the peculiar identity of India had to be built up for the sake of humanity. This meant that India would develop its own indigenous, non-western institutions. He is conscious of the weakness in the Indian society and makes a fervent plea to remove these. He says, "We must revolt not only against tendency towards Europeanisation but also against everything bad in India. This has been the spirit of Hinduism in the past, and there is no reason why it should not be in future also."[9] But he said that we cannot develop merely by following Europe—it would be through the cultivation of creative discipline (*tapasya*), a harmonised intellect (*buddhi*) and divine strength (*sakti*)—a process which was first started at Dakshineshwar by Sri Ramakrishna and Vivekananda. The movement which started with Vivekananda, according to him was the first visible sign of change and was yet to be completed.[10]

He lashed out against those liberals who according to him borrowed their ideas from the West and confined themselves to their western books.[11] He argued that either method was unsuited to the reality of Indian life. He believed that wasting money to send telegrams to England would not save India. He attributed the poverty of India to British rule and advised that the effect could only be removed by the removal of the cause, because the continuance of such a rule was fatal to the growth of self conscious life of the people and inimical to India's effort to carve out its independent destiny. Such an idea, according to him, was not based on hatred but on the conviction that any form of foreign domination is not in consonance with national development. He believed that nature is an organic whole and therefore changes must be introduced carefully and yet like an organism it must grow.

In reference to India, he criticised liberal movement and argued that to strike for anything less than a strong and glorious freedom would be to insult the greatness of India's past and the magnificent policies of the future. It might impede the struggle for political freedom but was something out of accord with the role India was destined to play in the spiritual regeneration of mankind. India must win complete freedom for that was the basic condition for the inner development of her soul. He declared: "Indeed, it is God's will that we should be ourselves, we should recognise ourselves." For him nationalism was a religion that had come down to India from God, and God himself was guiding the movement.[12] This analysis was the answer to the question. How could India win her freedom?

He discovered the reason for the slavery of India and attributed it to the preponderance of *tamas* (inertness) in the eighteenth century when the country according to him, abounded in traitors, oath-seekers and powerful men. He thought that the British rule came as a divine dispensation to punish India for her lapses and create a new awareness. In fact, even the repression unleashed by the British during the partition of Bengal was considered by him as a part of divine design. He said, "Repression is nothing but the hammer of God that is beating us into shape so that we may be moulded into a mighty nation and an instrument for his work in the world."[13] Culturally, Aurobindo argued, India had always been a nation but the political dimension had always been missing. India had been a nation "only in the sense of having a common soul-life, a common culture, a common social organisation, a common political head, but not a nation-state".[14] The spirit of political nationalism had only developed when the British came and a need began to be felt for social cohesion and harmony to counteract the challenge of the West. Otherwise, according to Aurobindo, Indian history had been a record of the succession of empires, each breaking up because they could not withstand the pressures of centrifugal forces. India had always lacked 'the political vigour which characterised the West'.

One cause, which more than anything else, contributed to the failure of the development of a strong nation state, according to Aurobindo, was the persistence of the village community. It prevented people, the real realm, from being a partner in the struggles of the realm, the triumphs, disasters and failures of the rulers either as citizens or as soldiers. These villages became little isolated Republics with no further interest than the payment of a settled tax. The British conquest, in a fit of absent-mindedness, trampled upon the autonomous character of the village life, and thereby removed the great obstacle in the way of national development. It destroyed villages and merged them into provinces. He criticized the attempt to revive the autonomous character of village life. Re-organisation of village was necessary but it should be done in such a manner that villages should feel that they are but imperfect parts of a single national unity, dependent at every turn on the cooperation of other members. He wrote:

The day of the independent village or group of village has gone and must not be revived; the nation demands its hour of fulfilment and seeks to gather the village life of its rural population into a mighty single and compact democratic nationality. We must make the nation what the village community was of old, self-sufficient, self-centred, autonomous and exclusive—the ideal national swaraj.[15]

He identified a further weakness in the Indian tradition. This weakness, according to him, was reflected in the divorce of spirit and matter that took place in India during the medieval period. He recognised that spiritualism had provided a continuity to the Indian civilisation. While so many civilisations like the Chinese or the Greek had perished, India, he thought, had survived all the catastrophies because its guiding principle was spiritual which had "made Indian civilisation a thing apart and of its own kind in the history of the human race".[16] In fact he attributed the rise of India to life and consciousness in the nineteenth century to the reaction against the materialistic and secularistic civilisation of the West. But like Vivekananda he believed that the Indian civilisation declined because people did not pay sufficient attention to the fact that the Spirit is all encompassing. The medieval saints glorified the Spirit but in the process divorced it from the processes of the material world, from the real life, needs and actions of the people through which it was revealed. While a concern for the spiritual was necessary, the higher transformation of society could not have been achieved for all unless people had conquered the realm of necessity by a transformation of the material itself. But Indians never learnt how to utilize the material for the realisation of the spirit.

This failure to realise the close relation between spirit and matter was combined with another folly. Indians came to the mistaken belief that the individual and social life could be ritualised in terms of a universal framework. This had found expression in social and moral codes, in religious dogmatism which destroyed the malleability and assimilative spirit of India, and ultimately led to decline.[17] People with no food in their stomach and no clothes on their body could not presumably have the time or the inclination either to think of their country's destiny or to remember her old time glories. While the ancients realised the virtue of happy spontaneity in a world of immense potentialities, their successors tried to bind down life with chains by making a provisional and imperfect compromise with the material and vital nature. A new consciousness which developed as a result of the interaction between the spiritual and the material, argued Aurobindo, would recover the spiritual heritage of the past and make it the basis of the development of India into an organised nation of the future. It would further create an atmosphere free from the self seeking anarchy characteristic of the medieval period.

A foreign government, he was convinced, would never allow complete self growth which entailed growth of political consciousness in the subject nation. It was obvious that the foreigners could last only so long as political consciousness could be stifled. The moment the nations become politically self conscious, Aurobindo prophesied, the doom of the foreign government was certain.

There is no need to go into a detailed discussion of the strategy suggested in this respect by Aurobindo. He was, convinced that there cannot be any question of pure or impure means when justice and equality are denied. It is only where liberty and a just equality are established that true good feeling can reign. He was convinced that those who deny liberty have no right to appeal to the higher feelings of morality.

III

Aurobindo had been deeply influenced by Lamprecht. Following him he believed that Society evolves through various stages such as symbolic type, conventional, individual and subjective, and lastly, supernatural when the rational soul attains its end. Every event in human history was viewed by Aurobindo in the context of this typology and his book *The Human Cycle* is an elaboration of this thesis by examples from the growth, development and decay of various civilisations. But while Lamprecht believed that it is a sort of a psychological cycle through which nations evolve, Aurobindo argues that such an analysis oversimplifies the complexities of the natural process and reduces it to a straight-jacket. However, he takes over the names which Lamprecht uses to reinterpret the historical process.

According to him, the Vedic age, was the age of symbolism. The symbolic marriage of Surya in the Vedic hymns signifies the fact that human figure is inferior to the divine and yet is constructed in its image. In the same way the symbolism of the relations between *Purusha* and *Prakriti* expresses the relationship between male and female principle in nature. Most of the time, according to Aurobindo, we do not appreciate this symbolism because we tend to interpret that age in terms of our own mentality. It is for this reason that we discover that Vedas were product of barbarism. But he believes that these were written by the seers specially commissioned to glimpse the divine truth and express it in human form. Aurobindo argues that this could be illustrated by considering *Purushukta* in which creator's body is more than an image.

The second stage comes when the symbolic society passes into conventional society. This society finds its expression in the four-fold caste system, birth, economic freedom, religious rituals, sacrament, and finally the four ashrams. But in due course of time this system too degenerates. The bogus pundits begin to masquerade under the name of *Brahmanas*, the aristocrats under the name of *Ksatriyas* to serve their own self-interest. The economic basis and the functional division break down; the system becomes corrupt and seeks to formalise everything, erects a system of rigid grades and hierarchies. So much so that the gulf between the convention and truth becomes intolerable. But great men reject this fiercely, "strike at the walls of the prison-house and seek by the individual reason, moral sense or emotional desire, the Truth that society has lost or burnt in its whited sepulchres".[18]

The third stage comes with the advent of the modern civilization based on individualism which is a revolt of reason against sacraments of the church and has found its culmination in the development of science and technology. It goes back to the beginnings of the European civilization when the free curiosity of the rational individual, inspires man to search for rational laws, to take delight in intellectual scrutiny and the facts of life by direct observation. It also inspires him to combine this with the Roman sense of 'the practical' so that life is ordered in harmony with larger principles. It rightly emphasises that man is not merely a member of a pack, a bee-hive, he is something his own. But unrestrained use of the individual reason without any recognisable standard of truth, according to Aurobindo, is dangerous as "it is likely to lead rather to a continual fluctuation and disorder of opinion than to a progressive unfolding of the truth of things".[19] The desire of change and individual self assertion may lead, firstly, to an exaggerated assertion of the will in each to have his own life, creating a serious anarchy of conflicting wills in society. Secondly, the attempt to create society on the basis of scientific laws, the biggest achievement of the individualistic society, may lead to logical suppression of that very freedom.

But, according to him if the latest psychological researches are any indication, we are in the twilight of another period of human psyche.[20] The lamp of this view of civilisation will turn towards the East where the individualistic cycle will be short-lived. This influence will be "in the direction of subjectivism and practical spirituality, a greater opening of our physical existence to the realisation of ideals other than the strong but limited aims suggested by the life and the body in their own gross nature". According to him, man can know himself only by becoming conscious, by more and more living in his soul and acting out of it rather than floundering on surface, by putting himself into conscious harmony with that which is believed to be his superficial mentality. The entire life moves towards a profounder subjectivism. The individual phase has led to exaggerated claims on behalf of will and power and has resulted in world wars. But in the new period an attempt will be made to so organise society that the individual will be able to discover his own talent. It will develop the objective and the subjective to a more sublimated form; on the one side, the moral and the intellectual life, and, on the other, the aesthetic; one standing for right the other for beauty. Beyond it all is the harmonised intelligence (*buddhi*) which is or should be the driver of man's chariot. It is a kind of illumination—not merely the dry light of reason, nor the most suffered light of the heart, but a lightning and a solar splendour.

He then examines the idea of aesthetic and ethical cultures in great details. According to him the Hellenic mind was dominated by a sense of beauty, "a clear aesthetic sensibility and a worship of the beautiful".[21] In philosophy and art it succeeded in arriving at a concept of the Divine. But it ignored the ethical, became impatient of the ethical rules which it mistakenly came to believe as a barrier in the expression of beauty. The ethical found its expression in the Roman empire. It was a unique attempt at character building, divorced from the sweetness of beauty which the Greeks admired. It testified to the fact that all great nations, in their formative periods, were products of the will, the character, the impulse to self discipline.[22] But Rome failed to develop humane and delicate side of human character. The result was that there was not much thought, art, poetry or literature in the early Rome. It seems as if these people deliberately avoided these, so much so that whenever Rome wanted a poet of war, it had to import one from Athens. They did not sufficiently realise that the human mind needs to think, feel and enjoy in order to expand. The Roman civilization sought to crib, cabine and confine it. Thus, while Greece had no true moral impulse, though it had some sort of a moral order without which it could not have survived, Rome has no conception of beauty. Whilst Greece did not realise that without character and discipline there could not be an enduring power in life; Rome did not realise that life demanded freedom and variation in order to develop. While one exclusively worshipped felicity (*ananda*), the other penance (*tapasya*), they did not sufficiently realise that both are not exclusive but complimentary in the process of living, history and transcendence.

He also rejected the enlightenment view that each culture is a stepping stone to higher one, for all are part of an ever ascending process. That is why, he argued, each nation has a potential which it develops in its own way; and we must never judge a nation by the criteria of another; that different nations embody different ways of living, are dominated by different temperaments, and in order to understand them we must see them from within.

His ideas bristle with some difficulties. On the one hand he believes in human essence which is creative. Men are the source of creative process and this human essence takes conflicting forms, develops in different directions. On the other hand, he seems to believe in a historical pattern in which events unfold themselves as a result of autodynamic forces. There is indeed a curious attempt to bring together the deterministic view and the concept of a creative dynamic individual. Despite his attempt to tide over difficulties, there is a vague feeling left in us that he has not been able to combine his faith in Hinduism and the results of natural science, the respect for qualitative view of life he inherited from the Indian tradition and the quantitative approach as expressed in Lamprecht. He seems to have a fascination for the spirit of India, aesthetic culture of the Greece, ethical ideals of the ancient Rome and the subjectivism of the Christian church and even more for science with its universalism and rational organisation. Yet he gives an impression that he is trying to escape the problem of reconciling inconsistent strains, by arguing for a synthesis in which all these still live side by side, each reflecting the Divine glory, but not properly assimilated into a system of epistemology or metaphysics. It is not to belittle the importance of his system, which is truly stupendous, but only to suggest that if he had explored the epistemological and metaphysical basis of his own thought, he would have arrived at a more satisfactory and plausible view of these relationships. All the confusions of Indian renaissance are richly reflected in his logical and suggestive works.

In political philosophy, however, liberalism, for him, was not welcome. He, indeed, viewed it as a triumph of the rights of man and the doctrine of political freedom. Its permanent achievement, according to him, was the doctrine of freedom so necessary for the realisation of the individual personality. But from his point of view, though it made for political freedom, it did not sufficiently realise the importance of the doctrine of equality, the organic character of the social whole and the individual's place in it. Although it destroyed the feudal system, the system it created was even worse than the disease it sought to cure. It, he pointed out, gave encouragement to commercial instinct and led men to believe that satisfaction of the vital and the sensual aspect is final. According to him, it reduces everything to merely a utilitarian device and makes everything in society a matter of private interest. It failed to appreciate that the individuals could attain their true dignity only through larger social aggregates. According to him, the philosophy of individualism is false because it fails to recognize that the individual is by nature a social being, he is a part of the cosmic process, and therefore can realise himself only through the instrumentality of society and nation. All larger social aggregates have a soul of their own, which is derived from the individuals composing them, and yet is independent, and all these are related through an intricate web to 'the wholes within wholes.' And the highest of human purposes is to participate in the larger whole for the welfare of all. The fundamental error of liberalism, he maintained, was to abstract the individual from society and to create parliamentary institutions on that basis.

He laments that socialism too had taken a purely economic form which, he thinks, is contrary to its true nature. It rightly adds the ideal of social equality to the ideal of political equality. It emphasises that men cannot be true to themselves unless there is equality of status and opportunity in society.[23] It rightly seeks to dispense with the hereditary right of property to the community as a whole. Aurobindo asserts that while freedom is not possible in an inegalitarian society in which unfettered individual liberty ultimately leads to operation of the law of jungle, it is also not possible in a unidimensional society organized around the principle of the superiority of the communal over individual interests. He points out that in such a society the individual comes to be completely absorbed by society, he becomes a cog in the machine and society comes to dominate each and every aspect of his life, not only the economic aspect but the entire mode of his experience. In a socialist society, the state eventually becomes totalitarian. In the beginning it attempts to combine some kind of individual freedom with some kind of collectivist control but, in the end, in its zeal to overcome the egoism of the individual life, succumbs exclusively to the latter. A yawning gap emerges between its theory and practice. While the liberal theory tries to secure liberty by making all politically equal, the socialist tries to secure equality by guaranteeing economic equality alone through the instrumentality of an over weaning state.

The upshot, according to Aurobindo, is that both have failed. In the change from liberalism to socialism, liberty had to be subordinated to the ideal of equality; for only so much liberty could survive as could be safely allowed with the individual getting enough room for his self without impinging on the equal right of others. It could not be allowed to endanger the egalitarian basis. But in the end one cannot fail to make the discovery that an artificial equality also has its irrationalities; its contradictions of the collective good, even its injustices and its costly violation of the truth of nature. Socialistic equality like individualistic liberty, shows Aurobindo, may turn out to be not a panacea but an obstacle in the way of the best management and control of life by the collective reason and will of the community.[24]

The ideal of brotherhood, so Aurobindo thought, squares better with the collective existence. But this ideal is to be pursued in the combination with the other two ideals of freedom and equality and not exclusively because comradeship without liberty and equality may also mean as sacrifice of the individual at the altar of collectivity. In such a case the only liberty left would be the freedom to serve society under the rigorous control of the state, something similar to what happened in Sparta or Rome early and under Hitler in Germany and Stalin in Russia recently. In Germany it gave rise to the ideal of the social democracy which had relegated democratic principle into background. In Russia socialism came to be identified with the total control of the entire life of society, in the professed interest of all. While in Russia the state had been turned into the dictatorship of the communist party in the name and on behalf of the proletariat,[25] in Germany Nazism went further and discarded both equality and liberty. Although its avowed aim was elimination of exploitation, in practice, it resulted in purges and concentration camps.

Aurobindo recognises that originally Marxism developed as a rational system, but now it has been turned into a gospel, "a collective *mystique*, an inviolable body of doctrines with all denials or departure treated as a punishable heresy, a social cult enforced by the intolerant party and enthusiasm of a converted people."[26] In fascism, in the name of national soul, the vital subjectivism had taken the place of the mystique in which both democracy and reason fell apart. The dictatorship of a party was replaced by the dictatorship of the Furher who imposed a rigid life in society. He called it "the end of the gate of reason".

In an ideal social organisation, according to Aurobindo, each individual must be given an oppurtunity to realise his potentialities in terms of his distinct nature and temperament through the instrumentality of society. He concedes that sometimes liberty of some is to be restricted to secure liberty of all. Liberty in isolation is a fiction. But anything which extols society at the expense of the individual ignores the complexity of man's life. It ignores that man has a soul which can be developed not through mechanical regulation by an external body but through self-regulation only. And this applies not only to the individual but also to the group, the class, and other larger social aggregates such as the nation, all of which develop their own soul in terms of greater and greater differentiation of the cosmic reality. According to him, a group soul too, develops by greater differentiation which implies diversity and variation in social life.[27] The State, in the ultimate analysis, is only a few individuals who govern in the name of all, and if this is so, argues Aurobindo, then these few men cannot be entrusted with absolute powers. Although Aurobindo pilloried liberal democracy rooted in the principle of individualism and right to property, at the level of institutions he, however, preferred democratic institutions because they provide full scope for individual variation while other kinds of institutions do not leave any elbow room to the individual. According to Aurobindo, man needs freedom so that he may grow, in its absence, he will remain a stunted being because regulation tends to inhibit free play of human life. In a fully regulated state, man is no different from an insect. He noticed that the state is menacingly growing into intolerable proportions and pointed out that a thorough-going scientific organisation of life can lead to complete regimentation.

Life, according to him, is a movement in which there is unfoldment of the developing force or energy (*shakti*) and it progresses through variations as its progress involves development and interlocking of diverse ways and forms.[28] The aim of humanity must be to find some common workable order of harmony and conçiliation amidst conflicts, wars and tensions. This is possible only when soul discovers its spiritual character and effects an upward transformation of life from inertia (*tamas*) to purity (*sattva*). In insisting upon a completely free development of the individual, individualism exaggerates the ego. In insisting upon the need for a rational order, collectivism subordinates the individual ego to the group ego. Aurobindo prophesied that in the next state of human evolution man will transcend these antinomies. He would once again assert his freedom in terms of the unity in diversity and diversity in unity and not on the basis of either his separate ego or the group ego alone.

It is noteworthy that Aurobindo also rejects anarchism because he believes that man is not an isolated being, he lives by relating himself to others. Society alone provides occasion for man to grow into perfection. Man's fall was not the result of the growth of social principles but the latter were introduced as a result of the fall. If he regards social principles as necessary for evolving to higher forms, something is required to regulate life because the crudeness of human instincts does not correct itself voluntarily. The compulsion my not have been used rightly by the realm of necessity. In any case, it is difficult to imagine how the anarchist ideal of a free-cooperative communism, a united life where the labour and property of all is there for the benefit of all, can operate in large and complex conditions of modern life and how can it be maintained without a group of men who are truthful and pious (*satvic*). It might have been possible in some remote golden age but man's nature is truly transitional, the rational being is truly middle. Therefore, he concludes:

The solution lies not in the reason but in the soul of man, in its spiritual tendencies. It is a spiritual, an inner freedom that alone can create a perfect human order.[29]

The true spiritual aim of life regards man not merely a body or life but a soul to the fulfilment of which the first two must act as vehicles.[30] It constantly reminds them of the higher possibilities that they should become visible members of the spirit. It, consequently, holds sacred all different aspects of life, viz., spiritual, psychic, emotional and material, and regard all forms of life as a means of a complex manifestation of the spirit. Aurobindo believes that such a view does not suppress evil by coercion alone but by emphasising that each of these aspects must grow to Godhood from within an atmosphere of "the widest air and the highest life". To quote Aurobindo:

A large liberty will be the law of a spiritual society and the increase of freedom a sign of the growth of human society towards the possibility of true spiritualization.[31]

Thus, Aurobindo points out, man in his upwards journey must have as much free space as possible. In this journey there are possibilities of error but it is through these errors that man grows in experience. The outcome of such a process is always a deeper experience. Each form of life or soul has its own potentiality, dharma, which must be followed; it applies to both human beings and their aggregates. Dharma for all consists in seeking truth dispassionately from one's own specific angle. Each soul can attain highest spirituality by following its own dharma. Similarly each form of knowledge can glimpse the truth by following its own mode of experience. Coercion only chains up the devil but does not change its essential character. True virtue comes only by finding a higher law by oneself. The spiritual ideal would "aim at establishing in society the true inner theocracy, not the false theocracy of a dominant Church or priesthood, but that of the inner Priest, Prophet and King".[32]

The importance of his attack on socialism, capitalism and anarchism lay in the fact that it not only expressed the political aspiration of India but also the profound changes which were coming in the political and intellectual climate of the West itself. It is this which gives Aurobindo's thought its distinctive flavour. He recognised the merit of all the contemporary ideological systems but did not take them wholesale. Instead, he took a leap and developed a new system altogether. The French revolution awakened us to the power of freedom. The Russian revolution was there as a watershed in the history of the world. The idea of equality caught the imagination of man and made the earlier exclusive emphasis on political liberty quite irrelevant. But what is significant is that the criticism of these doctrines by Aurobindo was almost on the lines which now the new left has taken up. Neither the abstract individual of the earlier liberalism nor the complete equality of the collectivist tradition could withstand the new historical and psychological pressures of society. Both doctrines had to be reconciled with nationalism which speaks in terms of the personality of aggregates in which individuals work for better social being. Aurobindo grasped the importance of the individual and his relationship to larger social aggregates as the central problem in contemporary philosophy. The importance of his ideas consist in the fact that he set us on a new trail, and gave us a new vision of man's place in life. In doing so, he has crystallised the anti-liberal and the anti-communist tendencies of the Indian national movement, and forced a thorough examination of both. This line of thought later found its practical expression in Gandhi's image of 'the oceanic circles'.

IV

Let us now turn to Aurobindo's ideas on freedom. He argues that when liberty is considered as a device to satisfy one's natural impulses without taking into account the similar impulses of others, it poses a difficulty for

..ll, because the liberty of one clashes with the liberty of another. The result is that the free running of many in the same field leads to chaos and collision. This kind of liberty glorified under the competitive system leads, as pointed out in the previous section, to an encouragement of a commercial spirit for the satisfaction of the vital—sensational activism.[33] The emphasis on the vital, according to Aurobindo, leads to a conflict in which we exhaust and corrupt ourselves. Dissatisfaction with this system leads to state socialism. But here also one is led to another extreme. The individual is forced to give up his freedom of action and possession to the state which in turn doles out regulated liberty to him. The system is admirable in theory, but, in practice, it tends to be very oppressive.

Experience has so far shown that the human attempt to arrive at a mechanical freedom only results into liberty of the kind which is enjoyed by some at the expense of others. Such a freedom has amounted usually to the rule of the majority by a minority of those who control economic and political power. Even the best machinery of this mechanical freedom yet discovered, according to Aurobindo, amounts to the selection of a body of rulers who tend to coerce all minorities or dissident groups. Mechanical freedom falsifies the value of the individual because it sets him against society; it falsifies the nature of the soul because it does not sufficiently pay attention to the ethical and spiritual aim of life as its sets bread against all this. Adherence to mechanical liberty, according to Aurobindo, is a proof that the real meaning of liberty has not yet been understood.[34]

What is his own notion of freedom? According to him liberty means the freedom to obey the law of our being, to grow to our natural self-fulfilment, to find out naturally and freely our harmony with our environment. According to him, perfect freedom is the inner freedom. It is spiritual or inner freedom which alone can be perfect—it is fulfilled in the freedom of the human soul, the deepest meaning of freedom is the power to expand and grow towards perfection by the law of one's nature or dharma which is not merely the fulfilment of mental and emotional but is also the flowering of the divine.[35]

He emphasises that any attempt to govern the life of the individual by an increasing light of thought rather than allowing it to be limited by its rough and imperfect actualities, is a distinct sign of advanced human progress. He prophesied that the true turning point will come with the further step which will initiate an attempt to govern life by that of which thought itself is only a sign and an instrument, namely, the soul, the inner being, which will make our ways of living a free opportunity for the growing height and breadth of its self-fulfilment. That is the real, the profounder sense of life and its fulfilment which we shall have to learn attain the idea of self-determination as the effective principle of liberty.

This concept of freedom, according to Aurobindo, is superior to all other concepts, for it neither subordinates the individual to the collective nor the collective to the individual. On the other hand, it seeks to synthesise the two. According to him, this idea of freedom, is not opposed to the ideal of a common authority or a state.[36] In an ideal society the respect for individual liberty and free growth of the personal being is harmonised with respect for needs, efficiency, solidarity and natural growth of the corporate life. Aurobindo follows an intermediate course between the two views, i.e. the rights are inalienable and the rights are conferred by society. Rights, according to him, are claims for the full development of the individual; they are principles of *Swadharma*. He argues that the primeval law and purpose is to seek one's own law. But it can not be realised in a community in which the individuals push themselves at the expense of others. In the very act of asserting freedom for themselves, they encroach on the free development of their fellow beings. If a real, spiritual and psychological unity were effected, Aurobindo thought, liberty will have no perils and disadvantages; for free individuals enamoured of the idea of liberty would be "compelled by themselves, by their own needs, to accommodate perfectly, their own growth with the growth of their fellows and would not feel themselves complete except in the free growth of others." He says that doubtlessly law of the state is a result of our imperfection. But while the advantages of law and compulsion in curbing evil propensities is obvious, the disadvantages are not so. The order created by law is always mechanical which is liable to break down as soon as the yoke is loosened and restraints withdrawn. An imposed order, if carried too far, inhibits the principle of natural growth. If we express and over standardise life, Aurobindo fears, we do so at a great peril because it tends to crush Nature's initiatives and differentiations and variations. He says that, "Dwarfed or robbed of elasticity, the devitalised individuality, even while it seems outwardly fair and symmetrical, perishes from within."

In fact he comes to the odd conclusion that anarchy is better than long continuance of a law which is not our own and which our real nature cannot assimilate. He is convinced that all repressive law is merely a makeshift. It is a substitute for the true law which must develop from within and be not a check on liberty. He argued that Human society progresses really and vitally in proportion as law becomes the child of freedom; it will reach its perfection when the individual life seeks its own self-development.

Just as the freedom for the individual consists in seeking its own self-development, in the same way the formal law and purpose of a society, community or nation is to seek its own self-fulfilment. As the free development of individual from within is the first condition for the growth and perfection of the community, so the free development of the community or the nation from within is the best condition for the growth of perfection of mankind. However, the law for the individual to perfect the individuality by free development from within also implies respect for the same free development in others. This law is to harmonise one's life with the life of other social aggregates and to pour oneself out as a force for growth and perfection of humanity. The law for the community or nation is equally to perfect its corporate existence by a free development from within, with full respect for and to aid and be aided by the same free development of other communities and nations. The law for humanity is to pursue its upward evolution towards the divine, taking full advantage of the free development and gains of all individuals and nations and groupings of men, to work towards the day when mankind may be really, and not merely ideally, a divine family. Aurobindo repeatedly emphasises that the ideal law of social development is one in which variety is the law, and it increases as society grows. The fulcrum of all the wholes, however, is the individual because everything in the nature is meant for the individual to develop his potentiality; he has a relative freedom to use or misuse in order to realise the law of his being.

Society, according to him, has to be a system of a mutual harmony. He reiterates that neither should the individual overlook society nor should society crush the individual because in this both can not fulfil themselves. "Every time the society crushes or effects the individual, it is inflicting a wound on itself and depriving its own life of a priceless source of stimulation and growth. The individual too cannot flourish by himself, for the Universal, the unity and the collectivity of his fellow beings, is his present source of stock."[37] Aurobindo elaborates that all things have their own law of development and they are all interdependent in terms of the law of variations. In the matter, variation is limited in type and form but in individuals it is further increased by variations in groups, types of species and supra-species. And in proportions, as life grows and still more when mind emerges, the individual arrives at a greater and more vital power of variation.[38] Everything in nature is an occasion for him to develop his potentiality, to use his freedom which can also be misused if he does so for his own ego. Therefore in nature freedom and rights are two basic forms which connect an individual to other individuals and help him to realise himself through the instrumentality of society in a process of what the ancients called, *Loksamgraha*, the holding together of the race in its cyclic evolution.[39] We must exercise our rights in the interest of humanity because rights are those things which are necessary for our free and sound development, and the development of humanity is inseparable from our own. Nazism was a denial of this truth. In it since the state became all powerful, the individual was crushed. The majority may accept a system but it is for the minority of scholars to emphasise the need for increasing differentiation and varied directions. The conditions which are necessary for the development of our potentialities from within are also necessary for the development of the world. In fact the expansion is not only to be outward or inward but also upward. Man must rise upward further in the same manner as he did from animal beginnings, and more into the spiritual and the divine.

According to him, liberty and equality appeared because the idea of humanity in an intellectual age has been obliged to appeal to the vital and physical kind of man rather than his inner being.[40] This age has limited its effort to revolutionise political and social institutions and to bring about such a modification of the ideas and sentiments of the common world of mankind as would make these institutions practicable; it has worked at the machinery of human life, much more on the outer world than upon the soul of the individual. He stresses that both freedom and equality are external attributes of the spirit. They can be acted only when we make an appeal to spiritual freedom. To quote:

The union of liberty and equality can only be achieved by the power of human brotherhood and it cannot be founded on anything else—when the soul claims freedom; it is the freedom of self-development, the self-development of the divine in man in all his being; when it claims equality, what it is claiming is freedom equally for all and the recognition of the same soul, the same god head in all human beings. When it strives for brotherhood, it is founding the equal freedom of self-development as a common aim, a common life, a unity of mind and feeling founded upon the recognition of the inner spiritual society. These three things are in fact the nature of the soul; for freedom, equality, unity are the eternal attributes of the spirit.[41]

He is very emphatic that the fulfilment of the individual is not the fulfilment of the vital, physical being but the full flowering of the divine in him to his utmost capacity.

Aurobindo's theory of freedom sometimes has great difficulties, because it becomes a play of logical abstractions. While at the logical level he combines freedom with larger social aggregates he nowhere explains as to who will decide what is freedom is case of a conflict. How are the boundaries of the individual, the family and province to be determined? The ideal of spiritual freedom may be all for the good but what kind of social, economic and political freedom must precede it? There is a full chapter devoted to the application of this idea in *Srimad Bhagwat*, but since no attempt was made to relate it to concrete social and political institutions, the idea remained abstract. Aurobindo's statement about economic and political freedom as basic preconditions of spiritual freedom are extremely vague. Starting with the assumption that these liberties are merely means to ultimate spiritual freedom, he fell early into the implication that such freedoms are not of much value. From passages such as the one relating to *Swadharma* it might be inferred that he often tended to confuse it with one's obligation in society—though this was not his intention is clear. He nowhere explains how to reconcile the doctrine of *Swadharma* with the doctrine of *Loksamgraha*, i.e. of working for the organisation and welfare of the world, for the latter upheld that men must concern themselves not only with one's station and its duties or with ones nation but with the organisation of society as a whole. While the first implies that no genuine conflict of interest can arise between the individual and society, the implication of second is just the reverse. Conflicts and cleavages are the unfortunate facts of life in this century and it is doubtful whether Aurobindo provides any guidance to solve the concrete problems of life. His general position is profound and full of possibilities but no attempt has been made to identify it with any line of action. The whole idea of Rama and Krishna as agents of history implies that society must be so organised that each is able to realise, to quote Aurobindo himself, "law of his own dharma". A clear theory at this point was necessary because he himself did not accept *status quo* in political life and did everything to change it. In spite of his tendency to idealise the basic elements of Indian polity, he was in fact a sharp critic of the actual state of Indian society.

The greatness of Aurobindo's system, however, lies in the fact that he presented before us a vision of the individual community life which is far different from both the individualist and the collectivist visions, by unequivocally declaring society as composed of, what I have called, "wholes within wholes", each of which has an individuality of its own and yet is subordinate to other wholes. In this way he resolutely refuses to allow either the individual to destroy society by his greed and cupidity or the state to destroy the individual or society. In providing a justificatory theory for legitimate 'differentiation' in society, and in insisting that the state is merely an instrument of social will, he provided enough safeguard against the misuse of power. But unfortunately he did not set out the institutional framework which would ensure such a state. He rejected parliamentary democracy but did not provide institutions which would take its place. The result was that when freedom came, the Indian nation did not have any other option but to adopt the Westminster model, even though people like Aurobindo and Gandhi were opposed to it. His insistence that Zeitgeist is the final arbiter in all matters, civilisations come and go, historical epochs follow one another, and in all the process of hope and tears the Zeitgeist unfolds itself, created an impression as if he was interested in obfuscating concrete issues of daily life.

V

A brief reference to Aurobindo's *Ideal of Human Unity* will be apposite. It first appeared in the 'Arya' (1915-18) in thirty-five serials from September 1915 to July 1918 and published in a book form in 1919. This was noticed in Indian nationalist circles, but received very little attention in the world of scholarship until recently. This lack of interest is difficult to explain, not only in view of the fact it was a major philosophical treatise on politics written by an Indian thinker, who at one stage in his life was himself very active and influential in the national movement, but also because it is a treatise on the lines of Hegel and Sorel which not only clarifies certain trends in human quest towards unity but also identifies the obstacles in the realisation of the ideal, and suggests both the solution best suited to our age and the conditions necessary for its achievement. It is this which has prompted the author to discuss Aurobindo's ideas in this book.

Aurobindo's attempt in this book was inspired by a conviction that the unity of mankind was the ultimate end of all our endeavours. He wrote that "the unity of mankind is evidently a part of Nature's eventual scheme and must come about". He attempted a concrete analysis of the conditions and safeguards "which will keep the race intact in the roots of its vitality, richly diverse in its oneness". He argues that the unity of mankind can be achieved neither by administrative nor by economic unity. It can be secured only be creating an enduring foundation, a new religion of humanity which would spring from the inner law of human life outlined above, for social and political forces are mechanical in character.

Behind his conviction lies the idea that since it is the law of nature that everything should move towards larger and larger aggregations, it is natural that the ideal of human unity should be the final culmination of the process. Nature, according to Aurobindo, never does anything at one moment, she is slow and patient in her action. "She takes up ideas and half carries them out, then drops them by the wayside to resume them in some future era with better combination." Mankind created many civilizations, each as rich as one would wish them to be, but each passes away, as each was a necessary stage in the process which must sooner or later end up in the ideal of human unity. The Roman empire, for instance, was able to develop an admirable organisation, based on the principles of security, order and material well-being, but it lost its colour and richness as it did not give sufficient importance to the individual. The system, in course of time, lost its vitality and died of stagnation.

At the moment there are two forces operating in nature with equal force. On the one hand, there is a force leading to greater and greater closeness, interrelation and interaction among the members of human race. And out of this comes collision and wars, demand for freedom and equality, giving rise to an equally forceful demand to reorganise our life on lines which would mitigate the ruinous consequences of wars and conflicts to the minimum. On the other hand, there is a force of common uniting element, which emerges in smaller units and leads them to seek larger unity, which is secured either by common sentiments or by external forces. This has happened, for instance in Italy, Germany and Africa. Along with these tendencies, there is also a new awareness of cosmopolitan sentiments. Aurobindo admits that at the moment this sentiment is quite nebulous and vague, not strong enough to check the old centrifugal forces. But there is, however, a new religion of humanity emerging in the modern minds, moving beyond the mechanical formulae of the past, and welding humanity together. Aurobindo held that this religion must sooner or later emerge victorious. Wars in the modern world might one day force mankind to unite in self-defence, mankind's choice will be "between that and a lingering suicide".[42] He adds that "If the human reasoning cannot find out the way, Nature herself is sure to shape these upheavals in such a way as to bring about her end."

VI

A presentation of political ideas more ancient than that attempted by Aurobindo appeared in Balbhadra Sahu's *Desik Sastra*.[43] It may be said that in this book he combined Manu's scheme of 'right' with Aurobindo's concept of nationalism. Manu had conceived of righteousness to be attained in a community and in its members, i.e. when each of its members seeks happiness or pleasure, which consists in the fulfilment of their separate aims, in accordance with their distinct nature and temperament.

Both the individual and the community are characterised by the predominance of three qualities—sublimate (*sattvic*), dynamic (*rajsic*) and inert (*tamsic*). Aurobindo had conceived of national right on the lines of the individual righteousness—which was neither a subjective morality of conscience, nor a biological community as a *Jati* nor merely a set of laws as expressed in formal institutions. He transcended all these in terms of notion of national community. Following Aurobindo, Sahu also argued that a national community is a moral community in the sense of determining the functions of its parts towards the fulfilment of the final end. Nationalism has become the spiritual urge which ought to control all men. The individual is integrally linked to this national community. If he pursues his self interest at the expense of the community, the community is destroyed and, along with the community, all his chances to enjoy pleasure. One of the reasons why the Indian civilisation declined was that Indians pursued their own self interest at the expense of the community, while the English people always gave more importance to the national interest. The result in the latter case was that England rose to be the strongest power.

Nationalism, according to Sahu, is the highest duty. It can be justified in terms of organic, utilitarian, metaphysical and spiritual arguments. From the organic point of view, the individual is an integral part of the collectivity and hence his interests are inseparable from the interests of the latter. From the utilitarian point of view, nationalism is not merely 'the greatest good of the greatest number', it is, in fact, greatest good of the community as a whole. From the metaphysical standpoint, anyone who sacrifices himself for the sake of the nation enjoys the bliss of heaven. Spiritually, it helps us to rise above our lower qualities and become a true man of action. The rise and fall of a national community is compared to appearance and disappearance of a matter in the physical world. It is a natural, organic and living evolution. Existence of a common culture, language, state or polity may add strength to the national bond but none of these factors is a necessary precondition for its existence.

Like an individual every nation is composed of two fundamental elements—*Chitti* and *Virat*. *Chitti* is transmitted through heredity in addition to many other characteristics. It is a conscious mental faculty and is preserved in terms of a desire for highest bliss. The character of a nation, like that of an individual, is also determined by the nature of the consciousness prevalent at a time, when it is to uplift a nation it partakes of divine consciousness, and when it gets corrupted it becomes identical with the demonic one. There may be setback but it is the first show of endurance and patience in the face of all odds. The demonic consciousness, according to Sahu, is a result of the mixture of races. It can triumph but its victory is always due to the fact that it does not have the capacity to survive for long in the community.

Virat is a natural outcome of *chitti* of a community and helps her to defend herself against all odds. It develops in the light of the life force provided by the *chitti*. All worldly efforts of a community in the direction of organising and defining itself are created and recreated by the *Virat* only. It manifests itself in the social and political organisation of the community. In its absence there is disorder, a society stops functioning and decadence sets in.

In the light of these two concept, "national right", continues Sahu, consists in "preservation and enhancement of *Chitti* and *Virat* and destruction of all those factors that lead to the weakening of the two". It is something of the national character. If the individual is constituted by his relations with the nation, morality consists in following the qualities necessary for its survival. Each nation as well as each individual should be free because without such a freedom they cannot develop themselves in terms of their own law of being. Human life is in intermediary stage between the animal status and the divine life. He identified freedom with *Swaraj* or self-government and argued that it was a reflection of the divine freedom in human life. Divine freedom is that stage when the nation provides everything at one's will, while the animal stage is one where one is dependent on others for the fulfilment of one's needs. Like Sukra he argued that human freedom consists in the fulfilment of one's interest without internal or external interference. It is possible only where man does not have to depend on anybody for the fulfilment of his natural interest. It is this which demands that both the individual and the nation must control their own desires, preserve and enhance their own *virat*. One needs to have certain preconditions before one can enjoy this freedom: a comfortable means of earning, place to live, and freedom and vitality of action. If all these four conditions are available in the community, they are also naturally available to the individual.

According to Sahu, there are three aspects of freedom—governmental, economic and material. Governmental freedom is possible when the ruler never does anything against public welfare. Economic freedom is possible when money does not play either a positive or a negative role in hindering the natural interest be it of the community or the individual, natural freedom means non-interference in those matters which are not harmful to others. While governmental freedom depends upon good rulers who govern for the welfare of the people, economic freedom depends on a society in which everyone is free from the supremacy of wealth. Only that wealth is justified which is earned through *right* means and is spent for the good of society. Wealth should not be allowed to corrupt individuals, because when it dominates it leads to disparities in life and disturbs social harmony. Besides, Sahu goes on, there must be no admixture of blood. Where the rulers are weak, and racial mixture takes place, economic disparities disturb social harmony. A good polity is one in which the individual is free to develop his virtues in accordance with his situation or its duties. The state, its laws and institutions, its social system, legal system and *usages* should help all in leading this life. The state should not dominate. It should not unnecessarily interfere in our daily life. It must constantly strive to adjust itself to these individuals who are wholes in themselves. It is often accorded a higher place because it regulates the activities of other institutions. Every state has an outer body of institutions and an inner spirit. The presence of the inner spirit makes it a part of the system and provides it with a set of moral aims. These aims or goals provide organising principle to the life within the state. But the state is not a whole in the sense that part are completely dependent on it. Parts too have a consciousness and moral principles of their own. The state, in its natural form, therefore, is an organ like stomach in human body that works to resolve conflicts and ease complexities of life. At the level of the state, self-rule is the form of organisation in which people are led by one's own tribal instinct.

According to Sahu, the form of government is not important; it can be hereditary or representative. The important thing is that the substance of the polity is decided on the basis of the predominance of any of three qualities—the sublimate, the dynamic, the inert. Although the form of government is not very important, Sahu goes into great details about the forms of government, some of which are clearly outdated. Governments can be classified into such categories as *Brahmana, Prajapatya, Daiva, Manava* and perverted form as *Asur, Rakshasha, Paishach* and *Pashava*. The classification is based on the predominance of the three qualities in various proportions as stated earlier. *Brahmana* is that kind of polity in which the sublimate element is predominant while the worst form, *Pashava*, is that kind in which the inert is predominant. The general characteristic of the good form, according to him, is that there is an identity of interest between the rulers and the ruled; a form of government in which the ruled are fearless and a general atmosphere of peace, obedience and satisfaction prevails. In the perverted form there is a wide gap between the interests of the ruler and the ruled, both fear each other and there is a general atmosphere of mutual distrust, discontentment and conflict. Where the *virat* completely disappears from a polity, it leads to the rule of the selfish. One important way to harmonise social relationships, according to him, is the caste system. Its chief merit is that it establishes an order in which the social balance is preserved by assigning specific duties to all. He respects the ideal of the *Bhagwat Gita* "Better one's own dharma though destitute of merit, than the dharma of another well discharged, better death in the discharge of one's own dharma, the dharma of another is fraught with danger." According to him, this ideal helps in preserving the general spirit of peace and contentment in society and also in developing the virtues of a good organisation. However, his idea of caste is not that of succession on the basis of heredity. It is not a rigid system and one's position in it has to be decided on the basis of education and desert.

A good economic system is also necessary to preserve a polity. The functional division of society under the caste system helps in preserving the social virtues of *varna*. Sahu is in favour of barter exchange of goods. It is justified on the ground that it helps to encourage the production of useful goods essential for the community and automatically checks inflated claims. The barter system must be combined with cow economy. He argues that cow is not merely important from religious point of view, it is also important in terms of cow products—milk and butter. A country is greater in proportion to the quantity of milk and butter available in it. The legal system should not be harsh. He quotes the *Dharmasastras* as saying that a legal system based on coercion is demonic in character. The natural course of law, according to him, must help the individual to function and perform his duty in two ways—motivating him to do the desirable and prevent him form doing the undesirable. In course of both these the natural process of law must encourage the individual to live a life as if it were form of a prayer. If the natural law fails, one is expected to repent for his acts of commission and ask for forgiveness of society. Should that also fail, state coercion is applied as the last remedy. Following the ancient thinkers he argued that the application of law should change according to the time and circumstances. The legal interpretation in his scheme is the prerogative of the council of worthy or those who are accustomed to the spirit of the Vedas.

Thus in his scheme there is a nation and its soul which is integrally related to the soul of the individual. The national soul assigns a place to each individual in terms of his stage of life, because the individual, too, has his own soul, a consciousness of its ends, and freedom for him consists in the development of this soul in terms of his distinct nature and temperament.

This is possible by finding a correct relationship of one's soul to the group soul so that we are able to pursue the law of our being by transcending our individual ego in the pursuit of the welfare of all. It is, however, not clear what happens when the will of the individual and the state run counter to each other. The individual cannot be free unless there is a whole host of institutions dividing the power of the state, and associations mediating between the state and society. Sahu grasps this importance of mediation when he compares the role of the state to the stomach in the body. He also realises that not every state can pursue our moral ends. The state may be in a decadent condition, it may even have selfish rulers who would trample upon the freedom of the ruled. Therefore, he rightly recognises that there is a morality which transcends the state and to which the state must constantly adjust itself. The state must adjust itself to the moral needs of the society composed of the individuals who have their own moral and spiritual ends to seek. The state can promote spiritual life only indirectly, i.e. by removing obstacles in its growth. We cannot surrender ourselves completely to the state whatever its quality of governance because, in the ultimate analysis, in order to attain true *Swaraj* we must realise our aims on our own.

If we were to venture on any criticism it would take the following direction. The institutional arrangement suggested by Sahu is weak in so far as it is outdated. While living in twentieth century he is still obsessed by the values of primitive barter economy, justifies caste-system, and recommends eugenics to preserve racial purity and suggests astrology as guide to rulers. We have realised through painful experience of totalitarian regimes in the twentieth century that some of these ideas are full of mischief. It is safer to construct institutions than to rely on the good intentions of rulers however noble. Even the Vedic seers emphasised the role of organisation of the state because they knew that no man of power could be entirely trusted. And that is one of the reasons why thinkers like Aurobindo, Roy and Gandhi thought of decentralisation of the state. Sahu does not adequately realise the importance of such institutions in building up a good polity. It is through these institutions alone that the state as a moral ideal is concretized; it is through them that both the rulers and the ruled are disciplined into the arts, graces and cultures of social communion.[44]

This traditional-intuitive-philosophical approach found a clear expression after independence in the writings of K.P. Mukerjee. His writings provided a justification of Hinduism in general and classical political institutions in particular. Mukerjee argued that society alone is moral and the state is merely an agent established by society for the achievement of this moral purpose. The state "is wedded to the realisation of a moral purpose, viz., to the making of justice available to all on equal terms", and political science must be "the science of justice or dharma." Deriving his inspiration from classical writings with their "transcendental view of spiritual reality", he made an emphatic plea that the policies of the state must conform to the principles of natural law of which freedom, justice and growth are parts. He says, "Nothing is absolutely settled in a creative universe, it is not a planned machine, it is rather like a creatively planning organism."[45] He is quite aware that the story of mankind does not conform to this view of the relationship between the state and morality and yet he would argue that ideas are none the worse for not being found in practice.

He criticised the West for its industrialism, capitalism, imperialism and nationalism. He refers to this pattern as the Nici-ethos order of things which came to its real climax in 1914. He made a plea for socio-ethos of socialism and the cooperativeness of a real world order. He wrote, "our social ideal can be pursued morally only by democratic socialism and through the instrumentality of a world state". In the light of this he defended the welfare of a socialistic state. However, what is interesting, and perhaps incongruous, is the fact that he connects this argument with the defence of the caste system in its classical form. It is true that the state in ancient India had a constitutional or even democratic basis at least theoretically, but it needs to be explained how this system degenerated and came to align itself with tyranny. There is a certain amount of chauvinism and irrationalism when he accuses western political thought of being responsible for the war. Even the Hindu thought did not eliminate war. If political thought of ancient India is any guide, constant tendency to anarchy was a problem which was greatly aggravated during medieval times. He no where comes to grips with the accusation that the major weakness of the Hindu thought was that it did not pay sufficient attention to institution-building in society which alone can provide effective safeguards against whimsical exercise of authority.

NOTES

1. Karan Singh, *Prophet of Indian Nationalism: Study of the Political Thought of Sri Aurobindo Ghosh 1893-1910* (London, Allen and Unwin, 1963), p. 136.
2. Quoted by Karan Singh, ibid., p. 183
3. Aurobindo, *The Ideal of Karmayogin* (Pondicherry, Aurobindo Ashram, 1913), p. 66.
4. Aurobindo, *The Human Cycle*, etc. (Pondicherry, Aurobindo Ashram, 1952), p. 218.

5. Aurobindo, *The Ideal of Karmayogin,* op. cit., p. 21.
6. Ibid., p. 22.
7. Ibid., p. 28.
8. Ibid., p. 6.
9. Ibid., p. 28.
10. Ibid., p. 20.
11. Haridas, and Uma Mukherjee, *Sri Aurobindo and the New Thought in Indian Politics,* Calcutta (FKL Mukhopadhyaya, 1964), p. 3.
12. Aurobindo, *The Ideal of Karmayogin,* op. cit., p. 6.
13. Aurobindo, *The Human Cycle,* op. cit., p. 100.
14. Ibid., p. 287.
15. Haridas and Uma Mukherjee, op. cit., p. 281.
16. Aurobindo, *The Human Cycle,* op. cit., p. 253.
17. Ibid., p. 303.
18. Ibid., p. 14.
19. Ibid., p. 21.
20. Ibid., p. 26.
21. Ibid., p. 123.
22. Ibid., p. 127.
23. Ibid., pp. 268-69.
24. Ibid., p. 273.
25. Ibid., p. 275.
26. Ibid., p. 276
27. Ibid., p. 281.
28. Ibid., p. 290.
29. Ibid., pp. 295-96.
30. Ibid., p. 305.
31. Ibid., p. 306.
32. Ibid., p. 116.
33. Ibid., p. 104.
34. Ibid., p. 600.
35. Aurobindo, *The Ideal of Karmayogin,* op. cit., pp. 44-5.
36. Aurobindo, *The Human Cycle* etc., op. cit., p. 382.
37. Ibid., pp. 58-9.
38. Ibid., p. 81.
39. Ibid., p. 83.
40. Ibid., p. 85.
41. Aurobindo, *Complete Works* (Pondicherry, Aurobindo Birth Centenary Library), 1972, vol. IX, p. 764.
42. Ibid., p. 770.
43. Balbhadra Sahu, *Desik Sastra* (in Hindi) (Almora, 1921).
44. K.P. Mukerjee, *The State* (Madras, Theosophical, 1952).
45. K.P. Mukerjee, *Implications of the Ideology Concept* (Bombay, Popular, 1955), p. 119.

CHAPTER 10

THE SYNTHETIC VISION: GANDHI

Gandhi is a very complex figure in the history of modern thought. The complexity largely springs from the fact that he was not only a man of thought but also the supreme leader of the nationalist movement in India for over three decades. During his lifetime, this man turned the national movement which was hitherto confined to a few sections of society, into a truly mass movement. He formulated a strategy of political action which was destined largely to determine the form of natural protest and struggle against the British, reaching its culmination in the independence of India in 1947. He was certainly not the first to formulate the policy of Swadeshi and boycott, but the way in which he integrated it with the idea of a non-violent satyagraha was unique. Gandhi was not only a man of action but also a prophet of modern India who truly attempted to transcend the class conflicts of society by devising a method which, for the first time, brought about the national aggregation of an all-India character. The fact that he created an ideology of national struggle which transcended class divisions, and, further, devised a political strategy to achieve this ideal in the minimum possible time, is the secret of his remarkable and enduring place in the history of thought.

However, we are not concerned so much with his strategy, which was truly remarkable, or his understanding of the class relations in society, which though dated was full of insight and effectiveness, but with his idea of the individual community relationship, concepts of society, freedom and the state, technological civilisation and the question of alternatives. Gandhi had a profound faith in the grandeur of the simple man. He was deeply involved in the freedom movement and, therefore, did not have sufficient time to write a book on political philosophy. His writings are diffuse and repetitive, except in *Hind Swaraj* which he wrote before he plunged headlong into the national movement. But, despite all this, all his writings have a coherent vision of man and society. In a way, while Aurobindo developed the idea of national identity, synthesising tradition and modernity, East and West at the grandiose level of metaphysics and abstract philosophy, Gandhi did so at the level of the common man. He was the son of a Dewan in a small state of Gujarat, and was brought up in an atmosphere in which Jainism had intermingled with Vaishnavism. Quite early in his life he had also come in contact with the writings of Ruskin and Tolstoy and was influenced by them. He assimilated from Jainism the emphasis on non-violence, from Vaishnavism the catholicity of outlook, from Ruskin and Tolstoy their contempt for industrial civilisation and ideas on passive resistance. There was also the background of his struggle in South Africa and the nationalist movement in India. Gandhi was a very effective writer too. He had a style of his own, Biblically simple, elegant and yet very effective.

We have referred to the coherent vision of Gandhian thought. It is reflected in two aspects, in his critique of the modern civilisation, and in his search for alternatives to the present structures such as the state, technology, and property. These two aspects of his thought are complementary and inseparable in all that he wrote. Liberals had a tremendous faith in man's progress. They had repudiated tradition, religion and customs and had prized rationalism and science. Their's was the philosophy of the advancing bourgeois civilisation. In India, as we have seen, while liberals had sung paeans in the glory of the British raj, conservatives were alarmed at the prospect of the European culture, particularly its materialistic dimension finding a foothold in India. They thought that the ancient civilisation of India would perish if it so happened. The idea of a calculated, rational, self-interest appeared pernicious to them and as totally disruptive of human relationships and community-way of life. Indian civilisation, they thought, was based on a more satisfactory view of man's place in the cosmos because it had given due place to spiritualism and the search for the soul. They were convinced that materialism imported from the west would destroy this by releasing forces towards atomisation as well as mechanisation of life. They feared that the pursuit of unbridled self-interest in the form of material interest would accentuate conflict in society. Such a society would turn its back on the tradition and go headlong in blindly imitating the West and, as a consequence, repeat the macabre consequences of a philosophy such as growth of capitalism, atomisation of society and the alienation of the individual, mechanisation of life and increasing unemployment as had happened in Europe. They had argued that spiritualism and traditional institutions could preserve the social cohesion and values which India had nourished and cherished. This outlook was reflected in some of the movements in the late nineteenth century and was shared by all conservative sections of Indian society.

Gandhi, too, shared this scepticism of modern civilisation, but instead of harking back to tradition he tried to look for an alternative. Like Vivekananda and Aurobindo he had welcomed the destruction of those institutions which has drained Indian society of its life. He particularly found the exploitation of the scheduled castes repellent and did more than anyone else to improve their social status. But Gandhi also denounced the evil consequences of political democracy and the industrial revolution, which according to him, were based on self-interest. Gandhi had a deeply religious outlook. In fact he had himself said that religion and politics were inseparable. But it must be remembered that by religion he did not mean sacrament and priestcraft, but rather a quest for ethical values such as truth and non-violence. He dismissed liberal democracy as a fish market, parliament a prostitute, in which people compete for their own self-interest.[1] While he believed that consent was the basis of all good government, he wished to conceive the ideal state as the rule of selfless individuals. According to him, the English people were governed by a parliament which was full of ostentation, pomp and show and in which decisions were not taken on the basis of wider interests. He condemned it as sterile and barren. He repeated Carlyle's indictment of it as a talking shop in which people play fantastic tricks on each other. He had published in Gujarati a translation of Plato's *Apology* and there is no doubt that he was deeply influenced by Plato's idealism and concern for moral values. According to him, democracy as practised in Britain, was bad because it believed in counting of heads, those who won 51 per cent votes carried the day. The minority had to submit to the majority. Gandhi shared enthusiasm of his predecessors like Vivekananda and Aurobindo on consensus and cooperation which transcended the majority principle and pursued the welfare of all. Like a true democrat he always thought power resides in the people. But for him institutions and procedures were not as important as the substance of democracy. Democracy, according to him meant that the weakest should have the same oppurtunity as the strongest. He complained, democracy had come to mean party rule, or to be more exact, rule in the hands of the Prime Minister who often lacked honesty of purpose. In it, he held each party thrives in horse-trading and sensationalism which is blown out of all proportions by the press.

Gandhi further argued that subordination of life to materialism had led western democracies to the exploitation of the colonial world. He was aware of the fact that the ruling classes had shared their exploits with the masses but concluded that "masses are being exploited by the ruling class or castes under the sacred name of democracy": He added, "shorn of all the camouflage, the exploitation of the masses of Europe is sustained by violence".[2] He was against imperialistic exploitation of the peoples of Asia and Africa by the democracies of the west and identified the rise of Nazism and Fascism as a culmination of this process in Western democracy. He wrote "at best it is merely a cloak to hide the Nazi and the fascist tendencies of imperialism".[3]

His critique of modern civilisation was no less trenchant. He was a votary of the ancient ideal of simple, moral and pious life. Praise for such a life is all-pervasive in his writings. He was a firm believer in God and thought that only the simple and the pure can communicate with Him. Brought up in a deeply religious environment, he yearned for spiritual emancipation. He declared: "For me morals, ethics, and religion are convertible terms. A moral life without reference to religion is like a house built upon sand."[4] His religion was the religion in the service of mankind. He had said, "I do not know any religion apart from human activity. It provides a moral basis to all other activities which they would otherwise lack, 'reducing life to a thing of sound and fury', signifying nothing." In this he was deeply influenced by the bhakti cult and the *bhagwat* tradition. He was one of the few leaders of modern India who intensely believed in a personalised God and exploited the richness of this concept to the full. Following it, he examined the modern civilisation subjectively, in terms of its impact on the immediate concerns of the common man; and this largely explains his misjudgement and exaggeration on so many points. He never tried to construct a philosophical system and never separated his moral concerns from personal experience.

Gandhi loathed the material civilisation and particularly detested the industrial revolution. He believed that it was destroying deeper values. He was convinced that Rome suffered a fall when it attained too much material affluence. So did Egypt. The descendents and kinsmen of the royal and divine Krishna too fell when they became too rich. Gandhi declared that "the modern civilisation represents forces of evil and darkness, it is immoral". "The last war has shown", wrote Gandhi, "as nothing else the Asuric nature of civilization that dominates Europe today. Every canon of public morality has been considered too foul to be uttered. Europe today is only nominally Christian. In reality it is worshipping Mammon".[5] He reiterated this idea again and again. This craze for the material had, he bemoaned, led to the ever-widening circle of wants without any sense of direction or purpose. He pointed out that science is meaningless because it does not provide any answer to the question "What shall we do and how shall we live. This craze for wants had led to series of wars, imperialism, colonisation, loss of sense of moral prestige and human justice and decline of deeper spiritual values." Indeed the more important reason for this was his concern for culture of society and preservation of Indian values.

The reaction against industrial society of the west and the glorification of the rural life, however, had a more pragmatic reason behind it. He thought that in a predominantly over-populated, rural society in which people depended on agriculture, the introduction of labour-saving devices would play havoc with the life of the people. However, as years rolled by his opposition to technology and industrialisation decreased in ferocity. He began to welcome any form of industrialisation which would not increase unemployment and destroy the village craft as well as the simplicity of rural life. He said that every machine that helps the individual has a place but, to quote him, "there should be no place for a machine that concentrates power in a few hands and turns the masses into mere machine minders, if indeed they do not make them unemployed". He thought that besides saving us from the ills of technology, the small industries would provide immediate employment. Gandhi indeed repudiated both machine and property as a means of power. Indeed so great was his revulsion against the industrial society that he condemned the doctrine which seeks to displace the synthetic medicine of earlier times. He even rejected railways which, according to him, had become a vehicle for the spread of moral corruption in society. He was clear that the railways had been introduced in India not to serve popular interest but to strengthen the foundations of the British imperialism. In fact, even in labour-saving machines he pleads more for communal ownership. For instance he wrote: "If we should have electricity in every village home, I should not mind villagers plying their implements and tools, with the help of electricity. But then the village communities or the state would own power houses just as they have their grazing pastures." According to Gandhi, "the whole emphasis must shift from power to service: production is inevitable but it must be not for private accumulation but social service".

II

His antipathy to all forms of power is reflected in his ideas on the state and property. He said, "I look upon an increase in the power of the state with the greatest fear, because, although while apparently doing good by minimising exploitation, it does the greatest harm to mankind by destroying individuality, which lies at the root of all progress."[6] The state to him represented "violence in a concentrated form". He argued, "The individual has a soul, but as the state is a soulless machine, it can never be weaned from violence to which it owes its very existence."[7] He preferred man to live by the exercise of his will than by force of habit. Like the ancients, Gandhi too believed in *swaraj*—a condition in which the individual would be the complete master of himself. As a result, he saw all power as a limitation on our capacity to seek *swaraj* which he thought lies at the root of progress.

Gandhi shared Rousseau's enthusiasm for the General Will. Both had respect for the community. But while Rousseau confused community with the state, Gandhi kept them separate. Rousseau thought that the General Will was an end result of a political process, "sublime reason which is beyond the understanding of the vulgar". For Rousseau the existence of the state is necessary to create and nurture a life of virtue. According to him, there could not be any justice or morality outside the state. This was quite different from the position of Gandhi who always looked with suspicion on all forms of power particularly political power.[8] While for Rousseau, in the civil state natural liberty is replaced by "civil liberty" and man becomes a moral being, for Gandhi despite his emphasis on mass participation, "no society can possibly be built on a denial of individual freedom".[9]

He also accepted the distinction between the state and society and often contrasted the spiritual dominance of Indian society with political dominance of western society. While he described western political power as a "brute force", the ancient Indian society was glorified where "kings and swords were inferior to the sword of ethics".[10] He thought that politics encircled people, "Like the coil of snake" from which one could not get out, no matter how much one tries. He made it one of his missions to "wrestle with the snake".[11] It is for this reason that for him *swaraj* was always something more than mere political freedom: it meant, to quote Dalton, "India's spiritual liberation through a fundamental change in each individual's moral perception".[12] Dalton further says, "Politics and law were inevitably, 'mechanical', 'external' and 'artificial' and usually, corrupt and degraded. For both Tagore and Gandhi the price must be paid in self-sacrifice, for that alone could produce the internal self-purification required for *Swaraj*."[13]

He launched a vigorous attack on the concentration of power in the state. He did not mind so long as the state confined itself to the maintenance of law and order and allowed full scope for voluntary activities of the members. He was convinced that the individual freedom alone can make a man voluntarily surrender himself completely to the service of society. If it is wrested from him, Gandhi argued, "he becomes an automation and society is ruined". He further wrote, "No society can possibly be built on a denial of individual freedom. It is contrary to the very nature of man."[14]

He thought that freedom lies at the root of progress. According to him, every man is born with certain innate tendencies. Every person is also born with certain definite limitations which he cannot overcome and consequently, everyone is not fit for all kinds of work. This leads to unnecessary and wasteful competition. An ideal social order is one in which there is no distinction of high or low and "in which each is guaranteed the fruits of his labour on the one hand and prevented from pressing upon his neighbour on the other".[15]

He toyed with the idea of a non-violent state on the lines of Ashoka and believed, though quite naively, that such a state is capable of defending itself against any combination based on armed forces. Such a state, Gandhi postulated would be a purely defensive state and would only do as much as is necessary to let people do what they want to. It would certainly not concern itself with health, and education, which must be better left to private initiative. The interference of the state in such matters would, Gandhi was convinced, introduce an immoral element in a moral field in so far as the state represents coercion. According to him, it is immoral for the state to interfere in the fields which are beyond its normal jurisdiction. Such a non-violent state would be based on a willing consent of the people and will represent near unanimity in society. It cannot be majority of one but "nearer 99 against one in a hundred". He was, however, hopeful that such a state would be possible in India.

The argument against the centralization was quite over-vigorous at times. It was a moral argument, and was based on the idea that centralisation of power destroyed man's urge to see his own *swaraj* in terms of his distinct genius. It also destroyed similar urge in various other wholes in society. He also thought that centralization would increase violence in society. Therefore, "if India is to evolve along non-violent lines, it will have to decentralise", because "centralisation as a system is inconsistent with a non-violent structure of society".[16] Gandhi was against not only centralization of political power but also against centralization of economic power. He lamented the fact that the tendency in modern industry was towards large scale production and later large scale control. In such a case there was bound to be a conflict between the rich and the poor.[17] Decentralisation, on the other hand, Gandhi thought, would induce people to realise their responsibility and be non-violent. It was based on a notion of cooperation and social feeling. Gandhi envisaged that the amount of non-violence used would be a mark of an advanced society. That is why he made a clear distinction between his state and an anarchist state. He was prepared to be classified as an anarchist provided the objectives are achieved without violence. His state is a form of society characterised by self rule and self-regulation, by voluntary help and a spirit of sacrifice as against competition and coercion which characterise the modern state. He wrote: "Political power means the capacity to regulate material life through national representatives. If national life becomes so perfect as to become self-regulated, no representation becomes necessary. There is than a state of enlightened anarchy. In such a state everyone is his own ruler. He rules himself in such manner that he is never a hinderance to his neighbour. In the ideal state, therefore, there is no political power because there is no state."[18] In such a state there would be no army, navy, police, courts or laws.

He looked back nostalgically on *Ramarajya* which for him personified the idea of self-help, sacrifice and discipline. He wrote, "Rama did justice even to a dog. By abandoning his kingdom and living in the forests for the sake of truth, Rama gave to all the kings of the world an object lesson in noble conduct. By his strict monogamy he showed that a life of perfect self-restraint could be led by a royal householder. He lent splendour to his throne by his popular administration and proved that *Ramarajya* was the acme of *swaraj*. Rama did not need the very imperfect modern instruments of ascertaining public opinion by counting votes. He had captivated the hearts of the people. He knew public opinion by intuition as it were. The subject of Rama were supremely happy." He thought that such a *Ramarajya* is possible even today. He even regarded Abubaker and Hazrat Umar like Rama. In concrete terms, *Ramarajya* for him meant: politically, the removal of the control of the British army in every shape and form, economically, freedom from the British capitalists and capital as well as from their Indian counterparts. Morally, it meant freedom from armed forces. He was convinced that a country governed by even its national army can never be free because, "its so called weakest member can never rise to his full moral height".[19] He declared "the humblest must feel equal to the tallest".

But he was quite aware that it is not possible to create such a state in the immediate future, that the ideal can never be fully realised "in the present state of iniquitous inequalities in which a few roll in riches and the masses do not get even enough to eat".[20] And, therefore, for the immediate, he conceded, corercion could be used in extreme circumstances. A state is good according to Gandhi, when "the people are governed the least". He thought that "the nearest approach to purest anarchy would be a democracy based on non-violence".[21] In such a state there will of course be railways, police, navy, army, courts and laws but all these will function as an aid to the people rather than as bureaucratic instruments of oppression. Gandhi pointed out that the future of civilisation depends on progressive diminution in the use of violence. He was convinced that the increase in the powers of bureaucracy stifles all sources of initiative. For this he pleaded for decentralisaiton of power in society by the introduction of the system of panchayat raj turning each village or units of villages into a republic. Indeed, the connection between his glorification of rural life and the pachayati raj is very intimate. Gandhi was a rustic and was very clear in his mind that the ideal non-violent society should be based on rural rather than urban basis. So great was his contempt for urban centres that he thought that they represent violence, coercion and exploitation in concentrated form, while villages are based on the ideal of happy spontaneity in which all voluntarily cooperate with each other. According to him, a rural civilisation based on the idea of village republics will be strong enough even to resist a megalomaniac such as Hitler who, he wrote "could not devastate even hundred thousand non-violent villages". And if he did so, Gandhi was convinced, "he would himself become non-violent in the process".[22]

Gandhi thought that the autonomous bodies should be the substance of the new state as this is the only means for ensuring variety and freedom on the one hand, and preventing bureaucratic oppression on the other. It was a continuation of a tradition which started with Vivekananda and was then developed further by Aurobindo and Tagore.[23] This was an application of the doctrine of unity in diversity, or diversity in unity as Aurobindo called it, as the basis of Indian life. Both Vivekananda and Aurobindo had emphasised that conflict could be replaced by cooperation grounded in an enlightened sense of spiritual unity. Gandhi's own experience in South Africa, where he had succeeded in resolving a legal dispute by discovering common interest, had taught him "the beauty of compromise". The autonomous institutions, based on the principle of decentralisation, Gandhi hoped, would develop spontaneous energies of the people while training them in cooperative action. Panchayat republic would be a flexible response to social requirements and could be a link in social groupings or organisation around the concepts of autonomy and cooperation. He, therefore, pleaded that these panchayats should be given full powers.

Every village has to be self-sustained and capable of managing its affairs. However, the Gandhian ideal of self-sustained village would not exclude dependence on, and willing help from, others. But Gandhi was convinced that in an ideal arrangement it would be "free and voluntary play of mutual forces". Gandhi thought that such a society is inevitably cultured because in it everyone knows his wants and also realises that no one should want anything that others cannot have with equal labour." He summed up his organisation of society thus:

In this structure composed of innumerable villages, there will be ever widening, never ascending circles. Life will not be a pyramid with the apex sustained by the bottom,... But it will be an oceanic circle whose centre will be the individual always ready to perish for the village, the latter ready to perish for the circle of the villages, till at last the whole becomes one life composed of individuals, never aggressive in their arrogance but ever humble, sharing the majesty of the oceanic circles of which they are integral units....[24]

He further said that "the outermost circumference will not wield power to crush the inner circle but will give strength to all within and derive its own strength from it".[25]

III

Similarly he also hated concentration of economic power. He loathed modern society in which a few thrive at the expense of the many. He even welcomed bold action to prevent such a sordid situation. He thought that it was a necessary result of modern materialistic civilisation. In a sense, the worship of mammon, he thought, "has given rise to a school which has been brought up to look upon materialistic advancement as the goal and which has lost all touch with the finer elements of life". Like Marx he put great emphasis on labour which, he believed, is the real wealth and gives rise to money. He thought that "the real owner of wealth is one who puts in a certain amount of labour with conscious productive aim".[26] It is because of this that he believed that the labour has a unique place in life and enjoined that no one should eat even a single meal without doing some labour. Such an approach, he was convinced, would naturally minimise inequalities and also safeguard against "unexpected change of fortune", and "go a long way towards the acquisition of fearlessness and thus towards an upliftment of our national character".[27] It would also prevent unnecessary accumulation of economic power.

In fact, Gandhi totally rejected the institution of property. He always thought that property was an obstacle in the realisation of God. He quoted a verse of Premchand to Gangabehari whose property had been stolen, "It is a blessing that the chains have broken, it will now be easier for me to find Shri Gopal." In another letter to Champabehari R. Mehta he wrote, "We have no right to possess a single pie, whatever we possess is as good as stolen property. Since all people in the world are thieves, possessions are not looked upon as theft. That, however, should not blind us to truth."[28] However, Gandhi was conscious that such a position would be too unrealistic in the present circumstances. Therefore, he declared that if property is "lawfully acquired",[29] it is entitled to protection. His ideas on property were an outcome of the traditional faith in the principle of plain living and high thinking which had implified that man's happiness really lies in contentment. He who is discontented, however, much he may possess, becomes a slave to his desires. Gandhi wrote, "And there is really no slavery equal to that of his desires."[30]

It is in this light that Gandhi's ideas on trusteeship should be viewed: they are essentially a concession to the fraility of human mind. He thought a nationalist zamindar or a capitalist would try to live like a non-zamindar or a non-capitalist. He will regards his tenants or workers as his co-proprietors. He will hold his zamindari or industry in trust for them by making a moderate contribution for the use of his labour or capital. Gandhi was sure that if people seriously think over it and constantly try to act up to it, then life on earth would be much better. He admitted that absolute trusteeship is an abstraction and is equally unattainable. "But", he wrote, "if we strive for it, we shall be able to go further in realizing a state of equality on earth than by any other method".[31] How about state ownership? Isn't it better than private ownership? Gandhi admitted that it was better, but he rejected it on grounds of violence. He declared "It is my firm conviction that if the state suppressed capitalism by violence, it will be caught in the coils of violence itself, and will fail to develop non-violence at any time."[32] He concluded, "what I would personally prefer would be not a centralisation of power in the hands of the State, but an extension of the sense of trusteeship, in my opinion the violence of private ownership is less injurious than the violence of the state".[33] But should the zamindars and capitalist refuse to become trustees, and state ownership, becomes unavoidable, Gandhi declared, he would support a minimum state ownership.

It is very difficult to say how far Gandhi was influenced by Marx. He himself claimed that he had read Marx. He wrote: "I have to reduce myself to the level of the poorest of the poor. That is what I have been trying to do for the last fifty years or more, and so I claim to be a foremost communist."[34] The differences are clear on two points. First, while Gandhi rejected property as something antithetical to spiritual progress, Marx did not reject property as such, he merely rejected the property which is based on exploitation and fosters inequality in society. Second, the major difference was around the problem of means. Though the entire tenor of Gandhi was against property, he too acquiesced in the institution, albeit reluctantly, by conceding one's right to earn property by lawful means. But, as against Marx, he was quite emphatic that the new society is to be achieved only by non-violent means. It is true that he contemplated the possibility of the state nationalising key industries and other means of production in case the capitalists refused to turn into trustees which he thought they would. But on the whole he was convinced that they would heed to his call. "I shall bring about", he wrote, "economic equality through non-violence, by converting the people to my point of view and by harnessing the forces of love as against hatred".[35] His contempt for use of violent means was based not only on the fact that he thought power was dangerous, that evil means had an inevitable tendency to enter into ends and corrupt them. That is why he insisted on non-violence and satyagraha over the concepts of boycott and passive-resistance. He wrote that, means to be means, must always be within our reach, and so *ahimsa* is our supreme duty. If we take care of the means, we are bound to reach the end sooner or later. He had derived these ideas from Thoreau, Emerson and Tolstoy as well as Jain tradition. He was also immensely influenced by the Sermon on the Mount. His ideas on trusteeship sprang from his faith in voluntary action as well as his fear of the state. He thought that while apparently doing good by minimizing exploitation, the "state does the greatest harm to mankind by destroying individuality, which lies at the root of all progress". He further said, "we know of so many cases where men have adopted trusteeship, but nowhere the state has really lived for the poor".[36] While Marx wanted to transcend class conflict by abolition of private property altogether, Gandhi seems to resolve it by converting men of property into trustees.

Behind all that Gandhi said lies the assumption that much can be done by change of heart, by establishing the connection between spiritual values and material conditions. Change of heart is the first and the most important course in the Gandhian scheme; though he also recommended change of material environment by pleading for decentralization of economic and political power. But, since material conditions are the result of man's spiritual disease, the real cure lies in changing man's psyche in which even the reform of the material conditions also helps. By decentralization of economic and political power as a corollary of change of hearts, Gandhi hoped to produce a new individual as well as a new society. Educate a man to truth and non-violence, and by truth, man will transform material conditions for the good of all, was his dictum. Material conditions and individual character are two sides of the same coin in which the individual character has a greater precedence because it alone has the capacity to transform material conditions on a permanent basis. A change of material conditions without corresponding change of heart will not yield results. Indeed, in some cases, when due importance is not given to means, it may permanently destroy all possibilities of good. While Marx was impatient of the world, Gandhi thought that there was no need to loose hope; things could still be improved by patience and understanding; otherwise attempt to transform material conditions by force and violence is likely to remove all possibility of good life.

But where he differed from the communist aim was, once again, on the problem of means. It is for purity of means that Gandhi developed his unique ideas on Satyagraha, which is not merely a negative way of opposing violence by non-violence but a positive method by which the whole society is reconstructed on the basis of love and search for truth. Satyagraha consists of two words, i.e. *Satya* which means truth and *agraha* which means insistence "force", "request" or "strength". A practitioner of Gandhian philosophy opposes violence by non-violence as well as by the strength of his moral convictions, to bring home the truth of his position to the opponent. According to Gandhi it is not merely a way of resisting authority but also a way of using love and moral strength to vindicate truth in society. Gandhi was convinced that violence breeds an attitude of revenge in the vanquished which eventually leads to further violence. It also inflicts enormous injury on others. On the other hand, use of *satyagraha* may involve suffering of the *satyagrahi* himself. This highlights that *satyagrahi* is not merely trying to win or pursue his own private interest but is seeking the larger good or truth which Gandhi thought was God himself. He said, "There is no way to find truth except the way of non-violence." While violence creates barriers between people, divides them, non-violence enlarges lines of communication and ties them in a new moral bond based on love and humility. To quote Horburgh, "Gandhi's quest for self-realisation is the pursuit of a way of life that incorporates all the truth to which men have yet attained and which continues to strive towards absolute Truth. This is communal enterprise."[37] Truth is to be attained by mutual love and sharing and not by fighting each other. However, if there was a choice between violence and cowardice, Gandhi always favoured the former. He declared that "though violence is not lawful, when it is offered in self-defence or for the defence of the defenseless, it is an act of bravery far better than cowardly submission. The latter befits neither man nor woman. Under violence, there are many stages and varieties of bravery. Every man must judge this for himself."[38] When once we have grasped this point, Gandhi was convinced, final victory is beyond question. As pointed out earlier, he even went to the extent of suggesting that a non-violent resistance would have succeeded against Hitler also. Gandhi was convinced that capitalism inevitably leads to exploitation of poor and that the latter's emancipation is desirable. He appealed to capitalists to give up wealth and work for the good of masses.

Hence the indictment of the state, property and industrialisation. The whole basis of society with its inequalities, coercive state and competitive capitalists is vicious. He declared, "If plain life is worth living, then the attempt is worth making."[39] His numerous ideas on this are diffused and vague. His realism as a political strategist is amply contrasted by the utopian elements in his thought. But if asking of question is as important as answering them, Gandhi certainly raised almost all the important questions which confront modern civilisation, namely, the question of bureaucratic oppression, statism, increasing use of violence, the hideous consequences of big technology. He, however, did not realise that the part of his gospel was largely unsuited to the precarious conditions of modern civilisation. He was largely concerned with the interests of the poor. For the prophet of modern India, the ideas of the minimum government as well as trusteeship provided the answer. He of course believed that some key industries were necessary. He no where enumerated these industries. The general assumption was that where a large number of people had to work together, state ownership was necessary. But he was convinced that dispossession of the monied made by force was not proper. Instead they should be invited to cooperate in the process of conversion to the state ownership. He wrote, "They are no *pariahs* of society, whether they are millionaires or paupers. The two sources of the same disease. And all are men 'for a that'".

He was of the opinion that the virtue of socialism was that it regards all members as equal, none low, none high. In the individual body the head is not high because it is at the top, nor are the soles of the feet low because they touch the earth. Just as the parts of the individual body are equal to each other, so are the members of society. But he was quite emphatic that since socialism is pure as crystal, it requires crystal like means to achieve it. "Impure means", he wrote, "result in an impure end." According to him the prince and the peasant will not be equalised by cutting of the Prince's head. Such a method is based on untruthfulness and cannot lead to socialism. He was convinced that true socialism can be established by *satyagraha* alone. He wrote, "It is the highest and infallible means, the greatest force. Socialism will not be reached by any other means. *Satyagraha* can rid society of all evils, political, economic and moral."[40] At another place, he declared, "under my plan the state will be there to carry out the will of the people and not to dictate them or force them to do its will. I shall bring about economic equality through non-violence, by converting the people to my point of view, by harnessing the forces of love as against hatred."[41] He even thought that the establishment of socialism or communism was inseparable from one's own personal life. He was convinced that one cannot hope to bring about economic equality if "he owns fifty motor cars or even ten bighas of land". Every socialist worker, according to him, must reduce himself "to the level of the poorest of the poor". He saw his own life as an attempt to do this and that is why he claimed himself to be the foremost communist. Herein lies the essence of difference between Marx and Gandhi. Both favoured economic equality but while Marx did not give much importance to means and considered personal life irrelevant to the wider struggle, Gandhi thought that only truthful means, combined with a sincere application of the ideal to one's own private life, would lead to a genuine socialist society. He thundered, "To my knowledge there is no country in the world which is purely socialistic. Without the means described above the existence of such a society is impossible."[42]

In his economic ideas, Gandhi appear singularly aware of the appalling selfishness of the controllers of industry and the state and to the urgent necessity of a clean but effective administration in the state to ensure the conscious diffusion of an economic and political power. As a critic of modern society, Gandhi's ideas are compelling. His critique of modern industrial society and his analysis are full of great insights. His ideas on the relationship between means and end are particularly thoughtful. No one has put a better case on these points than Gandhi. To cope with the problems of modern civilisation, including those of industrialisation and increase in the state power, one must take account of Gandhi. His criticisms can be answered but they cannot be ignored. However, there are two points on which we feel there is a regression in his thought to the medieval world. First, he overlooked the importance of power. In practice he was quite conscious of the positive role power could play and did more than any other man to put power at the centre of Indian society. And yet in theory he was quite naive and ignored what Vyasa and Kautilya had said about the importance of the state not only in maintenance of law and order but also in hindering hinderances to the development of the individual.

Doubtlessly power can be misused but, as the ancient believed, the solution was not in weakening power but in ensuring against its abuse. Secondly, his harsh language against the industrial society gives an impression as if he denounced the role of scientific knowledge in human life and yet it is not clear how would he like India's problems to be solved without science and technology. Vivekananda and Dayananda had reinterpreted the traditional thought in a more positive way. What is more, they were quite conscious of the fact that knowledge is power and it is in terms of knowledge, scientific and spiritual, through which society could be transformed for the better. Even when Dayananda gave a call to go back to Vedas, he had precisely this point in mind. He was contrasting the positivism of Vedas with mysticism and the attitude of the life-negation of the medieval world. It is not certain whether Gandhi denounced science and technology, but the overall impact of his ideas on these points was negative and dated. He raised the right questions but did not provide realistic answers profound enough to combine both the short term and the long term interests.

In reacting against utopianism of Gandhian thought people went to the other extreme: they went for the evils of centralized power and big technology increase. There is no doubt that there is a need for greater diffusion of economic and political power, greater equality in social relationships, a wide concern for moral values. These are all demanded by modern life, and more so when the increasing use of technology has brought to fore the evils of centralization of both economic and political power. The entire trend of modern society points to realism in the questions which Gandhi asked. But in denying the importance of knowledge and contrasting it with wisdom, in not seeking a better technology rather than condemning it outright, Gandhi virtually threw the baby with the bath water. Technology, for good or evil, possesses the only hope we have of eventual fulfilment of human needs, increase in knowledge, the only way by which good and bad moral orders or good or bad political organisations can be distinguished and related to the ongoing process of society. Only by greater knowledge of all aspects of life and by application of better and more humane technology, of course in terms of greater diffusion of political and economic power, a humane, more differentiated and creative civilization can be created. Without good life, power is dangerous. But without power, there is no possibility of ever building up good life. Knowledge (*gyana*) too is one of the forms of power (*shakti*) in knowledge-tradition in India pointed out earlier, along with the other two powers leading to prosperity (*aishwarya shakti*) and creative dynamism (*teja shakti*). He did not explore the possibility of bringing a better system into being with a far smaller degree of violence or corercion than had occurred in the West by development of a new kind of technology. Today, there is not one technology but many varieties of it and if we make a conscious choice in the context of human needs and a sense of right, we can definitely hope to ensure justice, equality, and the widest opportunity for full development of human beings. In this sense his ideas were reactionary. This explains why when his own magnetic and towering personality was not there, his ideas were thrown overboard and the Indian political leadership turned to other streams of thought for inspiration. This is also a reason why the influence of the Sarvodaya and Bhoodan movements which were launched by Jayaprakash Narayana and Vinoba Bhave did not capture the imagination of the people in the way in which Gandhian ideas were able to do. The events after independence perhaps diversified and obscured his vision. One group among his disciples accepted the centralised state and bureaucracy as inevitable consequences of modern civilisation. They acquiesced in state socialism and technological change. They helped in the creation of a massive state structure which interfered in most aspects of life. When these disciples tried to strike a break with the past, they turned to liberalism, socialism and communism for inspiration and laid the foundation of a centralised welfare state. In a deeper sense this was inevitable. But if Gandhi had combined the progressive and forward looking buoyancy of Vivekananda's vision with his ideas on the individual community relationship and clever political strategy, he would have pointed a direction better suited to a peaceful adaptation of the enduring elements in the traditional way of life to the problems of industrialising society. His political strategy was constructive and truly great. He stands as a great statesman in the first half of twentieth century. In his thought he raises profound problems of our times. A disquiet with the growing political power of the state and the concentration of economic and technological power in the hands of the few is there in him. His influence on nationalist thought was great. He brought a great deal of utopianism to bear on politics. His view of life was full of compassion, his morality puritan. In thought he made a major contribution by highlighting problems of the twentieth century and thereby insisting that politics, industry and technology should be subordinated to the ideals of life.

NOTES

1. M.K. Gandhi, *Young India*, 3 November 1927.
2. Ibid., 3 Sept.1925.
3. *Harijan*, 18 May 1940.

4. Ibid., 3 Oct. 1936.
5. *Youth India,* 8 Sept. 1920.
6. *Harijan,* 12 Dec. 1938.
7. *Works,* vol. 51, p. 318.
8. See, Dennis Dalton, *Indian Idea of Freedom* (Gurgaon, Academic Press, 1982).
9. *Harijan,* 1 Feb. 1942.
10. Loc. cit.
11. Works, XVII, p. 406.
12. Dennis Dalton, A.J. Wilson (Eds.), *The States of South Asia* (Honolulu, University Press of Hawaii, 1982), p. 182.
13. Loc. cit.
14. *Works,* vol. 73, pp. 93-94.
15. *Works,* vol. 59. p. 30.
16. *Harijan,* 18 Jan. 1942.
17. *Works,* vol. 58, p. 28.
18. *Young India,* 2 July 1931.
19. *Harijan,* 5 May 1946.
20. Ibid., 1 June 1947.
21. Ibid., 21 July 1940.
22. Ibid., 4 Nov. 1939.
23. See, Dennis Dalton, op. cit., p. 183.
24. *Harijan,* 28 July 1946.
25. Loc. cit.
26. Ibid., 25 March 1939.
27. Ibid., 19 Jan. 1947.
28. *Works,* vol. 41, p. 412.
29. Ibid., vol. 52, p. 218.
30. Ibid., vol, 73, p. 94.
31. Ibid., vol. 59, p. 318.
32. Loc. cit.
33. Ibid., p. 319.
34. Ibid., 31 March 1946.
35. Ibid., 31 March 1946.
36. Works, vol. 59, p. 319.
37. Horshburgh, HJN, *Non-violence and Aggression: A Study of Gandhi's Moral Equivalent of Work* (Oxford, 1968).
38. *Harijan,* 27 Oct. 1946.
39. Ibid., 1 Sept. 1946.
40. Ibid., 20 Sept. 1947.
41. Ibid., 31 March 1946.
42. Ibid., 13 Sept. 1947.

CHAPTER 11

THE HUMANIST AND SOCIALIST VISION:
M.N. ROY, NEHRU AND LOHIA

While Aurobindo and Gandhi were developing ideas of 'transform-ation' through reconstruction, M.N. Roy began with the idea of fundamental revision of Marxism only to finally abandon it altogether in favour of 'radical humanism'. Roy had much in common with Vivekanada, Aurobindo and Gandhi, but he sharply differed with them in his preoccupation with Marxism, and particularly in his concern for materialism for which his predecessors had some sort of a contempt. But while Gandhi was able to win the leadership of masses for almost three decades, the theoretical finesse of M.N. Roy in Marxism and other forms of European thought as against not having anything to do with dominant currents in Indian thought, kept him at a distance from the mainstream of political life in India. And while the ideology of reconstruction was to prove appropriate to the situation of the first-half of the twentieth century in India, Marxism, and later the radical humanism of Roy, was to remain confined to an esoteric circle.

Like most Bengali thinkers of his time, M.N. Roy started as an admirer of Vivekananda. He was a part of terrorist movement but soon got fed up with it and turned to communism for inspiration. He rose very high in the international communist movement and many a time crossed swords even with Lenin. The profundity of his understanding of India was accepted by the latter. But after the rise of Stalin his frustration with communism also began. He always thought Marx was right in emphasising the importance of matter, in his idea of class struggle and the need for a revolutionary action. But he did not accept materialistic interpretation of history which he thought had an element of both determinism and idealism. Not only that the economic crisis predicted by Marx for bourgeois society did not develop but also, Roy thought the communist prophecy of a classless, stateless society did not come true in the first communist state, i.e. in Soviet

Russia. Indeed he thought that while the bourgeois society survived all vicissitudes, the state socialism turned oppressive and tyrannical in Russia. Instead of the state disappearing or even restructuring itself in terms of diffusion of political power, it had become enormously strong. Power had been concentrated in the State. Rejecting the materialist interpretation of history he thought that the ideas have an autonomy and history of their own. He accepted that they do arise in material struggles of life but once arisen they acquire a certain amount of autonomy and work in different ways in different situations. He reacted sharply against both idealism in Marx's dialectics and determinism in his view of history in which one stage inevitably succeeds another. Marx had indeed provided a powerful method of understanding societies, their power structure and process of change. But his very genius made a dogma out of dialectic, which Roy feared, turned into determinism and fatalism and became an obstacle in our understanding of the historical process. Roy emphasised the need to change this, to emancipate the creative elements in the Marxist thought from the rigid framework of determinism and dialectic, to bring theory once again in relation to new experiences since the revolution. He argued that we must see Marx's materialist interpretation in the new light of a changed world situation; the communist thought must be rid of its utopian legacy. The task according to him, was to take advantage of the new situation and prepare for the good of the downtrodden from the point of view of economic and political democracy. The conditions in society had changed. While liberalism led to the tyranny of the rich, culminating in Fascism and the total state, communism had led to another kind of disappointment because it had failed to create sufficient barricades against the abuse of the state power. In Russia it had led to Stalinist terror and denial of freedom to people. The ideologies, Roy concluded, had become great deceptions. He was aware that Marxist prophecy about the decomposition of the bourgeois social order had not come true. The class struggle had not intensified as predicted. Instead, a large middle class had come into existence which would not be included in the class of the proletariat. This middle class was indeed much different from what the orthodox Marxists thought of it. Instead of collaborating with the bourgeoisie with whom it shares many ideas, the middle class was actually revolting against the economic relations and political practices of the bourgeois society.[1] It had become an agent of social transformation.

In fact, as pointed out earlier, Roy traced the distortions of Marxism to the Marxist denial of the independent existence of ideas. He was convinced that ideas have a logical development of their own and we can trace this development with reference to social movements anywhere. He wrote, "I categorically reject the view that ethical values, cultural patterns, movements of ideas, are mere ideological super-structures raised to justify established economic relations."[2] According to him, ideas have a causative force. He thought that Hegel was nearer the truth than Karl Marx when he declared that the history of philosophy is the history of civilisation.

Roy discovered traces of idealism in economic determinism which had within it some kind of a dualism. He pleaded that the concept of causality must be freed from the fallacy of dualism if it is to withstand the onslaught of positivism. Causality was conceived by him as a function of the physical and social process. According to him, causality is not an empirical, but a logical concept. But economic determinism cannot be established either empirically or logically. He also found the ideal of a classless, stateless society fallacious. According to him, a classless society would be stagnant since Marxism regarded class struggle as the only lever of history. "In a classless society," Roy tried to establish, "the dialectics of history will cease to operate, progress will come to a standstill, humanity will die."[3] In practice, according to him, exactly the opposite had happened. In the name of the dictatorship of the proletariat, the State, according to Roy, smothered all opposition. The very fact that the state had not withered away showed that "economic relations do not constitute the whole of human life, or that even under communism they are not equitable".[4]

He was of the opinion that Marxism cannot be strictly applied to history. The economic view of history only throws light on one aspect of history. But, Roy argued, history must be studied as the process of "integral human evolution—mental, intellectual, social". In this, a new class no less than new economic relations inspire destruction of the established economic relations and the creation of new ones. He admitted that the cultural traditions of Germany or of any other country which fell a victim to Fascism, might have been determined by economic conditions. But it was wrong to connect the consequences of economic backwardness causally with monopoly capitalism. He attributed this to the failure to appreciate the role of ideas in history.

He particularly blamed communist party for the way the revolution had gone. He argued that a party deliberately forged as the instrument for capturing power would not lead men into freedom. It sooner or later turns into an internal dictatorship. This is what happened in Russia. All opposition was suppressed in the name of discipline. "The individuality of its members," wrote Roy, "was scarified at the altar of the collective ego of the party and a party is the archetype of the society it proposes to build."

Roy believed that a good party is one in which every member of the party becomes conscious of the total experiences, thereby becoming a full-grown individual. In the way in which communism was established, Roy bemoaned, political practice had degenerated into a vain struggle for power. In the name of the collective ownership, it simply transferred power from one class to another. The capitalist ownership was replaced by a proletarian ownership. The net result is that power still remains in "private" hand, because it is vested in one class and not the entire society. Roy wrote:

We must realise that not only parliamentary democracy was a failure, but the Marxist theory of democracy was fallacious, dangerously so.[5]

Roy found Marxist theory teleological. Since, according to him, Marxism believed that history is made by the operation of the productive forces, one obvious conclusion is that there is very little that man can do, there is no alternative in Marxism to recognizing 'necessity'. This Marxist identification of freedom with some mysterious forces of production, according to Roy, means slavery for the individual. According to him, Marxism had become a new faith, and by conversion to it, "man willingly surrenders his right to freedom, and cultivates a cynical attitude to morality".[6]

But in revolting against liberalism and communism, Roy did not turn to the dominant traditions in Indian thought. Gandhi exasperated him. He could never sympathise with Gandhi's denunciation of the industrial society. For Roy, there could be no freedom, equality or democracy if we reject modern technology. He had contempt for idealism or revivalism of any kind. He did go to ancient sources but only to find support for his kind of materialism in *Lokayata*. He thought that materialist philosophy alone provided the basis for any future progress. He identified the eternal quest for freedom with struggle for existence. Starting with modest beginnings, Roy argued, we have come to the twentieth century technology which has provided us with powerful instruments for the conquest of nature. Science, according to him "is a search for truth, and it is the result of man's quest for freedom".[7] Any other philosophy, according to him, would take us outside the physical universe, "into the wilderness of a mystical metaphysics over which presides God".[8] But Roy's materialism is different from the Marxist materialism in so far as he recognised the autonomy of the mental world, the world of ideas, in the context of the physical nature. He writes, "In building up a social philosophy on the basis of materialism, we do not allot a subsidiary role to ideas. Originating in the pre-human state of biological evolution, emotion and intelligence and decisive factors of social and historical progress."[9] This modification in the Marxist view alone, asserted Roy, can enable us to conceive of universal human values in the context of a rational scheme of the physical universe.

Roy wanted to establish a radical democratic state wedded to the idea of freedom as conceived by materialist philosophy. He was clear in his mind that this state is an ideal but he thought that ideals alone provided incentive to action. He confessed that we cannot predict the future with any certainty. Even the fathers of the Russian revolution could not do it. A party deliberately forged as the instrument for capturing power could not help members to grow into freedom. Roy was convinced that his state wedded to the ideal of 'radical humanism' provided the best chance for freedom.

Roy regarded man greater than any means of production as the latter are his creations. Excessive emphasis on the means of production is the major defect in Marxism. The result is that it enslaves man to the means of production. According to Roy, if we do not regard man as central, we land up in idealism or mysticism. He wrote, "Freedom is the supreme value because the urge for freedom is the essence of human existence."[10] Roy accepted humanism because humanists had always approached life from the assumption of the sovereignty of man. It is man's unique capacity of knowing, as distinct from the common biological property of being aware, which endows him with powers not to rule over others but to create freedom for the benefit of humanity.

Roy conceived of a decentralised state. Unlike the communists, he proposed an organisation of democracy which would enable the people as a whole to become sovereign so that no political party is able to capture power on any pretext. He believed that over-emphasis on power in revolutionary politics had led to negation of freedom; the means had become the end. As a result the dictatorship of the party was justified in the name of communism. In all such situations, power is captured by the party in the name of the class, and then it is monopolised by a relatively small group in the name of the party. Clarifies Roy, "as power is never voluntarily abdicated, freedom for all is impossible. The collective ego-nation, class—is invented to justify this perpetual slavery of the majority." It is remarkable that in this Roy anticipated the new left thinking of our time by about thirty years.

But this does not mean that he accepted the system of parliamentary democracy. Like Gandhi, he too believed in communitarian politics. He, too, regarded the parliamentary democracy as a variant of dictatorship, albeit, the dictatorship of the monied classes over others.[11] Democracy began with two admirable principles of individual freedom and popular sovereignty. But in practice it deviated from those principles. While Rousseau argued that only institution which can claim to embody the General Will should be considered a democratic institution, in practice no attempt was made to organise such a will. Instead, democracy, took the form of delegation of power from the people to some agencies. In the French Revolution itself Robespierre claimed that he represented the General Will and hence justified his imposition of terroristic regime. The laudable theory of the General Will became the moral sanction for a dictatorship. In England, parliamentary democracy started with the recognition of individual rights. But it also soon degenerated into a scramble for power. According to Roy, even there different political parties compete for power and the people are completely forgotten. In this process, the rich acquire a leverage and turn democracy to their advantage. In practice both popular sovereignty and the individual freedom are negated. The sovereign individual is merged in the party and becomes subservient to the party machine. The parties in turn become vehicles for promotion of the ambitions of certain individuals. Democracy, according to Roy, further divides society into elite and masses. Representatives alone are considered competent to rule. Ruling becomes an exclusive prerogative of experts. There is no possibility for the individual to exercise his sovereignty unless he belongs to the elite.

The individual community relationship had been the fundamental problem of politics. Roy did not regard the individual as the antithesis of society. If this kind of relationship is inevitable, Roy declared that social progress is not possible because then we cannot harmonise interests through institutions of parliamentary democracy. In modern times, Roy lamented that the individual has completely disappeared not only from bourgeois but also from revolutionary thought. He rejected Nazism and Fascism because of their denial of the sovereignty of the individual. They reduce the individual to a mere cog in the machine, and, worse still, "endow this vast machinery [the state] with collective ego".[12] For Roy, neither the abstract concept of the nation nor that of the class could be extolled at the expense of the individual.

Roy recognised that the state is an essential organisation of society. The Marxist idea of the stateless society is a utopia which can never be attained. Biological and anthropological researches, Roy argues, have shown us that society is created by the individual. The individual comes first, "he is prior to society; society is the means for attaining an end, which is freedom and progress of the individual".[13] A wrong conception of this relationship has led to divorce of ethics from political practice. In the beginning each individual was alone. But in course of time, as a result of his struggle for existence, men realised that only together, they could carry on the struggle for existence successfully. Here Roy rejects the social contract view that once primitive people met at one place and entered into a contract to create a society. According to Roy, society comes into existence more by accident than by design. In order to combat the forces of nature, primitive men felt the need for cooperation and from this sprang the society as we know it. Purpose was injected into life by the development of consciousness and intelligence which were themselves products of the struggle for existence.

What is the purpose of the struggle? For Roy, it is freedom. At first to escape from the burden of environment so that man could be free from the forces which threatened his existence in this world. This urge for freedom was the basic biological urge which has enabled man to move from primitive state to still higher stages of existence. Doubtlessly there have been ages when society tried to throttle this freedom. But, according to Roy, man struggled for freedom throughout ages: he is still struggling. The establishment of parliamentary democracy was the first stage and that of socialism the second. Both failed. In parliamentary democracy power nominally belongs to the people. Socialism tries to establish a higher form of democracy but is frustrated by the emergence of the dictatorship of the party.

According to Roy, a free community could be conceived only on the basis of freemen. Any other notion of freedom is a fraud. In a good society, man should be able to unfold his own potential with the help of collective effort. Society is necessary because it alone enables the individual to realise his potential. But since the individual has become too helpless in the modern democratic, industrialised state, Roy would organise society around groups and people's communities. According to him these groups should be replicas of the state. Since they will be small and many, the state will not be able to crush the individual. On the other hand, Roy firmly believed man would have greater freedom to develop in small organisations. These groups would constitute the pyramidal structure of the state.

In a real democracy, Roy was convinced, there is no need for transfer of power, or delegation of power. Power belongs to the people, and should always remain in their hands. "Delegation of Power", writes Roy, "to a small minority necessarily means abdication of power as had happened in Russia. In the name of the class or the nation, the party became a new ruler; the proletarian state became its vested interest." But for Roy there can be no progress without individual freedom. In an ideal system, Roy thought, "there will be no contradiction between collective responsibility and individual liberty; social obligations will be voluntarily undertaken and discharged, in quest of individual freedom, by upholding his or her potentialities, that is to say, by asserting individuality, each member of society will increase his social utility and thus contribute to the sum total of collective well-being and progress".[14]

The creation of such a diffused polity shall be accompanied by the simultaneous creation of diffused economy so as to eliminate the possibility of exploitation. Such a society, according to Roy, will ensure an economy minimum to all. This economy will be based on "production for use and distribution with reference to human needs". Roy recognised that "a potential organization is necessary but once the basic necessities have been fulfilled the purpose of the state" should be no more than to maintain conditions under which it will not be necessary for any man to kill another.[15] The state must ensure equal possibilities to all its citizens of acquiring knowledge and developing intelligence. A harmonious society can exist only when we start with the assumption that every individual is capable of rational judgement and the purpose of the social organization is to allow the individual to unfold his potential. According to Roy, the state "will become harmonious in proportion as the individual grows as a free human being capable of making rational as well as moral judgements".[16] He was conscious of the fact that in a large country with millions of inhabitants, rule of the people, by the people was not possible. It was for this reason that he pleaded for indirect democracy in terms of peoples' committees. At the time of elections, the members of these committees will not be required to vote for anyone coming from outside; they will nominate members from amongst themselves. He asserted that while parliamentary democracy divides us into atomised individuals, the 'new democracy', as he called it, will make this freedom concrete by restoring popular sovereignty to them. The individual citizens will be discussing and planning local affairs in the framework of similar neighbouring committees, together constituting the country known as India and for whose administration they will feel responsible. This network of local communities will be the instrument through which the electorate will exercise influence over the decisions of the state. "The State," writes Roy, "will not then be able to become an all powerful Leviathan, because state power will be decentralised, being largely vested in the local republics. In other words, the state will in this way become coterminus with society."[17] Roy was particularly hopeful that such an experiment had a great future in India. In

Western countries democracy has already been imposed from the above. But in India democracy had a chance which it did not have in the East. He even toyed with the idea that the existing Panchayats could be built up as units of organised democracy.

Roy was a humanist and following Renaissance thought he accepted man as a point of departure. He accepted the principle of the sovereignty of the individual and tried to integrate it with democratic theory. His 'new democracy' was a direct result of his faith in the sovereignty of the individual. It was also a result of his deep anguish at the failure of the existing ideologies and institutions in enlarging man's freedom. Humanism appealed to him because it gave an important place to freedom in political equations. Until now, to quote Roy again, "political thinking had emphasised the state; the social welfare was considered as something bigger than the individual welfare. But state or society were no more than mere sum total of the welfare of the individual." He writes at another place, "No freedom, no welfare, no progress or prosperity can be actually experienced except by individuals."[18] Anything else is a fraud. One of the merits of the humanist politics, according to Roy, is that it started with the rejection of the whole game of fighting for political power according to the old rules of the game. Starting with the assumption that man is rational and moral, the humanist, according to him, goes by the rule of reason and ensures that in politics no one should be able to deceive others and drive masses like dumb-driven cattle.

Roy writes:

Then the time will come when a centralised Leviathan can no longer pose as democracy, but a democratic state composed of a number of local democratic republics will rise in which direct democracy is a reality. It will come into being not by passing of laws, not by imposition from above, but because local democracies will be in existence as a political reality and give the impress of their structure on the state as a whole.[19]

What can one conclude from this?

Roy was no longer in favour of a communist revolution. He was a socialist of a kind but was deeply opposed to all forms of totalitarianism. He undoubtedly made a call for revolution. But, unlike most revolutionaries, he paid greater attention to the loss of freedom and individuality in the modern society of which economic problems are an important part but do not exhaust it. Although he believed that the class struggle was a reality, he was opposed to the organisation of movements for freedom on party lines, particularly because political parties, according to him invariably ended up in Stalinism or Fascism. He rejected liberalism and Marxism alike, though for different reasons and as against them favoured a new kind of humanism combined with a radical restruction of political institutions so that power was exercised directly by the people.

In relation to humanism, his objectives were of libertarian kind. It is important to note here that despite Roy's fulminations against Indian political tradition in general and Gandhi in particular, the scheme of the new society given by him is broadly similar to that of Gandhi, which highlights the fact of a remarkable continuity in the Indian thought.[20] Although he rejected Gandhi's religious views as well as his antipathy to modern industrial society, he himself pleaded for a decentralised polity broadly on Gandhian lines and made it the fulcrum of his vision. There is also a certain distrust of the state. Both Gandhi and Roy emphasised self-regulation as the highest kind of freedom and both believed that such a freedom is possible only through an ascending circles of community organizations. Where Roy sharply differed from Gandhi was in his acceptance of modern technology. In doing so he was presumably not aware of his own contradictions; he could not realise that the logic of big technology would inevitably lead to centralisation of power and, hence, could not be reconciled with the kind of decentralised polity and economy he was propagating. A polity of Roy's kind demands a different kind of technology and it is in this context that the debate about small or appropriate technology acquires significance. Roy was indeed a troubled conscience and tried to utilise every branch of knowledge in the service of the ideas of rationality, freedom and equality. But precisely because he tried to sit on too many stools, of biology, psychology, anthropology, physics and politics, all at the same time, that he could not help a fall. From revolution at all costs, he moved to position when he would say "no" if any change had the possibility of ending up in totalitarianism.

He was, throughout his life, torn by his commitments to rational, secular, revolutionary tradition of Marxism and his painful practical experiences. At the end from a practical leader he turned into a utopian thinker. He presented himself as a determined rationalist thinker and yet his book *Reason, Romanticism and Revolution*[21] is a highly romantic work. The best portions are those where he makes an impassioned plea for freedom. But he nowhere convincingly defines what he means by freedom. How can reason help us to arrive at one concept of freedom? How can the idea of self-regulation be combined with the increasing interdependence of life? Reason is seen to have divided mankind because we all tend to view things from our own particular angles. Roy did not realise that reason is a means to an end. It works in terms of certain assumptions and paradigms of knowledge. Roy gave us no method of distinguishing right from wrong reason. He was indeed scarcely aware of the problem of paradigms. There is no room for tradition either in his scheme of things. This is important because while Gandhi could refer to good and bad in tradition as an anchor sheet, Roy could not do so. It was, therefore, all the more necessary for Roy to forge clear connection between his theory of rationality, freedom and new democracy. In the absence of a clear distinguishing criteria of rationality, even the dictators could plead that they were following the dictates of reason and trying to create a moral society. It is also not clear whether Roy would accept everything that goes on the name of science. Assuredly, Roy himself offered a package of institutions, namely, local republics organised around peoples' committees. But in the absence of a clear theory of reason and morality in which he seems to have grounded his 'new democracy', such committees could be far worse than the dictatorships at the top. The most repressive systems in the world have been practised at the lowest levels, in small, closed societies. The most atomised societies have sometimes been no less repressive. We are not saying that the ideal of local republics is false but unless there is a clear perspective of rationality and morality, and their relationship to technology, on the one hand, and the institutional arrangements of society, on the other, there is every likelihood of our facing greater difficulties than Roy ever anticipated.

II

By the middle of the twentieth century, Indian thinkers began to move specifically towards socialism, which while deriving its inspiration from the development of socialism in the West, would yet incorporate the specificity and identity of Indian society. In the beginning there were people like Bankim, Tagore, Aurobindo, Vivekananda who had denounced the materialism and individualism of the liberal political philosophy of the West. People like Lala Hardayal and Ramakrishna Pillai had already contributed weighty arguments in favour of some sort of Marxism in *Amrit Bazar Patrika* (1903) and *Modern Review* (1910) of Calcutta. But this kind of socialism which tried to combine Hinduism with Socialist and particularly Marxist thought had only an ephemeral existence and petered out in the twenties of this century. There was a kind of socialism in Gandhi but for the most part it remained in the background largely on account of the exigencies of the freedom movement.

More serious activity in this direction started in 1934 with the establishment of the Congress Socialist Party.[22] In 1936, in his inaugural address Acharya Narendra Deva defined Marxism as the basis of the new party. He said, "Socialism has only one form, one principle and that is Marxism." This was, however, not acceptable to the Indian Marxists who denounced it as a bourgeois conspiracy and thought that it would be an impediment to the development of Marxism. For sometime an attempt was made to integrate this party with the Communist party. But the attempt proved abortive because people like Masani insisted that such integration could be possible only if the Communist party was prepared to lose its identity.

It is, however, through the fusion of Integralism, Gandhism, Marxism and Democratic Socialism that the new opinion for socialism had been created. Vivekananda had laid the foundations on which the Indian socialists were destined to build. He advocated two principles: First, the Indian nation had its own identity and only that programme of social change would succeed which was based on the recognition of this fact. Second, the removal of poverty and upliftment of the downtrodden, particularly the scheduled castes, was the agenda for the future. Time was destined to emphasise both these principles though in immediate terms these principles received scant attention from the liberals in Indian politics. Gandhi recognised the value of both these principles and argued that these principles could be effectively implemented only in a decentralised polity and a decentralized economy based on the recognition of the importance of cottage and small industries. Gandhi has also denounced the role of the system of private property based on greed and cupidity. He always thought that this had led to the crisis of the Western civilisation. Gandhi's writings were a powerful denunciation of the modern industrial civilisation in terms of a fine vision of the holistic man. However, there was an anarchic streak in him which made him despise state socialism. As against this he had emphasised the importance of the principle of spiritual freedom and the autonomy of the individual. But after 1930, the weaknesses of Gandhi's programme became apparent. New ideals were needed if the Congress movement was to retain its hold over the working class. The Socialist Revolution had already taken place in Russia and had fired the imagination of people like Nehru and Jayaprakash Narayan. The formation of the Communist party as well as the Congress Socialist party served to precipitate issues. People began to see socialism as a central force in the modern world. Economic factors were seen as the important directing forces. Democratic Marxism was accepted as the basis of the new creed.

Both Jayaprakash Narayan and Narendra Deva tried to combine Marxism and Democracy. In 1949 Narendra Deva welcomed the Communist revolution in China as something far superior to anything before. Both were keen on left unity. The whole aim was to indigenize Marxism.

But change came in 1952 at a Panchmarhi session of the party in which Ram Manohar Lohia forcefully expounded the thesis that the Indian society must develop on its own. According to him, the new creed could not be developed on the basis of a borrowed creed. What was needed was an independent Socialist ideology which would be free from weaknesses of socialism in Europe. He argued that the aims of European socialism were bound by ethnocentric considerations, and therefore, it took into account the interest of the European nations only, and very rarely of the nations outside the European framework.[23] International communism had become merely a post office and did not take account of the specific and peculiar problems of the Third World. All this had resulted, Lohia believed, in an imbalance in the international order. While in Europe the development of socialism had been gradual, constitutional and distributive, in other parts of the world it had been revolutionary, extra-constitutional and production-oriented. It had become clear that the structural constraints play a very important role. And, therefore, Lohia was convinced that the character of socialism here could not be the same as in Europe. In Europe, as a result of progress, the main problem was of redistribution whereas in other countries even the structures for production did not exist.

While the aim of constitutional change is good, Lohia argued, the pace of socialism will have to be changed according to difference in circumstances. What the European socialism lacks is "ethos" and "elan" with the result that it no longer has the boldness of earlier socialist thought. The result is that both Socialism and Marxism have failed to free the individual in his private and social life.[24] These have given rise to meaningless structures and closed societies taking the world on to the brink of a world war.[25] Lohia declared that Marxism is full of internal contradictions. He argued that a powerful movement cannot be based on the thoughts of one person alone. He particularly lashed out against the attempt of Marx to lay down the laws of history starting from feudalism to socialism. He faulted Marxist idea on capitalist development on two grounds. First, Marx did not properly appreciate the linkage between capitalism and imperialism. Marx sympathised with the people in the colonies but since he did not probe deep enough he remained tied to the interests of the imperial powers. Instead of being the highest stage of capitalism, Lohia argued, both capitalism and imperialism develop simultaneously from the very beginning as is clear from the development of America, Japan and Germany. From the beginning capitalism is driven to seek external source of power and it builds itself up on exploitation of others by exporting goods to these colonies. The textiles produced by Lanchashire Mills were consumed in India. Secondly, the picture of capitalism painted by Marx is that of the Western Europe which could develop on the basis of exploitation of colonies; it does not take into account the fact that there is a world outside Europe; it makes no attempt to explain various formations in the erstwhile colonial countries. According to him, capitalist formations all over the world are related to each other and cannot be separated.[26] Lohia also criticised the doctrine of surplus value. He thought that while this doctrine took into account the form of exploitation in the developed countries, it did not sufficiently consider its shape in the colonies. The form of exploitation in both the situations has been very different. The nature of demands also varies in the two contexts. In the case of colonies 99 per cent of labour is transferred in the form of surplus value, while in the developed countries it is only 10 per cent. It is for this reason that the surplus value in both the cases cannot be taken together.

He was indignant against tendencies towards centralization in government and industry which he was convinced lead to unemployment. According to him, capitalism does not lead to the impoverishment of the working class as Marx had predicted. In Europe capitalism had led to a steady improvement in their standard of living and the working class was gradually turning into the middle class.[27] Lohia was aware that class struggle plays an important role in history. He refers to various phases of acute inequality which was reflected in the history of class struggle. But the important missing point in Marxism, according to him, is the form and sequence of the class struggles. He differed with Narendra Dev and Sampurnananda who viewed class struggle in internal dimensions only and did not take into account its external linkages.[28] Following Toynbee, Lohia argued that class struggle within society is linked to class struggle outside. According to him, Marx did not sufficiently appreciate the differences between those who are exploited internally and those by the outside agencies in rich countries. If he had done this he would have talked of socialism at home and poverty abroad. The whole drift of Lohia's argument here was that Marx did not sufficiently take into account the peculiar and specific conditions in the third world. He did talk of an Asiatic mode of production but it was a device to evade the basic issues. There are doubtless references to colonies in his treatment of the Asiatic mode of production but as in other matters, Marx could not separate this from his treatment of the interest of the Western nations. This is why he failed to enunciate principles which would decide the relationship between the two. But, Lohia argued, an adequate social theory must take into account this relationship. Indeed, Lohia concluded, Marx lacked a theory of nationalism which alone would have enabled him to see differences in national situations.

Lohia did not accept Western liberalism either. He regarded freedom as important. The replacement of the doctrine of negative liberty by positive liberty had already prepared the way for its actualization. But Lohia thought that liberalism was the ideology of the rich. Its individualistic elements led to foundation and development of capitalism based on the ideas of private property and profits. In our times, it has led to centralisation and mass production and profits. Lohia opposed this by the ideas of decentralization, social welfare, small machine- technology and economic equality. Since capitalism is based on the idea of profit, it leads to unemployment and war. The capitalist always want cheap labour which can be made available only when where there is unemployment.

Lohia held that capitalist competition leads to increased selfishness and avarice which are opposed to social equality and prosperity—the twin foundation stones of a socialist order. Socialism is superior to capitalism because it is not based on the idea of the use or exploitation of others for one's own aggrandizement or enrichment. He agreed with Sampurnananda and Acharya Narendra Dev that sometimes the capitalists go to the extent of sacrificing the freedom of their own country for their own selfish ends. It is this which explains, Lohia continues, why a section of capitalists in France welcomed the invasion of Hitler. He stresses that capitalism is a reactionary doctrine which, in the third world, gives protection to profit, black marketeering and exploitation. The whole history of the development of capitalism is full of this.

Lohia had firm faith in democracy as a government of the people but he opposed the tendency of democracy to lean on elitism. In a country like India where there is so much of poverty and caste distinctions, he was convinced that it leads to increase in powers of the upper classes: democracy applies to these classes only and has no meaning for the masses. He agreed with thinkers like Laski who believed that the political democracy has no meaning in the absence of economic democracy. If democracy is to succeed it is absolutely necessary that there must be increased production and effective distribution. While Jayaprakash Narayan had talked of the importance of the democratic decentralisation and adult franchise as a basis of "corporate democracy",[29] and Narendra Dev had referred to "distinct national traditions", Lohia talked of adapting it to the peculiar socio-economic conditions of India. Freedom in India, he emphasised is to be combined with the need to provide bread to all. Both are not contradictory. They are inseparable. Both can be achieved within the framework of social democracy. Lohia was of the opinion that neither political freedom can be sacrificed for the sake of economic freedom nor the latter for the former. Each has a place of its own.

It is here that Lohia thought that the Gandhian ideas had a great relevance to India. Though he rejected Gandhi's belief in God and his attempt to reconcile religion to politics, he hailed Gandhism as the great invention of the twentieth century, more powerful than even the atomic bomb. Lohia gave a call to combine socialist principles with the four Gandhian ideas, viz., *satyagraha*, ends and means principle, small machine technology and political decentralization. *Satyagraha* is superior to both constitutional and revolutionary methods. In a country where there is so much of poverty, constitutional methods are always tardy. He also rejected revolutionary methods because the result is never permanent. On the other hand, he believed, *Satyagraha*, combining moral and spiritual principles with pragmatic considerations leads not only to the achievement of aims but also to the purification of those who struggle. He had all praise for the way in which Gandhi experimented with the method of *Satyagraha* in Africa or during 1942 movement.

Gandhi had emphasised that means are more important th..n the ends. According to him, the nature of our achievement would depend on our methods: both are inseparable, they are two sides of the same coin. Following Gandhi, Lohia also argued that truth cannot be achieved on the basis of falsehood, one nation's freedom cannot be achieved on the basis of the sacrifice of the other.[30]

The most important contribution of Lohia is his development of the concept of political decentralization. A truly non-violent society can be achieved only on the basis of decentralization. In a centralised society the human beings are relegated into background and lose their freedom. Gandhi had said that State is good which governs the least. On the other hand, a decentralised polity provides full scope for the development of the individual potentiality. Lohia called his own scheme of decentralization as "Chaukhamba Model" in which the authority would be dispersed in villages, districts and provinces. Cenralization leads to dictatorship and whimsical exercise of power. It is contrary to democracy, whereas decentralization provides every one opportunity to express on and concretize one's will. It thus stakes democracy from the elite to the masses. The gap between the rulers and the ruled is bridged. On the one hand, it prepares future rulers, on the other, it creates effective mechanisms to control the present rulers.

It must be remembered that this scheme of political organisation is linked to a similar scheme of economic organisation of production and distribution. In the absence of decentralized economy, Lohia argued, there would be increased bureaucratization in which human beings will become cogs in the machine and the political system would take place of human values. He, therefore, pleaded that economic planning must be done at the grassroots upwards. He firmly believed that a centralized economy whether of the capitalist or of the Marxist type cannot solve the problems. He, however, emphasised the need of collective control over the means of production so that while there is check on increase in private property, the collective property on the whole is also increased. He, therefore, pleaded for the nationalization of foreign companies, need for chartered accountants and declaration of income by all. A decentralised economy, according to Lohia, will be more efficient as it would be based on willing participation of the workers who must be made partners in the scheme.[31] Where Lohia differed from other socialists in India was not so much in the scheme of decentralization as in, first, the enunciation of principles, and, second, in his emphasis on social freedom along with political freedom. He was clear that without necessary reforms in religion and social system, no enduring political changes could be conceived. He wanted the creation of a society in which individual freedom would thrive and his passion for socialism was a product of the belief that capitalism is based on a denial of individual freedom.

III

A different type of socialism emerged in the ideas of Jawahar Lal Nehru. The British socialism particularly its Fabian variant was his starting point. Then he came in contact with the communists and turned inevitably with good will towards communism which, he thought, "for, whatever its faults, it was at least not hypocritical and not imperialistic".[32] And yet his reverence for the rich cultural heritage of India was so deep and profound that he could not abandon it for either socialism of the Fabian kind or communism of the Russion variety.[33] That is the reason he did not adhere to anyone particular brand of socialism but tried to combine them all to suit the genius of India.[34]

Nehru was the leading exponent of socialism in India. Although there were other thinkers or activists more profound than Nehru, it was largely because of his influence that socialism found its roots in the Congress. It was at his instance in 1927 that the Congress committed itself to socialism. It was at his instance that Congress adopted socialist economic programme at Karachi session. It was at his instance again that socialism became the guiding and directing principle of the Congress policy after Independence. As he had occupied a powerful position in the Congress throughout, it was natural that his ideas would influence the organization. For him socialism was not merely an economic doctrine. He declared in 1936: "It is a vital creed which I hold with all my head and heart."[35] He was convinced that there was no other way of ending appalling mass poverty and suffering in the country. To quote him:

I work for Indian independence because the nationalist in me cannot tolerate alien domination. I work for it even more because for me, it is the inevitable step to social and economic change. I should like the Congress to become a socialist organization and to join hands with other forces in the world who are working for the new civilization.[36]

Though not systematic philosopher, Nehru had a vision of life which was based on socialism, not as a doctrinaire theory or as a textbook maxim but as a new way of life. British socialists had already advanced from John Stuart Mill to Webbs, Shaw, Cole and Laski. Nehru also followed the trend.

Like British socialists Nehru started by attacking capital as the sole fruit of human labour. He shared their belief that the system of land-holding in India was peculiar as it was marked by the concentration of land power in few hands. But he also believed that the rural character of the Indian economy distinguished it from that in the West. Nehru concentrated his attack on capitalists and landlords both of whom, he thought, were responsible for the poverty of India. He was also opposed to imperialism which had led to increasing impoverishment of the country. He thought that the Indian problem was but a part of the world problem of imperialism— "the two are indissolubly linked together".[37]

Nehru was not a very original or systematic thinker. He certainly did not add new ideas. And yet he was important because he implemented the existing ones with vigour and hustle by espousing the cause of controls and nationalisation, land reforms and co-operative farming, heavy industry and distributive justice within the parameters of a planned economy. He was convinced that the conditions of masses—the peasantry, the landless labourers, the workers, the shopkeepers, the artisans, cannot change by a mere change in government; what was required was a change in the social fabric itself, a new way of life involving an end of vested interests in land and industry. There was the other kind of socialism which was preached by Jayaprakash and Lohia which advocated an indigenous version of it. But this was adopted only by a small minority. It is certain that Nehru provided the official ideology of socialism for the next thirty years.

But his socialism was inevitably tied to democracy. He believed that far from being antithetical both were complimentary to each other. He declared, "We talk of a welfare state and of democracy and socialism. They are good concepts but they hardly convey a clear and unambiguous meaning."[38] Democracy and socialism are means to an end, not the end itself. He did not want socialism without freedom or freedom without socialism. We talk of the good of society. But, he asked, is this something apart from, and transcending, the good of the individuals composing it? If the individual is ignored and sacrificed for what is considered the good society, is that the right objective to have. He argued, "I do not see why under socialism there should not be a great deal of freedom for the individual, indeed far greater freedom than the present system gives."[39] It is for this reason that Nehru emphasized the value of the methods of peaceful democratic pressures against the methods of destruction and extermination. It is for this reason again that communists often irritated him. He did not like, to quote his own words, their dictatorial ways, their aggressive and rather vulgar methods and their habit of denouncing everybody who did not agree with them.[40]

At the theoretical level he argued that since India was not Europe, the ideas of the latter could not be transplanted wholesale into the Indian soil. For him two urgent needs in India were independence and transformation of rural economy. Both these objectives could not be achieved in terms of the logic of industrial proletariat. He was convinced that if socialism was to succeed in India it would have to grow as a response to Indian conditions. "Nothing is so foolish," he argued, "as to imagine that exactly the same process takes place in different countries with varying backgrounds."[41] He threw aside the theory of surplus value and class-war. He totally abhorred 'ruthless suppression' of political dissent and 'whole sale regimentation of society'. To this he also added the traditional Indian concern for moral values, its concern for the quality of the individual and the concept of *dharma* underlying it. He considered revival of some aspects of this philosophy of life necessary. Indeed he wanted socialism with a humane face and was convinced that it was possible to alter human life without a violent overthrow of the existing system. Even if there was a conflict in society, the best way was to resolve it by peaceful means.

Nehru's ideas served as a bridge between democratic socialism of the Fabian type and Gandhian idea of '*swaraj*' and '*welfare*'. It was largely under his influence that the doctrine of the welfare state came to be generally accepted creed within the Congress. The ideal of Swaraj was combined with that of socialism. He firmly believed that one could not exist without the other. He adopted the position that the best democracy is one in which production is controlled for the welfare of all, in which there is equality of opportunity and what is produced is distributed equitably in society.

While Gandhi was primarily concerned with moral revolution through a change of heart, Nehru was primarily concerned with institutional, social and economic reforms. His faith in parliamentary democracy was unshakeable and it is through this that he pleaded for socialization of property. The system of graded taxation, Nehru thought, will necessarily arm the state with great funds which it must use for developmental schemes. The best state which would be in a position to do this cannot be the old *laissez-faire* state of the British Raj, which according to him largely served imperial interests. Such a state is a thing of the past, it is too inefficient. He was also opposed to a capitalist state. He was convinced that "capitalism necessarily leads to exploitation of one man by another, one group by another, and one country by another." For him opposition to imperialism and exploitation also meant opposition to capitalism. It cannot be communist state either if such a state included authoritarianism and regimentation.

Nehru was conscious of the limitations of both capitalism and communism and wanted to avoid their demerits in the model of development he envisaged. In a country where there is so much of mass poverty, squalor and inequality he could not think of any other solution than socialism combined with representative institutions. Communists and socialists alike had pleaded for controls to replace the present profit system by a higher ideal of co-operative service. Nehru continued this tradition. But he was against following slavishly any dogma or any other country's example because, he believed, circumstances differ and different circumstances might demand different solutions. He pointed out that, armed with a philosophy which reveals the inner working of history and human relations, and with a scientific outlook to guide him, the socialist tries to solve the problems of each country in relation to the world. He was convinced that there could not be a welfare state in India unless the national income went up.[42] He agreed that while socialism and communism might help India to distribute its existing wealth, but in fact, there was not much of it to be distributed, there was only poverty to distribute.[43] According to him, India must produce wealth as well as divide it equitably. In both agriculture and industry, therefore, the primary test was whether the wealth of the country had been increased for eventual redistribution.

His welfare state demands a state which is neither based on feudal incompetence nor on capitalist selfishness. Welfarism demands a purely democratic-socialistic state. The wealth must be controlled in the interest of the whole society. Violence, monopoly and concentration of wealth in a few hands are produced by the present economic system. The only alternative, Nehru was convinced, is offered to us in some form of socialism. The state should be able to dictate conditions to the owners of wealth. Only such a state will be able to secure the welfare of the poor. Then, and then only, there will be economic equality without which political democracy cannot flourish; then and then only the gap between the governors and the governed will be bridged—the gap, which was so large in the British system. He was averse to revolutionary socialism because while he wanted to remove the scourge of poverty, he was equally concerned to preserve human values of a free and humane society. His socialism could be achieved only through a combination of state intervention and popular will expressed through democratic institutions. He had said, "I do not want India to be drilled and forced into a certain position because the costs of such drilling are too great: it is not worthwhile; it is not desirable from my point of view."[44]

This welfare state, according to Nehru, demands a mixture of socialist principles mostly with a fair share of capitalism. This mixture is achieved through planning. It demands that resources must be properly harnessed and deployed in a planned way. To this end, the state should plan through its democratic institutions and co-ordinate the various activities of the nation so as to avoid waste and conflict and attain the maximum result. Planning, he suggested, would deal with production, distribution, consumption, investment, trade, income, social services and all other activities which act and react on each other. This concept of mixed economy became the mainstay of his political creed. The source of his inspiration here was the Russian Revolution. As early as 1938 the Congress had appointed a National Planning Committee with Nehru as its Chairman. Its report became the first testament on economic planning in India.

Nehru was right in thinking that India's salvation lay in the adoption of socialist ideas and practices. He largely succeeded in making the Congress accept those ideas through various resolutions from time to time. His approach to social transformation was extremely cautious. It was gradualist, it relied on controlled but slow model of mixed-economy of which Mahalanobis report was a typical example. He had argued for the importance of a gradual change of social conditions by an assertion of controls and permits over profit, so that the socially created wealth leads to better wages and better economic conditions for the worker and peasants. He was firm that private sector should work within the parameters set by national objectives. The control of the private sector should not be confined to more dividends and profit but should also include all the strategic points in the economy of the country. To quote him "A democratic collectivism need not mean an abolition of private property, but it will mean the public ownership of the basic and major industries...." Such a system of democratic collective will needs careful and continuous planning and adaptation to the changing need of the people.[45]

Here his critics accused him of introducing centralization in government which only served the interests of politicians and bureaucracy and very rarely those of the masses. They argued that planning failed largely because he relied on corrupt and incompetent bureaucracy to administer developmental schemes from above, and that since planning meant control of individual life, it was alleged, Nehru adopted a scheme which was a negation of freedom. The latter charge seems difficult to sustain. Assuredly no one was more conscious of the value of freedom and democratic institutions than Nehru himself. The whole scheme of planning was adopted only to create conditions in which all could equally enjoy their freedom. It is true that bureaucracy was not an adequate instrument for the purpose but for a political party which did not have its own cadres, perhaps there was not much of an alternative when it came to policy implementation. He knew that the Congress constituted as it was could hardly be an effective instrument of revolutionary transformation. Even when he was the Prime Minister he made no attempt to convert the Congress into a cadre based party. Sometime he had the best of relations with those who were not prepared to accept his ideas. All his life he oscillated between his admiration for the USSR which despite its failures, had "unfolded a new order and a new civilisation as the most promising feature of our dismal age",[46] and his reverence of the representative institutions of the West.

And yet one must confess that despite the charm of his personality and the great hold he had on masses, Nehru did not achieve as much as he wanted to. Nehru's opponents accused him of applying platitudes when a drastic solution was required. The combination of radicalism in principle and conservatism in practice was quickly woven into the fabric of Indian society. We began to be called "a soft state". Because of his failure to take hard decisions, the structural compulsions of the polity based on an alliance of middle class with agrarian vested interests generated their own contradictions. Under his leadership Congress was a vehicle through which integration took place in the process of aggregating various interests. But it also tended to reflect cleavages between society, economy and polity rather than make an attempt to transcend them. He was able to retain the support of urban and rural elite but in the process was not able to help the lower classes and castes in their plight and degradation as much as he wanted. More often the system was tilted in favour of the dominant classes. We shall have to find reasons for all this. How is it that despite the fact that he had massive popular support, he could not effectively implement his own ideas? Was the failure on account of his personality or was it due to structural constraints in the polity? Or, was it because of some short-comings in his own ideas on state and socialism? Did they suit Indian conditions or did they require modification?

What is significant, however, in the socialist rationalist vision is the organic view of the individual community relationship. Society is conceived as a whole in which individuals are also smaller wholes with their own identity. Real social progress is interpreted in terms of the opportunity given to the individual to develop, "provided the individual is not a selected group but comprise the whole community".[47] And, therefore, the individual welfare cannot be separated from social welfare. Society provides meaning and value to his life. The traditional ideas of service of others as well as of welfare state became the inspiration of this model. The greater interest must precede smaller interest. Welfare of others is at once the motto of socialism. It is in this logical way that Lohia expressly used the metaphor of wholes' of Aurobindo and traditional Indian thought. Socialism means the triumph of the idea of a self conscious rational organization of society, it means the control of social activities by the "reason of the community". "The touchstone," declared Nehru, "should be how far any political or social theory enables the individual to rise above his petty self and thus think in terms of the good of all. The law of life should not be competition or acquisitiveness but cooperation, the good of each contributing to the good of all. In such a society the emphasis will be on duties not on rights, the rights will follow the performance of duties."[48] The liberal leaves each member to follow his own lead, hoping that somehow these conflicting interests would be harmonised when everyone pursues his own rationally calculated interest. The socialists in India, on the other hand, in ideas similar to Aurobindo and Gandhi, love the group as well as the individual, but unlike the western socialists, are not much enamoured of the state power. They emphasise private property as well as need for cooperative associations, though the state must own the larger units; it must certainly control others in order to prevent the exploitation of the community by certain individuals. The difference between Lohia and Nehru is that while Nehru believed in state-control and central planning, for Lohia such a scheme could only mean the increasing bureaucratization which is the negation of democracy. For the latter as for Gandhi, the state must exist as community of communities; as a coordinator of vertical and horizontal organisations. In term of these the state must ensure both economic and political democracy. One without the other is meaningless. It is vain to argue that man should have a vote unless he is able to exercise it freely and at the level nearest to him. The simultaneity of parliamentary democracy, economic planning and decentralised state will ensure this. While Nehru concentrated his attention on the state control of production, Lohia stressed diffusion of power, so that socialism does not make the state a bureaucratic machine regimenting and controlling the life of the individuals as a servile state would do. Such centralization, according to Lohia, is sure to ruin democracy because the existence of a national elite is the negation of democracy. It is because of this that he argued that the need for decentralised democratic institutions was as important as the control over industry. Real power must be given to various levels of government and society. An acceptance of this latter idea, which the socialist of Nehru type have generally ignored, can alone lead to a more adequate socialist theory suited to India. State socialism without some diffusion of power is just capitalism writ large, the gap between the rulers and the ruled is as great as in capitalism. The other model is based on an awareness of the need for a system of control of the lives of the citizens as a short term measure to secure welfare of all. This is the system of controls which gives due consideration to distinct needs and aspirations of diverse pluralities, and wholes in society. There is indeed no guarantee that the smaller groups would avoid tendencies towards bureaucratization, corruption and centralization. But these groups have in their favour the federal thought which, as can be seen from the development of thought in the last fifty years, has remained a powerful strand in modern Indian thought of all varieties. The integralist concerned with the integrated spiritual development of life, finds in this a welcome ally, to combine autonomy with dependence. The groups in democracy may find in it the only way to preserve their own identity as a part of the larger system.

Gandhians see in it an effective way to control state power. In any case this seems to be the only solution to reconcile the state control with individual and group autonomy in a democratic polity. The problem can be solved not by weakening the state but by consolidating it in the form of a model of a diffused polity in which each whole has sufficient power to develop its own identity as a part of the larger wholes.

NOTES

1. M.N. Roy, *Beyond Communism,* ed. Philip Spark (New Delhi, Ajanta, 1981), Reprint, p. 27.
2. Ibid., p. 38.
3. Ibid., p. 42.
4. Loc. cit.
5. Ibid., p. 90.
6. M.N. Roy, *Politics, Power and Parties* (New Delhi, Ajanta, 1981), Reprint, p. 8.
7. M.N. Roy, *Beyond Communism,* op. cit.
8. Ibid., p. 38.
9. Ibid., p. 43.
10. M.N. Roy, *Politics, Power and Parties,* op. cit.
11. Ibid., p. 87.
12. M.N. Roy, *Beyond Communism,* op. cit., p. 83.
13. Ibid., p. 87.
14. Ibid., p. 100.
15. M.N. Roy, *Politics, Power and Parties,* op. cit., p. 37.
16. Ibid., p. 38.
17. Ibid., p. 61.
18. Ibid., p. 120.
19. Ibid., p. 128.
20. See, Dennis Dalton, *Indian Idea of Freedom* (Gurgaon, The Academic Press, 1981).
21. M.N. Roy, *Reason, Romanticism and Revolution* (Calcutta, Renaissance Publishers, 1962).
22. Sampurnananda, *Samajwad* (Kashi Bhartiya Gyan Peeth, 1960), I.
23. R. Lohia, *Marx, Gandhi and Socialism* (Hyderabad, Navhind, 1963), p. 321.
24. R. Lohia, *Will to Power and Other Writings* (Hyderabed, Navhind, 1956), p. 91.
25. R. Lohia, *Marx etc.,* op. cit., p. 243.
26. Ibid., p. 16.
27. Ibid., p. 6.
28. Sampurnananda, op. cit.

29. See, Jayaprakash Narayan, *Socialism, Sarvodya and Democracy* (Patna, 1973), p. 277.
30. R. Lohia, *Marx etc.* op. cit., p. 122.
31. See, Jayaprakash Narayan, op. cit., p. 46.
32. S. Gopal (ed.), *Jawaharlal Nehru: An Anthology* (New Delhi, Oxford, 1980), p. 295.
33. Ibid., p. 292.
34. Loc. cit.
35. J. Nehru, *An Autobiography* (London, Iohnlane, 1936 ed.), p. 163.
36. J. Nehru, *India and the World* (London, Allen & Unwin, 1936), pp. 83-4.
37. S. Gopal (ed.), *Jawaharlal Nehru: An Anthology* (New Delhi, Oxford, 1980), p. 295.
38. Ibid., p. 285.
39. J. Nehru, *Where Are We* (Allahabad, K. Labiston, 1939), p. 59.
40. J. Nehru, *An Autobiography,* op. cit., p. 163.
41. J. Nehru, *Where Are We,* op. cit., p. 60.
42. S. Gopal (ed), op. cit., p. 292.
43. Loc. cit.
44. J. Nehru, *India & the World,* op. cit., p. 259.
45. J. Nehru, *The Discovery of India* (Calcutta, Signet, 1946), pp. 635-36.
46. S. Gopal (ed), op. cit., p. 260.
47. S. Gopal (ed), op. cit., p. 285.
48. Loc. cit.

CHAPTER 12

THE VISION OF COSMOPOLITANISM: RABINDRANATH TAGORE

Tagore was a great writer who has left an indelible mark on literary and social thought in this country. He wrote novels, poetry, drama, at once spontaneous and profound, truly capturing the greatness of Indian tradition amidst confusion and contradictions of everyday life. His voice stood for India and yet it had a vitality which cannot be confined to one particular country or tradition, and as such it reverberates with cosmopolitanism. Combined with his political temperament, his love for music and capacity for lyrical writing, it reinforces faith in the eternal and everlasting, in reason and goodness which have universal qualities. It is this extraordinary aspect of his writings which won him the Nobel Prize. He was celebrated in his life time as a great Indian literature, admired and even revered by people like Gandhi and Nehru. Gandhi called him *Gurudeva*.

Tagore was full of patriotism and wanted India to realize her potential, but he never confused patriotism with hatred for others. To the end he remained indomitably independent and committed to the ideal of the universal man. He always had in mind a new civilisation based on reason and goodness in which the individual will not be oppressed. He revolted against the humiliation and degradation of man by any organization of commerce or power or a sawage and arbitrary misgovernment which he identified with imperialism. Nowhere this aspect of his thought come out more clearly than in his brilliant essays on nationalism and on some aspects of the Non-cooperation Movement.

II

Thinkers like Aurobindo, did not take into account the harmful consequences of unbridled nationalism, Aurobindo was not sufficiently conscious of its connections with power, commerce and technology. But Tagore revolted against militant and aggressive nationalism. He thought that it was an inevitable consequence of modern science. It is true that like Aurobindo he was also deeply imbued with the spirit of India. He was firmly convinced that India had a unique personality of her own which ought to be preserved. For instance, when he talked of society being more important in India than power as in the west, he was clearly for the restoration of the spiritual genius of India. But it was more of a cultural approach than one tied to political nationalism. He compared nationalism to a hydraulic press whose pressure is impersonal and hence completely effective.[1] He noticed a clear and unmistakable link between technology, dehumanization and increasing megalomania in political life. A nation in the sense of political and economic union of a people was, for him, "that aspect which a population assumes when organized for a mechanical purpose".[2]

According to Tagore, technological orientation drives man to join society for self-preservation. This makes society mainly an aspect of power and as a collectivity it does not have much to do with the pursuit of higher ideals. As science advances, society grows more complex. It leads to greater wealth and development of technology and with it man's selfishness also increases. Nationalism is a result of this process. It is a cruel epidemic of evil which is eating into the moral vitals of mankind.[3] It embodies selfishness in a concentrated form for, once it arises, it excludes every other ideal. It becomes synonymous with power which has no consideration for human ideals like freedom and equality. It even leads to dissolution of personal humanity.[4] What arose as a consequence of our need for self-preservation, thus, ultimately becomes by virtue of blind pursuit of power and commerce a Frankenstein to devour humanity. Tagore was aware of the power of organization which turns mechanics into parts of the machine with no tinge of pity or moral responsibility.[5] He knew that the British imperialism had this hideous side when he declared: "This abstract being, the Nation, is ruling India".[6] At another place, he wrote, "It is a steam-roller, formidable in its weight and power, having its use, but it does not help the soil to become fertile."[7] He distinguished British imperialism from earlier imperialisms. In the case of earlier imperialisms, according to him, "their texture was loosely woven leaving big gaps"[8] through which our own life ran its own course. There were many things which were distasteful but the areas of freedom enjoyed were quite wide. In the case of British imperialism the area of freedom became very narrow. He thought that the chains of organization which were forged by the West were more relentless and unbreakable than have ever been manufactured in the history of mankind. He noticed another defect too. In the name of efficiency the British imperialism had led to the starving of the life of the personal man into that of the professional. He wrote, "man with his mental and material power far outgrowing his moral strength, is like an exaggerated giraffe whose head had suddenly shot up miles away from the rest of him, making moral communication difficult to establish".[9] It is remarkable that Tagore indicted imperialism in such a powerful fashion and even made it responsible for dehumanization of commerce and politics leading to "the conscience of a ghost and the callous perfection of an automation".[10] He was convinced that such a nationalism will never hold the voice of truth and goodness. "It will," he declared, "go on in its ring dance of moral corruption, linking steel unto steel, and machine unto machine, trampling under its tread all the sweet flowers of simple faith and the living ideals of man."[11]

While Tagore truly grasped the connection of nationalism with commerce and technology, he did not sufficiently realise that even the consciousness of one's distinct group identity could also lead to nationalism. Indeed that is how nationalism had been viewed by Rousseau. Or, alternatively, it could also be a result of popular upsurge against an alien rule. When people are exploited, they begin to realise the importance of freedom. It begins to dawn on them that their group has certain special features quite distinct from others. Tagore himself was conscious of this and yet he failed to draw a distinction between imperialism or militant nationalism and nationalism *per se*. In the thought of Vivekananda, Aurobindo, Tilak or Gandhi nationalism was not merely a reaction against the British rule but also a resurgence of the spirit of India, a spiritual necessity as Sri Aurobindo would view it. It formed a part of their vision of human unity—a vision in the execution of which India, they thought was destined to play an important role by virtue of her great spiritual heritage. They viewed the Indian independence as a link, albeit a necessary one, in our quest for world unity. According to them, Indian unity could not exist in abstract. It had to be built in terms of the unity of the smaller wholes, each representing the magnificence and splendour of the diversity inherent in nature. Unity devoid of diversity and differentiations is mechanical and destroys the vital springs from which springs the cosmic dance, the dance of Shiva. Tagore did not realize that far from being the embodiment of the selfish spirit, nationalism, in the above sense, enables the individual and the smaller groups to rise above their selfish interests.

Tagore was of course, conscious of the importance of diversity. Otherwise he could not have maintained that each nation had a vitality and genius of its own. He contrasted the East and the West for each represented different aspects of the cosmic reality. He recognised that the West had succeeded in guaranteeing material requisites of life to its people. The people in the West were, on the whole, more honest. But despite these achievements, Tagore denounced its nationalism which, according to him, had turned into imperialism destroying spiritual harmony everywhere. He indeed made a distinction between the *spirit* of the West and the *nations* of the West.[12] While the spirit stood for freedom, the nations forged chains around nationalism by destroying conditions necessary for it to flourish. Instead of spiritual harmony, nationalism created conflicts and wars and forged weapons to use them in the most barbaric manner. Tagore gave a remarkable analysis of nationalism and imperialism. But he confused nationalism with militarism and ignored that it was a group instinct, which nationalism represented, which raised man out of his selfishness and inspired him to sacrifice his own life for others.

Tagore's attack on nationalism came out sharply in his attack on Gandhi who, he thought, through boycott and civil disobedience, had opened up Pandora's box in the Indian political life. It is not that Tagore was unaware of the greatness of Gandhi. He was the first to call him 'Mahatma'. But while Gandhi was a politician first and a seer afterwards, Tagore was first a seer and could not accept any deviation from the lofty ideal of human brotherhood. He stood for cosmopolitanism which he identified with universalism but did not realise that this ideal could be actualized only in a society of equals. Otherwise it would only lead to freedom of the few powerful nations at the expense of others. Neither militarism nor cosmopolitanism but a path which recognises the holistic character of levels and stages of human existence can lead to a better society.

III

Tagore's conviction that the awakening of India was a part of the awakening of the world, and that no nation can take an isolated view of its own country, sprang from a particular interpretation of Indian philosophy. He was convinced that there was no word like 'nation' in the Indian languages. For him India's fight was a spiritual fight and not a fight for 'swaraj' as it was interpreted by the nationalists. In this spiritual fight liberation from the meshes that man has woven around him, the meshes of national egoism, appeared a hinderance, a veil of *maya* to delude ourselves from our real path. In his famous attack on Gandhian non-cooperation movement, he pointed out that it had at its back "a fierce joy of annihilation which at its best is asceticism, and at its worst is that orgy of frightfulness in which the human nature, losing faith in the basic reality of normal life, finds a disinterested delight in an unmeaning devastation".[13]

He had learnt from Raja Ram Mohan Roy that there was, at a fundamental level, a spiritual unity through all differences. In such a situation truth is based not upon rejection but on perfect comprehension. He could not comprehend Gandhi's argument that rejection could be as much an ideal as acceptance of a thing in Indian thought, that while *mukti* draws our attention to the positive, *nirvana* to the negative side of truth. Gandhi had, in fact, held that all religions teach that two opposite forces act upon us and that the human endeavour consists in a series of eternal rejections and acceptances. He, therefore, replied "Non-cooperation with Evil is as much a duty as cooperation with Good."[14] For Gandhi non-cooperation was the nation's notice that it was no longer satisfied to be in subjection. But to Tagore nationalism was a form of self-indulgence and greed. The real solution of India could not be found in either economic solution or political solution because, he wrote, "This creation can only be the fruit of the *yoga*, which gives outward form to the inner faculties." He was particularly unhappy with burning of foreign clothes. He was convinced that a political revolution meant only taking a short-cut, but it does not reach the goal. *Swaraj* cannot be attained by blind obedience to an outside power, but "only by the realization of self in the light of intellect".[15] He declared "that which fails to illumine the intellect, and only keeps it in the obsession of some delusion, is its greatest obstacle."

Tagore believed in the supremacy of reason and attributed India's decline and fall to the fact that the Indians had surrendered their right to reason and to judge for themselves to the blind forces of *sastric* injunctions and social conventions. We refused to cross the seas because Manu said so. We refused to eat with the Mussalman because it was prohibited in *sastras*. According to him, injunctions issued in the interests of the organization lead to denial of independent judgement and generate ill-will against those who will not follow them. It is extremely easy to over-power inner freedom in the name of outside freedom. People begin to follow the dictates of leaders and politicians without even understanding the issues at stake. In such a state man is forced to give up all legitimate questions and to blindly follow the path of obedience. But Tagore asked: what is the use of such a *swaraj*? According to him, "Our mind must acknowledge the truth of the intellect just as our heart does the truth of love."[16] Aspirations and emotions must be there, but no less must be study and thought and for it, wrote Tagore, "the economist must think, the mechanic must labour, the educationist and statesman must teach and contrive."[17]

Tagore defined freedom as "complete awakening, in full self-expression".[18] This, according to him, would be possible when truth is allowed to come from all sides. For him both the call to efficiency and will to wealth and power ought to be subservient to this. Sparta tried to narrow herself down to one particular purpose but she lost. Gandhi had argued that man is today becoming a slave of greed in the name of efficiency. But to Tagore while it is true that there is danger of being stunted by big machines, there is an equal danger of being stunted by small machines like *charkha*, because if one is obliged to play it very day, one suffocates the mind, which is no less valuable than the cotton thread. We must acknowledge the supremacy of mind with its diverse powers and relate it to our diverse needs and temperaments. He declared, "those for whom authority is needed in place of reason, will invariably accept despotism in place of freedom".[19] According to him, only those will be able to attain *swaraj* and keep it who have realized the dignity of self-reliance and self-mastery in the spiritual world—"those whom no temptation, no delusion, can induce to surrender the dignity of intellect into the keeping of others".[20] Otherwise the state of mind thus engendered will only raise angry passions, obscuring the greater world of our vision.

Tagore had raised important issues. We are now realising the significance of what he had said. Indeed both Gandhi and Tagore represented the immediate and long term perspective of Indian things. There was no fundamental difference. While Gandhi recognised the force of what Tagore had said, he felt that as a leader he could not ignore the immediate issues, for "when all about me are dying for want of food, the only occupation permissible to me is to feed the hungry".[21] To a people 'famishing and idle', wrote Gandhi, "the only acceptable form in which God can dare appear is work and promise of food and wages".[22] He thought that in burning foreign clothes, he was in fact burning his shame because at that moment India had nothing to share with the world save her degradation, pauperism and plagues. Tagore's critique of Gandhi was powerful and vitriolic in its own way, but Gandhi's reply was no less touching and profound. For Gandhi Non-cooperation also meant refusal to cooperate with the English administration on their own terms. He wrote, "A drowning man cannot save others. We must try to save ourselves. Indian nationalism is not exclusive, nor aggressive, nor destructive. It is health-giving, religious and therefore humanitarian. India must learn to live before she can aspire to die for humanity. The mice which helplessly find themselves between the cat's teeth acquire no merit from their enforced sacrifice." The difference in the two approaches to truth can be best summed up in Gandhi's own inimitable style:

The poet lives in a magnificent world of his own creation—his world of ideas. I am a slave of somebody else's creation—the spinning wheel. The poet makes his *gopis* dance to the tune of his flute. I wander after my beloved Sita, the charkha, and seek to deliver her from the ten-headed monster from Japan, Manchester, Paris, etc. The poet is an inventor, he creates, destroys and recreates. I am an explorer and having discovered a thing I must cling to it. The poet presents the world with new and attractive things for day to day. I can merely show the hidden possibilities of old and even worn out things. The world easily finds an honourable place for the magician who produces new and dazzling things. I have to struggle laboriously to find a corner for my worn out things.... I may say in all humility that we complement each other's activity.[23]

NOTES

1. Rabindra Nath Tagore, *Nationalism* (London, Macmillan, 1950), p. 17.
2. Ibid., p. 17.
3. Ibid., p. 16.
4. Ibid., p. 11.
5. Ibid., p. 12.
6. Ibid., p. 13.
7. Ibid., p. 25.
8. Ibid., p. 33.
9. Ibid., p. 35.
10. Ibid., pp. 37-8.
11. Ibid., p. 41.
12. Ibid., pp. 15, 20.
13. *Truth Called Them Differently (Tagore Gandhi Controversy)*, Compiled and edited by R.K. Prabhu and Ravindra Kelker (Ahmedabad, Navjivan, 1961), p. 20.
14. Ibid., p. 39.
15. Ibid., p. 54.
16. Ibid., p. 61.
17. Ibid., p. 63.
18. Ibid., p. 64.
19. Ibid., p. 66.
20. Loc. cit.
21. Ibid., p. 76.
22. Ibid., p. 77.
23. Ibid., p. 109.

CHAPTER 13

THE INDIVIDUAL, COMMUNITY AND POLITICAL ORDER: AN OVERVIEW

The relationship between the individual, community and political order in ancient Indian thought, specially as reflected in the dominant modes of thinking, can be viewed in a variety of ways. We can approach it philosophically in terms of monism (*advaita*), dualism (*dvaita*) and monistic-dualism, in terms of one cosmic being (*purusha*) or in terms of male (*purusha*) and female (*prakriti*) principles of Samkhya or in terms of wild pantheism or naturalism in which every thing—Sun, Moon, Stars, Ganges, beasts, flowers, are intra-cosmic Code in their own right. One can explore it as a great cosmic dance (*rasa nritya*) or a play (*lila*) or in seemingly vulgar and, therefore, perhaps senseless forms epitomised by certain varieties of *tantra*. Many and diverse relations of history cohere in India in which the doctrine of unity and differentiation at different levels finds a marvellous and at times somewhat baffling expression. I do not wish to explore all the dimensions of this rich tradition except one, namely, what I have called, that of 'integral pluralism'. I have tried to demonstrate elsewhere[1] that Indian society has envisaged an altogether different vision of the individual/community relationship—a vision, not of part and wholes but of wholes existing within wholes in a suitable relationship of autonomy and subordination. Most thinkers in India believed that the ideal of community relationship in India was that of complex "communal freedom" as Aurobindo conceptualized it, or that of 'Oceanic circles' as Gandhi envisaged it to be. Recently, eighteenth century historians have amply demonstrated,[2] how this was not merely an ideal but an actuality even as late as the eighteenth century. In this chapter, we shall try to unfold the structure of the individual community relationship. We shall also discuss the connection between it and political order. It also works out the implications of this view for political philosophy in terms of the argument that although Indian thinkers were able to discern ideal structural arrangements, they largely failed to evolve an objective political authority as a focal point of our limited temporal existence. Indeed this has been the chief despair of political life in India. Needless to add that the importance of the theme springs from the fact that the Indian society is still largely organised around some of these principles.

I should like to highlight two important points about the following discussion. Most of the terms used in ancient literature describe a number of things at the same time. For instance words like *dharma* or *kama* or *artha* have different meanings in different contexts. There are equivalents in English that will bring out the variety of meaning these terms contain. They include right order, specific activities, function, goods of life. For instance everything has its own dharma. And it also refers to a certain notion of universal moral order. It is a very elusive word to translate varying between an activity, a moral principle and even a stick according to the emphasis of the context. Sometimes it is very similar to law, at other times it reminds one of Plato's concept of *techne* It is very difficult to decide how the meaning of the terms in specific activities is related to science, morals, economics and politics. I have used the meaning I think most appropriate in the context of an overall understanding of Indian thought. But this would also explain a couple of inconsistencies that appear at different places.

Scholars in the west have built on five centuries of sustained history of ideas. We in India are just starting a tradition as far as political thought is concerned. Some scholars like Beni Prasad, Altekar and K.P. Mukerjee did try to unearth a tradition. But in their case, political science remained no more than a nationalist response to European political thought. They wanted to reply to the imperial argument that the Indians were not fit to govern themselves. And, therefore, there was a deliberate attempt to prove that ideas of democracy and freedom were not alien to India, most of these ideas had already been discovered and conceptualised by the political thinkers in ancient India, and hence Indians were qualified for freedom. The scholars were not so much interested in an examination of the tradition from within, in term of its own logic, as in demonstrating that the conceptual apparatus of European political science was already a part of the tradition of political thinking in India.

Every view of the individual-community relationship springs from a certain view of the individual and the over-arching cosmic process to which he belongs. According to most ancient Indian texts belonging to the dominant tradition, such as the *Manusmriti* and the *Mahabharata*, the correct view of life was based on a subtle combination of institution, experience and reason. There is reason to believe that Indian thinkers were "seers" and when they spoke they were merely describing what they experienced as a basic drive in Nature (*Prakriti*) consisting of truth (*sattva*), energy (*rajas*) and necessity (*tamas*) and their desire and will to cohere and transcend these in search of a permanent principle amidst all the diverse processes of existence (*jagat*). This line of thought was itself based on the assumption that there are levels of experience from gross (*sthula*) to subtle (*sukshama*) to causal or the most subtle (*karana*). The knowledge of the last one was available only to a chosen few who had undergone a great disciplining of mind as well as body for the sake of mind through severe penances, spiritual practices and a life of contemplation. We are not concerned here with the subtle and the causal[3] as that would take us beyond society and politics. The governing principle of social and political thinking in these texts, however, was a search for a social order which would correspond to the cosmic order of which they had spiritual glimpses. The causal described as '*Para Brahma*' was beyond our immediate senses. It was the subjects matter of *paravidya*. Suffice it to say that the world was a result of the interplay between the *Purusha* and the *Prakriti* leading to greater and greater differentiation—a porcess, in which each unity, whole or individual had a certain identity of its own and the fulfilment for each consisted in the perfection of this identity through cosmic cycles.

According to this tradition, therefore, each individual is an autonomous agent seeking fulfilment of his identity which alone can provide bliss (*ananda*) to his life.[4] Its pursuit is ordained by nature and destiny of man. Of course, it has many shades and levels. On the one hand, at the grossest level under the broad rubric of '*kama*', it may be purely physical and may consist in mere fulfilment of 'sex-desires' or other 'necessities' of biological or physical existence by the individual. On the other hand, it could be of a higher level which comes out from activity leading to surplus (*artha*) for the service of others (*dharma*). While the individual was entitled to use his own wealth or surplus (*artha*) the ideal situation was one in which he used it to transcend the immediate in search of the infinite bliss (*moksha*). In all this there is a feeling that some kinds of joys are higher than others. The higher kinds are the ones which are good not merely for the individual himself but for all.

We have spoken of the individual as a potentially autonomous agent. Indian thought refers to this state as '*swaraj*' which, according to it, is the highest stage. This concept dates back to *Atharvaveda* and has been the source of inspiration for many of our national leaders like Tilak and Aurobindo. In the tradition, *swaraj* has been interpreted differently to mean disciplining oneself, freedom from necessities, transcending both inertness and activity or attainment of release from the cycle of birth and rebirth. But generally in the literature on the statecraft it has been used in a very mundane sense, namely a condition in which we are not dependent on others at all for our survival or fulfilment. It means, to quote Sukra, "complete control of oneself and independence from others". Sukra justified by saying, "Great misery comes of dependence on others. There is no greater happiness than from self rules."[5] When no one is able to dominate us against our will or basic nature, it is called *swaraj*. It is in this sense that the authors of both the *Atharvaveda* and the *Sukraniti* share the same vision. This notion of autonomy is different from individualism which is often used in a derogatory sense. While individualism compartmentalises life into parts and treats individuals as objects to be exploited by each other, on the basis of our causal understanding, and for our own pleasure or self-interest, the autonomy view sees individuals as persons existing in larger space with their distinct identities trying to achieve inwardness through greater communication with all. It is believed that such a communication can take place only where our mutual dependence is reduced. It is surprising but nevertheless true that their vision has been simulated in Plato's *Republic*.[6] Glaucon had asked Socrates not only to define justice but also to demonstrate that the man who followed justice was always better than the one who followed injustice. At the end of the *Republic*, Socrates in his own characteristic fashion replied that while all other types of men are dependent on external aides for their fulfilment, a man of justice is not so because he is self-contained.

For the attainment of joy or a state of bliss man seeks goods, services, occupation, richness, honour, glory and fame. He engages himself in different activities in order to ensure the achievement of the objects of his desires. Each individual is a whole in himself with his own distinct nature which he derives from birth and temperament and develops in course of adapting his nature to life process. But this individual having his own distinct identity as defined by his nature and temperament is not Hobbesian. He is related to other individuals and groups of other individuals such as the household, clan, tribe, village, province because all these are natural (and not conventional) conditions which provide a setting in terms of which his life acquires meaning and substance. They are a part of both his psychology and biology and direct him to ethics and economics, politics and history.

Man's relationships entail rights as well as duties. But here the concept of rights and duties are different from their counterparts in the liberal tradition in the West. In the Western tradition the classic case was stated by John Locke who thought there are certain natural rights which are innate and no one can deprive us of those rights. Duties, according to him, are not parts of nature except in so far as they flow from the principle of mutuality. Indian thought, too, recognised the tension between the claims of the individual and society as a whole. But it tried to resolve it in a more complex manner, viz., first by connecting him to the concrete functions one performs in society, and secondly, by relating him to the cosmic process of which he is an integral part.

All individuals occupy a definite position in terms of functions they perform from which their rights and duties flow. Here the primacy is on duties. Rights are capacities to perform duties appropriate to functions. Duties presuppose consideration of others. Rights in the western liberal traditions are "claims" against others. But, according to the Indian view, the individual cannot be defined by his functions alone because he does not perform one function; he is a member of a number of wholes and he has to play his distinct roles in all of them. As a member of society he has to offer sacrifices to intra-cosmic Gods, serve his parents, provide hospitality to guests and protection to the weak. The governing principle of both rights and duties at this stage is that of welfare of others *(upkar)*[7] and the welfare of the larger group must take precedence over the smaller group. In order that all are able to lead a life of contentment and joy according to their own nature, life is based on the principle of give and take. This nexus of duties as a condition of functionality constitutes an organised bond of mutuality.

There is a second level where the individual is able to seek a relationship with cosmic order. It should be recalled that when one differentiates himself into many, each of the differentiations called 'soul', in due course of time, attains its distinct identity, which could even be called destiny in its own way, and, therefore, in the ultimate analysis, it is the individual or each whole alone which has to protect his own soul. In such a situation where it is no longer possible to do so, the individual is permitted to run against the tide of society. In the civic order, Krishna calls upon the members of the Kuru Court to destroy the unjust King.[8] In the context of the social order, the story of the sage Valmiki and the seven sages calls upon us to stick to the righteous path. In the context of the cosmic order, the *Manusmriti* calls upon us to abandon the world for the sake of the soul if necessary.

It has been said that there is no notion of the individual in Indian thought. For instance, Dumont, has argued that the individual has no existence outside the framework of the caste. In all what the individual does he is bound by caste obligations. There is only one situation in which he transcends caste, namely that of a Sanyasin. This view places excessive emphasis on caste and has led to grave misunderstanding about the character of the Indian society. Caste is undoubtedly important but so as *ashram, shreni,* village, *Kula, Jati* and above all, *dharma.* Indeed, in the *Ramayana* and the *Mahabharata,* and also Puranic literature, there is a notion of a hero which gives life and substance to existence in this world for, the *Mahabharata* declares, it is on the shoulders of the heroes that rests the mother earth. Indeed so great has been the importance attached to the hero that all morals and poems are sought to be explained through their lives, be it the limited and exuberant personality of Rama or the unlimited personality of full-man Krishna or the non-dimensional personality of Shiva.[9] Indeed, the rigidity of the caste system was not the cause but the effect of breakdown of political order. The fixation with caste in its present form has made us ignore the profound metaphysical and ontological assumptions underlying the complexities of Indian society and philosophy which conceive of various relationships in society from many angles and at different levels of existence.

This ideal of the individual-community relationship was based on the assumption that, although men differ in nature and temperament, each of them must try to develop himself and realize his soul through seeking greater and greater intercourse with other members as a part of cosmic reality. Everything has its place, every individual has his work, every caste its duties and functions, and the social systems should be such as would cohere them by larger and larger wholes within a symphony so that the identity of each of these wholes develops. Each whole, according to this view, has its own sphere and function and all of them together produce rhythm which finds its expression in the enrichment of the mainfold character of life. An attempt is made to define good or truth (*dhruva satya*). But since it was assumed that the subtle (*sukshma*) and the causal (*karana*) were beyond the comprehension of most of us, we had to make do with possible truth (*vyavaharika satya*). In the *Mahabharata,* from the absolute truth we move to a notion of truth which does not harm any one or, to put it positively, which promotes the welfare of all. It was thought that just as every individual, family or community has its own identity or distinctive quality, the larger wholes too have a personality of their own, and good is defined in terms of the relationship in which each whole stands to the other for the unfettered benefit of all of them. The large whole is neither a numerical summation nor does it derive its importance merely from its location outside the smaller wholes which compose it in the sense of superseding them all. It is located outside in so far as it acquires an identity of its own. This identity is not based on annihilation of the identity of smaller wholes but cohere in their richness and variety and attains to its fuller realization by permitting them a realization of their own. Not that individualism of the some kind involving some notion of individuation is not possible in some streams of Indian thought. But whatever the kind or variety, every important stream of Indian thought postulates that the individual as a whole exists within a complex of other inter-locking wholes, a complex in which each whole has a relative autonomy and yet is related to other wholes for self-development. The autonomy of each whole must be compatible with and complementary to determination of the autonomy of other wholes and ultimately to community itself which has its own specificity, its own moral values and kinds and levels of development. Viewed from this angle, the dichotomy between the individual and community disappears; indeed they begin to appear as indivisible aspects of totality. One example is that of the caste system. The caste system was supposed to represent this principle of One in many. The *Brahmans* were concerned with knowledge. The *Ksatriyas* with courage and valour so that they could provide protection to the weak. Third class was that of *Vaisyas*. They were the people concerned with the satisfaction of necessities of life, agriculture, craft and trade. The fourth class was that of *Shudras* who were more of instruments of production for other classes. This division was originally meant to be functional, in which each caste was complementary to other castes. All the four classes were compared to different parts of the *Purusha*[10] in which there could be no question of inequality. All parts were vital and one could not be healthy without the health of others. All this obviously led in later times to a variety of occupations. But let me add that I do not wish to justify this institution. We all know that this functional division based on the principle of complementarity gave place to a division based on birth and heredity and destroyed the happy spontaneity of the conceptual scheme. The earlier system held out a promise of freedom in terms of distinct functions, nature and temperament but its conversion into a hereditary scheme completely nullified all such prospects and indeed legitimised the worst kind of social practices. Various historical reasons account for this development. But one which immediately strikes is that Indian thinkers failed to devise a mechanism whereby they could identify people in terms of their potential and arrange for their transfer from one caste to another.

There is another example which does not suffer the stigma attached to the caste system. It is the household which is a smaller republic in which both the husband and the wife as *Pradhan* and *Purusha* with their own clear identities, are construed as two sides of the same coin. While they mutually depend on each other, they work to promote welfare of all. In the act of creation they are one and in everything else they are one in two and two in one, two distinct bodies and souls acting in a state of potential conflict and yet acting, interacting together. If Kalidas's portrayal of *Raghuvansham* is to be believed, parents are expected to retire when they have played their innings and children who have become adults take their places. Though the children are bound by their obligations, they too have their own identities to realise. We know that what we are describing is an ideal situation and Indian life in the last one thousand years at least has been based on its denial but the ideal as a pure type embodying the aspirations of a people has its significance also.

Buddhism and Jainism introduced a certain amount of individualism similar to atomism of the West into Indian thought. To some extent Kautilya too did so specially when he gave the impression that what mattered was the individual success or satisfaction only and nothing else. Similarly, Jainism rejected the hierarchical view of cosmic structures and believed that the individual is his own creator of happiness or unhappiness; he alone is responsible for his own actions. In view of this it enjoins the individual to seek his individual salvation by destroying all his *karma* particles by his own efforts. Mahavira taught:

Soul alone performs actions, reaps their consequences, is born alone and dies alone, and alone does it move through the cycles of birth and rebirth.

I am always alone. No one is mine nor am I of any one. I neither see any one whom I can call mine nor do I see one who can be mine.

In this world there is a preponderance of meaninglessness. Here who belongs to whom? Who is mine and who is not. All relatives and non-relatives become so while moving through the cycle of birth and rebirth. But a time comes where there is neither a relative nor some one else.

Think that you are alone. No one was mine earlier and no one shall be hereafter. I delude myself into thinking that others are mine because of past *karmas*. In reality, I was alone earlier also, alone now and shall be alone in future.[11]

But Jainism was also led to compromise this stand and acquiesce in caste and ashram. Buddhism refused to do so and hence almost disappeared from India. For the most part Jains objected not to the Vedantic system but to the Brahmanical dominance in it specially outside the sphere of knowledge, in economy and politics, because it had led to the degeneration of the ancient society. They in a way reinterpreted the ancient belief to emphasise the importance of human effort in the cosmic process—which they, too, thought was an ascent towards salvation. But structurally and in essentials both Jainism and Buddhism could not distance themselves much from the brahmanical society. They, too, developed same rituals, practices and forms of worship. They did not abandon the idea of intra-cosmic Gods and Goddesses as is generally described in philosophy books. All they did was to extol the ideal of liberation (*mukti* or *nirvana*) above those stages in our ascent which would inevitably throw us back into the cycle of birth and rebirth once our merits (*punya*) were exhausted. But this was an ideal which other traditions, too, did not ignore. Indeed the difference between them all is one of emphasis and the fact is that in things like *mantra* and *tantra* these different traditions become hardly distinguishable. It could certainly be said of Amitgati and Kurndudacharya, indeed of the golden period of Jainism from seventh to twelfth centuries, that it was hardly distinguishable from other Hindu sects. Indeed, the proper contrast is not between Jainism or Buddhism or Hinduism but between two traditions within Hinduism—if at all such a thing existed, namely the *brahmanical* and the *Shramana* traditions (*paramparas*). In fact, few systems of speculation have given expression to the acceptance of multi-dimensional reality in the way in which Jain thought has done. The *Nyayavada* declares that there "are many points of view from which a thing can be looked at and that all these points of view are relative": the *Syadavada* is a logical consequence of this. It deals with various points of view from which one can look at reality. It recognises the possibility as well as the need of reconciling different contradictions. Such a relational logic as *Syadavada* would inevitably lead to a relational view of life: integral knowledge would imply integral philosophy and integral character. And yet Jains were not moral relativists because they too accepted the *brahmanical* hierarchy of values and enterprises leading ultimately to liberation from the cycles of birth and rebirth.

It is because of this way of thinking that in Indian philosophical tradition instances of total lack of discrimination have been quite rare. None of the traditions believes that this world or life exhausts our meaning or that there is only one path leading to self-realization. All of them legitimate a variety of ways in our search from *noetic* to *pneumatic*, ranging from polytheism to the highest kind of monism, from self-abnegation to participation in the divine drama (*lila*), from rigorous asceticism to *tantra* and *kapalika* orgies; its paradigm successfully gravitates in concentric circles, moving ever more slowly towards the same ideal. The typical Indian attitude to reality is reflected in the saying of Gita that "whoever comes to me through whatever ways reaches unto me"; or in the

Anekantavada of the Jains or the *Sunnyavada* of Buddhists: all of them believe that there are many facets of reality. It is revealed in the famous parable common to all Indian traditions of the elephant and the six blind men. Indeed, the earliest formulation of this, though in a negative form, is found in the Vedantic principle of "*neti, neti*" (not this, not this), in a positive form, in the principle of all inclusive reality or the formulation of *Acharang Sutra*[12] of Jains which describes the highest reality in terms of 'this and this'. But as pointed out above, specially in the context of Jains, the Indian thought did not accept moral relativism and postulated a hierarchy of values and activities (*purusharathas*), finally culminating in transcendence of causality (*mukti*). Relationships at each level are organised finally in terms of a point located outside the cosmic process as revealed through history. But the existence of this as a historical point outside the cosmic process does not mean that relationships are to be made uniform. Since there are many wholes, levels and cycles of existence, each has its own importance so long as it is not transformed into a higher level which will cohere the lower and yet not destroy it. It is a process in which everyone, of whatever religion or caste, in fulness of time will be able to attain the highest point of no return.

The social system reared on the fabric of such a world view has a remarkable cohesion. And yet, since the relative autonomy of different levels and practices, as expressed through different languages, religions, kinship groups have been legitimised, they might pull the individual in different directions, creating a profound complexity of relationships not clearly found in the modern thought. Therefore, the picture of society which finally emerges in India is qualitatively different from that in the West. While the relationships in the West are viewed as dyadic, in India they are multistructured. "Instead of an indivisibility, (the individual) the subject is a totality of opposites, empirically multiple, ontologically one."[13] In other words, society is conceived as a concrete illustration of the Upanishadic principle, 'One in many and many in one', working in terms of neither the individual nor the collective analogy but in terms of its distinctive type of a social organisation inherent in the concept of, what Gandhi called, "oceanic circles", each having an inner rhythm and dynamism of its own.

The ideas which link men, society, order, the non-human world and the cosmos in Indian society have a rare internal consistency, and constitute a powerful system. These ideas and assumptions are different from those of the Western civilization. These ideas are concerned not so much with coexistence of different and discordant parts but with a variety of different spheres of living which go up to make the social whole. Indeed, the limits of the oceanic circles extend from the inanimate, such as a stone (Indians believe that these too have life) to the farthest reaches of our cosmos, from the wholes within wholes, from Koestler's 'holons', to the galactic system. And, therefore, there is no question of treating the individual as a separate atom with no valency to combine and recombine. The individual does have his rights and interests but he is not supposed to be merely a rationally calculating creature always interested in a maximization of his utilities only. Calculation is necessary but it is subordinated to the wider ends of human existence, to the maximisation of his powers of autonomy through a combination of rules and virtue, the supreme objective being to attain self autonomy or self development or complete liberation (described variously as *moksha, nirvana, mukti,* and *parama pada*), possible only by cohering the triple qualities of nature (*prakriti*) or by cohering the socio-economic relationships in search of the universal.

II

This, however, should not mean that the Indian thought does not recognize any tension between the individual and the community. There is a tension inherent in the individual community relationship. This springs from the fact that different wholes and practices at different levels of existence are competing with each other for more goods, riches, power, honour and glory or even greater self identity—there is, for instance, a tendency to justify the claims of the bigger wholes at the expense of the smaller ones. But it is doubtful whether the ancient Indian systems emphasise the biggest whole at the expense of the individual in all situations. In the scheme envisaged in the *Manusmriti,* the smaller whole commands necessary authority and resources and performs most of the social tasks relating to itself at its own level. The larger whole ought to perform only the residual functions, or, as the *Manusmriti* tells us, functions which cannot be performed by the smaller wholes. Indian thought does no conceive of the individual autonomy apart from a cosmic order which would guarantee similar autonomies to other wholes. It recognises that since in this cosmic order different wholes have their own distinct identities which they are trying to realize, it is possible that they will come into conflict with each other or cut each other's throats, for while we all have the capacity for integral reasoning, there is no guarantee that we shall always be its servants. We are human beings amenable to pride on the one hand and extravagance and licentiousness on the other.

The ancients were conscious of the struggle for existence amidst various polarities. Few could have the ultimate truth. Most of us were satisfied with the knowledge which threw light on the struggle between these polarities. The ancients recognised that the identification and control of these tendencies was extremely important in discerning ways ultimately leading to truth. The seer, therefore, was not merely concerned with abstract issues of philosophy but with concrete forms which One assumes at different levels and the ways in which the lower level can be transformed into a higher one. Elements of right order (*daivika*) are therefore developed in relation to the wrong order (*asurika*). The first is spelled out in terms of the sustenance and development of life process (*khil jagat paripalanaya*)[14] so that each soul is able to fulfil itself, and the second, in terms of domination of all by one or some in which the rest are reduced to a state of servitude. In enunciating these ideas in different contexts, the ancients followed a complex method in which philosophy, allegory, mystic symbols and prayers, all have a distinct place. There is no one dominant paradigm of truth (*sat*) or right (*dharma*) either but various competing ones in which even an asura can through yoga be a veritable symbol of *dharma*—as indeed Rambhana, Bali and Kritiviryaarjuna were. Consequently, there are many types or orders in which one can live.

Since this mode of thought legitimises various paradigms of social living, it did not so much concern itself with forms of government (though there is some discussion at a number of places) as with ordering of soul as well as society. The seer is interested in society for the sake of the soul. Society is important because it is an immediate medium through which soul finds its expression. When society however well organised fails to help the soul, the ancient seer is no longer interested in the society. The comparative indifference of some of these thinkers to the details of the institutions-building is explained by the fact that they were convinced that societies would take care of themselves if the rulers were good and followed the path of righteousness.[15] Mere construction or repair of institutions will not do unless there were good rulers. So great is the importance of rulers that their character even defines the nature of the epoch. They can change, albeit temporarily, even a *Kalayuga* into *Satyayuga*. In society the institutions created by scriptures and conventions must continue. But the goodness of these institutions will depend not so much on traditions as on the character of the rulers. Good body is essential but its legitimacy is derived from its ability to serve a good soul.

It might be asked why should there be the paraphernalia of society if so much depended on the good character of the ruler? What kind of relationship is there between soul and the state? In contrast to the Greek thought which postulated that there is no difference between the structure of society and the structure of the state, both are interfused, the ancient Indians made a distinction between society and the state. Society is as organic as the individual. But the state is merely one of the organs of society performing a limited but important role. Its role is more or less like that of the stomach in the body concerned with the production and distribution. But there are other organs of the body like the head corresponding to which in society are the seers and the learned who are concerned with elicitation of truth. They hold up to every one, including the state, the paradigm of right order. This order is thus not entirely absorbed by the order of the state. The order of the state may have precedence over the other orders, but it is not the only order. It merely deals with law and order as well as the means by which the unacquired is acquired, the acquired is guarded well, and the guarded is distributed well.[16] There are various other institutions and organs of society which have orders of their own. Orders find their expression in various kinds of communities, groups, institutions, in the household, the clan, the *jati* and the *shreni*. Some of these orders are intimately connected with the state. The moral, cultural and spiritual spheres are outside the realm of the state. The state can reconcile their claims and counter claims. But there are orders which are beyond the state. In the Greek thought Aristotle identified good life with the state, but in the Indian thought the definition of good life, indeed the entire cultural and spiritual realm, lies outside the order of the state and sets standards for the right order of the State itself.

The custodians of the cultural and the spiritual realm as pointed out above, define the criteria of good order, provide legitimacy to it, and see that the state abides by this criteria. There is an awareness that none of the existing states could be perfect. But there are some examples like that of Ayodhya of Rama which came near it. During the *Mahabharata* war, none of the states had it and therefore while change of government takes place in Hastinapur, Dwarka of Krishna, of the Lord himself, is destroyed once the great sustaining soul departs. Human existence was not solely confined to political existence and, therefore, not in all cases restoration of soul demanded restoration or creation of a political order. But it was recognised that without the latter the first could not be easily achieved, because, in the absence of the political order the law of fish (*matsyanayaya*) will prevail. A ruler shall have done his job if he keeps himself clear of vices and is able to enforce righteousness and protect the weak. While normally the seers are not expected to take a stand against rulers, there are situations when they take up arms, as when they did against Vena to uphold the dignity of the soul. They killed Vena as a retribution for his tyranny and installed in his place Prithu who took a solemn oath to protect his subjects. The oath is testament of the idea of contract and highlights more the duties of the king than his rights.[17] "Protection of his subjects is the highest duty of the king, since compassion to all creatures and protecting them from injury has been said to be the highest merit."[18]

There is a natural need for order to reconcile conflicting claims in terms of the recognition of social obligations. God has created order in nature. Everything functions according to a fixed law (*rita*). Since there is an order in nature there should also be one in the realm of human beings, the former may not be so obvious to us but with some application of integral knowledge (*Jnana* and *buddhi*) we can always discern it. The principles which ought to govern social life are called *dharma*. While *rita* refers to causality of the natural process, *dharma* to the moral concerns of the human world. *Dharma* is *recht* and is conceived as the fulcrum of social life, as "the prime object and basis of truth".[19] It is a principle which makes it possible for the world to sustain and develop itself by providing *order* and *pattern* to its arrangements' "it is the eternal law that governs all human and non-human existence". "It is soul of all beings which discerns good and evil."[20] But *dharma* too is a complex principle which takes the existence of what we have termed as 'wholes within wholes' for granted. It is, therefore, a principle of both individual self-development and communal self-development. As for the individual, it is a principle of meritorious development (*abhyudya* and *nishreyasa*) according to one's qualities, conditioned by one's nature, temperament and potential towards higher and higher existence. And for the community, it means attainment of self-rule (*swaraj*) in terms of its own historical identity.

There is no doubt that the ancients were able to seize the problem of order by throat and adequately locate the state in it because, according to them, in this the role of rulership flows directly from the place of *Ksatriyas* and the activities assigned to them. *Dharma* also defines the limits of the state power. The recognition of the problem at an early stage in human civilization as a great achievement which requires no proof greater than the fact that even a man like Gandhi, again and again, reminded us of the *Ramarajya*. *Dharma* is the principle which creates order in anarchy of impulses, activities and institutions in terms of such virtues as friendship, love and service. It creates balance among *purusharthas, kama, artha* and *moksa*. It also harmonises various activities. It ensures that men do not swerve from the ultimate ideal of self-rule and transcendence in terms of the supremacy of knowledge. In the hands of the medieval saints emphasis on knowledge was replaced by devotion and faith. The principles of *dharma* although outside the realm of all other activities, regulates them all and hence the one who symbolizes it, be it Lord Vishnu in the transcendental realm, or a ruler in the human realm, combines in himself all the qualities of other intra-comsic or super-Gods, and yet as the Lord of Bhagvatam is bound by the rules he has himself created, the ruler too is enjoined to order himself by the principles of *dharma*. The difference between Lord Vishnu and a ruler is that while there is no remedy against Vishnu's transgressions, the ruler like Vena has to fear popular wrath; he cannot afford to hurt the weak for his own happiness, for the weak and the poor when tormented can destroy even the mightiest of kingdoms.

Indian tradition accepted monarchical order. It was defended in terms of unity of social organism and efficiency of government. There was consequently a tendency to exalt the person of the King over and above the community. He was often compared to Lord Vishnu and it was argued that it was his responsibility to provide leadership to his subjects. His powers in that sense were derived from God himself. The relation of the king to State was compared with that of God to the world. He was assigned an element of divinity.

However, for all practical purposes the relationship between the king and the people involved reciprocity of rights and obligations. Both were bound by mutual obligations and the coherence of all these constituted the organic whole of the community. In the community, people were bound to obey the law of the State. But similarly, the king owed his powers to the fact that he had a duty to serve the people. Kingship war instituted for the sake of the well-being of the people and not people for the sake of the king. Therefore the power of the king was rarely conceived as absolute, it was always limited by the purpose for which it was brought into existence. His task is to punish the wicked and reward the deserving, maintain what is there, to increase it and to distribute what has been increased. He is to maintain caste system. Whenever there is a breach in the performance of these duties, the kingship in proportion loses its legitimacy and degenerates into tyranny. The doctrine of the unconditional divine right of kings did not exist in India. Every obligation to obey commands of the king was contingent upon the rightfulness of the commands. People accepted that the authority of dharma was higher than that of the king and therefore people were not bound to obey an unrighteous king.

The protection of the weak is the special responsibility of the King. The *Mahabharata* says, "Do not, therefore, come into (hostile) contact with the weak. Thou should not regard the weak as always subject to humiliation. Take care that the eyes of the weak do not burn thou with thy kinsmen. In a race scorched by the eyes of the weak, no children take birth. The power of the weak is more powerful than even the greatest power."[21] The *Mahabharata* is full of passages which emphasise that the power of the state is not for "self-aggrandisement" of the ruler. It says that those who seek to enlarge or govern their kingdoms in unscrupulous ways very soon come to be regarded as a vermin in dead body.[22] At another place it says "The crooked and the covetous king who suspects every body and who taxes his subjects heavily, is soon deprived of his life by his own subjects or relatives."[23] Even the word *rajan* tends to identify the kingship with a ruler who pleases people. The word *rajan* is derived from two roots, *ranja* which means to please and *rajr* which means to shine.[24] These ideas were later elaborated in the *Sukraniti* which made a distinction between a righteous and unrighteous king: only righteous king could claim ordination by God.

Indeed, as Dharampal has argued in his *Civil Disobedience and Indian Tradition* (1971), the entire moral life of the epic is rooted in the sustenance of a legitimate order. It carries further the distinction between society and the state. The state is merely a means to an end. It almost appears as an artifact created by human beings (specially in the episode of Vena pointed our earlier) or serve a definite purpose and that purpose is the pleasure of the people. Once tyranny and violence reach a particular limit, and a person, whether an ordinary individual or a king, deviates from the righteous path, severe punishment must be meted out to him regardless of filial or other considerations. In the *Mahabharata*, Arjun becomes the vehicle of rebellion. He is enjoined by Krishna to take up arms for the sake of the welfare of all (*Loksamgraha*). The powers of the king are consequently limited by the purposes for which the kingdom came into existence. It is no wonder, therefore, that James Mill, the author of *The History of British India*, told in his evidence to a Committee of the House of Commons:

In the ordinary state of things in India (though under such government as that of India there was little of anything like a regular check), the princes stood in awe of their subjects. Insurrection against oppression was the general practice of the country, the princes knew that when mismanagement and oppression went to a certain extent, there would be revolt, and that they would stand a chance of being tumbled from the throne, and a successful leader of insurgents put in their place.[25]

Dharampal has recorded that even as late as the eighteenth century, both group and individual resistance against injustice were quite common in all parts of India. These were institutionalised in the practices such as *dharma*, *traga, koorh* and *ijara*. Both the rulers and the ruled shared a certain notion of justice, and a violation of this led either to the overthrow of the ruler or the threats of mass desertion by the ruled.

III

It must be confessed here that in the medieval period, there was doubtless a breakdown of this kind of order. The system became extremely rigid. Ancient ideals of kingship were replaced by a new system based on Islam. The office of kingship sometimes bordered on tyranny with the introduction of the Persian ideas and the emergence of the period in which the ancient order had to face the challenge of the new order. Although in some phases every effort had been made to harmonise political ideas and institutions with idiom of life and values which were acceptable to all, the problems faced by medieval authority did not leave much scope for it. Islam as embodied in the state was, at least in early stages an exclusivist doctrine. It had to be subservient to the needs and demands of an extending empire. On the other hand, Hinduism by this time had become a bundle of paradoxes: on the one hand there was an emphasis on life and its processes expressed through rituals and *Karma Kanda*, on the other hand it became highly individualistic, and any attempt to attain salvation through participation in community life was rejected. The search for inner light and personal salvation become more important than salvation through the performance of one's functions and worldly obligations. From time to time such as in *Puranas* or the *Ramayana* of Tulsidas and that of Kaniban, there is amply emphasis on performance of one's obligation to society. But on the whole the doctrine of life negation or complete self-surrender became dominant. The *bhakti* movement was a high watermark of this trend. God was conceived as an image of ecstasy which can only be experienced through faith and complete surrender. All else was considered transitory.

The whole period was marked by an acute awareness full of antagonism and conflict, of reconciliation to the new situation and despair. In Hindu society there was perhaps a breakdown of norms in which "the husbands and parents behave very cruelly". The Bhagvatam declared "The Goddess of Learning has now been living in the house of brahmanas devoid of dutifulness, and even the best of brahmanas are serving the *Ksatriyas* who treat the brahmana with contempt." Such a society could not be congenial to the development of political thought. A politically decentred India was unable to deal with foreign conquests. The result was that the linkage between the state and the rest of the society became extremely weak. With the establishment of Islamic power at the centre, the circles of social life became independent with very little interference of the state. This perhaps enabled the Hindu society to protect itself against the possible encroachments by the central ruler. Since caste did not have a centre it could not be captured by outsiders. Finding life difficult, people tended to escape into world of mysticism by ignoring the importance of good life here itself. Since the political sphere was thought as not directly concerned with the salvation of the soul, it was thought that it should be left to rulers. The integral view of the ancient times was compartmentalised. Since rulership did not matter from the point of view of earning spiritual merits, it could be left to smaller souls. While political power was delinked from social moorings its exercise became highly personalised. The traditional writings on politics and statecraft were almost lost. Kautilya mentioned about thorty-two ancient texts on politics. But most of these have not come down to us. This did not of course influence the common man. He was still concerned with the problem of his own livelihood. But since the mentors left him alone, he merely became a passive spectator of the intrigue of the courts of rulers and emperors in whose hands political power had become highly personalised. The influence of Persian ideas made the situation still worse. On the other hand, the breakdown of kingship led to rigidity of the caste system which, in turn, became the cause of decline of the ancient society. This process reached its nadir during the British period when an alien political system was superimposed on the traditional society. The rise of the British power created a deep cleavage between political and social wholes, deliberately destroying the indigenous idiom, values and institutions, and creating new institutions which destroyed the ancient ideal of the organisation of polity (*rajyasamgraha*). The nineteenth century renaissance was a creative revival of the ancient Indian ideal. It was articulated in the writings of Vivekananda, Aurobindo, Tagore and Gandhi.

People have often spoken of the absence of dominance of politics in Indian tradition. This view is not quite correct. In the early texts like the *Manusmriti* and the *Mahabharata*, politics is indispensable because in its absence the laws of fish will operate and there will be terrible anarchy. But there is a clear distinction between the function of the state and the dominance of the state. It was believed, as pointed out earlier, that society is an organism and the role of the state is more or less similar to the role of stomach in the human body in so far as it too takes care of the productive and distributive apparatus in society. It is a part of the body and cannot be equated with the body as a whole. It must take into account diverse customs and practices of different castes, regions and even families, and come to terms with the differentiated reality of the cosmic process. If the state fails in the performance of its functions, and if anarchy actually comes upon society, people are justified in disobeying it. Obedience is contingent on the king keeping his part of the contract. This position obviously had its merit as well as demerits. The merit lay in its clearly defining the limits of the kingship and sovereignty; its demerit consisted in its inability to allow the emergence of the notion of the king or political power as independent of civil society.

In the Western political tradition, one of the most important development in modern times is the emergence of the State as an overarching regulatory order which acquires an objectivity of its own. Hobbes assumes the necessity of a political authority outside the framework of the competition and conflict in the civil society. The authority of the state emerges in order to conciliate and reconciliate different interests. It is not a part of society. The contract is among the individuals and the sovereign is not a party to it. This disjunction between the state and civil society is clearly stated by Hegel.[26] The state becomes a realisation of the spirit because it alone transcends the particularities of the civil society and enables us to realise freedom of Law which is general and objective. In the Indian thought, on the other hand, for the most part the state is so much a part of the oceanic circles of social life that it fails to transcend particularities of the social existence. Like the state in the political philosophy of Locke, it is one of the organs entrusted with the task of mere execution of laws made within the realm of the civil society itself.

Manu, Vyasa and Kautilya are perhaps exception to this. In their writings, the state becomes autonomous of civil society. Indian thought develops both the concepts of authority and that of office. The king claims the right to final interpretation of scriptures. The state becomes a focus of political power of which the king is perhaps the most important element but not the sole element. In the state the king is distinguished from six other elements i.e., the people, the minister, the army, the treasury, the system of justice and his friends and enemies. The elements are regarded as limbs of the body which are mutually interdependent. It is argued that even a minor defect in any of them may be inimical to the whole body.[27] This was indeed a great leap forward towards the conceptualisation of the state which becomes an institution distinct from both rulers and subjects. That is why the king is not permitted to use treasury for his personal pleasure.

If he does so, he is regarded as a thief. The king is compared with a pregnant woman who is ever concerned with the welfare of her child. At times he is also compared to a wage earner. The king should show utmost compassion to his people who constitute, according to the *Mahabharata*, "the most impregnable fort". However, for most part the tradition failed to develop the idea of an objective sovereign authority existing outside civil society. The idea of kingship remained always bound up with the idea of office with very few institutional checks. In the absence of proper institutional checks on the powers of the king, the subjectivity of the civil society is replaced by the subjective will of the king and his advisers.[28] The importance of law as a general principle and institutions as effective mechanisms to sustain the law were generally ineffectual. So long as the king was good he governed in the interest of all, but when he was bad he became a tyrant from whom there was no escape except through rebellion. This largely explains both why the absence of political authority did not materially disturb Hindu social organisation and why the weaknesses of political centre made India vulnerable in the face of conquerors. It also made the state unable to prevent or impede the ascendency of powerful rural, ethnic and caste divisions. The aspiration of Modern India to consolidate itself into a modern state is being thwarted by the absence, except in the most ancient texts, of the idea of the state standing outside the civil society and yet regulating, or more appropriately, bridging all cleavages within it.

In this century we have witnessed the emergence of new barbarisms either in the name of the reasons of the state or of the individual rights or some such things; the Indian political vision, on the other hand, seeks to create order without destroying the differentiated orders of human life— provides a package of autonomy and differentiated life from a vision, which concentrates on mutuality so that some room is left for individuals, associations and institutions to realise their autonomy.[29] It is this kind of disposition which one finds in Valmiki and Vyasa, Sukra and even Kautilya. We have no reason to believe that it is an outdated perspective. We find its resurgence in the modern Indian thought: particularly in the writings of Aurobindo, Coomaraswamy and Gandhi. The centralised political institutions operating on the basis of the principles of either statism and collective will or of individualism and economic rationality do not do justice to man's yearning for autonomy (*swa*) in society and its interlocking institutions. The ideology of the present state envisages economic growth largely in terms of increasing production, or arranging distribution of goods for individuals *qua* individuals rather than *qua* members of community or a cosmic order. The result is that while the process of disintegration of the ancient community life continues, the social life is becoming increasingly serialized and the political structures are becoming more and more bureaucratic and centralized. One hears a lot about socialism but it is in practice wedded to the notion of the collective needs, rather than human needs specified in terms of the autonomy of the individual or his membership of a variety of communities, corporations and wholes. An attempt to bring political and social wholes in correspondence and communion with each other in terms of the recognition of the differentiated character of the wholes alone can stop the present process of disruption and strife in social life. This normative concept of human relationship has many principles which are unsubstantiated. The entire history of modern Indian thought is an attempt to render a convincing account of it. But it highlights the meaning of the distinct civilisational experience in India. It is my belief that some such view of the individual community relationship alone can provide a justificatory theory for a diffused polity (which Manu called *Rajyam Samgrahyam*) and a decentralised economy so that we are able to realise *swaraj* in our own distinct ways.

NOTES

1. V.R. Mehta, *Ideology, Modernization and Politics in India* (Delhi, Manohar, 1983). Also see *Beyond Marxism: Towards an Alternative Perspective* (Delhi, Manohar, 1978).

2. Dharampal, *Science and Technology in India* (New Delhi, Impex India, 1971).

3. This view is generally attributed to Samkhya philosophers but in fact lies at the basis of all the texts attributed to Vyasa who in subtle way tries to combine Smakhya and Yoga.

4. For a clear expression, Somedeva, *Nitivakyamritam* (Mysore, Government Press), 6, 5, 6.

5. See Sukra, *Sukraniti*, trans. B.K. Sarkar (Ahmedabad, 1923), III, 652-5, 656; *Atharva Veda*, trans. Damodar Satvalkar (Ahmedabad, Seadhyay Mandal), pp. 110, 161.

6. Plato, *The Republic* trans: H.D. Lee (London, Penguin), p. 99.

7. *Manusmriti*, IV: 240-2.

8. *The Mahabharata* trans: P.C. Roy (Calcutta, Oriental Publishing House. VII XCIX.

9. Rammanohar Lohia, "Rama Krishna and Shiva" in *Interval During Politics* (Hyderabad, Nav Hind, 1965), pp. 29, 50.

10. *Rig Veda.*

11. Quoted from "Jain Thought and Philosophy", *Illustrated Weekly of India,* Feb. 15-21, 1981, p. 19.

12. *Acharang Sukram,* trans. Kishan Lal (Ujjain, Jain Sahitya Samiti), Part IV, 3rd chapter, 140-41.

13. *Durga Saptashati,* chap. 4.

14. L. Dumont, *Religion, Politics and History in India* (The Hague, Mouton, 1970).

15. *Agni Purana,* chap. 38, 13-15.

16. *The Mahabharata,* op. cit., VII, 127-9.

17. Ibid., VII, LIX (59).

18. See *Manusmriti,* Chaps. VII, LXXI.

19. Valmiki, *Ayodhyakand,* trans: M.N. Dutta, 23-4.

20. Ibid., pp. 6, 18-25.

21. *The Mahabharata,* op. cit., vol. VII, chapt. XCI.

22. Ibid., vol. VII, chap. LLLVI (156).

23. Ibid.

24. Ibid., vol. VII, chap. XXXVII.

25. Quoted by Dharampal, "The Rediscovery of India", *Illustrated Weekly of India,* 15-21 June 1986, p. 10.

26. See Hegel's incisive commitments in *The Philosophy of History* (New York, Dover Publications, 1986), pp. 139-69.

27. *The Mahabharata,* op. cit., vol. VIII, chapter XC.

28. Hegel, op. cit., pp. 139-69.

29. See V.R. Mehta, *Beyond Marxism: Towards an Alternative Perspective* (Manohar, 1978). Also, Aurobindo, *The Foundations of Indian Culture.* op. cit., Also, Radhakamal Mukherjee, *Community of Communities* (Bombay, 1976); V.R. Mehta, op. cit.

SELECT BIBLIOGRAPHY

Abul Fazal : *A'in-i-Akbari,* 2 Vols., Calcutta, 2nd ed., Trans, Blochman, Corrected and edited by J. Sarkar, Asian Society of Bengal, rep., New Delhi, New Imperial Book Depot, 1965.

Aiyar, A Subramanya : *A Lecture on State Interference in Social Matters in India* (Pamphlet) Madras, 1891.

Aiyer, Aiyar, P.S. Sivaswamy: *Evolution of Hindu Moral Ideas*, Calcutta, 1935.

Allchin, Bard R. : *The Birth of Indian Civilization*, Harmondsworth, 1968.

Altekar, A.S. : *State and Government in Ancient India*, Delhi, Motilal Banarsidass, 1958 (first published 1949).

Appadurai, Arjun : "It's Homo Hierarchicus?" *American Ethnologist*, Vol. XIII, No. 4, 1986, pp. 745-61

Athenaeus : *The Deipnosophists*, Eng. Trans, Charles Burton Qulick (2nd and 3rd AD) London, Heinemann, MCMXXVII, 6 Vols.

Bandyopadhyay, N.C. : *Development of Hindu Polity and Political Theories*, ed. with introduction by Narendra Nath Bhattacharyya, New Delhi, Munshiram Manoharlal, 1980.

Banerjea, P. : *Public Administration in Ancient India*, London, Macmillan, 1916.

Banerjea, S.N. : *A Nation in Making*, London, 1925.

Basham, A.L. : *The Wonder that Was India*, New York, 1954.

Besant, Annie : *Ancient Ideals in Modern Life*, Benaras, 1909.

Bhandarkar, D.R. : *Some Aspects of Hindu Polity*, Benaras, 1928.

Bhagavata Purana, ed., V.L. Pans Kar, Bombay, 1920, tr. M.N. Dutta, Calcutta, 1895.

Bhagvata Purana, Geeta Press, Gorakhpur.

Bhatia, H.S. (ed.) : *Origin and Development of Legal and Political System in India*, 2 Vols., New Delhi, 1976.

Blake, S.P. : "The Patrimonial—Bureaucratic Empire of the Mughals", *Journal of Asian Studies,* Vol. XXXIX, No. I, Nov. 1979.

Bondruant, J.V. : *Conquest of Violence*, Oxford, Oxford University Press. 1958.

Bose, A.C. : *Hymns from Vedas*, New Delhi, Asia, 1966. "The Theory of Diplomacy in the Mahabharata", *Journal of Historical Research,* Vol. 2, 1960.

Brown, D.M. : *White Umbrella: Indian Political thought from Manu to Gandhi*,

Berkeley, University of California Press, 1953.

Burke, Edmund : *Mr. Burke's Speech on the 1st December 1983, upon the question for the Speaker's Leaving the chair in order for the House to Resolve itself into a Committee on Mr. Fox's East India Bill*, London, J. Dodsley, 1984.

Chattopadhyaya, D.P. : *Sri Aurobindo and Karl Marx*, Delhi, Motilal Banarsidass, 1988.

Chaudhry, H.C. Roy : *Advanced History of India*, Vol. III, London, Macmillan, 1961.

Das, Veena : *Structure and Cognition: Aspects of Hindu Caste and Ritual*, New Delhi, Oxford University Press, 1977.

Coomaraswamy, A.K. : *Hinduism and Buddhism*, New Delhi, 1975.

————: *Spiritual Authority and Temporal Power in the Indian Theory of Government*, New Heaven, American Oriental Society, 1942.

————: *The Dance of Siva*, Delhi, Asia, 1952.

Dalton, D.G. : *Indian Idea of Freedom*, Gurgaon, 1984.

Dandekar, R.N. : *Insights into Hinduism*, Delhi, Ajanta, 1979.

Dange, S.A. : *India from Primitive Communism to Slavery: A Marxist Study of Ancient Indian History in Outline*, 4th ed., New Delhi, 1961.

Daniel, Thorner : 'Indian Feudalism' in Rushtor Caulborn, *Feudalism in History*, Princeton, Princeton University Press, 1956.

Derrett, J. D. M. : *Religion, Law and the State in India*, London, Faber and Faber, 1968.

Devahuti, D. : *Harsha: A Political Study*, Oxford, Clarendon Press, 1970.

Dikshitar, Ramachandra : *Mauryan Polity*, Madras, University of Madras, 1932.

Dumont, Louis : *Religion, Politics and History in India*, The Hague, Mouton, 1970.

————: *Homo Hierarchicus*, rev. edn. tr., Marksainsbury L. Dumont, and Baria Gulati, Chicago, University of Chicago Press, 1980.

Dutta, M.N. : (Trans) *Ramayana*, 2 Vols., Calcutta: G.C. Chakravarti Dev Press, 1891-94.

Gandhi, M.K. : *Socialism of My Conception*, ed. Anand T. Hingorani, Bombay, Bhartiya Vidya Bhawan, 1957.

————:*Democracy, Real and Deceptive*, Ahmedabad, 1961.

————:*India of My Dreams*, Bombay, 1947.

————:*Collected Works*, 51 Vols., Ahmedabad, Navjivan.

Ganguli, B.N. : *Gandhi's Social Philosophy*, Delhi, Vikas, 1973.

Geoffrey, Ash : *A Study in Revolution*, Heinemann, 1968.

Ghoshal, U.N. : *A History of Indian Public Life*. Oxford, Oxford University Press, 1959.

————: *A History of Indian Political Ideas: Ancient Period and the Period of Transition to the Middle Ages*, Oxford, Oxford University Press, 1959.

————: *A History of Hindu Political Theories*, 1923.

————: *The Foundations of Indian Culture*, Pondicherry, Aurobindo Ashram, 1971.

Ghose, Sri Aurobindo : *Bankim Chandra Chatterji*, Pondicherry, 1954.

————: *The Rennaissance of India*, Pondicherry, Aurobindo Ashram, 1951.

————: *The Ideal of Karmayogin*, Pondicherry, Aurobindo Ashram, 1913.

————: *The Human Cycle & the Ideal of Human Unity,* etc., Pondicherry, Aurobindo Ashram, 1952.

————: *Complete Works*, Pondicherry, Aurobindo Birth Centenary Library, 1972.

Ghurye, G.S. : *Vedic India*, Bombay, 1977.

Gokhale, B.S. : *The Making of Indian Nation*, Bombay, Asia, 1960.

Gonda, J. : *Ancient Indian Kingship from the Religious Point of View,* Leiden, E.J. Brill, 1966.

Gopal S. (ed), *Jawaharlal Nehru: An Anthology*, New Delhi, Oxford University Press, 1980.

Habib, M. : 'Life and Thought of Ziauddin Barni', *Medieval India Quarterly*, Jan-April 1958.

Haithcox, J.H. : *Communism and Nationalism in India*, Princeton, Princeton University Press, 1971.

Heesterman, J.C. : *The Inner Conflict of Tradition* : *Essays in Indian Ritual, Kingship and Society*, Chicago, University of Chicago Press, 1958.

————:*The Ancient Indian Royal Consecrations*, The Hague, 1957.

Hegal, G.W.P. : *Lectures on the Philosophy of Religion*, Tr. E.B. Speirs and J.B. Sanderson, London: Routledge and Kegan Paul, 1895.

————: *Lectures on the Philosophy of World History*, tr. H.B. Nisbet, Cambridge, Cambridge University Press, 1975.

Heimsath, Charles H.: *Indian Nationalism and Hindu Social Reform.* Princeton, Princeton University Press, 1964.

————: 'Hinduism' in *Encyclopaedia Britannica*, Vol. VIII, 1974. pp. 889-908.

Horsburg, H.J.N. : *Non-violence of Aggression* : *A Study of Gandhi's Moral Equivalent of Wars*, Oxford, Oxford University Press, 1968.

Hussain, Abid : *The National Culture in India*, New Delhi, Asia, 1956.

Inamdar, N.R.: *Political Thought and Leadership of Lokmanya Tilak*, New Delhi, Concept, 1983.

Inden, Ronald : *Imagining India*, Oxford, Basil Blackwell, 1990.

Ikram, S.M. : *Muslim Civilization in India*, New York, Columbia University Press, 1964.

Iyer, Raghavan : *Utilitarianism and All that: The Political Theory of British Imperialism,* London, Grove Press, 1983.

Jayaswal, K.P. : *Hindu Polity* : *A Constitutional History of India in Hindu Times*, Calcutta: Butterworth, 1924.

Kakkar, Sudhir : *The Inner World*, Delhi, Oxford University Press, 1978.

Kalmer, G. : *Gandhism,* Budapest, 1980.

Kane, P.V. : *History of Dharmasastra*, 5 Vols., Poona, Bhandarkar Oriental Research Institute, 1930-62.

Kangle, R.P. : *The Kautilya's Arthasastra: A Study, Part III,* Bombay, University of Bombay, 1965.

Kantowsky, Detlef : Max Weber on India: An Indian Interpretation of Weber; *Contributions to Indian Sociology,* New Series, Vol. XVL, 1982, pp. 141-74.

Karve, D.G. : *Ranade: The Prophet of Liberated India,* Poona, 1942.

Karve, Iravati : *Hindu Society: An Interpretation,* Poona, Deccan College, 1961.

Karunakaran, K.P. : *Indian Politics from Dadabhai Naoroji to Gandhi,* New Delhi: Asia.

Kautilya : *Arthasastra,* ed. R. Shamasastri, Mysore, Mysore Govt. Oriental Series, 1909.

Kaviraj, Gopinath : *Bhartiya Sanskriti and Sadhana,* Patna, 1953.

Khan, Benjamin : *The Concept of Dharma in Ramayana,* New Delhi, Munshiram Manoharlal, 1965.

Kosambi, D.D. : *An Introduction to the Study of the Indian History,* Bombay, Popular Book Depot, 1956.

Kothari, Rajni : *Politics in India,* Boston, Little Brown, 1970.

Krishnaswami, A.S. : *Evolution of Hindu Administrative Institutions in South India,* Madras, University of Madras, 1931.

Kumarappa, B. : *Capitalism, Socialism or Villagism,* Benaras, 1965.

Law, N.N. : 'The Religious Aspects of Ancient Hindu Polity', *The Modern Review,* Vol. 22, 1917.

————: *Studies in Ancient Hindu Polity,* New York, 1914.

Lohuizen de Leeuw, J.W. Van : 'India and 1st Cultural Empire' in *Orientalism and History,* ed. D. Sinor, Bloomington, Indiana University Press, 1970, pp. 35-67.

Lohia, Ram Manohar : *The Wheel of History,* Hyderabad, Lohia Samiti, 1955.

————: *Will to Power & Other Writings,* Hyderabad, Navhind, 1956.

Madan, T.N. (ed), *Way of Life: King, Householder and Renouncer,* New Delhi, 1982.

Mahabharata, Geeta Press, Gorakhpur.

Mahabharata, ed. Kamchand Sastri, 5 Vols, Poona, Chirasala.

Mahabharata (critical edition) ed. V. Suk Shankar Press, Poona, 1927.

Majumdar, A.C. : *India National Evolution,* Madras, 1917.

Majumdar, Bimanlehari: *History of Political Thought from Ram Mohan to Dayananda (1821-84),* Calcutta, 1934.

Majumdar, R.C. : *Corporate Life in Ancient India,* Calcutta, 1918.

Manusmriti, With the commentary of Medhatuthi, Calcutta, 1932-34.

Marx, Karl : *Karl Marx on Colonialism and Modernization,* ed. Shlomo Avineri, New York, Doubleday, 1968

McCrindle, John Watson : *Ancient India as Described by Megasthenes and Arrian,* London, 1877.

Mehta, V.R. : *Ideology, Modernization and Politics in India,* New Delhi, Manohar, 1983.

————: *Beyond Marxism : Towards An Alternative Perspective,* New Delhi, Manohar, 1978.

Mishra, B.B. : *Polity in the Agni Purana*, Calcutta, Punthi Pustak, 1965.

Misra, G.S.P. : *Prachina Bhartiya Samaj evam Artha Vyavastha,* Jaipur, 1984.

Mitra, S. : *India : Vision and Fulfilment,* Bombay, Taraporevala, 1972.

Mookerji, Radhakumud : *Local Government in Ancient India.* Oxford. Clarendon Press, 1919.

————: *Nationalism in Hindu Culture,* London, Theosophical Publishing House, 1921.

————: *Chandra Gupta Maurya and His Times,* Delhi, Motilal Banarsidass, 1960.

————: *The Fundamental Unity of India,* New York, 1914.

————: *Community of Communities,* Bombay, 1976.

———— : *The Culture and Art of India,* London, 1959.

Moore, Barrington, Jr. : *Social Origins of Dictatorship and Democracy: Lord and Peasant in the Making of the Modern World,* Boston, Beacon, 1967.

Morrison, John : *New Ideas in India,* London, 1907.

Mukerji, D.P. : *Modern Indian Culture,* Bombay, 2nd edn., 1948.

Mukherjee, Haridas and Uma : *Bande Matram and Indian Nationalism 1906-1908,* Calcutta, 1957.

————: *Bipin Chandra Pal and India's Struggle for Swaraj,* Calcutta, 1958.

————: *The Growth of Nationalism in India 1857-1905,* Calcutta, 1957.

————: *Sri Aurobindo and the New Thought in Indian Politics,* Calcutta, Firma KL Mukhopadhyay, 1964.

Mukherjee, K.P. : *The State,* Madras, Theosophical Publishing House, 1952.

————: *Implications of the Ideology,* Bombay, Popular, 1955.

Mukerjee, Sandhya: *Some Aspects of Social Life in Ancient India,* Allahabad, 1976.

Mukherjee, S.N. (ed)., *Elite in South Asia,* Cambridge, Cambridge University Press, 1970.

Mukhia, Harbans : 'Was there Feudalism in Indian History?' *Journal of Peasant Studies,* Vol VIII, No. 3 1980, pp. 272-310.

Nandy, Ashis : *The Intimate Enemy: Loss and Recovery of Self Under Colonialism,* New Delhi, Oxford University Press, 1983.

Natrajan, S.: *A Century of Social Reform in India,* Bombay, 1959.

Narayan, J.P. : *Socialism, Sarvodaya and Democracy,* ed. Bimla Prasad, Patna, 1978.

Narendra Deva : *Socialism and the National Revolution,* ed. Yusuf Meherally, Bombay, Padma Publishers, 1947.

Narvane, V.S. : *Modern Indian Thought,* New Delhi, Orient Longman, 1978.

Nehru, Jawaharlal : *The Discovery of India,* Calcutta, Signet, 1966.

————: *An Autobiography,* London, John Lane, 1936.

Nilakanta Sastri, K.A. : 'Political Organization' in *A Comprehensive History of India.* III.I (AD 300-985), 1981, pp. 730-47.

O'Malley, L.S.S. : *Modern India and the West,* London, 1941.

Overstreet, G.D and M. Windmiller, *Communism in India*, Berkeley, University of California Press, 1959.

Pal, Bipin Chandra : *The New Spirit*, Calcutta, 1907.

————: *The Soul of India*, Calcutta, 4th edn., 1959.

————: *Speeches*, Madras, 1907.

————: *Swadeshi and Swaraj*, Calcutta, 2 Vols.

Pandey, D.P. : "Balban's Theory of Kingship", *Journal of Indian History*, April-Aug. 1977.

Pandey, G.C. : *The Foundations of Indian Culture*, 2 Vols., New Delhi, Books & Books, 1984.

————: *Jaina Political Thought*, Jaipur Prakrit Bharti, 1984.

————: *The Meaning and Process of Culture*, Agra, Shivlal Aggarwal, 1972.

Pant, A.D. : *Introduction to Beni Prasad's Theory of Government in Ancient India*, Allahabad, 1968.

Pantham, T. and Deutsch, K.L. (ed) : *Political Thought in Modern India*, New Delhi, Sage, 1986.

Parvate, T.V. : *Gopal Krishna Gokhale*, Ahmedabad, 1959.

Prakash, Satya : *A Critical Study of Philosophy of Dayanada*, Ajmer, 1938.

Prannath : *Economic Condition in Ancient India*, Allahabad, 1980.

Prasad, Beni : *Theory of Government in Ancient India (Post-Vedic)*, Allahabad, India Press, 1927.

Prasad, Rajendra : *India Divided*, Bombay, Hind Kitab, 1946.

Pusalkar, A.D. : *Studies in the Epics and the Puranas*, Bombay, 1955.

Radhakrishnan, S.: *The Hindu View of Life*, London, George Allen, 1980.

Raghuvanshi, V.S.: *Indian Nationalist Movement and Thought,* Agra, 2nd edn., 1959.

Ramaswamy, T.N. : *Essentials of Indian Statecraft*, London, 1962.

Rao, M.V. Krishna : *The Growth of Indian Liberalism in the Nineteenth Century*, Mysore, 1951.

Rao, K. Raghvendra : "Kautilya and the Secular State", *Journal of the Karnataka University* -7.

Rothermund, D. : *The Phases of Indian Nationalism and other Essays,* Bombay, 1970.

Roy, M.N. : *Politics, Power and Parties*, New Delhi, Ajanta, 1981,

Roy, M.N. and Philip Spratt: *Beyond Communism,* New Delhi, Ajanta, 1981.

————: *Reason, Romanticism and Revolution*, Calcutta, Renaissance Publishers, 1962.

Rudolph, Lloyd and Susanne Rudolph : *The Modernity of Tradition; Political Development in India*, Chicago, University of Chicago Press, 1967.

Sampurnananda, *Samajwad*, Kashi Bhartiya Gyanpeeth, 1960.

Sahu, B. : *Desik Sastra*, Almora, 1921.

Said, Edward : *Orientalism*, New York, Pantheon, 1978.

Sarkar, B.K. : *The Political Institutions and Theories of the Hindus: A Study of Comparative Politics*, Leipzig, 1922.

————: "Democratic Ideals and Republican Institutions in India", *The American Political Science Review*, Vol. 12, 1918.

————: "On Some Methods and Conclusions in Hindu Polity", *Indian Historical Quarterly*, Vol. 2, 1926, pp. 848-63,

Sarasvati, Swami Dayanand : *Light of Truth or An English Translation of Satyarth Prakash*, by Chiranjiva Bharadwaj, Allahabad, 2nd edn., 1915.

Saxena, R.N. : *Indian Social Thought*, New Delhi, Meenakshi, 1981.

Schwanbeck, Eugen Alexis : *Indica: Fragmenta Collegit,* Amsterdam, A.M. Hakkert, 1966.

Sen, M.L. : *The Ramayana of Valmiki*, Delhi, Munshiram Manoharlal, 1978.

Shah, K.J. : "The Concept of Dharma", *Journal of Indian Academy of Philosophy*, 12, I:3413

Sharma, D.S. : *Studies in the Renaissance of Hinduism in the 19th and 20th Century*, Mysore, 1951.

Sharma, J.P. : *Republics in Ancient India*, Leiden, 1968.

Sharma, R. : *A Socio-Political Study of Valmiki Ramayana*, New Delhi, Munshiram Manoharlal, 1971.

Sharma, R.S. : *Indian Feudalism 300-1200,* Calcutta, University of Calcutta, 1965.

————: *Aspects of Political Ideas and Institutions in Ancient India,* Delhi, 1968.

Shils, Edward : *The Intellectual Between Tradition and Modernity: The Indian Situation*, The Hague, Mouton, 1961.

Shiva : *Sri Aurobindo's Integral Approach to Political Thought*, New Delhi, Metropolitan, 1981.

Singer, Milton : *When a Great Tradition Modernizes: An Anthropological Approach to Indian Civilization*, New York, Praeger, 1972.

Singh, Karan : *Prophet of Indian Nationalism: A Study of the Political Thought of Sri Aurobindo*, London, George Allen, 1963.

Sinha, H.N. : *Ancient Indian Polity: A Study of the Evolution of Early Indian State,* London, Luzac, 1938.

Smith, W.C. : *Modern Islam in India*, London, 1943.

Somedeva, *Nitivakyamritam*, tr. S.Gupta, Jaipur, Prakrit Bharti, 1987.

Shay, Theodore L : *The Legacy of the Lokmanya*, New York, 1956.

Stokes, Eric : *The English Utilitarians and India,* Oxford, Clarendon Press, 1959.

Tagore, R.N. : *Nationalism*, London, Macmillan, 1950.

————: *Truth Called Differently*, Compiled and edited by R.K. Prabhu & R. Kalekar Ahmedabad, Navjivan, 1961.

Tilak, B.G.: *Speeches and Writings*, Madras, G.A. Natesan & Co.

————: *Sukraniti*, trans. B.K. Sarkar, Allahabad, The Panini Office, 1923.

Tarachand, *Influence of Islam on Indian Culture,* Allahabad, 1954.

Tahmankar, D.V.: *Lokmanya Tilak*, London, 1956.

Thapar, Romila : 'The State as Empire' in *The Study of the State*, ed., Henri J.M. Claessen and Peter Skalnik, The Hague, Mouton, 1981, pp. 409-26.

————: *From Lineage to State*, New Delhi, Oxford University Press, 1984.

Thapar, Romila and Percival Spear: *A History of India*, Harmondsworth: Penguin, 1966.

Topa, Ishwar Nath : *The Growth and Development of Nationalist Thought in India*, Hamburg, 1928.

Trautmann, T.R. : *Kautilya and the Arthasastra*, Leiden, 1971.

Tripathi, R.P. : *Some Aspects of Muslim Administration* , Allahabad, 1959.

Turner, Bryan S. : *Marx and the End of Orientalism*, London, Allen and Unwin, 1978.

Upadhyaya, Ganga Prasad: *Philosophy of Dayananda*, Allahabad, 1955.

Vajpayee, R. : *Brahaspati Rajya Vyavastha*, Varanasi, Chaukhamba, 1968.

Varma, V.P. : *Studies in Hindu Political Thought and Its Metaphysical Foundations*, Delhi, Motilal Banarsidass, 1974.

————: *Modern Indian Political Thought*, Agra, 1971.

Vigasin, A.A. and M.A. Samazavntsev : *Society, State and Law in Ancient India*, New Delhi, Sterling, 1985.

Vishnu Purana, Geeta Press, Gorakhpur.

Vishnudhamottra Purana, Bombay, 1912.

Vivekananda, : *Caste, Culture and Socialism*, Calcutta, Advaita Ashram, 1955.

————: *The East and West*, Calcutta, Advaita Ashram, 1967

————: *Complete Works,* Calcutta, Advaita Ashram, 1951.

Voight, J.H. : "Nationalist Interpretation of Arthasastra in India's Historical Writing", *South Asia Affairs*, No. II: *The Movement for National Freedom in India*, Ed. by S.N. Mukerjee, Oxford, Oxford University Press, 1966.

Vyas, K.C. : *Social Renaissance in India*, 1957, Bombay.

Weber, Max : *The Religion of India*, tr. H.H. Gerth and D. Martindale, Glencoe, Free Press, 1958.

Wellesz, Emmy : *Akbar's Religious Thought*, London, 1952.

Wolpert, Stanley A : *Tilak and Gokhale*, Berkeley, 1962.

Woodcock, George : *Gandhi*, Fontana, 1972.

Younghusband, Sir Francis : *Dawn in India,* London, 1930.

Zia-l-Barni : "The Fatawa-i-Jahandari", *Medieval Indian Quarterly*, Issue 1957-58.

Zimmer, Hein : *Philosophies of India*, New York, Meridian Books, 1956.

INDEX